The Rise of British Logic
Acts of the Sixth European Symposium
on Medieval Logic and Semantics
Balliol College, Oxford, 19-24 June 1983

edited by
P. Osmund Lewry, OP

This collection of fifteen papers from an international symposium held at Oxford in 1983 traces the emergence and development of a distinctive British tradition in logic and semantics from the twelfth to the fourteenth century.

In a programmatic study of origins Sten Ebbesen indicates that the terminist logic, which had emerged in France in the twelfth century, maintained its vitality in Oxford at a time when it was eclipsed by modist theory in Paris, then returned to the Continent with Ockham. For the thirteenth century, P. Osmund Lewry explores the characteristic preoccupation of some neglected Cornish masters with problems of extensionality, questions of existence and tense; Alain de Libera contrasts William of Sherwood's Oxford source, the <u>Magister abstractionum</u>, with the Parisian <u>Abstractiones</u> of Hervaeus sophista; C.H. Kneepkens finds some links with the Parisian tradition in Roger Bacon's treatment of meaningfulness and grammaticality, and Georgette Sinkler relates Bacon's account of grammatical dependence to his reaction against Lambert of Auxerre; Alessandro D. Conti discovers a nominalist reading of the Categories in Thomas Sutton.

While D.P. Henry shows how the Lesñiewskian Ontology may be applied to resolve the existential paradoxes of the Oxford masters and Boethius of Denmark, Francesco Bottin outlines the metalinguistic solution devised by the fourteenth-century Mertonians for paradoxes of truth and falsity. Ria van der Lecq presents William Heytesbury as continuing the Aristotelian theory of modality; Joël Biard reveals his innovatory influence with regard to the signification of imaginary objects. N.J. Green-Pedersen suggests that the fourteenth-century sophismatic exercises of Oxford were the matrix for the widely diffused handbooks of <u>consequentiae</u>. E.J. Ashworth traces the diffusion of <u>obligationes</u> texts after Roger Swyneshed. Stephen Read elucidates the conflict between nominalists such as Ockham and realists such as Burley and Wyclif by reference to twentieth-century discussions and the positions of Russell and Frege. Graziella Federici Vescovini pursues the reflections of Heytesbury on the border of logic and physics in Messinus of Coderonco. E.P. Bos detects John Hunteman's hand behind Paul of Mantua's rejection of Parisian teaching on the ampliation and restriction of terms.

The collection includes many detailed descriptions of unedited works, and newly edited material from writings of Nicholas and Peter of Cornwall, Richard Clive, Robert Kilwardby, Thomas Sutton and William Heytesbury. It is accompanied by a general index and an index of manuscripts cited.

PAPERS IN MEDIAEVAL STUDIES

7

THE RISE OF
BRITISH LOGIC

Acts of the Sixth European Symposium
on Medieval Logic and Semantics
Balliol College, Oxford, 19-24 June 1983

edited by

P. Osmund Lewry, O.P.

PONTIFICAL INSTITUTE OF MEDIAEVAL STUDIES

Canadian Cataloguing in Publication Data

European Symposium on Medieval Logic and
Semantics (6th : 1983 : Balliol College)
   The rise of British logic

(Papers in mediaeval studies, ISSN 0228-8605 ;
7)
Includes some text in French.
Includes index.
ISBN 0-88844-807-4

1. Logic - Great Britain - History - Congresses.
2. Logic, Medieval - History - Congresses.
I. Lewry, P. Osmund (Patrick Osmund), 1929-
II. Pontifical Institute of Mediaeval Studies.
III. Title. IV. Series.

B722.G7E97 1983   160'.942   C85-098316-9

Jan Pinborg
1937-1982
<u>in memoriam</u>

Contents

Preface

The work of the past five years has done much to sharpen our sense of a British tradition in medieval logic. Its roots may lie in the teaching of English masters in the twelfth-century schools of Paris, of which we have tantalizing glimpses in the descriptions of John of Salisbury. Though the British presence in Paris continued, the thirteenth century saw a growth in native soil, particularly at Oxford. There too it flowered in the early fourteenth century, and the writings of those illustrious scholars associated with Merton College became a pervasive influence in the later Middle Ages throughout Europe and especially in the universities of Northern Italy and the recent foundations in German lands.

Some lines of development had already emerged from papers read at the Fourth European Symposium on Medieval Logic and Semantics, held in the Netherlands in 1979, where the principal concern was with English logic down to the early fourteenth century;[1] more came from the Fifth Symposium, held in Italy in 1980, where the focus was on the diffusion of English works in the Italian universities in the fourteenth and fifteenth centuries.[2] Meeting for the first time in England, it was natural that the Sixth Symposium should seek to give definition to the picture with a study of the rise of British logic. This theme, broadly interpreted, was pursued in eighteen papers, fifteen of which have been edited for the present collection.

The topics addressed are as wide-ranging as the interests of this international gathering of scholars. Various as they are, however, they lend weight to the view that a certain conservatism in the British tradition before Ockham kept alive an interest in terminist logic from the twelfth-century Parisian schools and may have brought it back to the Continent after a period in the second half of the thirteenth century when it had been largely superseded there by the current preoccupations of the modistae. Oxford texts from the third quarter of the thirteenth century, particularly those of some nelected Cornish masters, show a characteristic concern with problems of extensionality, questions of existence and tense. The contributors to The Cambridge History of Later Medieval Philosophy, some of whom also contributed to this Symposium, have already done much to characterize the Oxford and Paris traditions in logic.[3] Now a comparison of the abstractiones

literature is presented as a kind of case-study, suggesting that William of
Sherwood, working at Oxford rather than Paris, was influenced by the
Magister abstractionum (in all probability Richard Rufus of Cornwall) and a
tradition with specific features distinct from those of Paris in the mid-
thirteenth century.   Roger Bacon, on the other hand, displays certain
features in his notions of grammatical congruity and completeness that may
link him with the Parisian tradition represented by Robert Kilwardby and
Master Jordanus; and in his account of dependence, in regard to the logic of
composition and division, may be reacting to Lambert of Auxerre.   Around
the last third of the thirteenth century, with Thomas Sutton's reading of the
Categories, there may even be the beginnings of an Oxford nominalism before
the time of Ockham.

The late thirteenth-century Oxford and Parisian paradoxes from the
language of existence may be susceptible of a modern treatment in the
symbolic language of the Leśniewskian Ontology, but the early fourteenth-
century Mertonians evolved their own distinctions of language and metalan-
guage to solve the paradoxes of truth and falsity in the insolubilia, rather
than resorting to the earlier explanations by a theory of signs.   Of this
group, William Heytesbury claims attention for his account of what
necessarily is, or will be, like the soul of the Antichrist.   It now appears to
be arguable that he did not depart from the earlier tradition but continued
the Aristotelian theory of modality.   Heytesbury's sophismata are seen as the
starting-point for a more original development: where reference to present
objects had been the paradigm of signification for Bacon and Ockham, he
begins that extended sense of signifying, found too in Henry Hopton's De
veritate et falsitate propositionum, where imaginary objects become a matter
of increasing concern.

The study of argumentation may have received a particular impetus in
British logic from the sophismatic exercises of the Oxford schools.   This
could explain the popularity of handbooks on consequences, widely copied in
Continental universities in the fourteenth and fifteenth centuries.   The same
reason may lie behind the spread of obligation literature from England.   Few
reactions have been discovered to Roger Swyneshed's new stipulation that
logical relevance is to be judged by reference to the initial position, but
Richard Billingham's work undergoes some adaptation and stands in a close
relation to the treatment in the standard logics of Oxford and Cambridge,
with echoes not only in Wyclif but in such European figures as Albert of

Saxony and Paul of Venice.

The conflict between nominalists and realists, represented in the fourteenth century by Ockham, on the one hand, and Burley and Wyclif, on the other, as exemplified in the explanations of promising a penny, has a striking modernity when read against the twentieth-century differences between Russell and Frege. There is also a freshness about Heytesbury's inquiries on the border of logic and physics, that seems to have attracted the Northern Italian masters. Angelo of Fossombrone's commentary has already received some attention; now it is the turn of Messinus of Coderonco, who taught at Bologna in the late fourteenth century. Another British influence, that of John Hunteman, may lie behind Paul of Mantua's criticism of the Parisian masters Albert of Saxony and Marsilius of Inghen. Paul's rejection of their account of the ampliation and restriction of terms, and his view that tense limits supposition to present objects, demonstrates the vitality of Oxford themes of the mid-thirteenth century in Italy at the end of the fourteenth century.

The Sixth Symposium was planned by Jan Pinborg, who had been active in these meetings from their inception. The early death of Jan, on 24 September 1982, took from us an esteemed colleague and a much loved friend. The directorship of the Copenhagen Institute of Greek and Latin Medieval Philology and the organization of the Symposium passed to Sten Ebbesen, who, ably assisted by Niels Jørgen Green-Pedersen, carried through the arrangements for a highly successful meeting. That success was in large part due to the hospitality of the Master and Fellows of Balliol College, Oxford, by whose invitation the participants met on ground where British logic had thrived long before Wyclif's time.

Acknowledgment is made here to the British Academy for a generous subsidy towards this meeting; also to those libraries whose manuscripts have been cited here, particularly to the Warden and Fellows of Merton College, Oxford, for edited material from MS 289, to the President and Fellows of Corpus Christi College, Oxford, for edited material from MSS D 119 and E 293 B, to the Prefect of the Vatican Library for edited material from MSS Chigi L.V.159 and Vat. lat. 3065, to the Redemptorist Fathers of Venice for edited material from MS 519, and to the Dean and Chapter of Worcester Cathedral for edited material from MS Q.13.

The contributors have borne patiently with many editorial interventions. Those from Denmark, the Netherlands and Italy, who had chosen to honour British logic by writing in a language not their own, have unprotestingly accepted correction to their English. Father Charles Principe, C.S.B., has kindly given assistance to ensure that the French is all it should be. Some measure of uniformity has also been imposed on conventions of citation and footnoting, not without sacrifice of national and personal styles. Full bibliographical references have been given on the first citation of a book or article or manuscript in each contribution. Abbreviations, apart from those that are contextually clear or introduced by individual contributors, have been limited to 'BGPTM' for 'Beiträge zur Geschichte der Philosophie und Theologie des Mittelalters' and 'CIMAGL' for 'Cahiers de l'Institut du Moyen-Âge Grec et Latin, Universite de Copenhague'. In editing texts, angle brackets, '<>', have been used for editorial additions, square brackets, '[]', for editorial omissions. Elsewhere, square brackets have occasionally been used for editorial comment, where they seemed more appropriate than parentheses.

Notes

[1]See H.A.G. Braakhuis, C.H. Kneepkens, L.M. de Rijk eds., English Logic and Semantics from the End of the Twelfth Century to the Time of Ockham and Burleigh: Acts of the 4th European Symposium on Mediaeval Logic and Semantics, Leiden-Nijmegen, 23-27 April 1979 (Artistarium Supplementa 1; Nijmegen, 1981).

[2]See Alfonso Maierù ed., English Logic in Italy in the 14th and 15th Centuries: Acts of the 5th European Symposium on Medieval Logic and Semantics, Rome, 10-14 November 1980 (History of Logic 1; Naples, 1982).

[3]Norman Kretzmann, Anthony Kenny, Jan Pinborg eds., The Cambridge History of Later Medieval Philosophy from the rediscovery of Aristotle to the disintegration of scholasticism, 1100-1600 (Cambridge, 1982). See particularly, Alain de Libera, 'The Oxford and Paris traditions in logic' ibid., pp. 174-187.

OXYNAT: A Theory about the Origins of British Logic

Sten Ebbesen

Institute of Greek and Latin Medieval Philology,
University of Copenhagen

The Sixth Symposium on Medieval Logic and Semantics is the third in a row to have British logic for its theme.[1] The original plan was to deal exclusively with the period before 1250, but experience shows that it is difficult to keep people from talking about the later periods instead. It is easy to explain why this should be so: there is much more philosophical meat in the fourteenth-century texts. In this paper I shall concentrate on the early period. I shall not solve any important problems, but content myself with sketching what problems I think ought to be solved and some possible angles from which to approach them.

The question which has more than any other directed attention to early English logic is that of the sources of Ockham's thought. Even great philosophers do not come out of nothing, and it is hardly probable that his genius alone was responsible for the appearance of a number of distinguished English thinkers with a distinctively English approach to philosophy. If we look at Parisian logic from the period 1270–1310, which has been fairly well investigated, there is precious little that can be seen to forebode Ockham — or for that matter Buridan. Semantics is dominated by the modist theory, in which intentional **significata** are the source of explanatory power. The notion of supposition, though known, plays next to no role in the discussion. The interest in particulars, in reference of terms; the recognition that to explain what information a proposition carries, the speaker's intentions must be taken into account; the obsession with the formulation of rules of what

The Rise of British Logic, ed. P. Osmund Lewry, O.P., Papers in Mediaeval Studies 7 (Toronto: Pontifical Institute of Mediaeval Studies, 1985), pp. 1-17.
© P.I.M.S., 1985.

you may infer from a proposition, be it ever so complex and the rules ever so counter-intuitive -- all these fourteenth-century characteristics seem to have no precursors in Parisian modistic thought. Indeed, the fourteenth-century English approach to logic looks much more like a continuation of the approach we find in the twelfth century, but which apparently lost its impetus in Paris when the Organon and the Aristotelian ideal of demonstrative science became the centre of interest and study.

John of Salisbury describes how a clever man when going to an early twelfth-century disputation would bring a bag of peas so that during an argument he could take out one pea for each negation and finally control whether a statement was positive or negative by seeing whether the number of peas was even or odd.[2] Reading fourteenth-century English texts, you may sometimes wish for a bag of peas, but not when reading late thirteenth-century Parisian ones. Now, if it is true that twelfth-century style in logic was discontinued at Paris, it becomes tempting to think that there was an 'old-fashioned' logic which lived on in England, to come back to France only when it had received a brilliant formulation from Ockham and his contemporaries and at a time when debates at Paris had shown the weak spots of modism, thus preparing people there for a different approach.

This way of thinking becomes even more attractive when we consider that the views of Roger Bacon have some salient similarities with those of Ockham and his like — Bacon was as radical as they in his insistence on the role users of words have in semantic explanations and in his rejection of 'common natures' and similar hypostatized or semi-hypostatized universals, and in many respects he adheres to the ways of the twelfth century. Thus the twelfth century had witnessed an attempt to classify nonsense-utterances that violate no rules of ordinary syntax with the ungrammatical ones. 'Every phoenix is flapping its wings' would be regarded as ungrammatical because the putative subject is not there — in fact it is not possible to say what it would be like without disregarding either the standard interpretation of 'every' or standard knowledge about phoenixes; in a present tense context 'every' and 'phoenix' are as incompatible as 'two' and 'man'. Bacon takes the twelfth-century view on this matter. The general trend in the thirteenth century is to grant grammaticality and propositionhood to such deviating sentences.[3]

Another fact pointing towards conservatism in England is that around

1300 the British still care to copy and/or revise old-fashioned textbooks of logic like <u>Logica 'Cum sit nostra'</u> — in one manuscript called <u>Summulae ad modum Oxoniae</u>. Part of, or at least a regular companion of these <u>Summulae</u> is a treatise on fallacies that one manuscript calls <u>Fallaciae ad modum Oxoniae</u>.[4] The first version of this treatise is likely to have been written in the first half of the thirteenth century, but the extant copies differ considerably between themselves, suggesting continuous use by several teachers. One teacher who used it as the basic text for a course on fallacies was Burley.[5] Two manuscripts preserve his survey of the fallacies, in which he follows the summulistic treatise step by step, but adds discussions of points of interest.[6] The relation between the two manuscripts is unclear, but a high number of small divergences and some major ones may betray the fact that the two manuscripts originate from different courses on the same subject and based on the same old textbook, though retouched, possibly by Burley himself. Another manuscript from the years close to 1300 contains the chapter on supposition from William of Sherwood's <u>summulae</u> (<u>Introductiones in logicam</u>) and a series of <u>dubia</u> on it, probably composed in the 1260s or 1270s.[7] Even an old Aristotle commentary was copied in the late thirteenth century.[8] This late use of old books suggests conservatism. But at the same time one feature points to the future: the way Burley uses an old summulistic treatise cannot but remind one of Buridan's revised Peter of Spain, with Buridan's own commentary, and the intensive use of revised and commented <u>Summulae</u> that followed.

Also, we may notice that Simon of Faversham (writing about 1280, it seems), while relying on Parisian sources and tradition for the most part, in one place refers to a view held by the man from Lincoln. The same view is ascribed to some Robert of Lincoln in an indubitably English work which is hardly later than 1200. This indicates that Simon was acquainted with old literature from his own country.[9] We know too that the <u>Magister Abstractionum</u> was still read in Ockham's England, some seventy years after he wrote those <u>abstractiones</u>, so reminiscent of both twelfth- and fourteenth-century texts in their interminable delight in logical intricacies.[10]

To repeat, the picture suggested by such evidence is this: before the advent of the New Logic between 1130 and 1150, a 'native' Western European logical tradition had grown up in France, a tradition of indulging in the analysis of intricate inferences and implications, and with a penchant towards extensional semantics. Another approach to logic, inspired by the new Aristotle and Greek and Arabic scholastic writings gradually eclipsed the native tradition in Paris, while this native tradition managed to survive to a greater extent in England, finally producing Ockham and, after being reimported to France, Buridan.

This story of the historical development is not a simple narrative about obvious facts. It is a theory that has inspired and can still inspire new research because it is in need of corroboration and implies some unproven and potentially falsifiable claims. Let me call the theory 'OXYNAT' — the 'OX' for Oxford, 'NAT' for native, 'Y' for y.

OXYNAT postulates that the new ideas that characterize Buridan, as opposed to the modists, were imported to Paris from England in the 1320s. But can we be quite sure that Buridan does not in important respects follow a tradition already developed in Paris in the first quarter of the fourteenth century? Very little is known about Parisian logic during the years 1310–1325. The same is true for English logic from the period immediately before Ockham. The search for dateable works must be continued and their doctrine scrutinized. For want of purely logical writings, it may be an idea to have a closer look at the commentaries on the Sentences. Also, a thorough investigation of the chronology of Burley's works is badly needed. He may have been an important link between Paris and Oxford, but his long career makes it uncertain how much of his production can be assigned to the years before Ockham became an important figure.[11]

Then there are the last three decades of the thirteenth century. According to OXYNAT, modism held sway in Paris during that period, supposition theory was neglected and so was the meticulous analysis of sophismatic propositions. This claim rests on an impressive amount of textual evidence. Yet, it might be worth asking whether we have been turning the blind eye to part of the manuscript material because modern scholarship has pursued certain limited goals, such as finding out what Parisian masters said about problems that had interested Thomas Aquinas, or investigating problems dealt with in certain genres -- quaestiones on Aristotle, for instance, or modistic grammatical works — or problems dealt with by authors of a certain nationality — Danes, for instance.

OXYNAT claims that there was continuous use of old-fashioned summulae in England throughout the thirteenth century and continuous exercise in old forms of logical analysis at the University of Oxford, and possibly in other places too in the British Isles. I have offered some evidence for accepting the claim, and more could be produced. But are we quite sure that the interest in old books that we find around 1300 was not a real renaissance rather than the result of a continuous tradition? Or could it even be that this antiquarian interest was restricted to a few people whose books happen to be preserved? If this could be plausibly argued, it would deal a serious blow to OXYNAT. In short, we need a survey of British manuscripts from the late thirteenth and early fourteenth centuries containing logical works of an earlier date. Where, for whom, etc., were these manuscripts copied?

We know that Britons who had studied and taught at Paris brought back to their native country ideas and works that they themselves had composed in Paris using Parisian models. Simon of Faversham is a good representative of that class of writers. I think I can see some English traits in the way he handles certain problems (such as consequences), but for the most part he is as Parisian as anyone could be. In fact, he does not shrink back from lifting whole quaestiones almost verbatim out of earlier Parisian works. His commentaries were copied, and presumably used, in England about 1290–1310.[12] OXYNAT allows for such things to happen, but the theory requires that there also be works from the late thirteenth and early fourteenth centuries less influenced by Parisian modism than Simon's, though not necessarily as non-modistic as Bacon's. Evidence has been accumulating these last years in support of the notion,[13] but there is much more to do. First of all, we need a catalogue of texts that we may be sure are British and date from the period. Much relevant information is already available, in particular thanks to P. O. Lewry, but it is scattered in several publications. Secondly, we need more analysis of the texts.

The same need for cataloguing and doctrinal analysis occurs when we turn to the period before 1270. OXYNAT was formulated under the impression that such material as we find in Magister Abstractionum was not written or read in Paris, at least not so late as in England.[14] On this point A. de Libera's paper in this volume will help to clarify the actual situation.[15] In a paper that I wrote a couple of years ago I argued that supposition was old-fashioned in France already when Peter of Spain wrote his Summulae.[16] I feel pretty confident that this was the case by 1250. OXYNAT then predicts that such English works as we may find from the decades around 1250 will contain more on supposition, etc., than contempo-

rary Parisian ones. But once again, in spite of impressive gains in knowledge
acquired these last ten years, it is very difficult to utilize the extant
sources. So few datings are secure. So often we do not know where a logic
book was written, still less by whom. Let me illustrate the difficulties with
a couple of examples:

(1) MS Oxford, Merton College 280 contains a commentary on the
Elenchi. It is a literal commentary with dubia. The Merton copy was
executed around 1300, and the script is decidedly English. The general
impression one gains from reading in it is that it is 'early', i.e., not much
later than 1250. This fits well with the colophon (fol. 37^v): 'Explicit
tractatus super librum Elenchorum datus a magistro Roberto Grostest (+ de
Lyncolnia, possibly in another hand).' Now, Grosseteste is one of those men
whose career is so long that identifying him as the author gives the author
several decades to choose between for a date of the work. And to make
things worse, the commentary is under suspicion of being misattributed to
Grosseteste because neither stylistically nor in the choice of subjects to
discuss does it recall other parts of his oeuvre.[17] The author uses the
notion of supposition quite often, though not the division into several sorts of
supposition,[18] but it is not possible to estimate the significance of this
feature as long as we cannot date the work within narrower limits than
about fifty years. If it is from the 1250's, the predilection for supponere
looks significant. If the date is 1210-1220, we are probably dealing with a
terminology that was also Parisian at the time. It is thus very dubious what
this commentary can tell us about early thirteenth-century English logic.

On the other hand, it does give some corroboration to OXYNAT, at least
if we believe that it was composed before 1260, because then it is an
instance of an old work copied about the end of the century or early in the
next. On one point we do perhaps get a glimpse of the continuity of the
English tradition. On fol. 6vb the texts says:

Quaeratur autem quomodo universaliter debeat exprimi duplicitas
omnium orationum secundum compositionem et divisionem. Et
quod non sit una duplicitas omnium talium orationum videtur:
quaedam (fort. quidam cod.) enim huiusmodi habent talem
duplicitatem in se de re vel de dicto, quaedam (fort. quidam cod.)
talem quod potest esse categorica vel hypothetica....

To speak about a categorical/hypothetical ambiguity in connection with the fallacies of composition and division is to the best of my knowledge unusual, but I can recall one other text that does so. It is Ockham's _Elenchi_ commentary.[19]

(2) MS Oxford, Bodl. Digby 24 contains a fragment of a literal commentary on the _Elenchi_ (fols. 93-102^v). De Rijk has dated the script to the early thirteenth century and boldly conjectured that this is the work of Edmund of Abingdon, who, Roger Bacon said, was the first to have lectured on the _Elenchi_ at Oxford.[20] For my part, I think the handwriting belongs to the second half of the century, and I am inclined to put the date of composition in the third quarter of the century, but I am not sure, and I have only weak arguments for an English rather than a French origin.[21]

For most people, Aristotle commentaries are not very attractive material on which to work, particularly if they are literal commentaries, but such commentaries do have some advantages for the historian of philosophy. The fact that any two commentaries on the same work have something in common -- the text they comment on and the problems it presents -- makes comparison between them much easier than between works which lack the restraints imposed by dependence on the same authoritative book. An example:

MS Digby 24 contains some questions on the _Sophistici elenchi_ (fols. 91-92^v). They show acquaintance with the modistic distinction between active and passive modes of signifying. Hence the date is likely to be after 1270,[22] but hardly many decades later. There is nothing redolent of Ockham except for a curious remark about written, spoken and mental sentences. The Digby author remarks that a grammarian must regard an amphibolic sentence as several sentences because there is a different construction in each sentence, and the grammarian's field is the disambiguated level of mental discourse. The logician, on the other hand, must take the amphibolic sentence as one sentence because he operates on the level of spoken or written language.[23] We have several Parisian discussions of amphiboly from the late thirteenth century. They all have to address the problem of surface simplicity versus semantic multiplicity, but they never introduce the three kinds of discourse. Hence the questions in MS Digby 24, suspected of being English because of the circumstances of transmission, do in an important respect live up to our OXYNAT-expectations about such works.

I think the commentaries might be of great value in an attempt to provide a relative chronology and a distinction between Continental and English material. In this connection I would also like to point to the possible use of scholia. Dating on the basis of script is particularly difficult when we deal with scholia, but at least we can tell when a hand is of the type we usually associate with England. Such hands do occur in several Aristotle manuscripts conserved in England or Paris. Do English-hand scholia have some particulary close connection with commentaries known or presumed to be English? I think the matter merits investigation, for if they have, comparison with scholia may help to establish the origin of commentaries about which we are in doubt. There is some evidence of such a connection, but I do not know how much it amounts to. I may mention that the fragmentary Digby commentary to which I referred above (MS Digby 24, fols. 93-102^V) overlaps in one place with a scholium in a Paris manuscript (BN lat. 16599) written in an English hand.[24] The collection of scholia on the Elenchi in MS Paris 16599 overlaps to a considerable degree with those of three other manuscripts (Paris, BN lat. 6289; Oxford, Magdalen College 187; Milan, Bibl. Ambros. H.131 inf.), at least two of which (the first two) are in English hands. MS Paris 16599 also contains a scholium referring to England. It says: 'Equivocals by chance are primarily associated with proper names, as when somebody is by chance called by some name in England, and somebody else by the same name in France.'[25] This may be significant. I think the matter deserves further investigation.

The problems of dating and discriminating between British and Continental (French) material become more and more difficult the further back we move towards the twelfth century. Even the handwriting ceases to be a clue.

OXYNAT postulates a connection between thirteenth-century English tradition and the tradition of the twelfth century, when presumably most or all philosophical schools were on the Continent. But when did logical teaching begin in England? To provide an answer to this question we need, inter alia, a fresh consideration of the relative and absolute chronology of all the logical works from the twelfth and early thirteenth century, brought to light mainly due to the efforts of De Rijk, as well as a reconsideration of the arguments for assigning them to definite places and schools. At the present stage of research, the literature on this subject is a maze. The arguments for date and origin proffered by the first investigators of the relevant texts are scattered over a large number of publications. Subsequent research has often suggested modifications of the original proposals, but frequently the new proposal is to be found in some footnote or as a parenthesis in a discussion of something else. It would be extremely valuable to have a simple list of the arguments advanced concerning each work. A critical investigation would, of course, be even more welcome. Relative chronologies have been established for some genres, such as tracts on syncategoremata and commentaries and treatises relating to Boethius' Topics and Aristotle's Elenchi, but how do the results obtained for each particular genre square with one another? A thorough investigation, or at least a clear survey of this complex of problems is a real desideratum.

It has been doubted whether it makes sense to speak of English versus French tradition before the middle of the thirteenth century,[26] but a good case has been made for this being possible.[27] It has also been argued that early thirteenth-century English logic is especially closely related to that of the twelfth-century Parvipontani.[28] Twelfth-century philosophical schools may have had little institutional community, but there obviously was such a thing as a school of thought. The adherents of each school would distinguish between nostri and others, and even produce lists of theses constituting their own philosophical creed (nostra professio).[29] The names applied to the followers of each secta are derived from points of doctrine (thus nominales), location of teaching activity (thus Meludinenses, Montani) or the name of the sect's founder (thus Adamitae). Presumably the last two categories reduce to one: Meludinenses meaning 'followers of the Robert who once taught in Melun.' Most (all?) the school names point back to the second quarter of the twelfth century and such masters as Adam Parvipontanus, Gilbert the Porretan, Robert of Melun, Alberic of Paris; but school allegiances apparently survived the masters by a generation or two.

If we assume that the tradition of teaching logic in England started in the second half of the twelfth century, the first teachers are likely to have received their training in France at a time when the sense of school identity was strong. It is also a plausible guess that Britons would show a preference for studying under teachers of their own nationality, such as Adam Parvipontanus and Robert of Melun, or under the spiritual heirs of these men — quite possibly other Britons. If so, a possible consequence would be that once the teaching tradition got established in England, it carried with it certain French sectarian tendencies, possibly keeping them alive even after they disappeared in France; or that at least the memory of the sectarian debates was kept alive.

As a matter of fact, a remarkable amount of our information about the Meludinenses and Adamitae derives from sources with some sort of connection with Britain. The Melun treatises Ars Meliduna and Secta Meliduna are preserved in English libraries.[30] John of Salisbury, Alexander Neckam and Jocelyn of Brakelond are other sources of information about the Meludinenses, and so are Glosa 'Promisimus' (the Priscian commentary in MS Oxford, Bodl. Laud lat. 67) and the Elenchi commentary in MS Cambridge, St. John's College D.12(87).[31] The author of this last-named work, whom I call Anonymus Cantabrigiensis, may in fact be one of the initiators of the British tradition. The manuscript transmitting his work was probably never outside England. Besides the Elenchi commentary it contains one on Priscian, written in similar hand(s) and with a similar lay-out.[32] This work contains such remarks as, 'If you are asked, "Where are you from?", do not say "Anglica" but " de Anglica",' and 'solecism is said to be thus called because hostages sent from Soloes to Rome began to speak broken Roman, as Englishmen do when in France.'[33] The internal evidence of the Elenchi commentary is ambiguous as to place of origin. We find the example 'The Seine is here and in Rouen', suggesting Paris or Melun as the place of composition. But we also find 'the king has just one castle in Rouen, therefore he has just one castle.'[34] If the text is from the twelfth century, as I strongly believe, the king would seem to be the king of England, as Rouen is in Normandy. If the author was an Englishman, perhaps teaching somewhere near Rouen, he may have brought more than the Elenchi commentary back to England, for he refers once to a commentary on the Topics.[35]

Anonymus Cantabrigiensis presumably wrote at a time when the philosophical sects still had active adherents, but the memory of them was kept alive far into the thirteenth century. As Lewry has recently pointed out, both Robert Grosseteste and Robert Kilwardby refer to a thesis held by the Adamites.[36] The Kilwardby text is from about 1240. It does not indicate intimate acquaintance with the old sect, but it does show that they left some sort of imprint on what thirteenth-century Englishmen wrote. Could there be a profounder influence?

As mentioned above, Parvipontan (Adamite) influence has been suspected. But what about the Meludinenses? Have they left no traces in the English

adam Parvipontanus

tradition? To answer this question we must, first of all, acquire a clearer picture of the doctrinal characteristics of each of the twelfth-century schools. Here, then, is one more line of research to pursue: gather the evidence for what was peculiar to each of the old philosophical sects. Quite a lot of material is already available, but scattered. More may probably be found, not only in unedited works on logic and grammar, but also in theological literature. After all, many of the controversies between twelfth-century thinkers were closely related to theological issues and the interpretation of such theological texts as Boethius' Opuscula sacra.

Perhaps the Seventh European Symposium on Medieval Logic and Semantics will throw more light on the philosophical schools of twelfth-century France, and thus indirectly on the tenability of OXYNAT.

Notes

1 See H.A.G. Braakhuis, C.H. Kneepkens, L.M. de Rijk eds., English Logic and Semantics from the End of the Twelfth Century to the Time of Ockham and Burleigh: Acts of the 4th European Symposium on Mediaeval Logic and Semantics, Leiden-Nijmegen, 23-27 April 1979 (Artistarium Supplementa 1; Nijmegen, 1981); A. Maierù ed., English Logic in Italy in the 14th and 15th Centuries: Acts of the 5th European Symposium on Medieval Logic and Semantics, Rome, 10-14 November 1980 (History of Logic 1; Naples, 1982). For the problems treated in this paper see also J. Pinborg, 'The English Contribution to Logic before Ockham', Synthese 40 (1979) 19-42; A. de Libera, 'Supposition naturelle et appellation: aspects de la sémantique Parisienne au XIIIe siècle', Histoire. Épistémologie. Langage 3/1 (1981) 63-77; idem, 'The Oxford and Paris Traditions in Logic' in Norman Kretzmann, Anthony Kenny, Jan Pinborg eds., The Cambridge History of Later Medieval Philosophy (Cambridge, 1982), pp. 174-187; P.O. Lewry, 'Robert Kilwardby's Writings on the Logica vetus' (unpublished Oxford Univ. D.Phil. thesis, 1978); idem, 'Robert Kilwardby on Meaning: A Parisian Course on the Logica vetus', Miscellanea Mediaevalia 13/1 (1981) 376-384; idem, 'Rhetoric at Paris and Oxford in the Mid-Thirteenth Century', Rhetorica 1 (1983) 45-63. Older literature may be found via the publications mentioned here.

2 John of Salisbury, Metalogicon 1.3.

3 See S. Ebbesen, 'The Present King of France Wears Hypothetical Shoes
with Categorical Laces: Twelfth-century Writers on Well-formedness',
Medioevo 7 (1981) 91-113.

4 On Logica 'Cum sit nostra' see L.M. de Rijk, Logica Modernorum 2.1
(Wijsgerige Teksten en Studies 16; Assen, 1967). The manuscript with the
names Summulae/Fallaciae ad modum Oxoniae is Oxford, Bodl. Auct. F.5.23;
see L.M. de Rijk ed., Peter of Spain (Petrus Hispanus Portugaliensis),
Tractatus (Wijsgerige Teksten en Studies 22; Assen, 1972), p. LXIX n. 2.
Edition of the Fallaciae by Clemens Kopp forthcoming.

5 I owe my awareness of this to collaboration with Clemens Kopp, who
recognized that the form of the Fallaciae used by Burley was close to that
called Fallaciae breves in MS London, BL Royal 12.F.xix and edited by
Clemens Kopp, 'Ein kurzer Fehlschlusstraktat: die Fallaciae breves (ad modum
Oxoniae), London, British Museum, Royal MSS 122 F XIX, 104rb-105vb',
Miscellanea Mediaevalia 15 (1982) 262-277. De Rijk, Logica Modernorum 2.1,
p. 446, had already suspected a role for Burley in the history of Cum sit
nostra. A more detailed investigation of Burley's use of the old summulae
might repay study.

6 MSS London, Lambeth Palace 70, fols. 134vb-144ra; Cambridge, Gonville
and Caius College 448/409, fols. 95-115. It would be highly interesting to
know the date of this work of Burley's. In some respects it resembles
Parisian works from the late thirteenth century, e.g., in its dubia concerning
equivocation, but the extensive treatment of the fallacies of composition and
division makes one think of Magister Abstractionum. Lots of sophismatic
propositions occur, such as 'Omnis homo si est Plato differt a Socrate.' Also
under figure of speech one encounters unexpected examples such as
'Quemlibet hominem videns videt asinum istius, ergo videns quemlibet hominem
videt asimun istius.' The earlier the tract can be dated, the more
remarkable these features are.

7 MS Worcester Cathedral Q.13, fols. 59vb-62va. The late Jan Pinborg
has left an almost finished edition of the dubia on Sherwood, which I intend
to publish soon (most probably in CIMAGL 1984). Notice the passage, fol.
60vb: 'Significatum est duplex: primarium et secundarium; primarium est
forma, secundarium est aggregatum. Si terminus stet pro forma, hoc potest
esse dupliciter, vel absolute vel pro aggregato relato', etc. There is a

remarkable similarity to the anonymous commentary on the Prior Analytics in MS Cambridge, Peterhouse 206, discussed in S. Ebbesen, 'Early Supposition Theory', Histoire, Épistémologie, Langage 3/1 (1981) 35-48, ibid., pp. 46-48.

[8] Robert Grosseteste (?), Comm. in Soph. elench., MS Oxford, Merton College 280, fols. 3-37^V. More about this commentary above, pp. 6-7.

[9] See S. Ebbesen, 'Jacobus Veneticus on the Posterior Analytics and some early 13th century Oxford Masters on the Elenchi', CIMAGL 21 (1977) 1-9, with corrigenda in CIMAGL 34 (1979) XLII; idem et alii eds., Simon of Faversham, Quaestiones super libro Elenchorum (Studies and Texts 60; Toronto, 1984), p. 14.

[10] See J. Pinborg, 'Magister Abstractionum', CIMAGL 18 (1976) 1-4. Edition by P. Streveler et al. in preparation.

[11] Cf. n. 6 above.

[12] See the preface to the edition of Simon's questions on the Elenchi mentioned in n. 9 above.

[13] See, in particular, S. Ebbesen, 'The Dead Man is Alive', Synthese 40 (1979) 43-70; Pinborg, 'The English Contribution...'; S. Ebbesen, 'Supraseg-mental Phonemes in Ancient and Mediaeval Logic', in English Logic and Semantics, pp. 331-359; P.O. Lewry, 'The Oxford Condemnations of 1277 in Grammar and Logic', ibid., pp. 235-278.

[14] Yet, it is clear from the structure of the late thirteenth-century Parisian sophismata that the genre developed from something like the English sophismata. After all, the Parisian ones start with a sophismatic proposition and usually have a very short probatio & improbatio before the quaestiones are taken up. Sometimes the probatio & improbatio are reduced to the formula 'probatio et improbatio satis patent', but still, this is clearly a relic of the original form.

[15] See below, pp. 63-114.

[16] S. Ebbesen, 'Early Supposition Theory.' See above n. 7.

[17] Until recently I innocently believed in the manuscript attribution; but my belief has been shaken by a letter from Sir Richard Southern, in which he pointed out the discrepancy between the dull Elenchi commentary and the strongly personal style of other writings by Grosseteste.

[18] Thus fol. 5vb (on Soph. elench. 4, 165b31-34); 'Et quod dicit de hac oratione "quicquid scit hoc scit", scilicet quod e[s]t scientem et scitum contingit hac oratione significari, sic est intelligendum, hoc pronomen "hoc" quod potest esse nominativi (-us cod.) casu[s] vel accusativi, et primo modo habet ordinari ante hoc verbum "scit[um]" ultimo positum, et supponit tunc pro sciente; secundo modo habet ordinari ex parte post, et supponit pro scito. Quia ergo supponere potest tam pro sciente quam pro scito ordinatum (ordinat tn̄ cod.) eo modo quo ordinandum est si tantum supponit pro sciente, recte dicit quod contingit hac oratione significari scientem ut <scientem et> scitum et scitum ut scientem.'

[19] F. del Punta ed., Guillelmi de Ockham Expositio super libros Elenchorum 1.3.6 (Opera philosophica 3; St. Bonaventure, N.Y., 1979), p. 35.

[20] De Rijk, Logica Modernorum 2.1, p. 4. De Rijk's argument for this is the presumed early date of the manuscript and the occurrence in the same manuscript of Magister Abstractionum, whom De Rijk identified as Richard Fishacre, a pupil of Edmund's, but, as we now think, Magister Abstractionum was rather Richard of Cornwall. Bacon's reference to Edmund occurs in H. Rashdall ed., Fratris Rogeri Bacon Compendium studii theologiae pars 1 ch. 2 (British Society of Franciscan Studies 3; Aberdeen, 1911), p. 34; cf. Ebbesen, 'Jacobus Veneticus...', p. 4.

[21] An English origin is suggested (a) by the occurrence of the text in MS Digby 24; (b) by the link between this text and MS Paris, BN lat. 16599, to be discussed below, p. 8. As for the date, some traits point to a time not much later than 1250, e.g., the claim that an equivocal term signifies per modum copulationis (fol. 95ra): 'Dico ad hoc quod dictio aequivoca plura significat per modum copulationis, tamen non est falsa simpliciter, nec danda responsio simpliciter, sed dividenda, et post divisionem danda responsio dupliciter; nec etiam falsa est simpliciter copulativa, sed plures, quare non interimenda est, sed dandae sunt ei plures responsiones.' Cf. S. Ebbesen, 'Can Equivocation be Eliminated?', Studia Mediewistyczne 18 (1977) 103-124. Similarly, the discussion of the intentio, modus agendi, etc., of the Elenchi,

and the use in that connection of the Boethian distinction between judicium and inventio points to an early date. On the other hand, a remark on fol. 97^V may seem to allude to a view similar to that of Giles of Rome (in the 1270s) about the fallacy of figure of speech: 'dicunt aliqui quod non est hic causa apparentiae sumenda eiusdem ad se sed concreti ad abstractum.'

22 MS Digby 24, fol. 92va: 'Significatio activa est proprietas vocis, ergo modus significandi active erit proprietas vocis sive ex parte vocis.

23 Ibid., fol. 92rb: 'Consequenter quaeratur utrum oratio amphibolica sit una vel plures. ... Ad quod dicendum quod oratio est tripliciter, sc. in mente et in scripto et in pronuntiatione. In scripto autem et pronuntiatione contingit eandem orationem amphibolicam significare multas formas, in mente autem nequaquam: alia enim constructio erit, quae secundum Priscianum est ad intellectum referenda; et propter hoc alia erit oratio secundum grammaticum; secundum logicum autem, qui considerat orationem prout est in pronuntiatione, erit eadem oratio.'

Notice that mental discourse also receives much attention in Ps.-Kilwardby's commentary on Priscianus maior (ed. K.M. Fredborg et al., CIMAGL 15 [1975]).

24 MS Digby 24, fol. 93va

'Sunt autem paralogismi'
(Soph. elench. 1, 164a21),
et magis dicit dicendo 'sunt
autem paralogismi' quam
si dixisset 'sunt autem par-
elenchi', quia paralogismus
dicit privationem syllogismi
et parelenchus
elenchi, et ad privationem
syllogismi sequitur privatio
elenchi, cum elenchus sit
syllogismus cum contra-
dictione...

MS Paris, BN lat. 16599,
fol. 102^r in mg.

Nota quod
magis dicit in littera 'sunt
autem paralogismi' quam
si dixisset 'sunt autem par-
elenchi', quia paralogismus
dicit privationem syllogismi,
parelenchus dicit privationem
elenchi, et ad privationem
syllogismi sequitur privatio
elenchi, cum elenchus sit
syllogismus contra-
dictionis.

25 MS Paris, BN lat. 16599, fol. 103^V in mg.: 'Aequivocatio a casu proprie invenitur in propriis nominibus, ut quando unus casualiter vocetur

aliquo nomine in Anglia et alius eodem nomine in Gallia.'

[26] See Pinborg, 'The English Contribution...', p. 37.

[27] See de Libera, 'The Oxford and Paris Traditions...'.

[28] Ibid., following a suggestion of De Rijk.

[29] See S. Ebbesen and Y. Iwakuma, 'Instantiae and 12th Century "Schools"', CIMAGL 44 (1983) 81-85; S. Ebbesen, K.M. Fredborg, L.O. Nielsen, 'Compendium logicae Porretanum', CIMAGL 46 (1983).

[30] Ars Meliduna in MS Digby 174; Secta Meliduna in MS London, BL Royal 2.D.xxx. See De Rijk, Logica Modernorum 2.1. Editions by Y. Iwakuma in preparation.

[31] For references see De Rijk, Logica Modernorum 2.1, pp. 281-282, 288, 290. The text from the Cambridge manuscript is printed in Ebbesen and Iwakuma, 'Instantiae...', pp. 82-84. See n. 28 above.

[32] On Priscian, fols. 51ra-79rb; on the Elenchi, fols. 80^{r}-111^{v}.

[33] MS Cambridge, St. John's College D.12, fol. 66rb: 'aut notat (sc. "de") processum originis vel quasi pro origine, ut "iste est de Angli<c>a." Et nota quod, cum tripliciter ponatur "de" localiter cum ablativo, secundum primum dumtaxat modum potest proferri ablativus subtracta praepositione in responsione facta ad adverbiales interrogationes, ut "Unde venis? -- Domo mea(?)", sed non similiter "Unde audivisti vocem? — Caelo" sed "De caelo". Nec dicendum est "Unde natus es? -- Anglica"' sed "De Anglica".
Fol. 51ra: 'Soloes enim erat in confinio duarum linguarum sita, quae cum utramque volebat sibi defendere utramque corrumpebat. Vel, ut aliis placet, a praefata civitate [i]obsides missi Romam balbutire incipiebant Romane, ut Anglici in Gallia. Unde inolevit mos ut quodlibet vitium in oratione soloecismus diceretur.'

[34] Anon. Cantab., MS St. John's D.12, fol. 89rb: 'Sencana est hic et Rotomagi, ergo aliquid est hic et Rotomagi.' Fol. 90va: 'Rex habet unum solum castrum Rotomagi, ergo rex habet unum solum castrum.'

35 Ibid., fol. 83va: 'hanc autem divisionem plenius in Topicis executi sumus.'

36 P.O. Lewry, 'Robert Grosseteste's Question on Subsistence: An Echo of the Adamites', Mediaeval Studies 45 (1983) 1-21.

2

Oxford Logic 1250-1275: Nicholas and Peter of Cornwall
on Past and Future Realities

P. Osmund Lewry, O.P.
Blackfriars, Oxford, and Pontifical Institute of Mediaeval
Studies, Toronto

Cornwall, the most south-westerly of the English counties, ending appropriately at Land's End, has long been a realm of legend and romance. It is
country heavy with the past and seemingly very little of the present, bearing
an uncertain future. At Tintagel, Arthur, the central figure of La matière
de Bretagne, is reputed to have been born, and the figure of 'the once-and-
future king' may fittingly preside over his fellow-countrymen who feature
here.

A Toronto examiner, desperate to find a question an unresponsive
candidate might answer, once asked, 'Who was Arthur?' After an ominous
pause, the candidate hazarded, 'An English king.' When the examiner offered
the qualification, 'A British king, perhaps', the candidate resentfully replied,
'Isn't that what I said?' But, of course, it was not what he had said, and as
the organisers of this symposium in their wisdom asked us to discuss the rise
of British logic and not of English logic, there might be a place for looking
first at those logicians who had a better claim than most to be regarded as
British. For Cornwall was the last retreat within England of the original
inhabitants of this island, only finally submitting to the Saxon invaders early
in the ninth century. Here until the turn of the eighteenth century some of
the natives still spoke the language of a Celtic people and preserved a
literature whose closest kin was in the former duchy of Brittany and the
principality of Wales. In particular, before extending my study, I should like

The Rise of British Logic, ed. P. Osmund Lewry, O.P., Papers in Mediaeval
Studies 7 (Toronto: Pontifical Institute of Mediaeval Studies, 1985), pp. 19-62.
© P.I.M.S., 1985.

to focus on two men from the remote south-west: Nicholas of Cornwall, who has no more solid existence in that guise than a name in a colophon, and Peter of Cornwall, who has found his modest place in that great medieval Who's Who, Emden's Biographical Register of the University of Oxford.[1]

Behind them both lurks an older figure, Richard Rufus of Cornwall.[2] This Franciscan master is to be carefully distinguished from at least three other thirteenth-century masters, probably all secular, known as 'Richard of Cornwall'.   One held benefices in the diocese of York from before 1214; a canon and then chancellor, he died by 1234.[3]   Another, of whom we know no more, was a party to the peace settlement between Northern and Irish scholars in 1252.[4]   The third 'Richard' was a master by 1233-34 and held benefices and a canonry in the diocese of Lincoln when Grosseteste was bishop.[5]   Adam Marsh, the first lector of the Oxford Franciscans ca. 1247-50,[6] commended the latter to Grosseteste for a prebend.   Already a master, a subdeacon since around 1240, and not unknown to the bishop, he is described as a man of honest conversation and unblemished repute, well-informed in humane and divine learning, but 'idiomatis Anglici carens promptitudine.'[7]   Adam himself came from Somerset in the West of England, Roger Bacon's county, where Arthur was laid to rest at Glastonbury, but to a Somerset man Richard was evidently something of a foreigner, 'rather slow in his use of English idioms.'

For those of high birth language may have been no problem, but the case of this master suggests that some Cornishmen may still have been hampered by unfamiliarity with English in his time.   Even without this disability, it is readily intelligible that as a 'foreign' group they may have sought intellectual guidance from their fellows at Oxford, much as Danes may have done in thirteenth-century Paris.   This may give some weight to the supposed link between the unknown Nicholas and the Franciscan, Richard Rufus.   To retrace ground quickly passed over at Leiden in 1979, there is reason to suppose that Nicholas is the author of an unascribed commentary on the Perihermeneias in MS Oxford, Corpus Christi College D 119.[8]   Quétif, Stegmüller and Glorieux all took this to be a work of Robert Kilwardby, for no better reason than that it followed a copy of his exposition of Priscianus minor.[9]   Certainly, its form of literal commentary is not dissimilar from that of Kilwardby on the Ars vetus, but the doctrinal agreement is to be explained by literal borrowing from his Parisian work.[10]   The second-hand character of this material is often betrayed by the formula 'Dicitur quod', with which this commentator reports Kilwardby's arguments. As with the preceding work, Kilwardby on Priscian, the hand is English — or should one say 'British'? — and of the second half of the thirteenth century. Of course that would be compatible with transcription in the English nation at Paris, but the manuscript has by rare good fortune preserved its original binding, and that fits a type that Graham Pollard regarded as characteristic of Oxford at that time, four thongs in short grooves on the inside of the boards and a 'chemise' of skin wrapped around the codex.[11] It seems likely, then, that the commentator was an Oxford master profiting by the circulation there of Kilwardby's Parisian logic course, since the latter had probably been at Blackfriars as a student from around 1245, before becoming regent master in theology in the mid-1250s.

Kilwardby on Priscian is preceded by a question-commentary on De generatione et corruptione, which opens (fol. 1ra): 'Quia pars non accipitur nisi per diffinicionem tocius, et de qualibet parte naturalis philosophie sit presens intencio, liceat parumper gracia illius de diuisionibus philosophie sub quadam breuitate sermonem facere.' This opening recalls that of the commentary on the Metaphysica preserved in MS Vatican lat. 4538 and two Oxford manuscripts, thought by Gedeon Gál to have been used as a source by Richard Rufus.[12] A discussion here of the unity of matter reflects interests current when Kilwardby composed his De ortu scientiarum around 1250. The question form is similar to that employed by Geoffrey of Aspall, a master active between 1243 and 1263.[13] It is plausible to see this too as an Oxford work of the 1250s, but nothing in the style suggests that it is either by Kilwardby or the Perihermeneias commentator.

When that commentator discusses the nomen infinitum, he employs the argument that both ens and non ens can be said of non-man, when being is taken as esse habituale.[14] He associates this way of talking with the theologians, among whom it is plausible to see Rufus, in view of Roger Bacon's criticisms of 'Richard Rufus and the fools of his time', documented by Sten Ebbesen in his article with that title.[15] A contrast is made between the logicians' way of talking, in which esse is linked with actual existence, and the broader way of talking of the theologians, in which esse may cover not only actual but mental existence of what is real or imaginary. Later the commentator discusses the problem of talking about a dead man. His solution is either to say that a material unity makes possible such talk, or to say the compound can be talked about truly because the terms are not equally posited, but first there is a man, then he is dead, so that while it would be fallacious to infer, 'He is a dead man: therefore he is a man', there is no fallacy in inferring, 'He is a dead man: therefore he is dead.'[16]

When I argued that this *Perihermeneias* exposition was not by Kilwardby, I had not seen the *Notule Nicholai Cornubiensis super librum Porfirii*. This is the title given to an exposition of the *Isagoge* in another Corpus Christi manuscript, E 293B, fols. 69[ra]–77[va]. This work exhibits similar features of style to the *Perihermeneias* commentary and borrowings from Kilwardby's Parisian course with the same formula, 'Dicitur quod'. The form of the colophon (fol. 77[va]), 'Expliciunt notule *domini* Nicholai Cornubiensis super librum Porfirii', indicates that Nicholas was probably not a friar-'dominus' suggests either a secular master, a bachelor or a monk. In this codex after various works on medicine and theology, Sacrobosco on the sphere, and pieces on algorism and the computus, there follows a monastic calendar (fols. 204[va]–205[vb]). This makes no mention of the patron of Oxford, St. Frideswide, but British saints are represented, Oswald, Alban, Chad, Aelphege, John of Beverley, Dunstan, Augustine of Canterbury, Leofred, Ethelwold and Kenelm, and for the black monks, St. Benedict, and the white monks, St. Bernard. Coxe described the next item (fols. 207[ra]–215[vb]) as 'De praedicabilibus, consequentiis etc. [ex Gul. Heytesbury, ut videntur, confecta] in fine mutil.'[17] In fact, although unascribed, it is part of the *Abstractiones Ricardi* sophistae.[18] The quiring of the codex makes it likely that much that has been assembled here was originally independent, but the *Abstractiones* are in the same late thirteenth-century hand as the Nicholas of Cornwall commentary, a fact which may strengthen the link with Richard Rufus of Cornwall. Here, one should recall, the discussion of the *sophisma* 'Omne coloratum est' leads to talk of an 'esse habituale siue commune esse' (fol. 207[va]), and in connection with 'Omnis fenix est' the *Magister Abstractionum* says, 'iste terminus "fenix" subponit pro non ente equaliter ut pro ente' (ibid.).

Emden has no entry under 'Nicholas of Cornwall' in his *Biographical Register*. The only Oxford master I have found who might qualify is Nicholas de Musele, who surely came from Mousehole, on the English Channel coast of Cornwall near Land's End. In 1275 he was granted a pension charged on the Cornish church of Pelynt. In 1276 he was a cleric of the London Templars, acting as a proctor for the diocese of Exeter in a dispute between his bishop and the abbot of Forde.[19] Can this be our Nicholas of Cornwall? Whoever he was, the common authorship of the *Isagoge* and *Perihermeneias* commentaries appears to be beyond question.

In regard to the _Isagoge_ Nicholas handles the case of a species with only one individual, much as in regard to the _Perihermeneias_, drawing on Avicenna's _Metaphysica_.[20]   In regard to the _Isagoge_, however, he adds that 'celum' is said univocally of the many heavens that there might be, and predicated of them _habitudinaliter_: that is to say, there is nothing in the notion of a heaven that prevents it from being predicated of many. This leads to the objection that if 'phoenix' is habitually predicated of many, and there is none but the unique phoenix actually existing, then it is a non-existent which is being taken according to this 'habitual' predication; similarly, a single man existing, the habitual predication of 'man' would relate to non-existent individuals, Socrates or Plato. Nicholas recognizes that some admit this argument, but he thinks it is still possible to say both with the phoenix and man that, with one individual actually existing, there is predication of many habitually but not of this non-existent individual or that, since there are no _appellata_ if the individuals do not exist. If one were to say 'Every man is an animal', when none exists, man in Socrates and Plato is habitually an animal, but by these individual names one would understand something that could be a man, for a form is manifold, being made many habitually by many matters, whether they are or not.[21]

Later Nicholas has a lengthy discussion of 'Sortes semper est homo.' Here he plays with a notion of being as a predicate that inheres less in man than in a man who is, but the attribution of 'man' to a non-existent Socrates carries with it the possibility of contradiction, in unpacking life from the attributed humanity. Also, if the proposition is true when Socrates does not exist, then the name should have supposition for past and future realities; but that leads to the false conclusion that one would not be able to amplify the supposition of 'man' by a suitable addition. With regard to the inference 'No man exists; therefore Socrates does not exist', Nicholas wavers between saying that this holds because Socrates is an _appellatum_ of 'man'; or that he is not an _appellatum_, but if he were to exist, he would be a man; or even that Socrates was a man and therefore does not exist. But a noun, he insists, is imposed to signify apart from any difference of time: therefore this noun 'man' is related indifferently to all its _supposita_, present, past and future, and as it is true to say 'This man is a man', so too 'Socrates is a man.' Alternatively, one could say that the passage to the individual can only be made for those which are present.[22]

With regard to 'Every man exists', Nicholas mentions the opinion of those who hold that there is a restriction by 'every', so that there is supposition only for those who actually exist, a division of 'man' according to its existing supposita. He also refers to a 'great controversy' (magna controuersia) whether the time consignified by the verb could restrict the subject. He apparently favours the view that restriction occurs through the predicate as such. Since the mind in making a composition takes the predicate after the subject, it can be attributed in this way or that, so that the subject stands under the predicate according to the way in which it is predicated. It would still be true to say that a man is white even if there were only one subject of which whiteness was predicated, and 'Every man exists' might be construed in the same way, in accordance with Boethius saying that subjects are such as predicates permit them to be.[23]

Now the dictum of Boethius to which Nicholas appeals is that which Roger Bacon, in his discussion of appellatio in the Sumule dialectices, says is falsely attributed to him and represents a common misunderstanding, into which he would judge Nicholas had evidently fallen. Around 1250 Bacon forcefully rejects any suggestion that the predicate contracts or restricts the subject: it only amplifies its supposition.[24] Nicholas, from his use of Kilwardby's Parisian course from around 1240, is certainly open to Parisian influences of the pre-modist period, but Kilwardby's course is all but innocent of discussions of the logica modernorum, and we do not know what influence the sophismata ascribed to Kilwardby may have had in England. Nicholas is apparently influenced by the thinking of those Oxford theologians who have a characteristic representative in his fellow-countryman Richard Rufus, but although the position on esse habituale is alluded to, it has not been embraced uncritically. Although, too, Nicholas accepts the omnitemporal imposition of terms, implied perhaps in what Bacon calls the sententia communis,[25] he is unwillling to say that there must be appellata for those who do not exist: if Socrates existed, then he would be a man. Also Nicholas admits a temporal contraction or restriction, but recognizes that it is the subject of great controversy and, like William of Sherwood, seems to be swayed by arguments on both sides.[26]

There is more on the Isagoge, attributed to 'Cornib.' -- presumably Cornibiensis. a Cornishman -- in yet another Corpus Christi College manuscript, D 230, fols. 57^r-59^v. This fifteenth-century manuscript has a collection of short notes by this master, with others ascribed to Albert, Scotus and Burley, but those said to be from a Cornish source do not resemble Nicholas's work and have no bearing on the questions at issue here.

Of more interest for present purposes is the sophisma 'Omnis homo est'
of the otherwise unknown Peter of Cornwall,[27] in the Worcester Cathedral
MS Q.13 of John Aston, identified as a Worcester Priory monk who studied at
Gloucester (now Worcester) College, Oxford, in 1294-95,[28] although some of
his texts, like that of Peter, are from around 1270. Peter asks first whether
'being' said per se can be predicated of what does not actually exist,
because it would then be verified without distinction of what is and what is
not; secondly, whether what is not could be said to be an individual of 'man',
so that Caesar not existing one could say Caesar is a man; thirdly, whether
a predicate could contract a subject so that it would have supposition only
for what exists; lastly, whether one could properly have truth with the
posited restriction.[29]

Peter is familiar with the notion of a being common to what is and what
is not and the connection sometimes made between the distinction ens nomen
and participium and esse essentiae and entis and esse habitu and actu, but he
says quite firmly (fol. 49va), 'Michi uidetur quod non debemus distinguere esse
per actum et habitum....' He thinks it unAristotelian to apply such a
distinction to being, which only has place where a subject is not sufficient of
itself but needs an object or an instrument. He regards it as false to say
that Caesar is a man. A word does not primarily signify a thought but a
reality, and that in the way in which it is apprehended, and primary
imposition is on a reality of nature. Although a corpse is not a man, it is
the same reality of nature that is being signified in saying in the past tense,
'Caesar was a man.' However, neither being present, nor past, nor future,
nor being simply speaking, are of the notion of a noun, and it is this absence
of temporal distinction which makes it essentially different from the verb.
Being in the present is thus only attributable to something which is. In
saying 'Homer is a poet', it is primarily 'poet' which is predicated, and then
the being of a poet according to his poetry. Similarly, in saying 'Caesar is a
man', it is primarily manhood which is predicated, and then the animated
being of a living man. Although, however, being a man is part of the
understanding of Caesar, to say he is a man is misleadingly to suggest his
present existence as a man.[30]

At the end of the sophisma Peter refers to that celebrated way of
talking according to which even if 'man' is imposed to represent present, past
and future supposita, yet it is used for present supposita alone with the verb
'is'; and similarly with the past and future tenses for past and future

supposita. By imposition 'omnis homo' stands at one and the same time for
all men existing or not, but it seems that there cannot be a single
distribution for all, because of the limits of different kinds of appellation.
The sense, then, is that all that goes to the understanding of a man is to be
understood, and more truly of those that exist than of those that do not.[31]

Peter makes one topical allusion: when someone says, 'Henry is king of
England', the predicate does not contract the subject by virtue of the
expression (de virtute sermonis) to stand for that Henry who is king, but that
is on account of use (usus loquendi).[32]   Henry III died in 1272 after a long
reign, and it is not implausible to place Peter's activity towards 1270.   His
discussion of whether the subject is contracted by the predicate goes beyond
Nicholas's, and in considering whether this occurs by the predicate conferring
on the subject its modus intelligendi,[33] he is probably betraying the influence
of the Parisian modistae on Oxford logicians.   Peter opposes the view of
those who hold that propositional composition is the principle of understanding the subject according to the requirements of the predicate, using the
argument that propositional composition is relational and the terms are the
principles for understanding the composition.   He then argues against a
temporal restriction of the subject by the predicate and for the understanding
of 'is' according to the primary sense of actual being,[34] aligning himself in
this way with Roger Bacon.

Enlarging our inquiry from the men of the south-west: William of
Sherwood came not from Arthur's realm but from the forest of Robin Hood.
Whatever influence he may have had on the Cornish masters, Nicholas and
Peter, he is also explicitly represented in the Worcester manuscript by his
tract on supposition (fols. 58rb-59vb) and the anonymous questions on his
work which follow (fols. 59vb-62va).   One of these is: granted it is true
that every man exists, how can it be true or false that Caesar is a man.
There is a view that 'Caesar' of itself always signifies what it was imposed
to signify, and as the composite signified no longer actually exists, it
represents a non-existent reality that has undergone physical corruption and
is only a man in a diminished sense.   The author mentions with approval the
distinction made by Geoffrey of Aspall between the imposition of a general
term without temporal differentiation and that of a discrete term such as
'Caesar' for a particular time.   With a proper name, the identity of
suppositum and significatum means that one decays with the other: there is
only a basis for a mental distinction inasmuch as the significatum is the

suppositum as it is represented to the mind. Finally, however, the author returns to a view like the initial one, making corruption of esse actuale a reason for saying that 'Caesar is a man' is entirely false when the suppositum has perished, but saying that 'Every man exists' is true by reason of the esse diminutum of the supposita of 'man'.[35]

Bacon, who approved of Sherwood, would be less happy about a diminished sense of being than about the stress this anonymous master places on a significatum perishing with the suppositum. Geoffrey of Aspall is better known as a philosopher of nature than a logician, and the author's somewhat gratuitous development of the physics of corruption suggests that he may have known more of Geoffrey's work than his logic. Where Geoffrey's activity is to be placed is not certain. He appears to have had an influence in Paris if, as Bazán thinks, Siger of Brabant abridged material of his in 1265-68 for the Compendium de generatione et corruptione.[36] While there is no mention of Geoffrey in the Chartularium of Paris, one may ask if Paris looked to Oxford for texts when the libri naturales began to be taught. Geoffrey was already a master when he witnessed Richard of Clare's licence for Walter of Merton's foundation in 1262.[37] Enya Macrae placed Geoffrey's studies and teaching in the period 1243-63.[38] He was a fellow-student with John Pecham, the Franciscan who as archbishop of Canterbury criticised Geoffrey in 1286 for his plurality of benefices,[39] but Pecham studied arts first in Paris, then in Oxford, and Emden thinks it was at Oxford that they were together.[40] Perhaps, like many Englishmen, Geoffrey studied and taught in both universities. Both Peter of Cornwall and the anonymous author of the questions on Sherwood could have been writing in the 1260s, even if Geoffrey's arts teaching were a little earlier, say in the late 1250s and early 1260s.

Together with the sophismata ascribed to Peter of Cornwall, the Worcester manuscript has others ascribed to Willelmus de Scardeburh (fol. 37ra)[41] and Berwyck (fol. 48ra), perhaps the Franciscan John de Berwick, lector in theology at Greyfriars, Oxford, around 1290.[42] Later, and separately, there is an unascribed sophisma, 'Omnis homo de necessitate est animal' (fols. 74ra-76ra), which discusses three points: whether the proposition 'Man is an animal' has existential import; whether truth is presupposed to such a per se predication; whether there is a being intermediate between actual and potential being, esse quidditativum, corresponding to the reality signified by a general term.

In regard to the first point, the author rehearses various arguments to prove either that there is no existential import or that 'est' does imply actual existence, and mentions various solutions: even if terms are without temporal differentiation, the verb contributes a temporal differentiation; or the term 'man' of its nature stands for what actually has existence in the present; or the verb in the present signifies indifferently any present but has to be verified for some one present, although not by virtue of the expression itself.   The last resembles Peter of Cornwall's account of 'Henry is king of England.'[43]

The author's own position is that 'Man is an animal' does not have existential import.   He supposes that a general term is imposed to signify a thing and not a species, and not a potential being but an actual being, and he identifies this with esse quidditativum, apart from any difference of time, signifying in present, past or future.   It is not imposed to signify a suppositum, though he says that it has supposition for what it signifies as a sign.   Sometimes it has supposition for a suppositum, sometimes for an intentio, and sometimes for a significatum.   His analysis of 'est' is into two elements, the reality signified, expressed by the all–embracing participle 'being', common to real being, substantial or accidental, and to intentional and potential being; the mode of signification by which 'est' is primarily said of real rather than mental being but still is able to signify any 'beingness' (esseitas).   Simply speaking, it is false to say 'Man exists' when no man exists, in view of the primary reference to real being, although reference to a merely mental being may also allow it to be true, as with a definition.[44]

Modist influence may be detectable in the author's three–layer structure of a real, mental and linguistic union involved in making a statement.[45]   The union in the statement 'Man is an animal' does not imply that a man actually and really exists but mentally and according to its presence (mentaliter et presentialiter): mental existence or signification is sufficient for the composition, since the existence and thought of a man is the existence and thought of an animal, in view of their identity.   To say that a man is blind, however, involves real existence, since there is no such identity between a sighted man and a blind man.[46]   A threefold sense with respect to present, past and future, implicit in definitional relations, is replaced by a single sense in talking about inherence of attributes in the supposita at a particular time.[47]

The opinion that 'Man is an animal' is true because a man of the past, present and future is an animal of the past, present and future, is only talking about the nature of the terms and says nothing about the nature of the verb 'is'. If 'is' signified real being, then the author contends it would always signify that the existence was one of a real presence. Even if all restriction is eliminated, a man of the past being an animal of the past, or a man of the future being an animal of the future, is not the cause of the truth of man being an animal, because pastness and futurity do not inhere in man as such but as a man who was or will be. 'Who was' does not diminish the form, because then the <u>suppositum</u> would not exist. Granted that no man exists, there would be no <u>supposita</u> such as the man of the past and future, but the man who was is an animal.[48]

Finally, the author says it is true to say that man is an animal, and no distinction of sense is to be made when a man exists, but when no man exists, a distinction is to be made between real and mental existence. Similarly, when no rose exists, 'A rose is a rose' or 'A rose is a flower' is to be distinguished in the same way. Since a term can be taken for the word itself, it is also true to say 'Man is man', even when no man exists, having regard to the words, but it is not true that man is an animal, for that has to be distinguished.[49]

The solution to the third problem in the <u>sophisma</u> opens with a note that <u>esse actu</u> is opposed both to <u>esse in potentia</u> and also to pastness and futurity, in such a way as to be the same as being present. There is no intermediate being corresponding to the reality signified by a term in the first sense unless what is signified is a figment of the mind like the goat-stag. Even the embryo and the sperm, which might seem to qualify as intermediate realities, are signified according to the actual being in regard to essence. Taken in the second sense, there may be an intermediate being in regard to existence. A general term is imposed to signify its reality in act according to its esssence, not with regard to what is actually present, past or future, but with regard to that actuality expressed by the definition. However, this act can be realised in the present, past and future: what was, had being; what will be, will have being. This act will be the more truly realised in any time as the time designated by 'is' is realised in any present. As the term is indifferent to any time, it will be equally realised in present, past or future: whence the name of the species will be eternally realised with regard to whatsoever individual, whensoever it is, since it does not determine one time rather than another. In this respect, there is an intermediate being for whatever is actual yet not determined to one time.[50]

In the final reply the author says that for demonstration not only being in the present is required, nor is potential being sufficient, but a being opposed to potency, which is common to any time. Because a term can be realised in the past and future, it does not include being in the present; and because it can be realised in the present, it does not include in itself past or future.[51]

The pervasive influence of these preoccupations at Oxford around 1270 is evident when one looks at the non-logical works in the Worcester manuscript. Thus the anonymous questions on the Physica, with which the codex begins, open with a discussion of the possibility of knowledge of realities of nature, where the anonymous commentator appeals to a perpetua aptitudo essendi (fol. 2rb) as the ground for knowledge for what does not actually exist. A proposition such as 'The rose is the most beautiful of flowers' is saved by adding its condition of truth, 'when there is a rose.'[52]

The questions on the Metaphysica here are by Richard Clive. This master probably came from the south-east rather than the south-west, since his associations are Kentish rather than Cornish; his name may derive from Cliffe near Rochester. Robert Kilwardby nominated him junior dean of Merton College in 1276, by which time Clive was already a Master of Arts. In 1297 he was confirmed as chancellor of Oxford.[53] As a theologian, the Worcester MS Q. 99 reveals his interest in the divine ideas,[54] but the questions in MS Q. 13, reported by John Aston, belong to an earlier stage of his career, probably in 1272 or soon after.

Here again one finds the question of an intermediate being between actual and potential being, but now describd in the earlier language of esse habituale, alluded to by Nicholas of Cornwall, as well as in that of esse quidditativum used in the anonymous sophisma, along with the Avicennian example of the seven-sided house.[55] Clive holds that imposition is without restriction to the actual or potential or to any particular time. Since a term has to signify a true aggregate, but not with respect to determinate time, it can extend its significatum to the most remote past and future, to aggregates which are equally true with those of the present. In saying 'man' the mind by virtue of the significatum understands this aggregate to be a true aggregate indifferently with respect to present, past and future.[56]

This means that one who thinks of a present man with respect to the past or future, understands 'man' in a diminished sense; one who thinks of a man, present, past or future, with respect to the present or past or future, has a true understanding of man. The temporally indifferent imposition means that the being signified by the definition is true being with respect to the present or past or future. Taking actual being for that time in which we are now, there is an intermediate being, which is indifferent to every time, called _esse essentiae_ or _esse habituale,_ and there are habitual significata corresponding to it. It is called 'habitual' because it consists in a certain habitudo with respect to any time whatsoever indifferently. To say or think 'man', then, is to express or conceive an aggregate of matter and form referring indifferently of itself to a suppositum of any time.[57]

Up to this point, Clive has been talking about a noun alone. In saying 'Caesar is a man', however, there is a determinate reference to one time, the present, as with 'was' and 'will be', which refer to the past and future. Clive notes that a general term is imposed to signify a true being; but what is signified by a general term is not a true being, because with respect to the past or future it is not now. Granted that no donkey exists, the general term 'donkey' would express being and signify a true aggregate while it was in some past or if it was still going to be in some future.[58] In the 1270s Clive is still faithful to a position that had been current at Oxford for twenty years or more: there is an omnitemporal imposition of terms and a habitual or quidditative being to cover realities that do not have an enduring existence in the natural order and may even only have supposita in the past or future, signified with the determinate time-reference of tensed verbs.[59]

A general term, he thinks, has the same signification whether the reality exists or not and irrespective of difference of time.[60] However, what is signified is not the same reality. A name is imposed to signify the true being (vera entitas) of a reality but not its actual existence: existence and differences of time, then, such as pastness or futurity are accidental. 'William' always signifies William invariably, even though the reality signified is not always the same; 'King Henry' always has the same signification, even if the apprehension that goes with the expression changes. When it is said now — presumably in 1272 or soon after — you will apprehend that Henry is dead, though not by the force of the expression itself but by something heard or seen. Existence or non-existence are thus apprehended accidentally.[61]

Clive's view is that a general term still signifies univocally if the reality does not exist, because of the indifference to various realisations, so that 'man' relates equally to past, future and present both with regard to what is signified and with regard to the mode of signification.[62] He distinguishes a twofold being, then, actual being and quidditative being. The latter, being common to past, future and present, is what Avicenna calls esse non prohibitum: nature does not prohibit that being which is signified by the definition. 'Man' signifies what a man is; that is it does not signify non-man. As such, it is indifferent to present, past and future, as Avicenna's seven-sided house is a universal even if there is no house of that kind.[63] Nothing univocally the same is common to being and non-being; yet although presence, futurity and pastness share equivocally in being that exists or in the notion of being, something of the general term has being in the past and will have being in the future, and by reason of this being it is contained univocally.[64]

Despite the interest of Clive's questions on the Metaphysica for the understanding of tensed statements around 1270, he leaves out any consideration of the restriction or amplification of terms. These feature, however, in the last work to be seen here, an unascribed commentary on the Analytica priora, which immediately precedes (fols. 165va-191va) in the Worcester manuscript the Divisio scientiae of John of Denmark. The latter, a master of the English nation who reacted against Ps.-Kilwardby, composed his work in 1280 and, as the colophon indicates, at Paris.[65] As has been noted elsewhere, the Analytica commentary has a prologue that is initially the same as that of Kilwardby on the Elenchi, a Parisian work, but it is in the later question form rather than the literal form used earlier by Kilwardby.[66]

The relevant question for present purposes occurs when the unidentified commentator asks whether the mode of necessity amplifies a term, so that added to a verb in the present tense it makes it stand for some past.[67] He relates the opinion of some who say that it can amplify for times but not for supposita and of others who say it amplifies for neither. A word, he says, is imposed to signify its reality in any time whatsoever but according to its species rather than as an individual instance. In this way its meaning persists, and the locution does not perish or mean more said by one than said by another. He is contrasting the permanent character of verbal types with the accidental features of their tokens. Similarly, a word always retains the mode of signification conferred on it by imposition, wherever or whenever it is uttered:[68]

When someone says 'He runs', I do not think of any determinate present time. You may say, then, that it has a common time from the one who imposes it. I say that it has it from the one who imposes it that whensoever and by whomsoever it is uttered, it consignifies the present, but not this present or that but that which is truly present with regard to the utterance. What I say about the present, I also say about the past and the future: that this expression 'He ran' consignifies the past that is past with respect to the utterance. Thus an expression, according to its species, receives from the one who imposes it that it should signify such a time with respect to utterance, present or past or future. Restriction (artatio) of this kind follows the species, but it is not something inherent in the species that it should determine a time if the expression does not have it to signify this time except in its utterance.[69]

What is being justified here is a general form of an expression that in the case of a present-tense verb makes it stand by a non-linguistic contextual restriction, from the time of its utterance, for a particular present, though there are many such possible presents; in the case of past and future-tense verbs, for the many pasts and futures with regard to the time of utterance.[70] Someone may say 'Socrates runs' without adverting to the fact that he is running on Wednesday, and although it is Wednesday, and there cannot be two days at the same time, the tense of the verb does not determine the time-reference. With respect to an utterance at time a, the verb only accidentally consignifies the present a, not according to its essence or by imposition.[71] Finally, in saying 'Every man of necessity is an animal', the mode of necessity does not amplify for all times in the way the quantifier 'every' amplifies for all men, but it signifies unlimited and continuing inherence of animality in men. There is not simply an amplification of the verb but of the whole proposition by reason of the mode and the inherence. Ampliatio, contractio and distractio are to be understood in the same way.[72]

This paper has reviewed the handling of certain related problems by the Oxford masters of the generation between 1250 and 1275. Earlier material is hard to find, and the accidents of survival may mean that the works studied here are unrepresentative, but a consistent preoccupation with these problems pervades this narrow swathe of texts, and illustrations readily came to hand. The Cornish masters may not have been a close intellectual community like the Danes at Paris, but at least in two figures, Nicholas and Peter, one sees a persistence of questions that exercised Richard Rufus, even if they dissented from his solutions. Although there is a continuing inquiry about an intermediate being between act and potency, there is no consensus about an esse habituale or quidditativum in dealing with terms that have no present appellata. One master has clearly emerged as holding that restriction of subject by predicate with which Bacon took issue.

Jan Pinborg's perceptive insights into the English contribution to logic before Ockham are supported by a closer study of these texts.[73] There is the tendency he noted to look to the non-linguistic factor of the context of utterance to explain restriction of reference. Although the omnitemporal imposition of terms is prominent, and nothing has been seen to match Bacon's ideas on the reimposition of terms, the distinction of token from type neatly separates the imposed tense of a verb from its time-reference in use. Parisian modist thought has only a slight impact in this period, and the striking characteristic of these Oxford works is the employment of the terminist language of amplification and restriction. The well-established scientific interest of the British is also reflected in the attention given to the physical structure of the realities that ground the truth of utterances.

Around 1277 the understanding of the dead Christ was a touchstone of orthodoxy, but in 1272 Henry III is a topical and less controversial case. Caesar is always safely dead, and just once, in the Perihermeneias commentary in MS Cambridge, Peterhouse 205, formerly thought to be by Kilwardby, I found his name linked with that of the once-and-future king: 'since a reality of the past, like Caesar or Arthur, does not exist, it does not have being.'[74] The commentator, I believe, may be John de Seccheville, a Master of Arts, possibly of Oxford, by 1248, when he was clerk to Richard, earl of Cornwall, rector of the University of Paris in 1256, possibly a member of the familia of Bishop Bronescombe of Exeter in 1265 after residence in Oxford, and a holder of a Cornish canonry in the 1270s,[75] when Nicholas de Musele was acting as the bishop's proctor. If this paper has raised false hopes of a Cornish logic, this instance may be offered as a sop to local pride.

Notes

[1] A.B. Emden, A Biographical Register of the University of Oxford to A.D. 1500 (==BRUO), 3 vols. (Oxford, 1957-59).

[2] See BRUO 3.1604-5.

[3] See ibid., 1.490-91.

[4] See ibid., 491.

[5] See ibid., 490.

[6] See ibid., 2.1225-6.

[7] J.S. Brewer ed., Adae de Marisco epistolae 34 (Monumenta Franciscana 1, Rolls Series; London, 1858), p. 135.

[8] See Osmund Lewry, 'The Oxford Condemnations of 1277 in Grammar and Logic' in H.A.G. Braakhuis, C.H. Kneepkens, L.M. de Rijk eds., English Logic and Semantics from the End of the Twelfth Century to the Time of Ockham and Burleigh: Acts of the 4th European Symposium on Mediaeval Logic and Semantics, Leiden-Nijmegen, 23-27 April 1979 (Artistarium Supplementa 1; Nijmegen, 1891), p. 248.

[9] See the discussion of this work in P.O. Lewry, 'Robert Kilwardby's Writings on the Logica vetus studied with regard to their teaching and method' (unpublished Oxford Univ. D.Phil. thesis, 1978), pp. 111-12, 133-47.

[10] See ibid., p. 146.

[11] G. Pollard, 'Describing Medieval Bookbindings' in J.J.G. Alexander and M.T. Gibson eds., Medieval Learning and Literature: Essays presented to Richard William Hunt (Oxford, 1976), pp. 50-65; ibid., pp. 56, 57 fig. 3, 59-60.

[12] This commentary, also preserved in MSS Oxford, Bodl. Lat. misc. c.71 and Oxford, New College 285, is discussed by G. Gál, 'Commentarius in "Metaphysicam" Aristotelis, Cod. Vat. lat. 4538, fons doctrinae Richardi Rufi', Archivum Franciscanum historicum 43 (1950) 1-34.

13 See BRUO 1.60-61.

14 MS Oxford, Corpus Christi College D 119, fol. 126vb: 'Potest dici, secundum sentenciam Boecii, quod terminus infinitus nichil ponit, respondendo huic racioni sic: quod nomen infinitum commune est ad ens et ad non ens, secundum Boecium, eo quod est maius hoc quod est et non est, ideo neutrum ponit; de eo tamen uere potest dici vtrumque et ipsum de utroque sumpto esse habituali.'

15 Ibid.: 'Posset tamen dici, ut dicunt tehologi, quod si sumatur esse communiter, prout communiter se habet ad quodlibet esse, sic bene sequitur "Est opinabile: ergo est", similiter, "Est animal: ergo est." Esse enim est "prima rerum creatarum", ut habetur in Libro de causis (prop. 4). Quod eciam esse sit communissimum patet, quia per quodlibet ei adiunctum contrahi potest. Supponendo tamen ut logici supponunt, scilicet quod "est" cum per se ponitur predicat esse actuale, tunc dicendum est ut prius dictum est.' Cf. Sten Ebbesen, 'Roger Bacon and the Fools of his Time', CIMAGL 3 (1970) 40-44.

16 MS Corpus Christi College D 119, fol. 135rb: 'Queritur an de alico sit verum dicere quod sit homo mortuus. Et videtur quod non, quia esse hominem et esse mortuum sunt incompossibilia, et incompossibilia de nullo sunt vera.
    Dicitur quod si sumeretur hoc ipsum "homo" in tali sermone simpliciter et pro sua forma, esset talis forma implicans in se opposita, set sic non sumitur hoc set pro sua materia.
    Potest dici quod utraque de nullo sunt uera, set hoc compositum, scilicet hominem mortuum <esse>, est verum de alico, quia in eo non ponitur utrumque.
    Si dicatur quod in eo equaliter est vtrumque, et sic equaliter poneretur utrumque aut neutrum, potest dici quod in hoc composito non se habet sic vtrumque compostium, cum vnum horum sit prius et reliquum posterius, et non econuerso.
    Ex hiis patet qualiter fallit hec consequencis, "Est homo mortuus: ergo est homo", et non ista, "Est homo mortuus: ergo est mortuus."' See too Sten Ebbesen, 'The Dead Man is Alive', Synthese 40 (1979) 43-70.

17 H.O. Coxe, Catalogus codicum MSS. qui in collegiis aulisque Oxoniensibus hodie adservantur 2 (Oxford, 1852), p. 129. Formerly one manuscript, MS Corpus Christi College 293 was divided into two in 1910, the

second volume, <u>B</u>, beginning wih the old fol. 128, for which there are now two foliations. The foliation in which the old fol. 128 is renumbered as fol. 1 is that used here.

[18] It begins (fol. 207ra), 'Nulla est affirmatio in qua vniuersale sumptum vniuersaliter predicatur, ut dicit Aristotiles, et hoc potest esse quia non predicatur vniuersale sumptum vniuersaliter...', and ends (fol. 215vb), '...et istud est falsum nisi decipiatur, ergo credit'. The catchwords there, 'falsum nisi decipiatur et qui dicit', show a continuation was intended. Fol. 216^r begins a collection of sermons in a smaller format and a different hand. This copy of the <u>Abstractiones</u> was not noted by Jan Pinborg, '<u>Magister Abstractionum</u>', <u>CIMAGL</u> 18 (1976) 1-4.

[19] See <u>BRUO</u> 2.1331.

[20] MS Oxford, Corpus Christi College D 119, fol. 129ra: 'Potest dici quod cum uniuersale aliquando dicatur actu de pluribus, ut homo, et aliquando potencia solum, ut fenix, et aliquando secundum racionem solum, ut sol et luna, habet tamen quodlibet uniuersale, quantum est de racione sue forme, aptitudinem ut dicatur de pluribus.' Cf. <u>Avicenna, Liber de philosophia prima sive scientia divina</u> tract. 5 ch. 1; ed. S. van Riet, 2 (Avicenna latinus; Louvain-Leiden, 1980), pp. 227-28.

[21] See below, pp. 43-44, Nicholas of Cornwall, text I. Cf. MS Corpus Christi College E 293B, fol. 71ra: 'Set tunc queritur quid est habitualiter predicari.

Dico quod hoc est huiusmodi cuius racio non prohibet ipsum dici de multis et esse in multis, et hoc est esse uniuersale secundum Auiscennam.'

[22] See below, pp. 44-46, Nicholas, text II.

[23] See below, p. 47, Nicholas, text III.

[24] R. Steele ed., <u>Sumule dialectices magistri Rogeri Bacon</u> (Opera hactenus inedita Rogeri Baconi 15; Oxford, 1940), p. 281: 'Ex hiis patet quod predicatum nullo modo contrahit subjectum nec restringit, set solum ampliat ejus supposicionem, vel racione significacionis sue... vel racione consignifica-cionis, scilicet temporis, ut verbum de preterito et futuro....

Set contra hoc est quod communiter dicitur "talis sunt subjecta qualia permiserunt predicata". Si exponatur hoc quod dico "talia" per contraccionem mendacium est simpliciter illud verbum, quo tamen modo exponatuur non est curandum. Si autem dicatur quod Boecius illud verbum dicit, dicenduum quod falsum est. Boecius enim dicit in libro de Trinitate quod "talia sunt predicamenta qualia permiserunt subjecta" ....Verumptamen non est contraccio predicati per ipsum subjectum, sicut patet, quare ex illo non debet concludi contraccio.'

25 Ibid., p. 277: 'Duplex tamen est sentencia de appellacionibus, quia quidam dicunt quod terminus appellat de se appellata presencia, preterita, et futura, et est communis entibus et non-entibus. Alii dicunt quod terminus est solum nomen presencium et nichil est commune enti et non-enti, sive preterito, presenti, et futuro, secundum quod dicit Aristoteles in primo Methaphysice.

Quia vero sentencia prima est communis, ideo primo discernamus eam.' Cf. Alain de Libera, 'Roger Bacon et le problème de l'appellatio univoca in English Logic and Semantics, pp. 193-234.

26 See Martin Grabmann, 'Die Introductiones in logicam des Wilhelm von Shyreswood (+ nach 1267)', Sitzungsberichte der Bayerischen Akademie der Wissenschaften, Philosophisch-historische Abetilung, Jahrgang 1937, Heft 10 (Munich, 1937), pp. 82-85; repr. in idem, Gesammelte Akademieabhandlungen 2 (Veröffentlichungen des Grabmann-Institutes NF 25/2; Paderborn-Munich-Vienna-Zürich, 1979), pp. 1336-9.

27 See BRUO 1.490.

28 See ibid., pp. 46, lviii.

29 MS Worcester Cathedral Q.13, fol. 48ra: 'Omnis homo est, etc. Probacio et improbacio patent vna cum solucione. Circa istud sophisma primo queratur utrum esse per se dictum possit predicari de non ente actu, quia si sic, tunc posset indifferenter uerificari pro entibus et non entibus; secundo, vtrum non ens posset dici indiuiduum hominis, et hoc est querere vtrum, Cesare non existente, Cesar sit homo; tercio, utrum predicatum uel aliquid in ipso possit subiectum contrahere ut tantum supponat encia. Istud problema est bipartitum, quoniam vno modo potest hoc queri de proposicione in se, non comparando istam ad alicam aliam; alio modo comparando istam ad suam negatiuam, "Nullus homo est." De hoc ultimo nichil tangetur. Vltimo

queritur an nunc posita restrictione possit proprie (proprio cod.) habere ueritatem.'

30 See below, pp. 48-49, Peter of Cornwall, text IV.

31 See below, pp. 49-50, Peter, text V.

32 Ibid.

33 MS Worcester Cathedral Q.13, fol. 49ra: 'Consequenter queritur de coartacione. Et quod predicatum non coartat subiectum uidetur: Sicut principia rei se habent ad rem, sic principia intellectus ad intellectum. Set principia rei ita se habent quod quando separata sunt, neutrum dat esse alteri, nec modum intelligendi. Ergo similiter erit de principiis intellectus. Set intellectus predicati distinctus est ab intellectu subiecti. Ergo non potest dare modum intelligendi ipsi subiecto. Set si predicatum restringeret subiectum, daret ei modum intelligendi. Quare, etc.

Dicitur quod intellectus predicati et subiecti, secundum quod distincti sunt, neuter dat modum intelligendi alii, set secundum quod constituunt vnum coniunctum. Vnde, quando debet fieri coniunctum, primo accipit intencionem predicati et postea intencionem subiecti uel econuerso -- non curo de ordine -- et in ista collacione secunda sunt simul.'

34 See below, pp. 50-52, Peter of Cornwall, text VI.

35 See below, pp. 52-53, Anon., Quaestiones super tractatum de proprietatibus terminorum Guillelmi de Sherwood, text VII.

36 B. Bazán ed., Siger de Brabant, Écrits de logique, de morale et de physique (Philosophes médiévaux 14; Louvain-Paris, 1974), pp. 38-39.

37 See P.S. Allen and H.W. Garrod eds., Merton Muniments (Oxford Historical Society 86 [1926]; Oxford, 1928), p. 8.

38 Enya Macrae, 'Geoffrey of Aspall's Commentaries on Aristotle', Mediaeval and Renaissance Studies 6 (1968) 94-134; ibid., p. 97.

39 See BRUO 1.60-61.

[40] See ibid., 2.1445–47.

[41] See ibid., 3.1652.

[42] See ibid., 1.180.

[43] See below, pp. 53–54, Anon., sophisma, 'Omnis homo de necessitate est animal', text VIII.

[44] See below, pp. 54–55, Anon., text IX.

[45] MS Worcester Cathedral Q.13, fol. 75[rb]: 'Set vnio rei cum re triplex est, realis, intellectualis et uocalis.'

[46] Ibid.: '...dicendum quod per istam, "Cecus videt", significatur cecus existere, quamuis per istam, "Homo est animal", non significatur homo actualiter et realiter existere set intellectualiter et presencialiter, quia sicut existencia hominis est existencia animalis et similiter intellectus hominis intellectus animalis, propterea existencia intellectualis uel significacio sufficit ad composicionem. Set homo cecus et homo uidens non sic se habent quod significatum vnius sit significatum alterius. Vnde inter cecum et hominem non est nisi existencia realis, et per verbum denotatur cecus presencialiter esse.'

[47] Ibid.: 'Tamen respectu suppositorum potest esse triplex sensus, respectu presentis, preteriti et futuri. Patet quod non est simile de terminis concretis de superiore respectu inferioris: generaliter omnia que significant inherenciam ita quod exigant existenciam in subiectis, in talibus non est sic existencia in subiectis ut diffinibile, et ideo accipitur pro vno sensu.'

[48] See below, pp. 55–56, Anon., sophisma, 'Omnis homo de necessitate est animal', text X.

[49] MS Worcester Cathedral Q.13, fol. 75[vb]: 'Dico ergo quod hec est uera, "Homo est animal", et non distinguenda homine existente; nullo tamen homine existente, distinguenda est. Similiter, nulla rosa existente, hec, "Rosa est rosa" uel "flos", similiter distinguenda. Vnde, cum terminus potest accipi pro uoce, hec est uera, "Homo est homo", nullo homine, etc., quantum ad uocem; non tamen est hec uera, "Homo est animal", set distinguenda.'

[50] See below, p. 56, Anon., sophisma, 'Omnis homo de necessitate est animal', text XI.

[51] MS Worcester Cathedral Q.13, fol. 76[ra]: '...dicendum quod ad demonstracionem non solum requiritur esse presentis, nec sufficit esse potenciale, set esse oppositum potencie ei sufficit, quod esse est commune ad quodlibet tempus, presens, preteritum et futurum. Quia saluabile terminus in preterito et futuro, ideo non includit presencialitatem; et quia saluabile est in presenti, ideo non includit in se preteritum vel futurum.'

[52] Ibid., fol. 2[va]: '...non existente rosa, possum scire quod rosa est pulcherrima florum cum ista determinacione, "quando est" ....'

[53] See BRUO 1.444-45; A.G. Little and F, Pelster, Oxford Theology and Theologians c. A.D. 1282-1302 (Oxford Historical Society 96; Oxford, 1934), pp. 257-58.

[54] Ibid., pp. 287-92, 296.

[55] MS Worcester Cathedral Q.13, fol. 120[vb]: 'Omne uniuersale perpetuum est, ut hoc uniuersale "domus" est perpetuum; ergo habet esse in suo perpetuo non actuale; nec potenciale, quia hoc non sufficit: habet ergo esse habituale.'

[56] See below, p. 57, Richard Clive, Quaestiones in libros Metaphysicorum, text XII.

[57] See below, pp. 57-58, Clive, text XIII.

[58] See below, p. 58, Clive, text XIV.

[59] MS Worcester Cathedral Q.13, fol. 121[ra]: 'Ad argumenta respondendum: Ad primum dicendum quod est medium commune respectu presentis, preteriti et futuri, et sequitur "Est in potencia: ergo non est", set non sequitur "Est in potencia: ergo nec est, nec fuit, nec erit." Esse quidditatiuum est medium siue significatum terminum siue habituale.'

[60] Ibid., fol. 125[rb]: 'Queritur utrum terminus communis significet idem re existente et non existente...in significando nullam respicit temporis differenciam: propter mutacionem differencie temporis non mutatur eius significatum.'

[61] See below, pp. 58-59, Clive, text XV.

[62] See below, p. 59, Clive, text XVI.

[63] MS Worcester Cathedral Q.13, fol. 125rb: 'Dicendum quod duplex est ens uel esse, scilicet quidditatiuum et esse actualis existencie. Esse quidditatiuum est quod communiter se habet ad preteritum et futurum et presens, et vocat Auicenna illud esse, "esse non prohibitum" in 5 Methaphisice sue, idest esse tale quod naturam non prohibet, et hoc esse indicat diffinicio. "Homo" significat id quod est homo, idest non significat non hominem, idest significat ipsum quod est hominis, idest ipsum quid est, et hoc est esse indifferens ad presens, preteritum et futurum, sicut uult Auicenna quod domus eptangula est uniuersale etsi non fit.'

[64] Ibid., fol. 125va: 'Ad secundum dicendum quod enti et non enti, secundum quod ens et non ens, nichil commune est vniuocum, tamen quamuis presencialitas et futuricio et pretericio equiuoce communicant enti existenti uel in racione entis, tamen quid termini communis, quia in presenti habet esse in presenti, et in preterito esse habuit, et in futuro esse habebit: et racione istius esse vniuoce continetur, racione precedentis equiuoce.'

[65] Ibid., fol. 200rb: 'Explicit sciencia modi diuisionis cuiuslibet sciencie a magistro Iohanne Daco Parisius edita.' Cf. A. Otto ed., Johannes Daci Opera 1 (Corpus philosophorum Danicorum Medii Aevi 1; Copenhagen, 1955), p. xxxix. On the dependence of John of Denmark on the Ps.-Kilwardby Super Priscianum maiorem (partial edition by K.M. Fredborg et al., CIMAGL 15 [1975]), see K.M. Fredborg, 'Roger Bacon on "Impositio Vocis ad Significandum"', English Logic and Semantics, pp. 167-91; ibid., pp. 176-77.

[66] See Lewry, 'The Oxford Condemnations...', p. 242 and n. 57.

[67] MS Worcester Cathedral Q.13, fol. 185ra: 'Vtrum modus necessitatis adueniens alicui termino ampliet eum ad tempora, ita quod adueniens uerbo presenti faciat ipsum stare pro alico preteriti.'

[68] See below, pp. 59-60, Anon., Quaestiones super libros Analyticorum priorum, text XVII.

[69] See below, pp. 60-61, Anon., Quaestiones, text XVIII.

[70] See below, p. 61, Anon., Quaestiones, text XIX.

[71] See below, p. 61, Anon., Quaestiones, text XX.

[72] See below, p. 62, Anon., Quaestiones, text XXI.

[73] Jan Pinborg, 'The English Contribution to Logic before Ockham', Synthese 40 (1979) 19-42; ibid., pp. 34-35.

[74] MS Cambridge, Peterhouse 205, fol. 28ra: '...cum res preterita, ut Cesar uel Aritirus, si non sit, non habet esse....'

[75] See BRUO 3.1661-62.

TEXTS

Nicholas of Cornwall
Notule super librum Porfirii

I (MS Oxford, Corpus Christi College E 293B, fol. 71^{va-vb})

Quarto queritur de secunda particula, scilicet species predicatur de pluribus differentibus numero. Hoc enim videtur falsum (f. 71^{v} inf. marg.), cum sint quedam species que solum salua⟨n⟩tur in vnico indiuiduo, ut fenix, sol, luna et celum.

Dicitur, sicut dicit Auiscenna (Prima philosophia tract. 5 ch. 1), quod (que cod.) est quedam species que actu saluatur in multis, ut homo; quedam uero non actu set potencia, ut fenix; quedam uero nec actu, nec potencia, set intellectu, ut celum. Si enim intelligerentur multi celi et non vnum, esset 'celum' vniuocum ad omnes, et sic quamuis quedam species non predicentur actualiter de pluribus, etc., predicantur tamen habitualiter. Sensus igitur diffinicionis est: species predicatur, etc., idest cuius racio non prohibet quin predicetur, etc. (f. 71vb)

Set tunc sic sequitur: a habitualiter predicatur de b, ergo b est a sumpta habituali predicatione; cum igitur 'fenix' habitualiter predicatur de pluribus, et non est nisi vnicus fenix actualiter existens, est igitur fenix non existens

fenix sumpta habituali predicacione; similiter, vno solo homine existente, homo
est species, predicatur igitur habitualiter de pluribus, etc., et sic erit Sortes
uel Plato non existens homo sumpta habituali predicacione.   Quod concedunt
quidam.

Potest tamen dici quod tam fenix quam homo, vno solo homine actualiter
existente, predicantur de pluribus habitualiter, etc.; non tamen de Sorte non
existente uel Platone, etc., cum non sint appellata hominis, ipsis non
existentibus, set sumendi sunt eius appellata sicut dictum est in fine tercii
Topicorum de singularibus huius, 'Omnis homo est animal', nullo homine
existente: sic homo habitualiter in Sorte et Platone est animal, et non
intelligatur per li 'Sortes' aliquid actualiter existens set aliquid quod potest
esse homo.   Forma enim multiplex est, habitualiter multiplicata per plures
materias, et hoc siue sint siue non.

II (Ibid., fol. 76^{rb-va})

Queritur primo de hoc quod dicit quod Sortes semper est homo.   Aut
enim intelligit per hoc quod semper sit homo siue sit siue non sit, aut quod
semper sit homo dum sit.

Quod non primo modo: Si enim hec esset vera, 'Sortes est homo', Sorte
non existente, tunc esset hec falsa, 'Omnis homo est.' Set quod hec sit vera
probacio sic: Quando vnum predicatum inest duobus subiectis vel videtur
inesse, sic cui minus videtur inesse inest et cui magis.   Set 'esse' est
quoddam predicatum quod quidem minus videtur inesse homini quam homini qui
est.   Sequitur ergo, 'Homo est: ergo homo qui est est'; et constat quod
sequitur econuerso: ergo iste due proposiciones conuertuntur, Homo est' et
'Homo qui est est.'   Erunt ergo iste conuertibiles, 'Omnis homo est' et 'Omnis
homo qui est est.' Set hec est vera, 'Omnis homo qui est est', ergo et hec,
'Omnis homo est.'...

Item, si hec est falsa, 'Omnis homo', constat quod est impossibile, et sic
quelibet talis esset inpossibilis, scilicet 'Omnis homo currit' et huiusmodi.
Nulla ergo proposicio de contingenti, scilicet vniuersalis affirmatiua, esset
vera vt nunc.   Quod est contra Aristotilem in Prioribus.

Et si dicatur quod quedam sunt vere cum inplicacione, verbi gracia,

'Omnis homo qui est albus est' et consimiles, et sic intelligit Aristotiles in mixtione, cum dicit vniuersales de contingenti esse veras vt nunc.

Contra. 'Omne b est a'; hec enim equiualet huic, 'Omne quod est b est a, et dicit Aristotiles quod hec et huiusmodi sunt false et non impossibiles.

Item, dicit Augustinus in libro De vita christiana (PL 40: 1033) quod omne nomen inponitur ab actu, ergo hoc nomen, 'homo'; ergo cui non contingit actu hominis, nec homo; set mortuo non conuenit actus hominis, ergo nec homo; ergo cum Sortes non existens sit mortuus, Sortes non est homo....

Item, si Sortes non existens est homo, Sortes est animal; et si est animal, est animatus; set scribit Aristotiles quod [in]animatum distinguimus ab inanimata per hoc ipsum viuere: ergo Sortes mortuus viuit. Quod falsum est: ergo non est homo.

Item, si 'Sortes' supponeret pro preteritis et futuris in talibus, 'Omnis homo est' — aliter enim non esset hec vera, 'Sortes est homo', Sorte non existente — tunc non contingeret ampliare supposicionem huius termini, 'homo', per apposicionem alicuius ampliatiui. Quod falsum est.

Item, si Sortes est homo, cum illud esse quod hic predicatur non posset esse nichil, aut dicit esse in materia — quod falsum est — aut in anima — quod non contingit, cum sit esse indiuidui, et nullum tale ingreditur animam — aut est preter animam et intellectum, et tunc est actu intellectus, quia omne habens esse preter animam est actu intellectus. (f. 76va)

Ex hiis racionibus videtur quod non intellexit Porfirius per hoc quod dicit 'Sortes semper est homo', ipsum esse hominem ipso non existente, set solum dum sit.

Contrarium videtur sic: Aristotiles in libro Predicamentorum arguit sic, 'Animal' predicatur de homine, ergo de aliquo homine; nam si de nullo predicatur, nec omnino de homine, et sic nullus particularis esset homo post mortem. Est ergo hec falsa, 'Homo est animal', nullo particulari homine existente; cui contradicit Aristotiles in quadam mixtione, cum dicit de necessitate homo est animal. Sic videtur ergo quod Sortes et Plato, etc., sit homo nullo homine existente, et qua racione vnus et quilibet....

Item, 'Nullus homo est: ergo Sortes non est' aut sequitur aut non. Si sequitur, Sortes est appellatum hominis. Si non sequitur, detur oppositum, 'Sortes est', tunc sic: 'Sortes est; Sortes fuit homo', hec est necessaria, ergo adhuc est homo. Hoc enim sequitur, cum impossibile sit illud quod semel est indiuiduum vnius speciei, ad minus ipso existente, transmutari in aliud, et datum est Sortem esse.

Ad hoc dicitur quod prima consequencia non sequitur, sicut nec sequitur 'Nullum habens oculum videt: ergo lapis non videt.'

Vel potest dici quod sequitur 'Nullus homo est: ergo Sortes non est', non quia Sortes sit appellatum hominis, set solum tenet propter hoc quod si Sortes esset, ille esset homo, eodem modo sicut hec, 'Nullus homo est risibilis: ergo nullus asinus est risibilis.' Oppositum enim conclusionis infert oppositum premisse sic: 'Omnis asinus risibilis', ex hoc non sequitur 'Ergo omnis asinus est homo'; et ex hiis sequitur 'Ergo homo est risibilis'; et sic prima consequencia est necessaria. Non tamen sequitur asinum esse appellatum hominis; solum enim tenet propter hoc quod sequitur asinum esse hominem si asinus est risibilis.

Sic dicentes reducunt entimema in silogismum sic: 'Nullus homo est; Sortes existens, Sortes est homo; ergo Sortes non est homo.'

Potest eciam dici quod bene sequitur 'Nullus homo est: ergo Sortes non est'; non tamen sequitur Sortes appellatum hominis, nec debet assumi hec minor, scilicet 'Sortes est homo', ad reduccionem eius entimematis in sillogismum set hec, 'Sortes siue homo', sic: 'Nullus homo est; Sortes fuit homo; ergo Sortes non est.'...

Item, nomen inponitur ad significandum preter omnem differenciam temporis, eo quod nomen significat illud quod significat in tempore; ergo hoc nomen, 'homo', indifferenter se habet ad omnia sua supposita, presencia, preterita et futura: quare sicut hec est vera, 'Iste homo set homo', et sic et hec, 'Sortes est homo.'

Aut quamuis nomen sic inponitur preter differenciam, indiuiduum tamen sub ipso non continetur (continuatur cod.) nisi pro presentibus.

III (Ibid., fol. 76va-vb)

Item, cum li 'homo' de se stet indifferenter (f. 76vb) pro presentibus, preteritis et futuris, non (uel <u>cod</u>.) contraitur cum dicit 'Omnis homo est'; stabit ergo pro presentibus, etc., et sic est hec falsa, 'Omnis homo est': quare hec est vera, 'Sortes est homo.'

Quod autem per nichil contraatur probacio: Quia non per hec, 'omnis', quia hoc ipsum 'omnis' ampliat terminum cui adiungitur. Et quod non per hoc verbum 'erit', tum quia magis commune non contraat minus commune; tum quia predicatum non contrait subiectum, quia si sic, esset hec vera, tribus hominibus currentibus, 'Omnis homo currit'; tum quia in illo communicant nomen et verbum, racione cuiuslibet posset fieri contraccio, et omnis contraccio fit racione alicuius conueniencie. Videtur igitur quod non contraitur 'homo' per aliquod hic positum.

Et dicunt quidam quod restringitur ex parte li 'omnis' (de hominis <u>cod</u>.) vt supponat tantum pro actualiter existentibus, quia dicit diuisionem hominis in sua supposita, et omnis diuisio est existencium in actu, quia solum actus diuidit.

Probabilius autem dicitur quod hec contraccio fit ex parte temporis consignificati per verbum, et hoc non est communius quam subiectum set minus commune, nec est hic predicatum. Et quod hoc sit verum potest haberi, vt videtur, ab Aristotile in libro <u>Elencorum</u>: aliter enim nunquam posset 'laborans' supponere pro laborante nunc et prius cum dicitur 'Laborans sanabatur', nisi contraetur per tempus significatum per hoc quod dico, 'sanabatur'. Et quia magna contrauersia est an tempus consignificatum per uerbum posset contraere subiectum, propterea posset dici quod hec contraccio fit a natura predicati qua predicatum est. Cum enim posterius accipiatur predicatum ab intellecto componente quam subiectum, et predicatum potest conuenire subiecto sic uel sic; nam componit intellectus predicatum cum subiecto secundum quod subiectum potest substare predicato sic uel sic. Et huius signum est quod si non esset homo preter vnum cui conueniret albedo, esset hec vera, 'Homo est albus.' Et hoc est quod dicit Boicius quod talia sunt subiecta qualia permiserunt predicata; consimiliter potest hic dici 'Omnis homo est' et in consimilibus.

Peter of Cornwall
Sophisma, 'Omnis homo est'

IV (MS Worcester Cathedral Q.13, fol. 49va-vb)

Michi uidetur quod non debemus distinguere esse per actum et habitum,
quia proprie loquendo ita dicere tantummodo distinguunt aliquid ubi ad hoc
quod alica operacio esset in actu non sufficiunt subiectum et predicatum que
intrinsecus respiciunt ipsas actiones, set indigent instrumento uel obiecto,
quibus deficientibus potest impediri talis operacio. Verbi gracia, distinguimus
de videre actu uel habitu. Vnde, ad hoc quod uideamus non sufficit
subiectum ut tale, set oportet quod fuerit instrumentum et obiectum. Et
similiter est in omnibus talibus que ita distinguntur, quia nunquam inuenitur
ab Aristotile distinctum penes actum uel habitum, quia ibi sufficit quod fuerit
principium ut subiectum ad hoc quod talis operacio fuerit in vsu et non
indiget obiecto. Similiter de lucere, et hoc quia lux respicit illud solum quod
est de intraneitate rei. Similiter est de esse, quia posito esse in nobis, non
oportet respicere ad extrinsecum ad hoc quod fimus. Propter hoc huiusmodi
differencie non proprie distinguunt esse.

Ad argumentum, opposita nata sunt fieri circa idem, dico quod alica
opponuntur ut priuacio et habitus et habent fieri circa idem, non tamen est
aliquid actu uel habitu, set est alica substancia simpliciter non concernendo
actum uel habitum, quia sic forma exigeret totum compositum pro subiecto,
quod falsum est.

Ad aliud problema, Est ne hec uera, 'Cesar est homo'? Dico quod falsa
est. Intelligatis eciam quod nomen semper significat vnum; siue non fuit
actu, siue alico modo, semper nomen idem significat. Et quid est hic? Dico
quod si vocamus intellectum speciem uel similitudinem rei, [quod] vox non est
primo modo signum illius intellectus; et si hoc significet alico modo, hoc est
equiuoce, set primo et principaliter significat rem. Non tamen significat rem
simpliciter set secundum quod apprehenditur. Et differt dicere rem secundum
quod apprehenditur et speciem rei, quia species est in anima per se ipsam, et
res est in anima per speciem et non est in anima ut in subiecto set in re
extra. Hoc supposito, primo inponitur ad significandum quandam naturalem
rem, et hoc secundum quod apprehenditur ab intellectu. Vnde eandem rem
significat quam prius, quia nisi ista esset, non posset uere dici quod Cesar
fuit homo, quod tamen uere dicitur. Et tamen illud cadauer non fuerit homo,
nec illa species fuit homo.

Hoc supposito, intelligatis quod nec presencialitas, nec pretericio, nec futuricio, nec entitas sunt de intellectu vocis, quia sic dico 'homo', rem significando (significato cod,) et nullam differenciam temporis determino, et per hoc differt nomen essencialiter a uerbo. Vnde, si res illa sit que significatur voce, tunc uere possum attribuere esse de presenti; set si res non sit, tunc non possum uere ei attribuere esse de presenti. Vnde pono quod hec sit falsa, 'Cesar est homo', quia illi rei que aliquando fuit et modo non est attribuitur esse, cum tamen illi non insit set infuit. Set si 'Cesar' significaret rem suam aliquando ut ens, aliquando ut non ens, tunc esset vox equiuoca. Set dico quod neque significat ut ens neque ut non ens.

Intelligatis eciam quod in talibus ubi (nisi cod.) predicatur hoc uerbum, 'est', tercium adiacens, illud quod predicatur est illud quod significatur per uocem appositam, quia ibi non predicatur nisi res illius quod predicatur. Hoc patet cum dicitur 'Homerus est (f. 49vb) poeta.' Primo predico hoc quod est poeta et postea esse quod debetur poete. Esse autem poete est esse secundum poesim, et hoc est esse in opinione uel in singnificato. Ita exponit Boecius illam proposicionem, et propter hoc non sequitur 'Ergo Homerus est.' Vnde, cum dico 'Cesar est homo', primo predico hominem de Cesare, et postea esse quod debetur homini, et illud est esse animati, quia per hoc quod dico 'homo', intelligo corpus compositum et postea copulacio esse Cesari per hominem. Tunc attribuo animam Cesari, et hoc est falsum, quia anima est ablata ab ipso, et ideo nullo modo habet ese animati.

V. (Ibid., fols. 49vb-50ra)

Ad aliud, de ueritate, dico quod secundum famosiorem modum loquendi vera est, quia secundum famositatem loquendi supposita encia tantum supponit. Et si imponatur 'homo' ad representandum presencia, preterita et futura, tamen vsus loquendi famosus est uti pro presentibus tantum quando adiungitur huic uerbo, 'est', sicut in aliis, ut 'Omnis homo currit'; similiter habens cum uerbo de preterito pro preterito solum; similiter cum futuro solum pro futuro. Similiter, fortassis, voluit Aristotiles in istam, 'b contingit esse a', habere duas accepciones propter vsum (f. 50ra) loquendi. Vnde nos, respicientes ad usum famosiorem, dicimus quod vera est. Fortassis, tamen, si consideremus eam secundum imposicionem, diceremus quod 'omnis homo' supponeret tam homines non entes quam entes simul et semel. Adhuc, quod plus est, si tantum consideremus uirtutem sermonis in talibus, 'Canna Romanorum', etc.,

non plus dicerem Cannam vnius generis quam alterius.   Vnde in omnibus
talibus famositas loquendi debet plus considerari quam uirtus sermonis.

Set uidetur quod non possunt simul vnica distribucione distribui, quia
continentur per naturam diuerse appellacionis.

Dico quod distribucio reducit omnia ad actum quibus intellectis
intelligitur et homo.   Vnde is est sensus: omne illud quo intellecto intelligitur
homo.   Et quia illud (in cod.) hominis uerius est in entibus quam in non
entibus, famositas loquendi est quod semper reducat ad actum ea que sunt
entis; nec ad hoc cogit uirtus sermonis.   Illo modo dicitur hec esse vera,
'Omnis homo est', non nisi respiciendo ad famositatem vsus loquendi.

Similiter, dicendo 'Homo est species', non magis supponit homo in anima
quam homo in actu set solum est propter hoc quod famose vtilis.   Similiter,
cum dicitur 'Henricus est rex Anglie', predicatum non contrahit subiectum de
uirtute sermonis ut stet pro illo Henrico qui est rex, set solum hoc est
propter vsum loquendi.

Et sic patent ad quesita circa hoc sophisma.

VI (Ibid., fol. 49ra-va)

Contra opinionem quorundam que est quod composicio est principium
intelligendi subiectum secundum exigenciam predicati, potest sic obici:
Composicio non est nisi quedam relacio, et relacio quicquid habet habet ab
extremis; non erit ergo composicio principium intelligendi relicum extremum;
set extrema sunt, principia intelligendi composicionem.

Item, et si composicio simul fuerit cum extremis, et hoc in re, tamen in
sermone distans est.

Item, quod tempus non possit coartare uidetur: Semper enim in qualibet
actione agens et passum sunt simul; set tempus ibi (ubi cod.) distinctum est a
subiecto, et ita non potest ipsum coartare.

Item, si tempus coartet subiectum, tunc nomen aliquando habebit tempus
pro consignificato.   Probacio consequencie: Quid est consignificare tempus nisi

simul cum principali significacione habere significacionem temporis?
Confirmacio huius est quia participium non semper consignificat idem tempus
quod habet exprimari a significacione, quia sic dicto, 'Sedens surgebat', non
solum consignificat tempus presens set eciam preteritum. Si igitur nomen cum
suo significato principali haberet tempus, tunc nomen consignificat tempus:
quod falsum est.

Item, si tempus consignificatum possit coartare propter hoc esse quod est
ex alia parte oracionis; id autem quod coartat racione consignificati est ex
eadem parte cum eo quod coartat; queritur tunc que est racio huius.

Item, cum condicio coartantis sit esse minus quam coartatum, si tunc
illud quod est in minus non coartat, multo forcius nec illud quod est in plus.
Set hoc uerbum 'potest' est minus quam hoc uerbum 'est' et non coartat.
Quare nec hoc uerbum 'est' quod est in plus.

Ad oppositum...(f. 49rb)....

Redeo ad sophisma, et dico quod omni modo hic copulatur esse actu, et
alius modus eius quod est esse vtrum sit aliquod esse quod sit habitu, aliud
ab illo esse quod dicitur esse potencia, alias queritur.

Ad primam racionem, que fuit hoc ipsum ens dicitur transcendens quia
transcendit omnia, dico quod non transcendens dicitur quia transcendit omnia
quoquo modo encia, set quia transcendit uere encia, ut encia in genere.
Vnde non pono ea que sunt habitu uel potencia uel intellectu esse in genere,
et propter hoc non transcendit ipsa.

Set quid contrahat ipsum quando per se ponitur, quin liceat ipso uti pro
omnibus ad que est commune? Et dico quod hoc facit condicio rei et
proprietas sermonis, quia pono omnes proprietates sermonum referri ad
placitum imponencium et ut encium. Si enim imponentes racionem habeant,
illa uoluntaria est. Vnde voluntas est principium eorum que fuit ad placitum.
Condicio rei est quod cum hec res inueniatur in multis, in quibusdam
complete, in quibusdam incomplete; proprietas sermonis, et hoc quantum ex
vsu est, exigit quod si per se sumatur, stabit pro eo de quo dicitur complete.

Set nonne assimilatur esse actu esse accidentis, et esse habitu esse
substancie? Dicendum quod esse habitu est esse essenciarum, esse actu est

esse entis. Set essencie dicuntur res incomplete respectu encium, et solum encia dicuntur completa. Principia enim non sunt completa nisi prout sunt in principiatis. Vnde non pono quod esse actu sit esse accidentis, set est esse substanciarum encium, et uerius conuenit substancie quam esse habitu. Compositum enim cui respondet esse actu est prima substancia, et non omnino dicitur prima quantum ad actum substandi, sicut ponunt quidam, set quantum ad racionem substancie. Similiter, si esse temporale et esse perpetuum essent eiusdem, tunc esse perpetuum esset uerius esse quam esse temporale. Set ista non est ex parte ista, quia esse habitu est esse essenciarum, et esse actu est esse encium, et propter hoc non oportet quod illud esse sit uerius. Hoc patet, quia uniuersalia sunt perpetua (f. 49va) et indiuidua corruptibilia, et tamen indiuidua sunt uerius quam uniuersalia et uerius esse habent, quia uniuersalia non habent esse nisi in anima uel in indiuiduo. Vnde esse actuale eternum est uerius esse quam aliquod aliud esse; esse enim actuale est eternum Dei esse.

Anon.

Quaestiones super tractatum de proprietatibus terminorum Guillelmi de Sherwood

VII (Ibid., fol. 62^{rb-va})

Qualiter hec potest esse uera uel falsa, 'Cesar est homo', dato quod hec sit uera, 'Omnis homo est'?

Sciendum quod primo modo est quid significet 'Cesar', uel aliquid uel nichil. Et potest poni quod 'Cesar', quantum est de se, rem ad quam primo imponebatur ad significandum semper significat. Vnde 'Cesar' significat quoddam compositum et representat, quantum est de se, ad quod representandum imponebatur. Quia tamen hoc compositum non est actu, id representare hoc est representare ens non actu. Et habet esse effectum in suis principiis, quia uel potest producere illam potenciam ad actum ut iterum sit compositum completum, quoniam armonia et proporcio corrumpitur corrupto singulari, quia cum manet armonia et proporcio respectu forme generalioris, alia alia possunt produci et potencia sopita in illa materia. Vnde dico quod res quam presentat est res non existens, quoniam representat compositum consequens esse defectum in suis principiis.

Contra. Compositum resolutum in suis principiis non est compositum.

Dico quod non est compositum uere set diminutum. Ponendo hoc, dico quod hec, 'Cesar est homo', similiter intelligenda est homo diminutus, quia compositum habet esse diminutum sub forma.

Alia opinio est magistri G. Haspale, et est satis bona. Ponit quod diuersimode ad (f. 62va) representandum significatum suum imponitur terminus communis et terminus discretus, quoniam terminus communis imponitur preter omnem differenciam temporis; terminus discretus imponitur ad tempus. Et quia in termino discreto idem est suppositum et significatum, corrupto supposito corrumpitur et significatum; tamen suppositum et significatum in termino discreto sunt diuersa secundum racionem, quia significatum dicitur vnde intellectui representatur, suppositum vnde actui substat. Vnde hic est suppositum, 'Sortes currit'; hic significatum, 'Sortes est indiuiduum.'

Alia opinio redit in idem cum priori, quoniam sic suppositum corrumpitur per suum esse actuale completum et non secundum suum esse diminutum. Vnde hec est falsa omnino, 'Cesar est homo'; hec autem vera, 'Omnis homo est.' Similiter dico quod incomplete participat formas superiores.

Anon.
Sophisma, 'Omnis homo de necessitate est animal'

VIII (Ibid., fol. 74^{ra-rb})

Omnis homo de necessitate est animal. Circa hoc sophisma primo querantur tria: primo, utrum per istam proposicionem, 'Homo est animal', significatur hominem esse, ita quod sequatur 'Homo est animal: ergo homo est'; secundo, vtrum per se in proposicione presupponat ueritatem proposicionis; tercio, utrum rei significate per terminum communem respondeat aliquod esse medium inter esse actuale et esse potenciale, ut esse quidditatiuum.

Circa primum, quod non probacio: Quia nec per naturam subiecti, nec per naturam predicati, nec per naturam aggregati significatur hominem esse. Per aggregatum non, quia nichil significatur per hoc aggregatum nisi quod animal, <quod> indifferens est ad omne tempus, attribuitur homini indifferenti presencialiter; non per subiectum, quia indifferens; similiter et predicatum.

Ad oppositum. Cum composicio non posset esse presens nisi per extrema et presencia; set hic est composicio presens, ergo et extrema presencia, cuiusmodi sunt 'homo' et 'animal': ergo per istam homo significatur actualiter esse.

Dicitur quod significatur hominem esse per Boecium: quando hoc verbum 'est' predicatur tercium, etc., et per hominem et animal significatur una res nature; et ideo significatur hominem esse.

Et per hoc respondetur ad racionem, quia predicat esse quod debetur extremis, cuiusmodi est esse reale, esse quod aptum natum est inesse animali est uerum esse reale.

Contra....

Aliter dicitur quod significatur hominem esse, et si res significate ex parte terminorum sint indifferenter, tamen componuntur per uerbum, et ipsum uerbum facit nomen stare pro presentibus uel pro aliis differenciis temporis... (f. 74rb)....

Aliter dicitur quod stat 'homo' presencialiter: per naturam termini in se, 'homo' significat uerum esse hominis hic (nisi cod.) cui actualis existencie. Cum homo sit in genere substancie uerum esse ei debetur....

Aliter dicitur quod non significatur hominem esse, quia uerbum presens significat indifferenter quodcumque presens, tamen pro alico vno habet uerificari set non de uirtute sermonis, sicut presens significat nunc esse, non tamen hoc nunc.

IX (Ibid., fol. 74^{va-vb})

Suppono quod terminus communis imponitur ad significandum rem non speciem; et non imponitur ad significandum esse potenciale set actuale, hoc est esse quidditatiuum preter omnem differenciam temporis et preter omnem significacionem in presenti, etc.; nec imponitur ad significandum suppositum, quia significacio est extra significatum.

Quarto, suppono quod supponit quod significat et non aliud; nec supponit nisi sicut signum. Terminus signum est.

Suppono, quinto, quod terminus aliquando supponit pro supposito, aliquando pro intencione, aliquando pro significato.

Hiis suppositis, uidendum est de natura huius uerbi, 'est', et primo in se. Nota quod in hoc verbo, 'est', duo sunt, scilicet res significata et modus significandi, et hec duo sunt, quia vnum non est aliud. Res significata est eadem cum re significata per participium sibi coniunctum.

Et cum nichil sit lacius ente, Aristotile in **Metaphisica**, nichil erit lacius hoc uerbo, 'est'. Res huius uerbi, 'est', est communis ad esse reale substanciale et accidentale, communitate tamen attribucionis, et similiter ad esse intencionale et potenciale. Et cum modus significandi non debet diminuere de re significata, modus significandi non diminuit de re uerbi: et sic modus significandi ad tria esse est communis, set per prius dicitur de esse reali quam intellectuali (f. 74vb) et quelibet esseitas potest significari, ut 'Homo est iustus', ut 'Homo est intellectus.'

Cum predicatur 'est' secundum, cum per prius significat esse reale actuale, tale copulatur esse, et propterea hec est falsa, 'Homo est', nullo homine existente. Si tamen referamus intellectum ad illud quod sermo permittit, hec potest esse uera, 'Homo est', nullo homine existente, quia esse potest esse intellectuale. Hoc uult Aristotiles in **libro Posteriorum** ubi uult quod diffinicio non requirit nisi esse intellectuale.

X (Ibid., fol. 75^{va-vb})

Vera opinio erat quod hec, 'Homo est animal', est uera, quia homo preteriti, presentis et futuri est animal preteriti, presentis et futuri. Isti loquebantur de natura terminorum et nichil de natura huius 'est', quia in vno sensu est uera. Dicunt quod est uera, set sic dicentes necessario habent concedere istam, 'Album est nigrum', 'Cecus est uidens', et dico quod utraque est falsa. Si per hoc uerbum, 'est', significatur esse reale, ut 'Homo est animal', semper significatur quod res significata sit presens et significatur ista existencia esse realiter presencia. Et sic quecumque causa accipitur, semper erit hec falsa, 'Album est nigrum'; quascumque causas habuerit proposicio, quando (f. 75rb) res predicati non inest subiecto, erit falsa, quia qualibet causa presupponit inherenciam rei predicati in subiecto. Et si circumscribatur omnimodo restrictio, homo preteritus est animal preteritum, homo futurus est animal futurum, non sunt cause ueritatis, quia homo non inest preteritas et futuritas in racione preteriti et futuri set homo qui fuit et qui erit. 'Qui fuit' non diminuit de forma, quia tunc non esset suppositum: posito quod nullus homo sit, non sunt supposita homo preteritus, homo futurus. Set homo qui fuit est animal: hic 'animal' presencialiter attribuitur, et est falsa.

XI (Ibid., fol. 76ra)

Vtrum termino vel rei significate per terminum correspondet aliquod esse medium inter esse actuale et potenciale. Nota quod esse actu dupliciter accipitur: vno modo opponitur esse in potencia, quia ens diuiditur in actum et potenciam; alio modo opponitur pretericioni et futuricioni, et tunc est presencialitas. Dicendum quod rei significate per terminum non respondet esse medium inter actum et potenciam, prout esse actu opponitur potencie, nisi significatum per terminum sit fingmentum. 'Yrcoceruus' imponitur ad significandum actu talis qualis sibi debetur et non potencia. Terminus, id quod significat, actu significat, ut 'materia' non significat in potencia ad materiam, quamuis materia, id quod est, sit in potencia; et similiter, 'embrio' et 'sperma' et omnia huiusmodi significant in actu — essencie, dico.

Si accipitur actu secundo modo, et iste actus est actus esse et non essencie, et sic rei significate per terminum respondet esse medium, quia cum terminus communis imponitur ad significandum rem suam in actu, non tamen in actu presenti uel preteriti vel futuri, set actu secundum quod opponitur potencie et dicitur 'actus essencie', et istum actum exprimit diffinicio. Iste actus potest saluari in presenti, preterito et futuro -- quod fuit habuit esse; quod uero erit habebit esse -- et adeo uere saluatur iste actus in quolibet tempore, sicut tempus assignatum per hoc 'est' saluatur in quolibet presenti: ex quo terminus indifferens est ad quodcumque presens, preteritum et futurum, in quodcumque eque saluatur. Vnde nomen speciei in eternum saluatur in quocumque indiuiduo, quandocumque fuerit, cum non magis vnum tempus determinet quam aliud. Vnde habet esse medium quod nominat esse oppositum potencie, non determinando aliquod tempus.

Richard Clive
Quaestiones in libros Metaphysicorum

XII (Ibid., fols. 120vb-121ra)

Quare, cum terminus significet uerum aggregatum, non tamen respectu alicuius temporis determinati, ideo significatum suum se extendit ad remotissimum preteritum et similiter ad remotissimum futurum, ut homo se extendit ad omne preteritum et ad omne futurum. (f. 121ra) Quia futurum respectu futuri est uerum ens, similiter est de preterito, ideo aggregatum preteritum et futurum respectu futuri et preteriti sunt adeo uerum aggregatum sicut aggregatum presentem respectu presentis: et ita omne suppositum preteritum respectu preteriti erit uerum aggregatum, et similiter est de futuro. Ex quo sequitur quod sic dicendo, 'homo', intellectu uirtute significati intelligit hoc aggregatum indifferenter respectu presentis, preteriti et futuri esse uerum aggregatum, et illud est esse quod significat iste terminus. 'homo', et similiter de quolibet alio termino communi; intelligere hominem respectu preteriti est intelligere uerum hominem, et similiter de aliis differenciis temporis.

XIII (Ibid., fol. 121ra)

Qui intelligit hominem presentem respectu preteriti uel futuri, diminutum hominem intelligit; qui uero intelligit hominem presentem, preteritum uel futurum respectu presentis uel preteriti uel futuri, intelligit uerum hominem. Et istud est uerum esse quod significatur per terminum communem, et istud est quod significat diffinicio, ut esse uerum respectu presentis uel preteriti uel futuri, quia imponuntur ad significandum uerum hominem siue aggregatum indifferenter respectu trium temporum.

Accipiendo esse actu pro eo quod nunc est in quo sumus, medium est esse, et est illud esse esse indifferens ad omne tempus et uocatur 'esse essencie' siue 'habituale', et ei respondent significata habitualia. Et dicitur 'habituale esse' quia consistit in quadam habitudine respectu cuiuslibet temporis indifferenter...

Proferre hominem est proferre aggregatum ex materia et forma respectu cuiuslibet temporis indifferenter, et similiter intelligere hominem est

intelligere uerum aggregatum respectu cuiuslibet temporis, et de se
indifferenter respicit suppositum cuiuscumque temporis

XIV (Ibid., fol. 121ra)

Ex hoc sequitur, ut uidetur quod potest dici 'Cesar est homo.' Verum
est, set compara similia similibus sic: 'Cesar est uel fuit uel erit homo', et
sic erit uerum dicere, quia uerificacio est pro uno tempore. Comparando
preteritum ad presens uel futurum, erit sermo falsus, ut 'Cesar est homo',
dato quod sit falsa. Facta tamen comparacione prout sub termino est, sic
erit uera, quia si hoc uerbum, 'est', esset commune cuilibet tempori, esset
hec uera, 'Cesar est homo.' Set nunc ita est quod hoc uerbum, 'est',
determinate se habet ad vnum tempus, et similiter 'fuit' et 'erit'.

Nota quod terminus communis imponitur ad significandum uerum ens; non
tamen est uerum ens id quod significatur per terminum communem, quia
respectu preteriti et futuri non est nunc. Vnde dico quod si ponatur quod
nullus asinus sit, adhuc iste terminus communis, 'asinus', habet esse et
significat uerum aggregatum, dummodo fuit in alico preterito uel adhuc si erit
in alico futuro. Terminus igitur communis uerum aggregatum significat.

XV (Ibid., fol. 125rb)

Ad primam questionem dicendum quod idem significat terminus communis,
re existente actualiter et non existente, et tamen illud quod significatur non
est eadem res. Racio huius est quia nomen non imponitur ad significandum
rei existenciam actualem, quia accidens est significare rei actualem
existenciam; consignificatur per tempus, set per nomen non consignificatur
tempus, nec ex significato: ergo non significat existenciam, nec alicam
differenciam temporis, quia hec accidencia sunt. Set imponitur ad
significandum ueram entitatem, sicut res nata est habere entitatem. Hoc dico
propter ea que habent esse in anima, etsi entitas rei actu sit uel preterita
uel futura, quia ista sunt ei accidentalia. Quamuis de re possit predicari
esse nunc, quia non est de eius essencia, ideo existenciam rei non significat,
nec pretericionem, nec futuricionem. Patet tunc quod idem significat; non
tamen id quod significat est idem. Et quamuis quid non semper existat actu,
tamen semper idem est quod significat, ut 'Willelmus' semper significat

Willelmum; quamuis uarietur accidentaliter, cum terminus communis quid significat quod inuariabile est, ideo idem significat.

Ad argumentum dicendum quod illud per uocem significatur quod per uocem apprehenditur; uerum est primo et per se semper idem significat, quamuis per apprehensionem uocis. Si igitur apprehenderis uiuum uel mortuum, hoc non est de significato uocis, set est per aliam apprehensionem, ut patet si Henricus rex est, per 'Henricus' semper idem significatur de ui vocis. Si nunc dicatur 'Henricus rex', apprehenderis mortuum, set non de ui vocis, set per auditum uel per uisum uel alio modo. Significat ergo primo et per se idem; tamen, aliquando per apprehensionem uocis accidentaliter apprehenditur existencia uel non existencia.

XVI (Ibid., fol. 125rb)

Ad secundam questionem dico quod significat vniuoce, re existente et non existente. Ad cuius euidenciam nota quid est vniuocum, quia 'Vniuoca sunt, etc.' Nec est sic intelligendum quod eadem res sit in homine et in asino. Set nota, quando imponitur aliquid ad significandum prout indifferens est res ad duo et ad neutrum determinatur, ita quod non magis appropriat sibi hoc quam illud, tale dicitur vniuocum, sicut 'animal' imponitur ad significandum rem incompletam indifferentem ad quamcumque speciem, quantum de se est; et ideo est diffinicio eadem secundum illud nomen, quod significat quiddam incompletum commune cuilibet: sic est vniuocacio. Sic in proposito, gracia exempli, 'homo' terminus communis est et equaliter comparatur ad preterita et futura et presencia, quantum est de significato suo; et similiter, quantum est de modo significandi, non significatur alicam differenciam temporis, set indifferenter, quantum de se est, respectum habet ad omnem differenciam temporis.

Anon.

Quaestiones super libro Analyticorum priorum

XVII (Ibid., fol. 185rb)

Dubium est de ista questione: quidam dicunt quod potest ampliare ad tempora, non autem ad supposita; quidam uero neutram partem opinantur, nec

quod ampliat ad tempora, nec ad supposita. Vt, tamen, aliquid videamus de
ista questione, primo videndum est quod tempus consignificat uerbum et
qualiter, et quid eciam significet modus necessitatis.

Circa primum nota quod imponens vocem ad significandum rem non
imposuit alicam uocem significatiuam a tali homine et in tali tempore
prolatam ad significandum rem ipsam, et quod natura alica uox consimilis idem
significaret, quia si sic, dubium esset audienti quid talis uox significaret si in
alico tempore proferetur, et ita periret locucio. Manifestum est ergo quod
imponit vocem vna imposicione generali ad significandum rem suam in
quocumque tempore proferetur, non in tali tempore uel tali; nec tali uoci uel
tali uoci nomen imponit, set speciei uocis inposicio facta est.

XVIII (Ibid., fol. 185^{rb-va})

Et ideo prolata hac voce, 'Currit', a te, non plus intelligo propter te
proferentem quam propter alium set propter imposicionem suam in hoc quod
referro eam ad impositorem primum. In quantum vox ab impositore signum rei
est et proferatur a tali uel a tali in tali tempore uel tali, accidit voci.

Secundum notandum est: Sicut impositor se habuit ad uocem significatiuam, sic se habuit ad imposicionem, modi significandi; sicut ad speciem
refertur uox in significando, sic et in modo significandi inponit in quocumque
loco et tempore, et a quocumque proferetur semper eundem modum
significandi retineret. Imponit eciam ut uox significaret rem mensuratam tali
tempore mensuratiuo, et per hoc excluditur dubitacio quod res mensuretur
tempore mensuratiuo et proporcionali magno uel paruo sicut rei decet in
mensurando.

Quod tempus presens? Imponit ne tempus presens quod fuit in
imposicione uel quod fuit in prolacione? Non. Si sic, cum non imponit
alicam vnam uocem determinatam set totam speciem ad significandum,
sequeretur quod aliquando significaret tempus preteritum, aliquando futurum,
et ita impossibile esset quod alica uox ab impositore habeat quod significet
aliquod tempus determinatum. Cum dicitur 'Currit', non intelligo aliquod
tempus presens determinatum. Dices ergo quod habet tempus commune ab
impositore. Dico quod habet ab impositore quod quandocumque et a
quocumque proferatur consignificet presens (f. 185va), non hoc tamen presens

uel illud set illud quod est uere presens respectu prolacionis.   Quod dico de
presenti, dico eciam de preterito et futuro, quod hec uox, 'Cucurrit',
consignificet preteritum quod est preteritum respectu prolacionis, et ita uox
secundum suam speciem recipit ab impositore quod significet tempus tale
respectu prolacionis, presens uel preteritum uel futurum.   Talis artacio
sequitur speciem.   Set quod tempus determinaret, hoc non posset inesse
speciei si uox non habet quod significet hoc tempus uel illud nisi in
prolacione sua.

XIX (Ibid., fol. 185va)

Si significaret tempus determinatum illud uel istud, non possit inesse
speciei imposicione vocis: relinquit uoci indeterminacionem ad prolacionem, et
sic relinquit voci indeterminacionem in significando, quia ex quo in eam quod
est prolacio relinquit indeterminacionem et in significando quod est effectus.
Prolata hac uoce, 'Currit', nunc, non habet ab impositore quod illa vox
consignificaret nunc determinatum tempus, quia sic coartasset quod in nullo
alio tempore significaret presens.   Et tamen habet, posito per impossibile
quod plura essent simul presencia respectu eiusdem temporis sicut sunt plura
preterita et futura, tunc hec uox habet a suo impositore quod consignificet
tempus presens respectu sue prolacionis; et iam positum est quod plura sunt
presencia simul: neutrum determinate significabitur, sicut 'Cucurrit' non
consignificat aliquod preteritum determinatum.   Dato quod uox haberet ab
impositore quod aliquod tempus determinatum consignicaret, et essent plura
tempora presencia simul, alterum non consignificaret.   Dicetur quod hoc
sequitur propter impossibile, posicionem scilicet plura presencia simul esse.

XX (Ibid., fol. 185va)

Dicat aliquis 'Sortes currit', non percipiens quod currit die Mercurii, nisi
quia dies Mercurii est, et non possunt esse duo dies simul.   Si uero
determinaret tempus, non sic esset.   Quod tempus consignificat?   Dico quod
non consignificat aliquod tempus determinatum nisi respectu prolacionis, quia
in tempore prolacionis non est aliquod tempus nisi a; ideo accidentaliter
consignificat presens quod est presens respectu a, et non est presens nisi a
uel quod est pars a: ideo dico quod quantum ad essenciam vocis et
imposicionem uocis non consignificabit a.   Vnde non sequitur 'Currit: ergo
currit in a' de vi uocis nisi supposito quod illud tempus sit a.

XXI (Ibid., fol. 186ra)

Ampliat ne modus ut stat pro diuersis temporibus, ut 'Omnis homo de necessitate animal', etc.? Dico, sicut pono ibi possibile contraccionem et similiter distraccionem, sic pono possibiliter ampliacionem. Non pono quod modus necessitatis ampliat sicut signum, ut hoc signum, 'omnis', adueniens termino significat ipsum stare pro omnibus. Talem amplificacionem non pono a parte modi quod faciat uerbum stare pro diuersis temporibus. Set sic ampliat cum aduenerit uerbo substantiui habenti inherenciam respectu temporis determinati: significat istam inherenciam continuari in infinitum, ita quod non potest deficere ab inherencia cum dicitur 'Homo currit' uel ponatur in a, nisi quia a non habebatur de virtute sermonis set ex necessitate materie. Ideo modus non ampliat respectu talis determinacionis, et ita per talem proposicionem totum significatur respectus ad quodlibet futurum, et non ponit ad non essendum in inherencia que est significata, et hoc significatur uirtute tocius circumscripto modo. Habes sic, dicto 'Homo est animal', quod animal inheret homini nunc, set modus adueniens facit continuacionem inesse respectu cuiuslibet temporis. Idem dico nunc quod et prius et adhuc plus. Sicut 'homo' significat in se vnum, cum dico 'homo in potencia', idem significat et plus, quia ampliat respectu termini. Similiter, cum dicitur 'Homo de necessitate est', uel idem significat uerbum et alio modo. Vnde uerbum solum non ampliatur, set est ampliacio in tota proposicione racione modi et inherencie. Non enim ampliatur uerbum quod in ipso racione adiuncti fuit ampliora tempora, set eodem modo intelligatur de ampliacione, contraccione et distractione.

3

La littérature des abstractiones et la tradition logique
d'Oxford

Alain de Libera
C.N.R.S., Paris

On connait deux oeuvres qui portent le titre d'Abstractiones:

   -- les Abstractiones magistri Richardi sophiste contenues dans plusieurs manuscrits dont Oxford, Bodleian Library, Digby 2, fols. 122^r-140^v; Digby 24, fols. 61ra-90rb; Brugge, Stadsbibliotheek 497, fols. 74ra-95va; Paris, BN lat. 14069, fols. 26ra-33ra.

   -- les Abstractiones Herviei (!) sophiste contenues dans le manuscrit latin 15170, fols. 48va-52va, de la Bibliothèque Nationale de Paris.

   De quoi s'agit-il? Le mot même d'Abstractiones est surprenant. S'il désigne, comme c'est vraisemblable, un équivalent de l'anglais 'abstract', nous avons affaire à un 'résumé', à un 'condensé', ou, comme on dirait aujourd'hui, à des 'extractions'. Autrement dit: plus qu'un florilège, mais moins qu'un traité. Ceci amène une deuxième question: à quoi les Abstractiones servent-elles? A qui sont-elles destinées? A leur propre auteur ou à un étudiant? Qui les a rassemblées matériellement? Ont-elles été notées au jour le jour ou redigées? Par le 'maître' lui-même ou par son bachelier? Peut-on distinguer ici, comme pour les Questiones entre reportation et ordination? Si oui, sur quels critères?

   Un moyen de tenter de répondre à ces questions nous semble être d'essayer de distinguer sur un plan strictement littéraire entre nos deux textes et quelques-uns des genres dont l'existence est couramment admise et

The Rise of British Logic, ed. P. Osmund Lewry, O.P., Papers in Mediaeval Studies 7 (Toronto: Pontifical Institute of Mediaeval Studies, 1985), pp. 63-114. © P.I.M.S., 1985.

solidement documentée. Dans l'état actuel des connaissances, ces genres, relativement voisins les uns des autres, sont les suivants:

. Distinctiones

. Sophismata

. Syncategoremata

auxquels on ajoutera l'entité intermédiaire que constitue, d'après son titre, la Summa de sophismatibus et distinctionibus de Roger Bacon.

Les syncatégorèmes constituent 'la base de la littérature des Sophismata' dans la mesure où la présence d'au moins un syncatégorème suffit à définir une proposition exponible, c'est-à-dire, du même coup, un sophisma, puisque 'la plus grande partie des Sophismata porte sur des propositions exponibles.'[1] La 'carrière des syncategoremata' dans la logica moderna permet donc d'opérer un premier classement à la fois historique et littéraire des formes concernées. C'est ce que fait N. Kretzmann dans son étude de la Cambridge History of Later Medieval Philosophy:[2]

With all the warnings and disclaimers appropriate to historical generalisations of vast scope and meagre detail, I suggest that the career of the syncategoremata within the logica moderna falls into three stages, the third of which is divided into two contemporaneous lines of development:

1. their emergence as the focal points of certain logical or semantic relationships or special problems of interpretation (in the twelfth century, especially the latter half);

2. their identification as a distinguishable set of topics worthy of development in separate treatises called, typically, Syncategoremata (from the last quarter of the twelfth century to the last quarter of the thirteenth);

3a. their assimilation into general treatises on logic, sometimes as a group, but sometimes dispersed in ways designed to associate particular syncategoremata with more general topics in logic to which they are appropriate; and

3b. their absorption into the sophisma-literature, where a particular syncategorema may serve as the germ of a paradox the interest of which is often associated with metaphysics or natural philosophy more than with logic or semantics proper (from the first quarter of the fourteenth century to the disintegration of scholastic logic).

Notre problème étant plus spécifiquement centré sur le XIIIème siècle, et, en l'occurence, sur sa première moitié, il nous faut cependant, tenter d'aller plus loin dans la caractérisation de ces genres, apparemment très éphémères, comme les *Distinctiones* et les *Abstractiones*, et dans l'analyse de leur spécificité par rapport aux genres mieux connus ou plus durables, comme les *Syncategoremata*.

LES *DISTINCTIONES*. Ce genre apparemment limité à la première moitié du XIIIème siècle est représenté par plusieurs oeuvres décrites par H.A.G. Braakhuis: deux figurent dans le ms Vat. lat. 7678, il s'agit des *Communes objectiones et responsiones* (fols. 73ra-82ra)[3] et de *Nomen dividuum* (fols. 82rb-88^{r}).[4] M. Braakhuis en a donné le plan détaillé, deel 1, pp. 35-36 et p. 37 de son ouvrage sur les *Syncategoremata*. La troisième texte: *Quoniam ignoratis communibus*, contenu dans les mss Vat. lat. 4546 et Barcelona, Archivo de la Corona de Aragón, Ripoll 109, fols. 278ra-309vb, a également été décrit par Braakhuis, d'après le manuscrit catalan.[5] Nous avons trouvé un autre témoin de ce texte dans le ms latin 16618 de la Bibliothèque Nationale de Paris, qui figure dans le catalogue de Delisle sous le titre de *Compilatio Durandi super logicam* et est effectivement attribué au fol. 165^{r} à un certain Durand de la petite Sorbonne. En fait, seul le texte des fols. 1^{r}-39vb a été compilé par le maître (vers 1335); le reste du manuscrit est antérieur. C'est notamment le cas du traité *Quoniam ignoratis communibus* donné aux fols. 109ra-135vb.

Les *Distinctiones* se présentent comme des recueils de règles sur le fonctionnement propositionnel des syncatégorèmes. Ces règles sont regroupées par termes et illustrées par des *sophismata*. Elles paraissent, en général, être mentionnées selon un certain ordre, qui, lui-même, semble épouser la physionomie d'un domaine de problèmes, implicite ou explicite.

Dans les *Communes objectiones et responsiones*, l'enchaînement du texte est assuré par des formules comme: 'Consequenter queritur de alia regula dictionis exclusive' (fol. 73va), 'Queritur de quadam regula dictionis exclusive' (fol. 74rb) ou 'Queritur de ista distinctione que solet fieri de disiunctiva coniunctione' (fol. 77rb). Une partie seulement des questions est explicite-

ment consacrée à des syncatégorèmes: de fait, plusieurs semblent concerner
davantage la théorie de la supposition en tant que telle. Toutefois, dans la
mesure où les problèmes alors discutés ont surtout trait à la quantification,
on peut estimer que c'est 'omnis' qui fournit implicitement le thème
directeur. L'enchaînement du texte dans <u>Nomen dividuum</u> paraît plus
directement articulé sur l'examen successif des propriétés des differents
syncatégorèmes. Songeons, par example, à la manière dont est introduite
l'étude de 'tantum' et de 'solus' (fol. 85vb):[6]

> Consequenter dicemus de dictionibus exclusivis. Sunt autem tres
> dictiones exclusive, scilicet '<u>tantum</u>' et '<u>solum</u>' et '<u>solus</u>'; exceptive
> autem '<u>preter</u>', '<u>nisi</u>'. De quibus est questio difficilis, propter quid
> dictiones exceptive sint prepositiones vel conjunctiones, exclusive vero
> sint nomina vel adverbia, et propter quid tantum dictiones exclusive sub
> nomine vel adverbio.   Ad hoc respondemus....

On peut donc bien dire, à grands traits, que les <u>Distinctiones</u> sont des
recueils de règles dont une partie notable concerne spécifiquement les
propriétés syntactico-sémantiques des <u>syncategoremata</u>.

<u>Quoniam ignoratis communibus</u> est-il ou non un recueil de 'distinctions'?
M. Braakhuis en doute: pour lui, il s'agit d'un texte parallèle aux <u>Syncatego-
remata</u>, dont le fil conducteur est explicitement fourni par l'examen des
syncatégorèmes:

> Op grond van het bovenstaande kan, zo komt me voor, het tractaat
> '<u>Quoniam ignoratis communibus</u>' als een soort paralleltekst van een
> syncategoremata-tractaat beschouwd worden.[7]

A l'appui de cette affirmation, on peut citer la transition du fol. 305rb du
ms Ripoll 109:

> Quoniam iam pertransivimus de communibus accidentis que circa dictiones
> syncategorematicas accidunt...circa signa distributiva inquiramus.[8]

Cependant ce passage reprend l'<u>incipit</u> dont voici le texte complet d'après
notre manuscrit parisien:

> Quoniam ignoratis communibus necesse est artem ignorare sicut vult

Aristoteles in libro _Elenchorum_, et in arte sophistica necesse est sic
communia cognoscere, ipsis ignoratis tota ignoratur scientia: propter hoc
aliquid de communibus determinare intendimus secundum possibilitatem
nostri ingenii non ad propria quecumque sophismata descendendo nec nova
nec inaudita dicere intendimus, sed _communes distinctiones_, que sepius
accidunt in sophismatibus, sicut posuerunt antecessores nostri, intendimus
in hoc.[9]

Autrement dit: ces 'distinctions communes', dont le domaine de législation est
la matière des _sophismata_, porte, si l'on met en relation les deux textes, sur
les 'dictions syncatégorématiques'. _Quoniam ignoratis_ semble donc partie
intégrante du genre des _Distinctiones_, même si l'ordre d'enchaînement des
items est donné par l'énumération — d'ailleurs relativement ordonné -- des
différents syncatégorèmes.

La _Summa de sophismatibus et distinctionibus_ de Roger Bacon, est une
étape intermédiaire entre les _Distinctiones_ et les _Syncategoremata_. Comme
les _Distinctiones_ c'est un recueil de règles d'ailleurs manifestement classées -
- comme dans _Quoniam ignoratis_ -- d'après les syncatégorèmes qui y figurent;
comme dans les _Syncategoremata_ les règles sont censées exprimer les
propriétés syntaxiques et sémantiques des termes syncatégorématiques.[10]

S'ajoutant à celle de _Quoniam ignoratis_ l'existence même de la _Summa_
nous oblige à revenir sur notre problème initial: l'existence des genres
littéraires que nous venons d'énumerer. Qu'est-ce-qui, au fond, distingue
véritablement les _Distinctiones_, la _Summa_ de Bacon et les _Syncategoremata_ de
Sherwood?

La seule différence, réele et inconstestable, réside...dans les titres
donnés par les médiévaux eux-mêmes aux différentes oeuvres. Ces
différences nous semblent pouvoir être expliquées de la manière suivante: Les
Syncategoremata supposent l'existence des sommes de logique dont la
sémantique est _explicitement_ fondée sur la reconnaissance d'une bipartition
entre les propriétés des termes catégorématiques et celles des termes
syncatégorématiques, reconnaissance qui entraîne une bipartition dans l'analyse
des bases de la sémantique: aux _Sommes_ les généralités sur les catégorèmes
considérés du seul point de vue de leur nature (substantif, adjectif) et de
leur fonction dans la prédication (sujet ou prédicat), aux _Syncategoremata_
l'approche nécessairement spécifiée des différents mot de la langue naturelle

susceptibles d'être considérés comme des syncatégorèmes: liste plus ou moins empiriquement définie, plus ou moins extensible, ici l'analyse des propriétés sémantiques d'un sujet dans telles ou telles conditions d'emploi intra-propositionnel, là l'analyse des propriétés sémantiques de tel mot particulier: 'omnis' ou 'vel' ou 'ambo'.

Ainsi donc, on peut risquer l'hypothèse suivante: les Distinctiones ont pour objet de dresser le bilan d'une pratique: il s'agit d'inventorier les règles utilisées dans la pratique de la discussion sophismatique et de dresser la carte de leur application. Dans les Syncategoremata il s'agit de compléter l'édifice d'une théorie: décrire pour chaque catégorie de syncatégorèmes définie sur la base de propriétés spécifiques (distributivité, copulativité, disjonctivité, etc.) l'ensemble des conditions dans lequel chaque terme qui relève de cette catégorie peut exercer ses propriétés et l'ensemble des conditions qui font que dans certains cas il ne peut pas, description qui fait donc dans le détail pour les termes outils ce que les Sommes ont fait avec une relative généralité pour les termes à contenu sémantique autonome.

Examinons à présent plus en détail nos deux oeuvres:

les ABSTRACTIONES MAGISTRI RICARDI SOPHISTE sont un recueil de 282 sophismes dont la plupart des copies datent 'des premières décennies du XIIIème siècle.'[11] 'Sophisme' a ici le sens de 'proposition ou d'expression présentant une difficulté logique.'[12] Chaque item se présente sous la forme d'un condensé, généralement très bref, d'un sophisma proprement dit: l'auteur discute et réfute les solutions de ses contemporains ('quidam dicunt'), les sophismata sont classés d'après les syncatégorèmes qu'ils renferment. Ce classement est le suivant et ne correspond à aucun des Syncategoremata actuellement connus.

(1)-(50): signa distributiva inter plures ('omnis', 'omne', 'quicquid', 'quilibet', 'quidlibet').
On remarque toutefois que des sophismata comme (38): 'Tu es aliud quam animal quod est Rome' ou (49): 'Album fuit disputaturum' n'ont pas de lien explicite avec le problème de la quantification. Leur présence s'explique uniquement dans le cas de (38) par dérive de la problématique de (37): 'Omne aliud quam animal quod et Sortes sunt duo differt a Sorte',

dans celui de (49) parce que ladite proposition sert à aborder des problèmes de quantification temporelle implicite.

(51)-(69): signa distributiva inter duo ('uterque', 'isti', 'decies', 'et', 'neutrum', 'uterque...reliqui', 'alter...reliquus', 'bis', 'duo'). On remarque à nouveau l'hetérogénéité apparente du classement: 'isti' n'est pas de soi un signe distributif duel mais seulement dans certaines conditions ('demonstratis duobus'), de même la présence de (56): 'Helena peperit decem filios' ne s'explique que par celle de (57): 'Helena peperit decies decem filios.' Par ailleurs, au simple énoncé des propositions, il est clair que les problèmes que l'on va affronter ne sont pas tous réellement des problèmes de quantification duelle, ainsi de (63) dont la difficulté repose manifestement sur la présence de vel: 'Uterque istorum est homo vel asinus' ou de (66): 'Uterque istorum est hicintus et alius est hicintus' dont la difficulté repose sur celle d'alius, autrement dit, dans un cas sur un problème de portée de la disjonction, dans l'autre sur des problèmes de coréférence.

(70): 'Plura pluribus sex sunt pauciora paucioribus sex' est isolé mais appelé par l'emploi de plura en (68) et (69) explicitement consacrés à bis et duo: (68): 'Bis duo sunt tria et non plura', (69): 'Duo patres et duo filii sunt tria et non plura.'

(71)-(77): signa distributiva inter partes integrales ('totus', 'quicquid', 'et', 'B', 'pars', 'quaelibet pars', 'tota...altera pars'). Ici c'est le lien des expressions considérées avec la notion de syncatégorème qui est très flou: 'pars' est un catégorème qui remplit une fonction de syncatégorème, qu'il soit lui-même préfacé d'un syncatégorème, comme dans (76): 'In qualibet parte animalis est anima', ou non, comme dans (75): 'Animal est pars animalis.' De même 'et' tântot présenté comme un disjonctif duel, n'a le sens d'un distributif intégral que dans le contexte d'emploi particulier de (73): 'Sortes et Plato sunt homines.'

(78): 'A' est B: est A, non est B; ergo A differt a B se rattache au groupe précédent...à cause de l'emploi des lettres 'A' et

'B', c'est-à-dire des 'appelations' 'A' et 'B' caractérisées comme distributifs intégraux en (74): 'Sor nascitur in B.'

(79)-(108): coniunctiones continuativae ('si').

En fait, la présence de si est l'unique dénominateur commun de phrases contenant toutes les catégories possibles d'expressions: catégorématiques ou syncatégorématiques ('hoc instans', 'necessarium', 'aliquid', 'ipsum', 'differt', 'A', 'de necessitate', 'ubique', 'non', 'nullus, -a, -um', 'nihil', 'verum', 'falsum', 'vel', 'id quod', 'quicquid').

(109) et (110) sont isolés.

(111)-(128): 'inquantum', 'quantocumque', 'qualecumque', 'quodcumque', 'quanto', 'tanto', 'quotiens'.

(129)-(144): coniunctiones disiunctivae ('nisi', 'vel', 'an', 'ne').

Certains sophismata reprennent des problèmes esquissés ailleurs. C'est le cas de (133): 'Nichil est verum nisi in hoc instanti' dont la parenté avec (79): 'Si aliquid est verum, est verum in hoc instanti' est évidente. D'autres concernent le statut et les propriétés des verbes épistémiques comme 'savoir' ou 'vouloir' plutôt que des propriétés de la conjonction disjoncitve an. C'est le cas de (136)-(142), de (143) pour 'vult' et de (144) pour 'tu scis'.

(145)-(168): signa negativa ('nullus', 'nihil'). Problèmes de double quantification.

(169)-(175): traitent pêle-mêle du verb 'negare', de 'aliud quam', de 'plus quam', de 'plura' et de 'pauciora'. Ces deux derniers termes ayant, on s'en souvient, déja fait l'objet d'un examen dans le sophisma (70). Encore faut-il noter que (173): 'Plura sciuntur a Sorte quam a solo Sorte' ne concerne pas reellement 'plura' mais bien plutôt la différence entre 'Sor' et 'solus Sor'.

(176): 'Infinita sunt finita' est isolé. Cependant sa place s'explique par l'emploi de 'totidem sibi' au (174) de la section précédente: 'Plura sunt vera de sibi totidem quam sunt vera de paucioribus se.'

(177)-(199): concernent les verbes 'incipit' et 'desinit'. On y trouve, toutefois, un sophisma comme (183): 'Sor vult esse similis Platoni' dont la présence s'explique uniquement par celle de (180): 'Sor desinit esse similis Platoni.'

(200)-(214): dictio exceptiva ('praeter').

(215)-(255): dictiones exclusivae ('tantum', 'solus').

(256)-(282): dictiones modales ('impossibile', 'possiblile', 'contingens', 'contingenter', 'necessarium').
On note la présence de (262): 'Sicut se habet homo ad non homo, sic se habet animal ad non animal' et de deux autres sophismata en 'sicut...sic': (263) et (264) dont la présence est exclusivement justifiée par l'analyse de (261): 'Sicut se habet impossibile ad non impossibile, sic se habet necessarium ad non necessarium.'

Comme on le voit, la structure des Abstractiones est assez clair: il s'agit d'un recueil de règles et de sophismata ordonnés d'après une classification des syncatégorèmes. Cette espèce d'anthologie thématique est aussi manifestement un répertoire de lieux, de thèmes et de doctrines brièvement caractérisées d'un trait ou d'une formule.

Répondant à la question préjudicielle: le genre des Abstractiones existe-t-il? nous disons donc que si les Distinctiones existent comme genre, alors les Abstractiones aussi. Et nous faisons l'hypothèse que ce sont des recueils pédagogiques vraisemblablement destinés aux enseignants des arts, contenant l'analyse et la discussion parfois argumentée d'un très grand nombre de sophismata et d'examples susceptibles d'être utilisés dans un enseignement oral ou écrit. Les recueils d'Abstractiones ne sont pas des formes littéraires concurrentes des Syncategoremata. On peut, de ce point de vue, les séparer aussi nettement des Distinctiones. Dans ces dernières, la part de la discussion et surtout celle de l'encadrement théorique sont nettement plus importantes: les règles sont enoncées et expliquées d'abord, les sophismata qui les illustrent vient ensuite. Dans les Abstractiones les règles sont le plus souvent évoquées au cours même de la discussion d'un sophisma. Un tout petit nombre d'entre elles seulement sert à introduire une réflexion.

Il en va de même dans les <u>Abstractiones</u> d'Herveus Sophista. Le recueil d'Hervé contient 298 <u>sophismata</u>, soit 16 de plus que celui de Richard, pour un texte pourtant nettement moins long. Le caractère d'aide-mémoire est, de ce fait, encore beaucoup plus accusé. La plupart des analyses sont restituées en style elliptique. <u>Probatio</u>, <u>contra</u>, <u>solutio</u> sont donnés en deux ou trois lignes d'une écriture relativement riche en abbréviations de toute sortes: on remarque notamment l'utilisation de '∅' pour 'instans' ou 'instantia'. Quelques références sont faites aux opinions courantes: 'ut solet dici', 'dicunt quod'. Certains <u>sophismata</u> sont developpés avec mention explicite d'une solution ('solutio'). L'auteur lui-même s'implique à plusieurs reprises: 'dico', 'dicunt quod... sed hoc nihil est.' Le classement des <u>sophismata</u> est à nouveau fourni par le groupement des syncatégorèmes, toutefois, comme Richard, Hervé ne s'interdit pas d'insérer tel ou tel <u>sophisma</u> par association avec tel ou tel élement secondaire d'un <u>sophisma</u> précédent.

L'ordre suivi par Hervé est assez largement parallèle à celui de Richard.

Si l'on compare les deux listes de <u>sophismata</u>, on observe, en effet, les 140 corrélations suivantes:

Richard	Hervé	Richard	Hervé	Richard	Hervé
1	35	40	52	74	47
10	2	41	18	75	51
11	1	42	19	76	50
13	12	43	34	78	53
14	10	44	29	83	81
15	11	46	30	86	106
17	5	47	32	88	109
18	6	48	57	94	110
23	13	50	33	95	111
25	15	55	60	96	136
28	23	57	69	97	87
29	24	62	41	99	88
30	22	64	40	100	85
31	16	66	38	101	86
35	27	70	260	102	92
36	20	71	46	103	91
37	17	73	45	104	93

Richard	Hervé		Richard	Hervé		Richard	Hervé
106	83		169	148		224	207
107	100		171	61		227	210
111	65		174	152		228	215
113	71		176	153		229	212
116	54		178	165		232	195
118	56		179	164		233	197
121	218		183	59		237	221
122	112		192	174		239	224
123	115		193	175		240	222
124	117		194	176		241	223
128	70		195	158		242	240
129	130		196	159		243	225
130	131		197	172		247	229
133	133		198	177		248	231
135	173		199	178		249	235
136	121		202	182		255	226
137	123		203	183		256	258
138	125		205	186		258	261
139	126		207	181		259	266
143	119		208	194		262	257
144	120		209	180		263	256
145	146		210	187		264	255
147	145		211	188		268	245
151	127		214	191		270	241
153	128		215	193		271	242
154	129		216	209		272	253
155	134		219	208		274	243
164	144		220	205		282	269
166	26		221	204			
168	137		223	206			

Autrement dit: quasiment la moitié des items de Richard le Sophiste est aussi traitée chez Hervé. Est-ce beaucoup ou peu? Les données statistiques sur la Logica Modernorum sont encore trop faibles pour qu'on puisse se faire une opinion. Toutefois, si l'on compare les Abstactiones avec les deux principaux traités De syncategorematibus dont le texte nous soit intégralement accessible, ceux de Sherwood et de Nicolas de Paris, on constate que le

nombre de <u>sophismata</u> discutés par les quatre auteurs est très bas: en tout 27
items:

Hervé	Richard	Sherwood	Nicolas
6	18	99	93
13	23	4	101
22	30	11	107
26	166	24	7
41	62	31	5
81	83	83	57
110	94	91	52
130	129	93	61
133	133	94	60
136	96	27	53
137	168	30	9
146	145	22	4
148	169	95	98
158	195	77	65
172	197	74	64
173	135	101	89
180	209	42	47+111
181	207	35	45
195	232	59	25
204	221	58	23
221	237	47	31
222	240	96	32
223	241	70	18+81
225	243	53	19
231	248	49	28
242	271	67	79
245	268	72	73+74

Ainsi donc: 1/10 seulement des <u>sophismata</u> traités par Richard se
trouvent également repris chez les trois autres maîtres.

Les proportions ne sont guère plus importantes dans les corrélations par
deux ou par trois. Toutefois il y a une incontestable homogénéité des
résultats:

Richard/Nicolas	: 60 cas
Richard/Sherwood	: 58
Hervé/Nicolas	: 55
Hervé/Sherwood	: 48
Richard/Nicolas/Hervé	: 43
Richard/Nicolas/Sherwood	: 34
Hervé/Nicolas/Sherwood	: 26

Si l'on considère le nombre de _sophismata_ traités dans chaque recueil (Hervé 298, Richard 282, Nicolas 119, Sherwood 108), on voit qu'un seul chiffre peut paraître significatif. De fait, les _sophismata_ traités dans les _Syncategoremata_ de Guillaume de Sherwood étant les moins nombreux, force est de constater que plus de la moitié des examples discutés par Guillaume sont traités chez Richard. Ceci ne prouve rien par soi. C'est toutefois un indice que les deux auteurs appartiennent à un 'même univers de doctrines'.

Quelques indices plus particuliers vont également en ce sens. Le fait notamment que Guillaume et Richard sont les seuls à discuter et à déterminer, de façon d'ailleurs strictement identique, le _sophisma_ 'Cuiuslibet hominis asinus currit' dont L.M. de Rijk a récemment rappelé l'importance pour les condemnations oxoniennes de 1277 _in logicalibus_. Un autre _sophisma_ caractéristique est le pittoresque 'Nullo currente crescunt tibi cornua fronte', qui, à notre connaissance, n'est attestée nulle part ailleurs.

En outre, Sherwood donne souvent l'impression d'avoir eu sous les yeux les _Abstractiones_ de Richard au moment de composer son texte. Souvent, en effet, il paraît se contenter de résumer rapidement le dossier déjà bien établi d'une question et d'apporter une solution qu'il ne développe que si elle s'écarte nettement de la solution ricardienne, comme s'il la supposait bien connue de son public. C'est, par example, le cas pour l'ensemble formé par:

Si Sortes necessario est mortalis non necessario est mortalis. (Sherwood 88, Richard 89)
Si omnis propositio est vera aliqua est falsa. (Sherwood 89, Richard 92)
Si nulla propositio est vera aliqua est vera. (Sherwood 90, Richard 92)
Si nullum tempus est, aliquod tempus est. (Sherwood 91, Richard 94)

C'est également le cas pour:

Omnis homo qui est albus currit. (Sherwood 3, Richard 31)

et:

Omnis homo est unus solus homo. (Sherwood 6, Richard 3)

Par ailleurs, il semble également qu'en plusieurs occasions Sherwood cherche délibérément à se démarquer du modèle que nous lui supposons.

Revenons sur quelques uns de ces examples:

(1) SI SORTES NECESSARIO EST MORTALIS NON NECESSARIO EST MORTALIS.

La présentation du sophisma chez Richard comprend une probatio et une improbatio. La probatio repose sur un passage a primo ad ultimum que l'on peut schématiser ainsi:

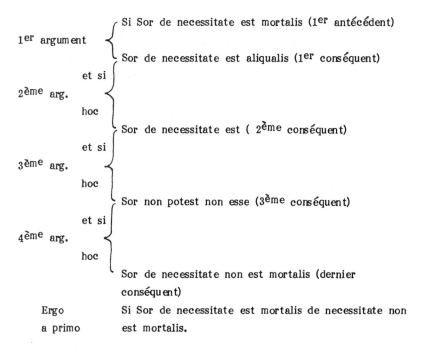

Si Sor de necessitate est mortalis (1er antécédent)

1er argument

Sor de necessitate est aliqualis (1er conséquent)

et si

2ème arg.

hoc

Sor de necessitate est (2ème conséquent)

et si

3ème arg.

hoc

Sor non potest non esse (3ème conséquent)

et si

4ème arg.

hoc

Sor de necessitate non est mortalis (dernier conséquent)

Ergo   Si Sor de necessitate est mortalis de necessitate non

a primo   est mortalis.

L'improbatio repose sur la règle des consequentiae: 'Sed hec est falsa, cum unum oppositum non antecedit ad suum oppositum'

La solution de Richard est qu'une proposition dont l'antécédent 'implique' c'est-à-dire contient des opposés, en l'occurence la possibilité de non

existence notée par 'mortalis' et la nécessité d'existence notée par
'necessario' (='non posse non esse'), le premier antécédent pouvant être
paraphrasé en 'Sor non potest non esse mortalis', une telle proposition, dis-je,
n'empêche pas de prendre comme conclusion 'ergo non necessario est
mortalis':

> Solutio. Licet concedi conclusio, eo quod in antecedente primo
> intelliguntur opposita, eo quod mortale significat posse non esse et
> necessario additum non posse non esse, et hec sunt opposita.[13]

On notera, toutefois, que Richard mentionne et discute une autre solution
qui, apparemment, rejette le sophisme et accepte l'_improbatio_ pour la raison
que l'antécédent n'implique pas réellement des opposés.   Dans cette
perspective, en effet, on distingue deux sortes de nécessité: celle correspon-
dant à la possibilité de la mort et la nécessité véritable exprimée par le
terme modal ('necessario'):

> ...quia cum necessitas respectu huius posse mori est necessitas deminuta
> et necessitas deminuta non significat non posse non esse, non significan-
> tur opposita in hoc sermone 'Sor de necessitate est mortalis.'[14]

Un second argument confirme que l'antécédent n'impliquant pas d'opposés,
la conclusion qui en est tirée n'est pas valide et le _sophisma_ faux:

> Et preterea hec, que per se insunt superiori, per se inerunt inferiori....
> Cum igitur mortale per se insit homini, per se inerit eidem homini, et,
> que per se insunt de necessitate insunt rebus, mortale igitur de
> necessitate inerit isti homini, et sermo significans de necessitate inerit,
> quod de necessitate inest....Hec igitur non significantur opposita.[15]

Richard concède cette solution ainsi que la réfutation de la _probatio_ qui
l'accompagne; la première inférence de la _probatio_ (le premier antécédent du
processus a primo ad ultimum) pèche par _fallacia secundum quid et
simpliciter_, puisqu'elle passe indûment d'une nécessité diminuée à une
nécessité absolue:

> Quod concedo dicendo, quod non valet 'Sortes de necessitate est mortalis,
> ergo de necessitate est aliqualis', sed est fallacia secundum quid et
> simpliciter, eo quod, cum dicitur 'Sor de necessitate est mortalis', est

necessitas condicionis, et hec est necessitas deminuta, ad quam non sequitur necessitas simpliciter, cuiusmodi significatur, cum dicitur 'Sor de necessitate est aliqualis.'[16]

De l'ensemble de cette discussion Sherwood ne retient qu'une petite partie. La probatio repose elle aussi sur un processus a primo ad ultimum:

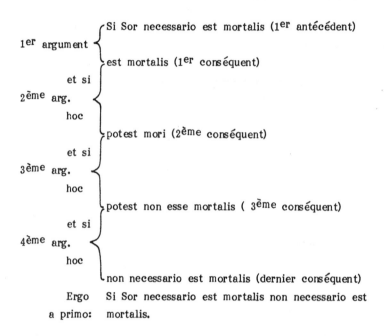

Ergo   Si Sor necessario est mortalis non necessario est
a primo: mortalis.

Ce processus est différent de celui de Richard, plus 'captieux'. Mais ce n'est pas la seule particularité du texte de Sherwood. De fait, le maître anglais ne fournit pas d'improbatio et il se borne à noter qu'il y a différentes manières de résoudre le sophisma: 'Et hic diversi diversimode dicunt.' La solution qu'il retient, sans autre discussion, est la première solution mentionnée par Richard: la conclusion a primo est logiquement possible puisque le premier antécédent 'implique' des opposés:

Possumus tamen dicere, quod in antecedente implicantur opposita, quia ratione ejus, quod est 'necessario', ponitur necessitas suae existentiae, ratione ejus, quod est 'mortalis', ponitur ibi possibilitas ad non esse; nec est inconveniens, quod ex ipso sequantur opposita vel etiam suum proprium oppositum.[17]

Comme on le voit, la présentation sherwoodienne du sophisma est un condensé légèrement retouché de l'analyse de Richard.

(2) SI OMNIS PROPOSITIO EST VERA NON OMNIS PROPOSITIO EST VERA. Le sophisma, manifestement apparenté au précédent, est à nouveau prouvé par Richard à l'aide d'un processus a primo:

> Si omnis propositio est vera, hec propositio est vera qualibet demonstrata; et si hec est vera, eius opposita est falsa; sed, si eius opposita est falsa, non omnis proposition est vera; ergo a primo: Si omnis propositio est vera, non omnis propositio est vera.[18]

L'improbatio est la même que la précédente: 'Sed hec est falsa, cum oppositum non antecedit ad suum oppositum.'[19] La solution est la réitération de la première solution proposée. Richard apporte, toutefois, quelques précisions supplémentaires (notamment l'allusion à la règle: 'Quidquid antecedit ad antecedens, antecedit ad consequens; quidquid sequitur ad consequens, sequitur ad antecedens' qui, on le sait, fonde la consequentia a primo ad ultimum):

> Solutio. Dicendum est hic sicut ad precedens. In hac enim 'Omnis propositio est vera' intelligitur opposita, scilicet, hec 'aliquam propositionem esse veram', et eius oppositam, et per consequens 'aliquam propositionem esse veram et non esse veram', quarum utraque naturaliter antecedit ad hanc 'non omnis propositio est vera.'[20]

Dans le cas présent, ce qui entraîne ('antecedit') l'antécédent entraîne aussi le conséquent, autrement dit: chacun des opposés contenus dans l'antécédent entraînant à la fois (ou aussi bien) cet antécédent et le conséquent de cet antécédent, il n'y a aucun inconvénient à admettre que l'antécédent entraîne le conséquent. Richard rejette donc l'improbatio 'sicut prius dixi', renvoyant par là à la solution donnée pour un autre sophisma (non traité par Sherwood) SI TU SCIS TE ESSE LAPIDEM TU NON SCIS TE ESSE LAPIDEM. Cette solution:

> Respondendum est improbationi per interemptionem. Ex tali enim antecedente, in quo intelliguntur opposita, naturaliter sequitur oppositum eius.[21]

fixe la terminologie de Richard et la nature de la règle qu'il applique et que présuppose aussi le texte elliptique de Sherwood: le terme de 'naturaliter' renvoie à la notion de 'conséquence naturelle' reliant un antécédent contenant deux opposés et en un conséquent opposé à l'antécédent.

On note que Richard ne reprend pas la seconde solution mentionée au sophisma précédent.

Guillaume de Sherwood discute notre sophisma sous la forme: SI OMNIS PROPOSITIO EST VERA ALIQUA EST FALSA. Le développement de l'analyse est en tout point comparable à la démarche suivie pour SI SORTES NECESSARIO EST MORTALIS NON NECESSARIO EST MORTALIS. La probation se fait a primo ad ultimum:

> Simile est hic: si omnis propositio est vera, tunc deum esse est verum; et si hoc, tunc sua contradictoria est falsa; et si hoc, aliqua est falsa; ergo, si omnis propositio est vera, aliqua est falsa.[22]

Aucune improbatio n'est mentionnée. La solution est identique à la précédente: l'antécédent contient des opposés. Toute la difficulté consiste à établir que l'antécédent contient bien deux opposés. C'est ce que fait Sherwood en quelques lignes:

> Et intellige, quod, cum ponere aliquam propositionem esse veram sit ponere suam contradictoriam esse falsam, tunc ponere omnem esse veram est ponere cujuslibet contradictoriam esse falsam, et haec est omnem esse falsam, et sic implicantur opposita in antecedente.[23]

Comme on le voit, il n'éprouve pas le besoin de préciser que le sophisma est acceptable. Le parallèle avec Richard n'en est que plus intéressant: la seule différence entre les deux textes est à nouveau la formulation (plus subtile?) de la probatio.

Le troisième sophisma du groupe: (3) SI NULLA PROPOSITIO EST VERA, ISTA PROPOSITIO EST VERA est également discuté par Nicolas de Paris. Richard prouve le sophisma par processus a primo:

> Si nulla propositio est vera, hec propositio non est vera; et si hec

propositio non est vera, eius opposita est vera; et si eius opposita est
vera, aliqua propositio est vera; ergo a primo: si nulla propositio est
vera, aliqua propositio est vera.[24]

Sa solution consiste, cette fois, à rejeter le sophisma comme faux et la
probatio comme fallacieuse. En effet, d'une part le deuxième argument ('sic
haec propositio non est vera, eius opposita est vera') n'est pas valable, qui
tire une affirmation d'une négation, d'autre part, la proposition 'haec
propositio non est vera' a deux causes de vérité: soit parce que la
proposition qu'elle désigne est fausse et son opposée vraie, soit parce que
cette proposition n'existe pas, auquel cas, son opposée n'est pas vraie non
plus (puisqu'elle n'existe pas). Dans ces conditions l'inférence 'si haec
propositio non est vera, eius opposita est vera' n'est valable que si la
proposition en question existe. Dans le cas contraire, elle n'est pas valable.
L'argument a primo ad ultimum ne tient donc pas, puisqu'il contient une
inférence entachée de fallacia consequentis:

> Solutio. Prima est falsa, et fallit hec consequentia: 'si hec propositio
> non est vera, eius opposita est vera', cum ex negatione non sequitur
> affirmatio. Quod enim hec non sit vera, possit esse, eo quod non sit,
> quia casu contingente non est vera eius opposita. Patet igitur, quod
> prior propositio potest habere duas causas veritatis, et non est vera nisi
> existente una illarum. Unde sequitur 'si eius opposita est vera, hec non
> est vera', et non convertitur, cum opposita est vera, hec non est vera',
> et non convertitur, cum possit habere aliam causam veritatis. Unde
> arguendo e contrario pono consequens.[25]

Guillaume de Sherwood présente explicitement le sophisma comme
illustration d'une situation où contrairement aux deux précédentes et malgré
l'apparente similitude des données, le processus a primo ne tient pas.

Ce processus, à nouveau modifié par rapport à celui de Richard, est le
suivant:

> Si nulla proposito est vera, tantum deum esse non est verum; et si hoc,
> sua contradictoria est vera; et si hoc, aliqua est vera: ergo a primo, si
> nulla est vera, aliqua est vera.[26]

Sa solution est, en revanche, strictement identique à celle du Magister

<u>Abstractionum</u>: le second argument -- i.e., 'si haec propositio (='tantum Deus est') non est vera, sua contradictoria est vera' -- n'est valable que si l'on suppose l'existence de ladite proposition. Or ce n'est pas une hypothèse conforme à la prémisse générale, puisque, précisément, celle-ci donne plutot à entendre qu'il n'existe aucune proposition, de par la convertibilité de 'esse' et de 'verum esse'. Dans ces conditions, il n'y a pas processus <u>a primo ad ultimum</u>:

> Et sciendum quod secundum argumentum non tenet nisi supponendo, quod aliqua propositio sit: haec autem non supponitur in prima, sed magis sua opposita, quia nullam esse veram est nullam esse, et propterea non tenet a primo ad ultimum.[27]

Bien qu'il ne le dise pas explicitement, Sherwood, qui rejette le processus, rejette donc aussi le <u>sophisma</u>, qui en est la conclusion.

Une fois de plus; Sherwood semble condenser les <u>Abstractiones</u> tout en précisant la formulation de la <u>probatio</u>. Le parallélisme des solutions ('non est vera nisi existente una illarum', 'non tenet nisi supponendo, quod aliqua propositio sit') n'en est que plus frappant encore.

Ce, d'autant plus qu'il est comme souligné par l'irreductibilité de la position ricardo-sherwoodienne à celle de Nicolas de Paris. Certes, le maître parisien ne consacre pas un développement exprès à notre sophisme, mais, comme il le range parmi les <u>sophismata</u> équiformes de <u>SI NULLUM TEMPUS EST, ALIQUOD TEMPUS EST</u>, on peut en conclure qu'ici comme la il rejette le processus, non parce que, comme chez Richard et Sherwood, l'un des arguments contenus présuppose une existence (ici celle d'une proposition, là celle du temps), mais parce que, d'une inférence à l'autre, le principe topique change ou a changé. Le <u>sophisma</u> est donc une illustration de la règle selon laquelle:

> Processus a primo ad ultimum...tenet, cum eadem est comparatio primi ad medium quae est medii ad extremum...sed, si mutatur habitudo, non debet sequi.[28]

Cette solution par la 'modification des relations' ('propter mutationem habitudinorum') est, comme on va le voir maintenant, une solution que Sherwood discute et rejette dans sa propre analyse de <u>SI NULLUM TEMPUS EST, ALIQUOD TEMPUS EST</u>.

Pour plus de clarté nous commencerons notre presentation par le texte de Sherwood:

(4) SI NULLUM TEMPUS EST, ALIQUOD TEMPUS EST. La version du processus _a primo ad ultimum_ dans l'édition O'Donnell est lacunaire. Il faut lire d'après le ms P:

> Si nullum tempus est, dies non est, et si hoc, nox est, et si hoc, aliquod tempus est; ergo a primo: si nullum tempus est, aliquod tempus est.[29]

La solution de Sherwood est la même que pour le _sophisma_ précédent (i.e., 'Si dies non est, nox est') ne tient que dans l'hypothèse où le temps existe, hypothèse précisément exclue par la première prémisse (i.e., 'nullum tempus est'): 'Dicendum quod secundum argumentum non est necessarium nisi supposito quod aliquod tempus sit et oppositum supponebatur in prima.'[30] Cette solution formulée, Sherwood en examine une autre.

'Certains', en effect, rejetant le processus _a primo ad ultimum_ pour la raison qu'il présente une discontinuité topique de la première proposition ('si nullum tempus est, dies non est') où le principe d'inférence est le topos du tout quantitatif, à la seconde ('si dies non est, nox est') où le principe d'inférence est le topos des contraires:

> Dicunt quidam quod non tenet talis processus eo quod in prima est locus a toto in quantitate, in secunda a contrariis, et sic non est continuus processus.[31]

Sherwood rejette cette solution.

La _probatio_ du _sophisma_ est identique chez Richard à celle de Sherwood:

> Si nullum tempus est, aliquod tempus est. Quod sic probatur. Si nullum tempus est, dies non est et si dies non est, nox est, et si nox est, aliquod tempus <est>; ergo a primo si nullum tempus est, aliquod tempus est.[32]

Sa solution est la même que celle du maître anglais ('prima est falsa') et pour la même raison: le second argument n'est pas valable. Dans sa démonstration, toutefois, Richard est moins clair que Guillaume. Certes,

comme lui il rejette l'inférence: 'Si dies non est, nox est' pour _fallacia_
consequentis (i.e., inférence d'une affirmative à partir d'une négative) et,
comme il l'avait déjà fait, il justifie plus généralement ce rejet par le fait
qu'une proposition admettant deux causes de vérité ne peut inférer l'une
d'entre elles:

> Fallit hec consequentia: _si dies non est, nox est,_ cum ex negativa non
> sequitur affirmativa et sequitur _si nox est, dies non est_ et non
> convertitur, cum antecedens possit habere duplicem causam veritatis
> quarum una implicatur.[33]

Toutefois, exprimant à son tour le problème de la prémisse additionelle, il
semble laisser entendre qu'ainsi reformulé le processus serait valable.   De
fait, il ne stigmatise pas comme Sherwood une _fallacia accidentis_ dans
l'argument total qui prendrait pour antécédent du second argument: 'si dies
non est et aliquod tempus est.' Il se contente de noter qu'ainsi formulé le
second argument est valable et que tel qu'il est formulé dans la _probatio_
(i.e., avec 'dies non est' comme second antecedent) l'argument total ne l'est
pas:

> Per consequens scimus quod ad propositionem que potest habere duplicem
> causam veritatis non sequitur una illarum, nisi distinguendo cum altera.
> Tenet autem hec consequentia: _si dies non est et aliquod tempus est, nox_
> _est._ Sed sic dico: si nullum tempus est, dies non est; et si dies non est,
> nox est; et si nox est, aliquod tempus est. Non sequitur ergo: si nullum
> tempus est, aliquod tempus est, nec est hec consequentia a primo ad
> ultimum eo quod non continuantur inter se propositiones. Continuantur
> enim in tali processu per hoc quod consequens huius precedentis sit
> antecedens in conclusioni sequente, cuius oppositum autem in proposito
> isto est.[34]

Sa position d'ensemble est donc assez voisine de celle de Sherwood, mais sur
un point essentiel -- celui de la prémisse affirmative additionelle -- Guillaume
prend une décision beaucoup plus rigoureuse que lui. Il n'est pas interdit de
penser que les _Syncategoremata_ reviennent ici sur une doctrine reçue à
Oxford mais jugée insuffisante par leur auteur. Il faut, en tout cas, souligner
que la position de Nicolas de Paris et des autres textes parisiens est
précisément celle des _quidam_ dénoncés par Sherwood, i.e., la solution par la
commutation des principes topiques.

Cette solution est particulièrement bien exposée par Nicolas de Paris dans la probatio qui décompose l'argument total en quatre inférences topiques distinctes:[35]

Premier Argument:	Si nullum tempus est, dies non est.	TOPIQUE DE LA DE-STRUCTION DU GENRE (a genre destructo)
Deuxième Argument:	Si dies non est, nox est.	TOPIQUE DES OPPOSES (ab oppositis)
Troisième Argument:	Si nox est, aliquod tempus est.	TOPIQUE DE L'ESPECE (a specie)
Quatrième Argument:	Si nullum tempus est, aliquod tempus est.	LOCUS A PRIMO AD ULTIMUM

Elle est également mentionnée comme la 'solution commune' dans les Syncategoremata de Jean le Page, quand il s'interroge sur le fait de savoir si tout argument a primo ad ultimum suppose une continuité dans l'argumentation topique:

His habitis, cum soleant fieri argumentationes a primo ad ultimum <...> queritur utrum necesse sit omnes consequentias esse secundum locum eumdem a specie vel sit possibile sumere conditiones secundum locum alium et alium.

Et dicitur quod omnes sumende sunt secundum eumdem locum, ut est hic 'si Sortes est homo, animal est; si animal est, corpus est; si corpus est, substantia est; ergo a primo: si homo est, substantia <est>.' Et per hoc solet solvi hoc sophisma: 'Si nullum tempus est, dies non est; si dies non est, nox est; et si nox est, aliquod tempus est; ergo si nullum tempus est, aliquod tempus est.'...Dicitur communiter quod non est argumentacio a primo ad ultimum, quia consequentie non sunt secundum locum eundem.[36]

Cela posé, la critique de Sherwood parait s'appliquer à cette opinion commune, telle qu'elle est mentionnée par Pagus, plutôt qu'à la solution de Nicolas de Paris.

De fait, Nicolas ne se contente pas de montrer qu'il y a 'mutatio habitudinum', c'est-à-dire application successive du 'locus a genere destructo', du 'locus ab oppositis' et du 'locus a specie', il précise en quoi cette 'mutatio' est ruineuse pour le processus, i.e., parce qu'elle rend équivoque la 'signification' du syncatégorème 'si': 'Cum hec dictio 'si' sicut syncategoreuma recipiat significatum ab adiunctis, manifestum quod equivoce tenetur in hiis locis.'[37] Or Sherwood n'a pas un mot pour relever cette 'équivocité' de 'si' dans sa présentation de la commutation des principes topiques.

Mais surtout, la véritable solution de Nicolas n'est pas la simple mention de la commutatio habitudinum. Au contraire, telle qu'il l'exprime (Braakhuis, 2.197[8-17]), cette solution est assez proche des lignes où Sherwood montre que le processus a primo pèche par fallacia accidentis.

Pour Nicholas, en effet, comme pour Guillaume, la probatio du sophisma souffre d'une erreur de l'accident. Ceci, dit-il, apparait clairement si remplaçant 'si' par 'quandocumque' on présente l'argument sous forme syllogistique, i.e.,

Quandocumque nullum tempus est, nox est
sed quandocumque dies non est, nox est;
ergo quandocumque nullum tempus est, nox est.

En effet, dans ce syllogisme, le medium ('diem non esse') se rapporte différemment au grand terme ('nullum tempus esse') et au petit terme ('nocem esse'). Dans le premier rapport, il s'agit de la simple relation d'inférence entre négation de l'inférieur (le jour) et négation du supérieur (le temps), laquelle ne présuppose évidemment pas l'existence du supérieur (le temps) pour être valable, alors que, dans le second, il s'agit d'une relation entre inférieur ou, si l'on préfère d'une relation entre l'absence d'un inférieur (le jour) et la présence corrélative de son opposé (la nuit), laquelle présuppose l'existence du supérieur (le temps) pour être valable. La dissimilitude dans le rapport du moyen terme au grand et au petit termes rejette donc le syllogisme dans l'erreur de l'accident:

Patet quod hic quod est diem non esse, quod est sicut medium, dissimiliter comparatur ad hoc quod est nullum tempus esse, quia sequitur negatio inferioris ad negationem sui superioris nichil supponendo, et ad hoc quod est nocem esse, sicut negatio unius oppositorum ad societatem alterius cum suppositione alicuius, scilicet quod tempus sit, aliter enim non sequeretur.[38]

Les solutions finales de Guillaume et de Nicolas sont donc très proches l'une de l'autre, toutes deux consistent à montrer que 'dies non est' ne se rapporte pas de la même manière au premier antécédent et au second conséquent. Toutefois, sur le plan littéraire, c'est évidemment de Richard que Guillaume est le plus proche.

Le traitement du sophisma par Herveus Brito est apparemment différent des analyses précédentes. Certes, la probatio est identique: 'si nullum tempus est, dies non est; et si dies non est, nox est; et si nox est, aliquod tempus est; ergo a primo: si nullum tempus est, aliquod tempus est.'[39] Mais la solution mentionnée et discutée par Hervé parait originale puisqu'elle consiste à rejeter le processus pour la raison qu'il y aurait utilisation de deux types de conséquences: la conséquence accidentelle dans le premier et le dernier arguments et la conséquence naturelle dans le deuxième argument:

Dicunt quod non est a primo ad ultimum distinguentes naturalem consequentiam et accidentalem. In prima et ultima conditionali, accidentalem. In media, in hac scilicet 'si dies non est, nox est', naturalem. Nox enim accidentale.[40]

En fait, cette solution reprend la notion de conséquence naturelle évoquée par Richard dans son analyse de SI OMNIS PROPOSITIO EST VERA NON OMNIS PROPOSITIO EST VERA. La seule différence est qu'elle l'utilise, cette fois, pour rejeter le sophisma et ce dans un cadre argumentatif 'parisien', qui est celui de la modification, non certes des principes topiques, comme chez Nicolas de Paris et Jean Le Page, mais celle, plus strictement logique, de la nature des conséquences. On sait en effet que la conséquence naturelle ou essentielle est celle où le conséquent est 'naturellement' compris dans l'antécédent et que, l'accidentelle ou positive est celle qui s'exprime dans les maximes (A) 'Ex impossibili sequitur quidlibet' et (B) 'Necessarium sequitur ad quidlibet.' La solution mentionnée par Hervé est donc logique et non dialectique, comme celle de Nicolas de Paris ou de Jean Le Page.

Dire que le premier et le dernier arguments sont des conséquences accidentelles, c'est dire que 'si nullum tempus est, dies non est' et 'si nullum tempus est, aliquod tempus est' tiennent l'une et l'autre leur validité de la maxime (A): 'ex impossibili quidlibet'; alors que, dire que 'si dies non est, nox est' est une consequence naturelle revient à dire qu'elle tient sa validité du fait que le conséquent ('nox est') est naturellement compris dans l'antécédent ('dies non est').

Hervé rejette cette solution.   En fait, selon lui, dans 'si nullum tempus est, etc.', 'tempus' ne désigne directement ou indirectement ni le jour ni la nuit mais l'absence et du jour et de la nuit, la proposition 'si nullum tempus est, aliquod tempus est' est donc fausse de quelque façon qu'on essaie de l'établir: 'sed dicimus quod hec est falsa, quia primum "tempus" iudicii neque dies neque nox.'[41]

Toutefois, il faut noter qu'Hervé fait une concession: si l'on développe l'argumentation sous la présupposition que le temps existe encore -- comme l'on fait, on l'a vu, Guillaume et Richard, tenants de ce qu'on a appelé la 'prémisse additionelle au second argument' (='et aliquod tempus est') -- la prémisse initiale est impossible, ou, ce qui revient au même, son opposée est nécessaire.   D'où par application de la maxime des conséquences positives ou accidentelles, le processus a primo ad ultimum est valable:

> Si autem volunt loqui tempore semper durante, sic necessarium est aliquod tempus esse, et ita impossibile est nullum tempus esse.   Unde cum ex impossibili quidlibet, necessarium ad quodlibet, et sic bene sequitur duplici de casu: 'Si nullum tempus est, aliquod tempus est.'[42]

Il n'est évidemment pas certain que le 'tempore semper durante' d'Hervé soit une allusion à l'introduction d'une prémisse additionelle affirmative. Toutefois, il parait difficile de lui donner ici un autre sens.   On voit donc combien les analyses et les solutions des différents auteurs sont ici entremêlées.   Cela n'en fait que mieux ressortir, encore une fois, la proximité littéraire des textes de Richard et de Sherwood.

Un dernier sophisma mérite de ce point de vue notre attention: (5) SI NIHIL EST, ALIQUID EST.   C'est le n° 27 de Sherwood et le n° 96 de Richard.   Le simple énoncé de cette différence montre que Sherwood ne le traite pas au même endroit que Richard.   Ceci confirme la flexibilité des classements et des groupements au sein même du genre des Syncategoremata.

Examinons rapidement ce sophisma également traité par Nicolas de Paris et Herveus Sophista.

Guillaume traite le sophisma à propos de la règle selon laquelle 'Negatio potest ferri ad diversa'; la probatio est une dernière fois le processus a

primo: 'si nihil est, nihil esse est verum; et si hoc, aliquid est; ergo a primo,
si nihil est, aliquid est.'[43]   Comme on pouvait s'y attendre, cependant, la
solution n'est plus la même; compte tenu de la particularité du premier
antécédent: 'si nihil est'.   Cette solution est la suivante: l'expression 'nihil
esse verum est' est ambiguë, du fait que 'esse' et 'est' peuvent être
composés ou divisés.   S'il y a division, la négation de 'nihil' s'arrête à 'esse',
s'il y a composition, elle s'étend à 'est': '...et significat divisio, quod negatio
sistat in ly "esse", composita autem significat, quod negatio transit ad ly
"est".'[44]   Dans le premier cas, 'nihil esse verum est' est une proposition
affirmative.   Elle n'est donc pas validement inférée de la prémisse 'nihil est',
puisque, comme on l'a déjà vu chez Richard pour SI NULLA PROPOSITIO EST
VERA, ISTA PROPOSITIO EST VERA, une affirmative que 'pose' quelque
chose, ne suit pas d'une négative qui ne 'pose' rien.   Ainsi le premier
antécédent est faux.   Dans le second cas, 'nihil esse verum est' est une
proposition négative dont le sens est: 'non est verum aliquid esse.'   Elle est
donc validement inférée de la prémisse, ce qui valide le premier antécédent,
mais invalide le premier conséquent ratione predicta, puisque, celui-ci a pour
conclusion une affirmative 'aliquid est verum'.

La solution de Guillaume est donc que le processus a primo n'est pas
valable, quel que soit le sens de 'nihil esse est verum', puisque, dans un cas
(sens divisé) c'est le premier antécédent qui est invalide, et dans l'autre (sens
composé) le premier conséquent.   La conclusion du processus 'si nihil est,
aliquid est' ne peut donc pas être établie.

On notera que le maître anglais renvoie au traité des Insolubilia l'analyse
des difficultés subsidiaires: cette analyse est absente de la version du De
insolubilibus contenue dans le ms Paris, BN lat. 16617, fols. 46^r-50^v, des
insolubles composés, n'aborde que les conjonctifs ('Deus est et ego dico
falsum.') et les disjonctifs ('Tu es asinus vel ego dico falsum.').

L'analyse de Ricardus Sophista est toute différente de celle de
Guillaume.   En fait, Richard traite le sophisma en liaison avec le groupe que
nous avons étudié précédemment.   Il conserve donc la solution qu'il a
appliquée jusque là.   Cette différence entre les deux maîtres montre
clairement que si Sherwood a utilisé les Abstractiones, il l'a fait très
librement.   Cette liberté va de pair, semble-t-il, avec une tendance à
supposer connu l'essentiel des thèses de Richard.   Si l'on considère
attentivement le texte des Abstractiones, on constate, en effet, que lui seul

permet de spécifier en quoi le sophisma renvoie bien à la problématique des 'insolubles', comme Sherwood se contente de le suggérer.

De fait, la probatio du sophisma ajoute, chez Richard, une prémisse latente dans l'enchaînement 'si nihil esse verum est, aliquid est verum', qui évoque immédiatement les difficultés esquivées par Sherwood. L'argument ainsi reformulé est le suivant:

> Si nihil est, nihil esse est verum; et si nihil esse est verum, hoc dictum 'nihil esse' est verum; et si hoc dictum 'nihil esse' est verum, aliquid est verum; et si aliquid est verum, aliquid est; ergo a primo si nihil est, aliquid est.[45]

La solution ricardienne est entièrement différente de la solution sherwoodienne, puisqu'elle reprend la notion de consequence naturelle: le sophisma est donc recevable — au titre de consequentia naturalis — puisqu'il a une prémisse ('nihil est') qui contient des opposés. On a vu, en effet, qu'une proposition contenant des opposés, c'est-à-dire une proposition 'impossible', impliquait 'naturellement' l'un et l'autre de ces opposés ('ex impossibile quodlibet'). Il suffit donc, pour Richard, de prouver que 'nihil est' est bien une proposition de ce genre, pour que, du même coup, le sophisme soit validé. Sa démonstration est la suivante: l'universelle, ici 'nihil est', contient l'indéfinie, ici 'ens non est', or 'ens', 'étant', signifie 'ce qui est', 'id quod est'; le sens de l'indéfinie est donc: 'ce qui est n'est pas', proposition qui manifestement contient deux opposés. Selon la définition de la consequence naturelle on a donc bien, au niveau de l'indéfinie: 'si ce qui est n'est pas, quelque chose est' et au niveau de l'universelle qui la contient: 'si rien n'est, quelque chose est':

> Solutio. Dicendum, quod sequitur 'si nihil est, aliquid est', eo quod in antecedente primo intelliguntur opposita hac ratione: In omni universali intelligitur sua indefinita, et in hac ergo intelligitur sua indefinita, et est 'ens non est', sed 'ens' est 'id, quod est'; ex quo sequitur: 'id, quod est, non est'; et hec sunt opposita, quorum utrumque sequitur naturaliter, et propter hoc dicitur, quod sequitur naturaliter 'si nihil est, aliquid est.'[46]

Cette solution est limitée au cas où 'ens' est interprété comme un participe, i.e., au cas où 'ens' signifie 'id, quod est': '...ens enim sumitur equiuoce participium et nomen, et secundum, quod est nomen, non est "ens" idem cum isto "quod est", sed secundum, quod est participium';[47] la distinction faite ici entre le sens nominal et le sens participial de 'ens' doit être soulignée. On sait, en effet, quel rôle joue la discussion de cette 'équivocité' dans la polémique baconienne contre Richard de Cornouailles. Il faudra s'en souvenir au moment de faire une hypothèse sur l'identité du Magister Abstractionum.

La solution par la conséquence naturelle étant limitée à une seule acception de 'ens', Richard propose une seconde solution, exactement opposée à la première, qui permet de rejeter le processus a primo en s'appuyant sur l'ambiguïté de 'nihil esse verum est.' Cette solution est, en plus developpé, celle que propose Sherwood: 'nihil esse verum est' peut être interprétée comme composée ou comme divisée. Dans les deux cas, cependant, l'enchaînement pèche, puisque, dans le sens divisé, c'est le premier conséquent qui est invalide, alors que dans le sens composé, c'est le premier antécédent. La raison de cette invalidité tient à ce que, pris au sens divise '[si] nihil esse est verum' est une proposition universelle négative, i.e., de quantité et de qualité identiques à la proposition de inesse correspondante: 'nihil est' (='nulla res est'), autrement dit c'est une proposition de re, alors que 'hoc dictum est verum' est une particulière affirmative, or, on sait qu'une affirmative ne résulte pas d'une négative. Dans le sens composé, en revanche, 'nihil esse est verum' est une affirmative de dicto dont la quantité est singulière mais, cette fois, c'est la prémisse 'nihil est' qui est négative. L'enchaînement est donc à son tour impossible, pour la même raison que le précédent:

> Aliter solvitur in proposito. Deficit enim illud consequens: 'nihil esse est verum' quia multiplex est secundum compositionem et divisionem. Et in sensu divisionis sequitur. Et fallit ista consequentia in illo sensu: 'si nihil esse est verum, hoc dictum est verum' quia, in illo sensu non subiicitur '⟨nihil⟩ esse' sed res, et est universalis et negativa, hec autem affirmativa: 'hoc dictum est verum', et affirmativa ex negativa non sequitur. In sensu compositionis, dicitur quod non sequitur 'si nihil est, nihil esse est verum', cum hec sit affirmativa in hoc sensu et antecedens negativa, et cum hec ponat esse et antecedens privet esse, et etiam cum ad illud antecedens non sequitur, idem affirmant et negant.[48]

Dans cette perspective, le seul enchaînement correct est celui qui mène de 'nihil est' à 'nihil esse non est verum.' De fait, si rien n'existe, il

n'existe non plus ni proposition ni _dictum_. Donc aucun _dictum_ n'est vrai,
dont évidemment 'nihil esse'. D'où: si rien n'existe, le _dictum_ affirmant que
rien n'existe n'est ni vérifié ni vérifiable, autrement dit: 'qu'il-n'existe-rien'
est faux si cette proposition 'rien n'existe' est vraie, bref: la proposition
'nihil est' est vraie quand ou si son _dictum_ est faux et ce dernier est faux si
ou parce qu'elle est vraie:

> Et sequitur: 'si nihil est, nihil esse non est verum' quia si nihil est, non
> est propositio nec dictum, ex quo sequitur nullum dictum esse verum et
> hec per consequens: 'nihil esse non est verum.'[49]

A cela on peut objecter que la proposition 'nihil esse est verum' est
vraie si 'nihil est' est vraie. En effet, 'nihil esse est verum' signifie qu'il en
est comme elle dit, et s'il en est comme elle le dit, elle est vraie selon
l'autorité d'Aristote pour qui, si Socrate est assis, la proposition qui dit qu'il
est assis est vraie:

> Sed <...> hec oratio 'nihil esse est verum' significat hoc esse verum,
> scilicet _nihil esse_, et quando nihil est, vera est oratio que dicit nihil
> esse, dicente Aristotele: 'sedente Sorte, vera est oratio que dicit ipsum
> sedere.'[50]

Toutefois, Richard semble concéder, en dernière analyse, qu'il en est du
dictum comme de la proposition _de inesse_ qui lui correspond. Si la
proposition est vraie, ce que dit le _dictum_ est le cas. Si elle est négative,
il est négatif. Si elle ne pose ou n'affirme rien, il ne pose ni n'affirme rien.
Donc si 'nihil est' nie l'existence de ce qui n'est pas, 'nihil esse est verum'
n'affirme rien et _n'est pas_ une affirmation. Telle qu'elle est ici formulée.
La solution définitive de Richard le Sophiste semble donc résider dans le
rejet du processus _a primo_, par blocage de l'inférence de 'nihil esse est
verum' à 'aliquid est verum':

> Sed sicut sedere et non sedere est sub hac affirmatione et negatione
> 'sedet', 'non sedet', nihil esse est sub hac negatione 'nihil est' tamquam
> res eius. Igitur ad esse unius sequitur esse alterius, quod concedo
> dicendo quod nec ponit esse sicut nec eius antecedens nec est
> affirmativa simpliciter: affirmare enim esse de eo quod est non esse, non
> est affirmativa esse, sed fallit sicut illud: 'nihil scio, ergo non scio
> me.'[51]

On voit combien l'analyse du Magister Abstractionum baigne dans la problématique des insolubles. On voit aussi pourquoi Guillaume laisse de côté tout ce développement: l'ensemble de l'analyse ne cadre pas avec la discussion de la modeste règle de négation que le sophisma est censé illustrer: 'negatio potest ferri ad diversa.' Mais on voit surtout combien, une fois de plus, les deux auteurs sont proches l'un de l'autre sur l'essentiel.

Le texte d'Herveus Sophista se présente comme le condensé, extrêmement réduit, des analyses de Richard et de Guillaume. Comme Sherwood, Herveus examine le sophisma à propos du fonctionnement de la négation.

En revanche, la présentation du processus a primo est la même que chez Richard (i.e., elle contient la prémisse additionnelle):

Si nichil est, nichil esse est verum; et si nichil esse est verum, hoc dictum 'nichil esse' est verum; et si hoc dictum est verum, aliquid est verum; et si aliquid est verum, aliquid est; ergo a primo: si nichil est, aliquid est.[52]

et sa solution à nouveau centrée sur le 'conséquent de la première conditionnelle' -- autrement dit la conclusion du premier antécédent dans la terminologie usuelle — i.e., 'nihil esse est verum' correspond à une synthèse de Richard et de Guillaume:

— si 'nihil' porte sur 'est' i.e., si le sens est 'aliquid est verum' le premier antécédent est valide.

-- en revanche, si 'nihil' porte sur 'esse' i.e., si 'est verum' est prédiqué du dictum 'nihil esse', le même premier antécédent est invalide, le sens étant: 'nihil esse est verum', ce qui bloque toute inférence. En effet, si rien n'existe, il n'existe rien de vrai ni rien de faux. On ne peut donc passer de 'nihil est', c'est-à-dire factuellement d'un état-de-chose où rien n'est vrai, à 'nihil esse est verum', c'est-à-dire factuellement à un état-de-chose où quelque chose est vrai, en l'occurence la proposition 'nihil est.'

Nicolas de Paris traite le sophisme en parallèle avec 'si nullum tempus est, aliquod tempus est', à propos de la mutatio habitudinum dans les processus a primo.

La présentation du processus est la même que chez Richard et Hervé. Toutefois on note que le terme d''enuntiabile' remplace ici celui de 'dictum' et que la topique de chaque inférence est précisée:

Si nihil est, nihil esse est verum (a propositione ad dictum); si nihil esse est verum, hoc enuntiabile 'nihil esse est verum' est verum (a convertibili);
et si hoc enuntiabile est verum, aliquod enuntiabile est verum, ([similiter] a specie);
et <si> aliquod enuntiabile est verum, aliquid est verum (similiter a specie);
et si aliquid est verum, aliquid est (similiter a specie).[53]

La formulation de Nicolas est intéressante, en ce qu'elle manifeste par un redoublement la contradiction entre la forme et le contenu de l'énonciation caractéristique des paradoxes de la sui-réflexivité.   De fait, Nicolas prend comme dictum de 'nihil esse est verum' non pas la proposition infinitive 'nihil esse' mais la proposition complète elle-même -- i.e., 'nihil esse est verum' — arguant de la convertibilité de 'nihil esse est verum' et '"nihil esse est verum" est verum.'   Cette convertibilité exprime le fait que la proposition 'nihil est' affirme à la fois sa propre vérité ('nihil esse est verum') et que le contenu de cette affirmation est le cas ou, si l'on préfère, qu'il en est bien ainsi qu'elle le dit ('"nihil esse est verum" est verum'). Autrement dit: c'est l'affirmation-qu'il-est-vrai-que-'nihil est' qui est vraie et non simplement que rien n'existe.   C'est cette affirmation qui, si elle est vraie, fait que quelque chose est vrai et non le fait que rien n'existe.   Seule l'affirmation que rien n'existe est vrai peut être vraie si rien n'existe, car le simple dictum 'nihil esse' ('rien n'exister') n'affirme ni ne nie rien et donc n'est ni ne peut être en lui-même ni par lui-même vrai ou faux.   La formulation de Nicolas fait nettement apparaître l'aspect paradoxal de l'inférence a primo: si ce-que-dit la proposition 'nihil est' est bien comme elle le dit, en d'autres termes, si l'enonçable 'nihil esse' désigne un état-de-chose effectif, l'affirmation même qu'il en est comme il est dit ne peut elle-même exister.

La solution de Nicolas n'est pas expressément développée car le maître parisien réduit le problème posé à celui qu'il a déjà résolu à propos de 'si nullum tempus est, aliquod tempus est.'

On peut donc schématiquement noter que pour lui le processus a primo est invalide à raison d'une équivocité de 'si' déterminée par la variation des principes topiques, variation dont chacune des étapes a été notée: a propositione ad dictum, a convertibili, a specie. La différence entre le sophisma et 'si nullum tempus est, aliquod tempus est' parait résider dans le fait que la présupposition d'existence (la suppositio alicuius; Braakhuis, 2.197 [16]) ne conditionne pas seulement le passage du premier antécédent au premier conséquent (comme dans 'si nullum tempus est, dies non est' valable absolument parlant, et 'si dies non est, nox est' valable si le temps existe) mais la position même du premier antécédent: 'si nihil est, nihil esse est verum' qui n'est valable que si '"nihil est" est.'

Que conclure de l'examen des sophismata que nous venons de voir?

Il serait évidemment aventureux de poser sur une aussi faible base statistique la thèse d'une dépendance stricte de Sherwood par rapport à l'univers doctrinal ricardien. Les particularités que nous avons notées nous paraissent cependant suffisantes pour justifier l'ensemble d'hypothèses suivant:

(1) Guillaume de Sherwood a pu connaître et utiliser ou, au moins, supposer connues de son milieu d'activité les Abstractiones Magistri Ricardi Sophistae.

(2) De ce fait, l'idée de l'existence d'une tradition oxonienne de la logique reçoit une confirmation directe puisque l'on sait que Sherwood n'a jamais enseigné en dehors d'Oxford, et que,

(3) les textes d'Herveus Sophista et de Nicolas de Paris semblent presenter plus d'affinité entre eux qu'avec les textes de Sherwood et de Richard.

Ceci ne signifie évidemment pas que Sherwood et Richard sont toujours d'accord. La différence le plus notable entre les deux maîtres semble être la suivante: Guillaume recourt apparemment le plus souvent possible à la 'solution' des sophismata par l'ambiguïté de composition et de division, alors que souvent Richard rejette purement et simplement les sophismata distingués par Guillaume. Cette tendance à traiter les problèmes syntactico-sémantiques de fonctionnement de syncatégorèmes au sein d'une théorie de la composition et de la division du sens propositionnel fondée sur le modus prolationis des énoncés semble être une caractéristique de la pensée sherwoodienne et sans doute à un degré moindre de la sémantique d'Oxford.

La tendance personnelle de Sherwood à résoudre autant que possible les sophismata par la seule considération du modus prolationis déterminant l'ambiguïté selon la composition et la division du sens propositionnel est nette dans les cas où, bien que d'accord sur le fond, Guillaume et Richard se séparent sur l'explication, c'est le cas par example de NEUTRUM OCULUM HABENDO TU POTES VIDERE rejeté comme faux par l'un et l'autre, mais expliqué par Sherwood en termes de composition et de division du sens, par Richard en considération du contexte extra-linguistique de l'énonciation.

La spécificité oxonienne de la solution par l'ambiguïté de composition et division est naturellement attestée par les cas où comme dans OMNIS PROPOSITIO VEL EIUS CONTRADICTORIA EST VERA Richard et Guillaume s'accordent à privilégier l'explication par le modus prolationis. Mais on peut aussi considérer comme probants les simples cas où le seul Sherwood a des solutions attestées avant tout chez Nicolas de Paris ou Herveus Sophista. C'est le cas, notamment, pour OMNE ANIMAL EST RATIONALE VEL IRRATIONALE analysé par Sherwood comme example d'ambiguïté de composition/division alors que Nicolas et Herve utilisent la notion d'inclusion entre la disjonction ('vel') et le quantificateur ('omne'), pour TU NON POTES VERE NEGARE TE NON ESSE ASINUS, ambiguë pour Guillaume, absolument vraie pour Nicolas, ou enfin pour SORTES DESINIT ESSE NON DESINENDO ESSE, interprétée par Guillaume en termes de composition ou de division alors que Nicolas s'attache à la référence temporelle de desinendo d'après une exposition de desinit déterminée en termes de supposition actuelle et de supposition secondaire.

L'hypothèse général de la représentativité de Guillaume et de Richard pour ce que L.M. de Rijk a appelé la 'tradition logique d'Oxford' nous conduit à poser, pour finir, la question sans doute la plus délicate: qui sont les auteurs des ABSTRACTIONES? Autrement dit: qui sont Ricardus Sophista et Herveus Sophista?

Le cas de Herveus peut être vite résolu. De fait, li n'y a qu'une seule hypothèse possible, celle de L.M. di Rijk. 'Hervé le Sophiste' doit être identifié avec le maître parisien mentionné par Jean de Garlande dans son

Morale scholarium, c'est-à-dire Herveus Brito, également connu sous le sobrique de 'Herveus Raucus'.[54] La candidature d'Hervé de Nédellec souvent appelé 'Herveus Brito' est évidemment exclue, comme, d'une manière générale, celle de tout maître de la fin du XIIIème et du début du XIVème siècle: l'appartenance des _Abstractiones Hervei Sophiste_ à l'univers des premières décennies du XIIIème siècle ne peut être sérieusement mise en doute, ni par le contenu littéraire et doctrinal, ni par l'analyse paléographique. L'identification présomptive d'Herveus Sophista avec Herveus Raucus ne nous apporte d'ailleurs aucune information supplémentaire car on ne sait strictement rien du personnage.   Tout ce que l'on peut dire est qu'il s'agit sans doute d'un maître ès-arts qui, contrairement à son confrère parisien Jean le Page, n'a pas enseigné la théologie.   De fait, Glorieux ne mentionne, ne cite aucun Herveus théologien dans son _Repértoire des Maîtres en Théologie_ à part de Nédellec.

L'identification de Ricardus Sophista pose plus de problèmes.   En effet, s'il y a pour Hervé défaut de candidat, il y a pour Richard possibilité de choisir entre deux auteurs.   On sait, en l'occurrence, que deux hypothèses ont été proposées, toutes deux anglaises et concernant des personnes relativement connues: Richard Fishacre (selon L.M. de Rijk) et Richard Rufus de Cornouailles (selon J. Pinborg).[55]   Dans l'état actuel des connaissances, il semble impossible de décider entre les deux.   Tout ce que nous pouvons dire est que la lecture des _Abstractiones Magistri Ricardi Sophiste_ ne nous a fourni aucune confirmation particulière, aucun indice si léger soit-il, en faveur de l'hypothèse de Richard Fishacre.   En revanche, nous pensons que deux passages au moins plaident en faveur de l'attribution à Richard de Cornouailles.

Le premier consiste dans l'utilisation par _Magister Abstractionum_ de la notion d'équivocité entre 'ens nomen' et 'ens participium', distinction alléguée par Richard de Cornouailles dans son _Commentaire des Sentences_, in III _Sent._, dist. 21: 'ergo differunt vivens, quod definit tempus presens, et vivus, quod nullam differentiam temporis definit', et stigmatisée par Bacon dès les _Summule dialectices_.

Le second consiste dans l'utilisation d'une autre distinction de Richard de Corunouailles, fondamentalement réprouvée par Roger Bacon, celle d'un sens existentiel et d'un sens non existentiel de 'esse' dans _OMNE COLORATUM EST_.   Dans ce _sophisma_, en effet, Ricardus Sophista rejette l'_improbatio_

('omne coloratum est, omne album est coloratum, ergo omne album est') pour
cause d'équivocité de 'esse' dans la majeure et dans la mineure. Dans la
majeure, selon lui, 'esse' a le sens d'être, pris comme acte ou opération de
l'étant, c'est-à-dire l'être en tant qu'il est, selon le texte du manuscrit
parisien, 'esse, eo quod est', ou l'être qui est étant, d'après le manuscrit
d'Oxford 'esse quod est ens', bref l'être actuel, alors que dans la mineure,
'être est le simple signe d'une relation conceptuelle entre les termes 'album'
et 'coloratum', autrement dit, l'être copule des propositions hypothétiques,
l'être _tertium adiacens_, qui autorise la prédication indépendamment de
l'existence. On sait que cette distinction entre être actuel et être habituel
est attestée dans le Commentaire des Sentences de Richard de Cornouailles,
in III Sent., dist. 22, qu'elle est acceptée par Sherwood dans l'analyse de
OMNIS HOMO DE NECESSITATE EST ANIMAL où, comme chez Richard elle
est reliée à la distinction entre 'distributio pro partibus secundum speciem' et
'distributio pro partibus secundum numerum', et qu'elle est violemment
rejettée par Roger Bacon, dans les Summule. Il semble donc bien qu'on aie
là un des principaux passages à verser au dossier des 'erreurs de Richard de
Cornouailles.'

Tout le problème historique est de savoir si Richard de Cornouailles a pu
soutenir cette distinction comme logicien, autrement dit avant 1250. De fait,
le témoinage de Bacon porte exclusivement sur son activité de lecteur des
Sentences à Oxford. Bacon ne dit mot de son activité de maître ès-arts,
activité qui, nécessairement doit se situer dans les années 1240, voire 1230,
si l'on admet avec Felder, Mandonnet, Davy et Charles que Richard a d'abord
lu les Sentences à Paris, avant 1247 pour Felder, avant 1241 pour
Mandonnet.[56]

On sait, toutefois, que la thèse de Mandonnet n'a aucun fondement
véritable: elle repose sur une simple confusion entre Ricardus et Rigaldus
(Eudes Rigaud) et elle a, à ce titre, été réfutée à plusieurs reprises.
Contrairement aux affirmations de Mandonnet, Richard de Cornouailles n'a
jamais participé à l'Expositio regulae demandée par le Général des
Franciscains élu au Chapître de Rome le 1er Novembre 1240, Aymon de
Faversham. L'explication de la Règle, connue sous le nom d''Exposition des
quatre Maîtres' a été faite par Alexandre de Halès, Jean de La Rochelle,
Robert de la Barrée et Eudes Rigaud.

Telle que nous pouvons la reconstruire, la chronologie de la vie de

Richard nous permets néanmoins de situer la période à laquelle il a pu rédiger les Abstractiones, si tant est qu'il en soit l'auteur. De fait, nous savons qu'il a quitté Oxford pour Paris en 1253 grâce à une lettre d'Adam de Marsh à Guillaume de Nottingham, nous savons également qu'en 1256, de retour en Angleterre, il a succédé à Thomas d'York, quatrième maître (1253-1256) de l'Etude Générale d'Oxford, et qu'auparavant, en 1248, Richard a successivement décliné ou négligé deux 'obédiences' qui l'appelaient à Paris. Nous pouvons donc dessiner le cadre suivant:[57]

1248	Richard est à Oxford
1250-1253	baccalauréat sententiaire à Oxford
1253	départ d'Oxford, lecture sententiaire à Paris
1256	entrée à l'Etude générale d'Oxford où les lecteurs 'commencent comme maîtres' ('incipiunt ut magistri').

Compte-tenu de la durée moyenne des études théologiques, on peut estimer que vers 1240-1241 Richard 'était étudiant en théologie depuis deux ou trois ans.' Il n'a donc pas pu enseigner les arts après 1240. Dans ces conditions, si les Abstractiones de Maître Richard le Sophiste ont bien été composées par le Franciscain Richard Rufus de Cornouailles c'est avant 1240, dans les années 1230. Ceci cadre assez bien avec le climat doctrinal que nous croyons y lire.

On notera dans cette perspective que le transfert de la distinction 'ricardienne' entre esse actuale et esse habitudinis à la question théologique de l'humanité du Christ in triduo mortis est attesté à la fois chez contemporains et confrères Franciscains Alexandre de Halès et Eudes Rigaud: Alexandre dans la Summa III, n° 165, Eudes dans son Commentaire des Sentences, in III Sent. dist. 22.[58]

Nous concluerons donc cette présentation de la littérature des Abstractiones par les trois thèses suivantes:

le Magister Abstractionem est plus vraisemblablement Richard de Cornouailles que Richard Fishacre, du moins si l'on s'en tient aux indications fournies par Roger Bacon sur la nature des 'erreurs de Richard Rufus' et sur leur chronologie.

Les deux recueils d'Abstractiones actuellement connus sont

indépendant l'un de l'autre mais présentent suffisamment de points communs pour que l'on puisse les considérer à la fois comme contemporains et comme concurrents, le recueil de Richard paraissant lié à la tradition d'Oxford, celui d'Hervé à la tradition de Paris.

Les Abstractiones de Richard ont connu une certaine diffusion, vraisemblablement à Oxford et à Paris par l'intermédiaire de la nation anglaise, elles semblent, en tout cas, avoir servi de manuel ou de répertoire à Guillaume de Sherwood dans la préparation de ses Syncategoremata.

Notes

[1] N. Kretzmann, 'Syncategoremata, exponibilia, sophismata' in N. Kretzmann, A. Kenny and J. Pinborg eds., The Cambridge History of Later Medieval Philosophy (Cambridge, 1982), p. 216.

[2] Ibid., p. 215.

[3] H.A.G. Braakhuis, De 13de Eeuwse Tractaten over Syncategorematische Termen, 2 vols. (Krips Repro Meppel: Nimègue, 1980), (=Braakhuis), 1.35-65.

[4] Ibid., pp. 66-73.

[5] Ibid., pp. 30-31.

[6] Ibid., p. 71.

[7] Ibid., p. 31.

[8] Ibid.

[9] Ms Paris, BN lat. 16618, fol. 109ra; cf. le texte parallèle dans Braakhuis, 1.410.

[10] R. Steele ed., Roger Bacon. Summa de sophismatibus et distinctionibus (Opera hactenus inedita Rogeri Baconi 14; Oxford, 1937). Le texte de Steele — au demeurant incomplet — est généralement peu fiable. M. H.A.G.

Braakhuis prépare une édition critique d'après mss Erfurt, Wissenschaftliche Bibliothek der Stadt, F. 135, fols. 60ra-84vb, et Oxford, Bodleian Library, Digby 67, fols. 117ra-124vb, déjà utilisé par Steele.

[11] L.M. de Rijk, __Logica Modernorum__ 2.1 (Wijsgerige Teksten en Studies 16; Assen, 1967), p. 71.

[12] Ibid., p. 62.

[13] Ms Paris, BN lat. 14069, fol. 32va.

[14] Ibid.

[15] Ibid.

[16] Ibid.

[17] Ed. J. Reginald O'Donnell, 'The __Syncategoremata__ of William of Sherwood', __Mediaeval Studies__ 3 (1941) 46-93 (=O'Donnell); ibid., p. 81.

[18] Ms Paris, BN lat. 14069, fol. 32[vb].

[19] Ibid.

[20] Ibid.

[21] Ibid.

[22] O'Donnell, p. 81.

[23] Ibid.

[24] Ms Paris, BN lat. 14069, fol. 32[vb].

[25] Ibid.

[26] O'Donnell, p. 81.

[27] Ibid.

[28] Braakhuis, 2.195 (2, 3-4, 8).

[29] Ms Paris, BN lat. 16617 (=P), fol. 40^V; cf. O'Donnell, pp. 81-82.

[30] O'Donnell, p. 82.

[31] Ibid.

[32] Ms Paris, BN lat. 14069, fol. 32vb.

[33] Ibid.

[34] Ibid.

[35] Braakhuis, 2.195 (11-13).

[36] Ibid., 1.187.

[37] Ibid., 2.196 (7-9).

[38] Ibid., 2.197 (12-17).

[39] Ms Paris, BN lat. 15170, fol. 50ra.

[40] Ibid.

[41] Ibid.

[42] Ibid.

[43] O'Donnell, p. 58

[44] Ibid.

[45] Ms Paris, BN lat. 14069, fol. 32vb.

[46] Ibid.

[47] Ibid., fol. 33ra.

[48] Ibid.

[49] Ibid.

[50] Ibid.

[51] Ibid.

[52] Ms Paris, BN lat. 15170, fol. 50va.

[53] Braakhuis, 2.195 (17-22).

[54] De Rijk, Logica Modernorum 2.1, pp. 50-51.

[55] Ibid., pp. 71-72; Jan Pinborg, 'Magister Abstractionum', CIMAGL 18 (1976) 1-4.

[56] Cf. sur ce point H. Felder, 'Les Franciscains ont-ils eu deux Écoles Universitaires à Paris?', Études Franciscaines 25 (1911) 604-607, et P. Mandonnet, 'Thomas d'Aquin, Novice Prêcheur, 1244-1246', Revue Thomiste 30 (1925) 510-514.

[57] Cf. A. Callebaut, 'Alexandre de Halès, O.F.M., et ses confrères en face des condamnations parisiennes de 1241 et 1244', La France Franciscaine 10 (1927) 263-267. Cf. également F.-M. Henquinet, 'Autour des écrits d'Alexandre de Halès et de Richard Rufus', Antonianum 11 (1936) 190-196.

[58] Sur ce point cf. Prolegomena in librum III necnon in libros I et II 'Summae fratris Alexandri', Alexandri de Hales, Summa theologica 4, lib. 3 (Quarrachi, 1948), p. CCXLIV.

Abstractiones Magistri Hervei Sophiste
(MS Paris, BN lat. 15170, fols. 48va - 52va)

(1) OMNE COLORATUM EST
(2) OMNE ANIMAL FUIT IN ARCHA NOE
(3) OMNE ANIMAL CURRIT

(4) OMNE SEDET

(5) OMNE RATIONALE VEL IRRATIONALE EST SANUM

(6) OMNIS PROPOSITIO VEL EIUS CONTRADICTORIA EST VERA

(7) OMNIS PROPOSITIO VEL EIUS CONTRADICTORIA EST FALSA

(8) OMNIS AFFIRMATIO VEL EIUS NEGATIO EST VERA

(9) OMNE ENUNTIABILE VEL EIUS CONTRADICTORIUM ET OPPOSITUM EST VERUM

(10) OMNE ANIMAL VEL NON ANIMAL EST SANUM VEL EGRUM

(11) OMNIS HOMO VEL ASINUS EST RISIBILIS

(12) OMNE BONUM VEL NON BONUM EST ELIGENDUM

(13) OMNIS HOMO EST ET ALIUS HOMO EST

(14) OMNE ALBUM EST ET ALIUD ALBUM EST

(15) OMNE VERUM ET DEUM ESSE DIFFERUNT

(16) OMNIS HOMO QUI EST ALBUS, CURRIT

(17) OMNE ALIUD QUOD ANIMAL QUOD ET SOR SUNT DUO, DIFFERT A SORTE

(18) SOR DICIT OMNE ENUNTIABILE IN A ET IN B

(19) SORTES VIDET OMNEM HOMINEM IN A ET IN B

(20) QUODLIBET ANIMALIUM ALIQUORUM EST NON HOMO QUORUM QUIDLIBET EST HOMO

(21) OMNIS HOMO ALBUS EST

(22) OMNIS HOMO EST ET QUIDLIBET DIFFERENS AB ILLO EST NON-HOMO

(23) OMNIS HOMO EST ET QUIDLIBET VIDENS ILLUM EST ASINUS

(24) OMNIS SCIENS EST ET QUILIBET SCIENS ILLUM ESSE GRAMMATICUM EST TANTUM TALIS

(25) OMNIS THEOLOGUS EST ET QUILIBET SCIENS ILLUM ESSE THEOLOGUM EST TANTUM TALIS

(26) OMNE CAPUD NON HABENS EST ALIQUOD CAPUD HABENS

(27) DEUS ERIT IN QUOLIBET INSTANTI NON EXISTENS

(28) OMNE NON ANIMAL QUOD EST HICINTUS EST LAPIS

(29) OMNEM HOMINEM VIDENS EST UNUM SOLUM HOMINEM VIDENS

(30) OMNIS HOMO MORITUR QUANDO UNUS SOLUS HOMO MORITUR

(31) POSSIBILE EST OMNEM HOMINEM MORI

(32) IMPOSSIBILE EST OMNEM HOMINEM MORI

(33) OMNE QUOD DEUS SCIVIT ADHUC SCIT

(34) OMNIS HOMO EST ANIMAL ET E CONVERSO

(35) OMNIS HOMO EST OMNIS HOMO

(36) QUIDLIBET EST QUIDLIBET VEL DIFfERENS A QUOLIBET

(37) UTERQUE ISTORUM EST SOR VEL PLATO, ERGO SOR VEL PLATO EST UTERQUE ISTORUM

(38) UTERQUE ISTORUM EST HICINTUS ET ALIUS EST HICINTUS

(39) UTERQUE ISTORUM EST TANTUM ALTERUM ISTORUM VIDENS VEL UNUM SOLUM HOMINEM VIDENS

(40) UTERQUE ISTORUM VEL RELIQUO QUORUM NEUTRUM DIFFERT AB HOMINE EST ASINUS VEL RELIQUO ISTORUM EST ASINUS

(41) NEUTRUM OCCULUM HABENDO TU POTES VIDERE

(42) ISTI CURRUNT ERGO UTERQUE ISTORUM CURRIT

(43) ISTI SCIUNT A ERGO UTERQUE ISTORUM SCIT A

(44) AB UTROQUE ENUNTIATUM EST VERUM

(45) SORTES ET PLATO SUNT HOMINES, ERGO TOTUS SOR ET PLATO VEL NON TOTUS SOR ET PLATO

(46) TOTUS SOR EST MAIOR SORTE

(47) SOR NASCATUR IN B

(48) HOMO EST PARS HOMINIS

(49) AFFIRMATIO EST PARS NEGATIONIS

(50) IN UNAQUAQUE PARTE ANIMALIS EST ANIMA

(51) QUELIBET PARS ANIMALIS EST ANIMAL

(52) QUODLIBET QUALELIBET DE SE TALI SCIT SE IPSUM ESSE TALE

(53) A EST, B EST A, NON EST B, ERGO A DIFFERT A B

(54) SOR INQUANTUM ANIMAL DIFFERT AB ASINO

(55) SOR INQUANTUM EST INDIVIDUUM DIFFERT A PLATONE

(56) QUANTO ALIQUID MAIUS EST, TANTO MINUS VIDETUR

(57) QUIDQUID AUDITUR A SORTE PROFERTUR A PLATONE

(58) NEGATO TE ESSE ASINUM, BENE RESPONDES: "FALSUM EST"

(59) SORTES VULT ESSE TALIS QUALIS EST PLATO, ERGO VULT ESSE SIMILIS PLATONI

(60) ISTI PUGNANT UT VINCANT SESE, ERGO PUGNANT UT VINCANTUR

(61) SORTES EST ALIUD ANIMAL A BURNELLO

(62) IESUS PEPENDIT INTER DUOS ALIOS LATRONES

(63) IDEM HOMINES VIDENT ISTOS

(64) INQUANTUM SUNT EQUIVOCA NON SUNT EQUIVOCA

(65) ALIQUID IN EO QUOD EST EQUIVOCUM EST UNIVOCUM

(66) ALIQUID IN EO QUOD EST ALBUM EST NIGRUM

(67) ISTI INCEDUNT BINI ET BINI

(68) BIS UNUM EST UNUM

(69) HEC MULIER PEPERIT DECIES DECEM FILIO

(70) QUANDOCUMQUE FUISTI SEDENS, FUISTI HOMO

(71) INQUANTUM DIFFERUNT, CONVENIUNT

(72) SI CANIS CURRIT, LATRABILE CURRIT

(73) SI MALUM EST BONUM, TU ES CAPRA

(74) SI MALEDICTUS EST BENEDICTUS, TU ES CAPRA

(75) SI ALIQUIS ASINUS EST RATIONALIS, TU ES CAPRA

(76) SI ALIQUIS ASINUS EST HOMO, TU ES CAPRA

(77) SI QUOD NIHIL EST LEGIT TU ES CAPRA

(78) SI QUOD NIHIL EST ACTU VEL POTENTIA EST ALIQUID TU ES CAPRA

(79) SI IMPOSSIBILE EST ALIUD QUAM ASINUM GENUISSE TE, TU ES CAPRA

(80) SI VERUM EST TE ESSE VEL ALIUD ESSE QUIDLIBET, TU ES CAPRA

(81) FALSUM EST VERUM SI ANTICHRISTUS EST

(82) NON SCRIBENS SCRIBIT SI SOR SCRIBIT

(83) SI VERUM EST TE CURRERE ET TE NON CURRERE, TE SEDERE ET TE NON SEDERE, TU ES CAPRA

(84) TU ES ALBUS ET TU ES NIGER SI TU ES TU, IGITUR TU CURRIS ET TU SEDES SI TU SEDES

(85) DEUM ESSE ERIT VERUM IN A SI A NON ERIT, QUIA NECESARIUM ERIT VERUM IN A. ET IDEO DEUM ESSE SI A NON ERIT, ERIT VERUM IN A

(86) B ESSE SI B NON ERIT ESSE FALSUM IN B

(87) NECESSARIUM EST ANIMAL CURRERE SI HOMO CURRIT

(88) IMPOSSIBILE EST TE SEDERE SI TU LOQUERIS

(89) IMPOSSIBILE EST TE ESSE IPSUM NISI SIS ASINUS

(90) SI FUNDAMENTUM VIDETUR A TE IN CAVERNA TU ES ASINUS

(91) SI AD HOMINEM ESSE QUOD EST VERUM SEQUITUR ABESSE QUOD EST VERUM, HOMO EST

(92) SI DE EO QUOD EST SOR VERUM EST IPSUM ESSE VEL NON ESSE, SOR EST

(93) SOR DICIT ID QUOD VERUM EST SI PLATO LOQUITUR

(94) ERGO SI DE SORTE VERUM EST IPSUM ESSE VEL NON ESSE, SOR EST

(95) ERGO SI AD HOMINEM ESSE SEQUITUR ANIMAL ESSE, HOMO EST

(96) SI DE ALIQUO EST VERUM QUOD DE NULLO EST VERUM TU ES ASINUS

(97) SI NICHIL EST ET TU ES ASINUS, TU ES CAPRA

(98) SI NICHIL ET CHIMERA SUNT FRATRES, TU ES CAPRA

(99) SI ALIQUID NICHIL EST NEC ERIT, TU ES CAPRA

(100) SI SOR EST, SI PLATO EST, SI CICERO EST, TU ES ASINUS

(101) SI ANIMAL EST, SI HOMO EST, SI MOTUS EST, CURSUS EST

(102) SI ALIQUIS HOMO EST QUIES TU ES CAPRA

(103) SI ALIQUA PROPOSITIO SINGULARIS EST INDEFINITA TU ES CAPRA

(104) SI ALIQUID EST VERUM QUOD NICHIL EST VERUM NEC EST FALSUM, TU ES ASINUS

(105) HOMO SI EST VIDENS TU ES CAPRA

(106) SI ALIQUIS DICIT TE ESSE ASINUM DICIT VERUM

(107) SI ALIQUIS DICIT TE ESSE SOR DICIT VERUM

(108) SI ALIQUIS DICIT TE ESSE ALIUD AB ASINO DICIT VERUM, SED SI DICIT TE ESSE CAPRAM DICIT TE ESSE ALIUD AB ASINO, ERGO SI DICIT TE ESSE CAPRAM DICIT VERUM

(109) SI QUIDLIBET EST NON-HOMO, HOMO EST NON-HOMO

(110) SI NULLUM TEMPUS EST, ALIQUOD TEMPUS EST

(111) SI NULLUS HOMO EST HICINTUS, ALIQUIS HOMO EST HICINTUS

(112) SIVE HOMO QUI EST ALBUS EST PLATO SIVE TU ES ASINUS, TU ES CAPRA

(113) QUICUMQUE DICIT TE ESSE THEOLOGUM, DICIT VERUM

(114) QUIDQUID CONTINGAT, SI TU ES ASINUS, TU ES CAPRA

(115) QUALECUMQUE EST ALIQUID, SI IPSUM EST ALBUM TALE EST ILLUD SI IPSUM EST NIGRUM

(116) QUALECUMQUE EST ALIQUID, SI IPSUM EST SANE TALE EST ILLUD SI IPSUM EST EGRUM

(117) UBICUMQUE EXISTENS EST ALIQUID, SI IPSUM EST ROME IBI IDEM EXISTENS EST ALIQUID SI IPSUM EST PARISIUS

(118) SOR DICIT A ERGO DICIT A ET B. SED A ET B EST C. SIT ITA. ERGO DICIT C

(119) DEUS PROHIBET NE FACIAS FURTUM, DEUS VULT NE FACIAS FURTUM ET QUIDQUID PROHIBET NON VULT, ERGO IDEM VULT ET NON VULT

(120) TU CAVES NE TIBI CONCLUDATUR ET TU VIS NE TIBI CONCLUDA-
TUR, ERGO IDEM VIS ET NON VIS

(121) TU SCIS AN OMNIS HOMO CURRAT QUONIAM TU SCIS NON OMNEM
HOMINEM CURRERE, ERGO TU SCIS OMNIS HOMO AN CURRAT

(122) TU SCIS AN SOR SIT SANUS. SIT ITA QUOD NULLO MODO POTEST
ESSE SANUS, ERGO TU SCIS AN IPSE SIT EGER

(123) TU SCIS AN DE MENTIENTE SIT FALSUM SORTEM ESSE IPSUM

(124) TU SCIS AN Δ ESSE IMPOSSIBILE SIT IMPOSSIBILE DE IMPOSSIBILI

(125) SOR SCIT AN PLATO SCIAT ALIQUID DE EO

(126) TU SCIS AN OMNE ANIMAL SIT RATIONALE VEL AN ILLUD SIT
IRRATIONALE

(127) NON ALIQUID EST ET TU ES ASINUS

(128) SI ALIQUID NON EST NEC ERIT ET EST ET ERIT

(129) NEC HOMO NEC ASINUS EIUS VIDENS ILLUM EST CAPRA

(130) NULLUS HOMO LEGIT PARISIUS NISI IPSE SIT ASINUS

(131) NICHIL EST VERUM NISI IPSUM SIT FALSUM

(132) NICHIL SEDET NISI CURRAT

(133) NICHIL EST VERUM NISI IN HOC INSTANTI

(134) TU SCIS QUOD NICHIL SCIS QUOD SI SCIS NICHIL SCIS

(135) ALIQUA SUNT QUE NULLA SUNT QUE NECESSARIA SUNT

(136) SI NICHIL EST, ALIQUID EST

(137) A NULLO ENUNTIATUM A NULLO VERE DICITUR

(138) IUDEI PIE INTERFECIUNT IHESUM

(139) SOR PERCUTITUR ITERUM A PLATONE

(140) TU VIDES ECCLESIAM SUPRA EQUUM

(141) SUNT DUO QUI DUO SUNT ET SUNT DUO QUI DUO NON SUNT, QUI
DUO SI DUO SUNT NULLA DUO DUO SUNT

(142) NICHIL VIDENS EST ALIQUID VIDENS

(143) ALIQUIS HOMO NON EST HICINTUS, ERGO HICINTUS NON EST
ALIQUIS HOMO

(144) NULLUS HOMO EST SI ALIQUIS HOMO EST

(145) NICHIL NICHIL EST ERGO NICHIL NULLA SUBSTANTIA EST

(146) NULLUS HOMO NULLUM ANIMAL EST, ERGO NULLUM ANIMAL
NULLUS HOMO EST

(147) SI TE NON ESSE ASINUM AFFIRMATUR AFIRMATIVA PROPOSITIONE
PROFERTUR

(148) TU NON POTES VERE NEGARE QUIN SIS ASINUS

(149) TU NON POTES VERE NEGARE QUIN DEUS SIT, ERGO TU NON POTES VERE NEGARE QUOD DEUS NON EST

(150) SOR ERIT ALTERIUS MODI QUAM PLATO EST

(151) PLURES HOMINES SUNT HICINTUS QUAM SUNT IN CIVITATE

(152) PLURA SUNT VERA DE TOTIDEM SIBI QUAM SUNT VERA DE PAUCIORIBUS SE

(153) INFINITA SUNT FINITA

(154) INFINITI HOMINES SUNT FINITI HOMINES

(155) PAUCIORA SUNT VERA DE TOTIDEM SIBI QUAM SUNT VERA DE PAUCIORIBUS SE

(156) DEUS DESINIT NUNC ESSE

(157) DEUS INCIPIT NUNC ESSE

(158) SOR DESINIT ESSE NON DESINENDO ESSE

(159) SOR DESINIT ESSE SI EST ET NON ERIT

(160) SOR DESINIT SEDERE SI SEDET ET NON SEDEBIT

(161) SOR DESINIT ESSE ALBUS, ERGO DESINIT ESSE COLORATUS

(162) DESINIT CURRERE, ERGO DESINIT MOVERI

(163) SOR DESINIT ESSE HOMO, IPSO MORIENTE, ERGO SOR DESINIT NON ESSE NON HOMO

(164) SOR INCIPIT ESSE ALTER ISTORUM

(165) SOR DESINIT ESSE ALTER ISTORUM, ERGO SOR DESINIT ESSE SORTEM VEL PLATONEM

(166) ISTE EXERCITUS DESINIT ESSE, ERGO MILITES DESINUNT ESSE

(167) ISTE POPULUS DESINIT ESSE, ERGO HOMINES DESINUNT ESSE

(168) ISTI SCOLARES DESINUNT ESSE ET QUICUMQUE SUNT TALES VEL TALES SUNT HOMINES, ERGO ISTI DESINUNT ESSE HOMINES

(169) OMNE ANIMAL DESINIT ESSE

(170) SOR DESINIT ESSE TALIS QUALIS EST PLATO

(171) TE SURGENTE DESINIS ESSE TALIS QUALIS ES

(172) SOR DESINIT ESSE ALBISSIMUS HOMINUM

(173) OMNE ANIMAL EST RATIONALE VEL IRRATIONALE

(174) DESINIT SCIRE SE NICHIL DESINERE SCIRE

(175) OMNIS HOMO INCIPIT ESSE

(176) OMNIS HOMO DESINIT ESSE

(177) DESINIT VIDERE OMNEM HOMINEM

(178) TU NON CESSAS COMEDERE FERRUM

(179) PLATO CURRIT PRETER SORTEM

(180) SOR BIS VIDEBIT OMNEM HOMINEM PRETER PLATONEM

(181) OMNIS HOMO PRETER SORTEM VIDET OMNEM HOMINEM

(182) DECEM ANIMALIA SCIUNT SE ESSE ALBA

(183) OMNIA DECEM PRETER UNUM SUNT NOVEM

(184) OMNE ENUNTIABILE PRETER FALSUM EST VERUM

(185) OMNE ANIMAL PRETER SANUM EST EGRUM

(186) QUOTLIBET PRETER DUO EXCEDUNT UNITATEM NUMERO

(187) OMNIS HOMO NECESSARIO CURRIT PRETER SORTEM

(188) UTERQUE ISTORUM PRETER UTRUMQUE DIFFERT AB ILLO

(189) OMNIS HOMO CURRIT PRETER SORTEM, ERGO SOR NON CURRIT

(190) QUATUOR PRETER DUO SUNT DUO, SEX PRETER TRIA SUNT TRIA, ERGO DUO NON SUNT DUO

(191) OMNIS HOMO EXCIPITUR PRETER SORTEM

(192) OMNE ENUNTIABILE PRETER UNUM EST VERUM

(193) SI ALIQUID CURRIT, ALIQUID NON CURRIT

(194) NULLUS HOMO VIDET ASINUM PRETER BRUNELLUM

(195) SOR SCIT TANTUM TRES HOMINES CURRERE

(196) TANTUM OMNEM HOMINEM ESSE HOMINEM EST POSSIBILE

(197) POSSIBILE EST SOR VIDERE OMNEM HOMINEM NON VIDENTEM SE

(198) HEC EST FALSA: TANTUM TU ES ASINUS, ERGO HEC EST VERA: NON TANTUM TU ES ASINUS

(199) EA QUE NON SUNT HOMINES SUNT ANIMALIA, IGITUR TANTUM NON HOMINES SUNT ANIMALIA

(200) A DE NUMERO ISTORUM QUORUM QUODLIBET DIFFERT AB EO QUOD EST IPSUM ESSE NON EST ILLUD

(201) SOR VIDENS OMNEM HOMINEM EST ILLE, ERGO SOR VIDENS SOR NON EST ILLE

(202) TANTUM HOMO EST IUSTUS, ERGO TANTUM HOMO NON EST IUSTUS

(203) TANTUM VIDES OMNEM CECUM, ERGO TANTUM VIDES OMNEM HOMINEM NON VIDENTEM

(204) TANTUM UNUM EST

(205) TANTUM UNUS HOMO EST UNUS HOMO

(206) TANTUM ALTER ISTORUM VEL RELIQUUS EST HOMO

(207) TANTUM DUO VEL TRIA SUNT TRIA

(208) SI TANTUM ALTER ISTORUM EST, UTERQUE ISTORUM EST

(209) TANTUM OMNIS HOMO CURRIT

(210) TANTUM VERUM POTEST ESSE VERUM

(211) TANTUM HOMO POTEST ESSE HOMO

(212) TANTUM VERUM EST IDEM VERO

(213) TANTUM HOMO EST IDEM HOMINI

(214) TANTUM VERUM OPPONITUR FALSO

(215) TANTUM VERUM EST VERUM

(216) TANTUM QUATUOR ESSE VERA

(217) "TANTUM PLATO DICIT VERUM."

(218) QUANTO PLUS ADDISCIS, TANTO MINUS SCIS

(219) TU DAS MIHI ID QUOD HABES ET DAS MIHI UNUM SOLUM DENARIUM, ERGO HABES UNUM SOLUM DENARIUM

(220) TU SCRIBIS MANU QUAM HABES ET SCRIBIS UNA SOLA MANU, ERGO HABES UNAM SOLAM MANUM

(221) SOLUS SOR EST ALBUS QUO PLATO EST ALBIOR

(222) SOLIUS BINARII PARS EST UNITAS ET NULLUS NUMERUS

(223) SOLA NECESSARIA NECESSARIO SUNT VERA

(224) SOLA NOVEM ANIMALIA SUNT ALBA QUI NON SUNT SOLA

(225) SOR ET ALII DUO SUNT TRES

(226) SOLUS SOR EST, SI SOR EST ET ALIUS HOMO SUNT

(227) A SOLO SORTE DIFFERT QUIDQUID NON EST SOR

(228) NON OMNIS HOMO EST ISTE HOMO ET SIC DE SINGULIS, NON ERGO OMNIS HOMO EST HOMO

(229) SOLUS SOR NON EST DIFFERENS A SOLO SORTE

(230) SOLUS HOMO EST INIUSTUS, ERGO SOLUS HOMO EST NON IUSTUS

(231) SOLUS GENITIVUS PRECEDITUR A SOLO NOMINATIVO, ERGO SOLUS NOMINATIVUS PRECEDIT SOLUM GENITIVUM

(232) SOLA ASSUMPTIO PRECEDIT SOLAM CONCLUSIONEM, ERGO SOLA CONCLUSIO PRECEDITUR A SOLA ASSUMPTIONE

(233) SOLA TRIA SUNT PLURA SOLIS DUOBIS, ERGO SOLA DUO SUNT PAUCIORA SOLIS TRIBUS

(234) SOLUS SOR VIDET SOLUM SORTEM, ERGO SOLUS SOR VIDETUR A SOLO SORTE

(235) SOLUS SOR VIDET SE

(236) SOR SCIT SOLUM PLATONEM SCIRE A, ERGO SOR SCIT A ESSE

VERUM ET QUIDQUID SCIT ESSE VERUM SCIT, ERGO SOR SCIT Δ, NON ERGO SOLUS PLATO

(237) IMPOSSIBILE SOLUM SORTEM SCIRE SOLUM PLATONEM SCIRE Δ

(238) SOLUS SOR SCIT Δ NON ERGO SOR ET PLATO SCIUNT Δ

(239) PLURA SCIUNTUR A SORTE QUAM A SOLO SORTE

(240) SOLA CONTINGENTIA ESSE VERA EST VERUM CONTINGENS

(241) CONTINGENTIA NECESSARIO SUNT VERA

(242) ANIMA ANTICHRISTI ERIT NECESSARIO

(243) QUICQUID NECESSARIO EST VERUM VEL NECESSARIO FALSUM EST NECESSARIUM VEL IMPOSSIBILE

(244) ALTERUM ISTORUM EST NECESSARIUM

(245) OMNIS HOMO NECESSARIO EST ANIMAL

(246) OMNIS HOMO NECESSARIO EST ALBUS

(247) NECESSARIUM EST OMNEM HOMINEM ESSE ALBUM

(248) ALIQUID EST IMPOSSIBILE ET IDEM NECESSARIO EST VERUM

(249) NECESSARIUM EST TE ESSE ASINUM ET TE NON ESSE ASINUM

(250) NECESSARIUM EST QUOD IMPOSSIBILE EST

(251) NECESSARIUM EST POSSIBILE VEL POSSIBILIA ESSE IMPOSSIBILE

(252) IMPOSSIBILE EST ALIUD QUAM ASINUM GENUISSE TE

(253) SOR DE NECESSITATE EST HOMO

(254) NON EST VERUM TE CURRERE, ERGO VERUM EST TE NON CURRERE. NON EST NECESSARIUM TE CURRERE, ERGO EST NECESSARIUM TE NON CURRERE, POSSIBILE EST TE NON CURRERE, ERGO NON POSSIBILE EST TE CURRERE

(255) SICUT SE HABET NOVENARIUS AD SENARIUM ITA SENARIUS AD QUATERNARIUM

(256) SICUT SE HABET PROPINQUITAS ET DISTANTIA MEI AD OSTIUM, ITA PROPINQUITAS ET DISTANTIA MEI AD ROMAM, ERGO PERMUTATIM: SICUT SE HABET PROPINQUITAS MEI AD OSTIUM ITA AD PROPINQUITATEM MEI AD ROMAM, ITA DISTANTIA AD DISTANTIAM

(257) SICUT HOMO AD NON HOMO, ITA ANIMAL AD NON ANIMAL SE HABET

(258) IMPOSSIBILE FUIT POSSIBILE

(259) IMPOSSIBILE EST TE SCIRE ALIQUID QUOD NON SCIS ESSE

(260) IMPOSSIBILE EST PLURA ALIQUIBUS ESSE PAUCIORA ILLIS

(261) IMPOSSIBILE EST TE SCIRE PLUS QUAM SCIS

(262) IMPOSSIBILE EST TE SEDERE ALIBI QUAM SEDES

(263) POSSIBILE EST NON SEDENTE SEDERE

(264) ANTICHRISTUM ESSE HOMINEM QUI NON EST

(265) IMPOSSIBILE EST OMNE NESCITUM A TE SCIRI A TE

(266) IMPOSSIBILE EST DICI QUOD IMPOSSIBILE EST DICI

(267) QUICQUID EST VERUM SCIRI A TE EST VERUM

(268) POSSIBILE EST SORTEM SCIRE QUICQUID PLATO SCIT

(269) OMNE ANIMAL ESSE HOMINEM EST POSSIBILE

(270) NEGATUM APELLARI "LIGNUM" EST VERUM

(271) POSSIBILE EST QUOD NEC POSSIBILE EST NEC IMPOSSIBILE EST QUOD SI POSSIBILE EST VEL IMPOSSIBILE EST, TU ES ASINUS

(272) CONTINGENS EST QUOD NEC CONTINGENS EST NEC NON CONTINGENS EST, QUOD SI CONTINGENS EST VEL NON CONTINGENS EST, TU ES ASINUS

(273) VERUM EST QUOD FALSUM EST QUOD NEC VERUM EST NEC FALSUM EST QUOD SI VERUM EST VEL FALSUM EST, TU ES ASINUS

(274) IDEM EST A QUOD B

(275) NECESSARIUM EST A ESSE B, TAMEN IMPOSSIBILE EST B ESSE A

(276) IMPOSSIBILE EST A VIDERE B, ET TAMEN A VIDEBIT B

(277) IMPOSSIBILE FUIT A VIDERE B ET EST ET ERIT, ET TAMEN A VIDET B

(278) A ERIT BONUM VEL FUIT, TAMEN IMPOSSIBILE EST A ESSE BONUM

(279) A EST PARS B ET A EST C , ERGO C EST PARS A ET A ESSE C SUNT IDEM, ERGO C EST PARS B

(280) SOR CURRIT IN A ET A EST ANTE B, ERGO CURRIT ANTE B

(281) A EST, B EST, A NON EST B, ERGO A DIFFERT A B

(282) A ET B SUNT C, ERGO A EST C VEL PARTIM DE B

(283) PANIS ET VINUM COMEDUNTUR A TE

(284) A ET B DIFFERUNT ET NON IMPOSSIBILE EST A DIFFERE A B, SIMILITER B DIFFERE AB A

(285) TU VIDISTI A, HOC AUTEM C HOMINES, ERGO TU VIDISTI C HOMINES

(286) DESTRUCTO A, DESTRUCTUM EST B

(287) SIMPLICITER IDEM A ET B, ERGO SI ALTERI VERE ADDATUR C ET ALII

(288) OMNINO IDEM SUNT A ET B, ERGO AD QUODCUMQUE SEQUITUR A SEQUITUR B

(289) SOR DICIT A, SIMILITER B, UTRUQUE EST C ET ECONVERSO, ERGO DICIT C

(290) NECESSARIO EST A NON ESSE B ET TAMEN IMPOSSIBILE EST B NON ESSE A

(291) A OMNINO EST IDEM QUOD B, ERGO NON DIFFERT A B

(292) A VIDET B ET TAMEN IMPOSSIBILE EST B VIDERI AB A

(293) A EST ET PRIUS NON FUIT, ERGO INCIPIT ESSE

(294) DESINIT

(295) A EST NECESSARIUM, ERGO EST VERUM

(296) NECESSARIUM EST A ESSE TALE QUALE EST B, ERGO NECESSARIUM EST A SIMILE B

(297) IDEM EST A QUOD B, PENITUS NECESSARIUM EST A ESSE, TAMEN IMPOSSIBILE EST B ESSE

(298) A FORE EST NECESSARIUM, ERGO A FORE SEMPER ERIT VERUM

4

Roger Bacon's Theory of the Double Intellectus: A Note on the
Development of the Theory of Congruitas and Perfectio in the
First Half of the Thirteenth Century

C.H. Kneepkens
University of Nijmegen

1. Introduction

The interest historians of mediaeval grammar take in the development of the
theory of congruitas and perfectio is of relatively recent date. In the past
two decades, the views of grammarians of the second half of the thirteenth
century and of the early fourteenth century have received particular
attention from scholars.[1] The studies and editorial observations by, for
instance, Jan Pinborg, G.L. Bursill-Hall, John Trentman and L.G. Kelly
contain valuable observations and discussions of the views held by the
modistic grammarians,[2] while in the first part of his contribution to the
Fourth Symposium, P. Osmund Lewry dealt extensively with the positions held
by the late thirteenth-century Oxford masters William de Bonkes and Thomas
Cherminstre and by the anonymous authors of the Oxford grammar textbooks'
Notandum quod octo sunt partes' and 'Innata est nobis'.[3]

In his discussion of the first two propositions in grammar that were
condemned by Archbishop Robert Kilwardby on 18 March 1277 at Oxford,
Father Lewry also touched on Roger Bacon and his view on congruity and
perfection or completeness, as expressed in the Summa gramatica, and his
theory of the double intellectus: the intellectus primus and secundus (or
'secundarius', as one of the manuscripts reads).[4] In the present paper I
intend to examine in more detail Bacon's contribution to the development of

The Rise of British Logic, ed. P. Osmund Lewry, O.P., Papers in Mediaeval
Studies 7 (Toronto: Pontifical Institute of Mediaeval Studies, 1985), pp. 115-
143. © P.I.M.S., 1985.

intend to examine in more detail Bacon's contribution to the development of the doctrine associated with these notions, and I would like to pay special attention to the theory of the double intellectus, which has been relatively ignored in modern literature.   But first I shall briefly sketch the views on congruitas and perfectio held by Petrus Helias and Petrus Hispanus (non-Papa), the author of 'Absoluta cuiuslibet', since acquaintance with the writings of both of these earlier grammarians formed part of the grammatical luggage of every thirteenth-century grammarian.

2. Congruitas and Perfectio in the Writings of
Petrus Helias and Petrus Hispanus

2.1 Congruitas

The mediaeval notion of congruitas reaches back through Priscian to Apollonius Dyscolus' KATALLELOTES.   It forms an essential part of Priscian's definition of 'oratio', sc. 'ordinatio dictionum congrua', but one looks in vain for a definition or description of the term itself in Priscian's writings.   The grammarians who were active before Petrus Helias used to define congruitas on the level of grammatical government and concordance.[5] Actually, it covered what some modern linguistics scholars call 'grammaticality'.

Petrus Helias introduced an important distinction in the notion of congruity namely that between congruity secundum vocem and congruity secundum sensum or sensu.   The former, the vocal congruity, corresponds with the traditional notion of congruity: it concerns the correct combination of case, gender, and person in the construction.   The congruity secundum sensum is new to this grammatical context.   Petrus calls a construction 'congrua sensu' if and only if it offers something intelligible or non-nonsensical to the hearer.   But, Petrus stipulates, one must be careful not to confuse the notion of falsity with that of nonsense or nugatory speech.   The judgement about truth and falsity belongs to the domain of the logician, whereas the grammarian has to decide on meaningfulness and nonsense.   Thus he allows that the sentence 'Homo est lapis', which is undoubtedly false, is congruous secundum vocem and also secundum sensum, since it is intelligible.[6]

A traditional category of nugatory constructions is that in which an adjective noun of second imposition enters into construction with a substantive of first imposition.   Although such constructions are congruous secundum vocem, they were rejected as ungrammatical by Petrus because of their lack of sense. At nearly the same period Alberic of Paris and John of Salisbury condemned constructions of the same type on the same grounds,[7] e.g. — I quote from Petrus' Summa — 'Socrates habet ypoteticos sotulares cum categoricis corrigiis.' So it appears that Petrus Helias' congruitas secundum sensum displays a great resemblance to the modern notion of meaningfulness. Like some modern linguistics scholars too,[8] Petrus Helias indicates the possibility of an utterance being congruous secundum sensum, i.e., in meaning, but at the same time incongruous secundum vocem and vice versa.

There is, however, an interesting restriction to Petrus' application of the congruitas secundum sensum as compared with the modern use of the term 'meaningfulness'. Petrus holds that there are constructions in which the sensus is correct and congruous but the vox incongruous, in which nevertheless something is offered to the hearer that he can grasp 'rationabiliter' from the utterance;[9] such a construction, he asserts, has to be accepted by the grammarian.[10] On the face of it, it seems that Petrus has in mind all those constructions that suffer from vocal incongruity but are interpretable. But we must note that Petrus Helias does not mention here ungrammatical constructions of the type 'dominum venit', which could be considered meaningful, as the utterance 'The boy call his mother' might be considered to be an interpretable but ungrammatical sentence. On the contrary, Petrus' example is 'turba ruunt', often used in order to illustrate a figurative construction. Moreover, Petrus asserts that where the meaning is correct and congruous but the vox incongruous, one is confronted with a figura. So it turns out that in this discussion Petrus only has in mind the class of figurative constructions.

Petrus Hispanus (non-Papa),[11] whose Summa on Priscianus minor must have been far more influential than the work of Petrus Helias on the same text, is very pronounced in his opinion. He introduces into this discussion Priscian's statement that every construction has to be referred to the intellectus vocis[12] and emphasizes the absolute predominance of the meaning component in the notion of congruity. Not only traditionally condemned sentences of the type 'homo hypotheticus habet cappam affirmativam', but also such sentences as 'tu es homo qui es asinus' or 'lapis non diligit filium suum' have to be rejected by the grammarian, although no objection can be made about the merely vocal part of the sentence.[13] However, not all twelfth-century grammarians held this view. The student who wrote the Glose 'Promisimus'[14] informs us that this position was typical of the school of Petrus Helias. His own master, whose glosses he reports, taught that the congruity of a sentence only depended on the concord of the grammatical accidentia and that his opinion was that the grammarian has to accept a sentence like 'iste est fortior se.'[15]

2.2 Perfectio

The notion of grammatical perfectio has a similar history to that of congruitas. It also reaches back to Apollonius through Priscian, who translated Apollonius' 'AUTOTELES LOGOS' with the Latin 'oratio perfecta', defined as a sentence that gives rise to a complete or perfect understanding in the mind of the hearer. A necessary condition for such a sentence is that it consist of at least a substantive noun (ONOMA), say a nominative subject, and a verb (HREMA). So an oratio is not complete or perfect without a noun and a verb. This notion also occurs in the definition of 'oratio' Priscian gives in the second book of his Institutiones. According to Priscian, an oratio is 'a congruous arrangement of words that shows a complete or perfect sense' (perfectam sententiam demonstrans).[16]

In the early commentaries on Priscianus minor the oratio perfecta was identified with the constructio, and so the definition of 'oratio' was also applied to 'constructio'. Moreover, the glossators appended the clause 'quantum in ipsa est' to their definition in order to avoid the objection that, e.g., a sentence like 'Socrates legit' must be called incomplete or imperfect since 'legit' is a transitive verb that normally requires an object to satisfy the mind of the hearer.[17] Nevertheless, the mediaeval grammarians considered these sentences to be complete since they consist of a subject and a verb, a suppositum and an appositum in their terminology.

Unlike William of Conches, who rejects this identification of oratio with constructio,[18] Petrus Helias follows the glossators in their view of constructio but with a slight, though for our subject important, modification. Petrus drops the part that deals with perfecta sententia from his definition of construction since, in his opinion, a construction such as 'homo albus' is correct and congruous — 'competens' is the qualification he uses — but not complete. Following Priscian, Petrus holds that normally an oratio has to consist of a noun, or suppositum, and a verb, or appositum, in order to be complete or perfect.[19] At the end of his Summa Petrus returns to this subject in his discussion of government.   Here he argues that the verb requires the nominative case because it carries this case with it into the construction 'for the completeness of the construction' (ad perfectionem constructionis).[20]

So it appears that in the second half of the twelfth century a distinction is made in the notion of congruity between the vocal congruity and the congruity in meaning: the vocal congruity corresponds to the modern notion of grammaticality, whereas the congruity in meaning roughly covers the modern notion of meaningfulness.   Some influential grammarians held the view that both of them must normally be present in a proper construction or sentence; the congruitas secundum sensum, however, can occur without vocal congruity but only in figurative sentences.[21]   In order to be complete a sentence has to consist of at least a suppositum and an appositum.   The question whether perfectio presupposes congruitas is not explicitly posed by these grammarians.

3. Roger Bacon

3.1 Bacon and congruitas

Before we turn to Bacon's views on congruity and perfection, we must recall that Bacon is not always as systematic as we should like him to be. Sometimes he does not give an explicit answer to the question posed, or one has to guess the opinion Bacon holds himself from his remarks in a later quaestio.

Although the contents of Bacon's Summa [22] show an undoubted affinity with Priscian's last two books in certain respects and Bacon's references to instruction in logic clearly point to the class-room, this work is not a series of lectures on Priscianus minor, as its editor, Robert Steele, surmised.[23]   Jan Pinborg's characterisation of it as a collection of grammatical sophisms dealing with various constructions, is more to the point.[24]   The greater part of the Summa consists of discussions on figurative constructions.   They are preceded by some introductory quaestiones of a more general character, which are often referred to in the treatment of the constructions themselves. It is in the section immediately preceding the discussions of the figurative constructions in speciali that Bacon deals with the notions of congruitas and perfectio in their mutual relationship.

Bacon has arranged the subject-matter in three main quaestiones. First he deals with congruity, secondly with perfection, and finally he discusses the relationship between the perfectiones he has distinguished and the intellectus primus and secundus.[25]

In the first quaestio Bacon inquires whether a figurative construction is simply incongruous or not. In fact, Roger's own answer is given in the arguments of the next quaestio, with regard to the perfection of figurative speech.[26] It appears that Bacon distinguishes between two kinds of figurative sentences. There are figurative sentences that have an impropriety deriving from a conflict between the obligatory grammatical form and their meaning, resulting in what would be called in modern terminology 'an improper surface structure', but nevertheless exactly express the meaning intended by the speaker. However, notwithstanding the circumstance that there is an excuse for their incongruity — 'figura est vitium cum ratione' — these sentences are judged to be simply incongruous, but congruous in a certain respect (secundum quid), since they do express the intention of the speaker — who is deemed to be a wise man — in a more congruous way than proper constructions would have done. The other category consists of figurative sentences that also have a conflict between form and meaning; now, however, it does not result in a deviant surface structure but in a correct one that does not exactly express the meaning intended by the speaker. Bacon's instance of this type is Virgil's 'ceciditque superbum Ylion et omnis homo FUMAT Neptunea Troia',[27] in which verse 'fumat' is considered to be a form of the indicative mood of the present tense — which it is, indeed — but used here instead of a form of the perfect tense 'metri causa'. Bacon leaves this category out of the discussion. Such sentences are simply congruous but incongruous secundum quid. So, according to Bacon, it appears that only a deviance in the verbal structure of a sentence, i.e., on the level of the modi significandi, is responsible for simple incongruity.

3.2 Bacon and the perfectio orationis

More attention is paid by Bacon to the perfectio orationis. In the first quaestio on this matter he inquires whether a figurative construction   is perfect or not.[28] For a good understanding of this problem we must bear in mind that in Priscian's definition of 'oratio' the notion of congruity precedes that of perfection. In the opinion of Bacon and other mediaeval grammarians this should imply that normally a sentence cannot be called perfect without being congruous. On the other hand, Bacon is confronted with a category of figurative sentences that, as we have seen, are simply incongruous but at the same time, as was generally accepted, able to generate a 'complete' or 'perfect' meaning in the mind of the hearer. Moreover, these sentences are found in the works of the most authoritative writers.

Bacon's solution is complex. Some utterances may be congruous but imperfect, as, e.g., 'homo albus'; some perfect but incongruous, as is the case with a figurative sentence. But this solution is not wholly satisfactory, and Bacon argues that the notion of perfection can be interpreted in two ways: either sui generis and altogether apart from congruity, so that it forms no part of the definition of 'oratio'; or conceived as a part of congruity, which, in its turn, then functions as a sort of genus. In the latter case congruity is a necessary requirement for a perfect or complete sentence. In the case at issue of figurative speech, Bacon asserts that it is perfect but not on the grounds of the perfection that belongs to it at the level of the modi significandi, i.e., that perfection that presupposes congruity, but on those of the perfection of the signified meaning only (absolute), the perfection that belongs to the level of the significata.

So Bacon arrives at two possible perfectiones in a sentence, distinguished according to their subjects: a perfection on the part of the significates and a perfection on the part of the modi significandi. We must bear in mind, however, that at both levels perfection always concerns sentences that are composed of both a suppositum and an appositum: for a sentence this is the primary and most traditional claim on perfection.

Bacon now investigates the relationship between the two notions of perfectio,[29] and he poses the question whether a distinction based on vox and intellectus would be fitting, as, he alleges, many grammarians grant. A long discussion follows, in which Priscian's statement that every construction has to be referred to the intellectus vocis, plays an important role.[30] After a series of arguments in favour of this distinction, it is argued, inter alia, in the series of reasons against this view: that the vox non-significativa is left out of consideration here;[31] that as far as the vox significativa is concerned, the same correspondence exists between the vox and the intellectus as between the intellectus and the res; and that since the intellectus is entirely proportionate to the res, what holds good of the vox also holds good of the intellectus.[32] Further reasons are adduced to argue that if there is a perfectio vocis, there also has to be a perfectio intellectus, and vice versa, so that a distinction between vox and intellectus must not be allowed in this context.[33]

Bacon's answer relies on the distinction in intellectus, the meaning, between intellectus primus and intellectus secundus.[34] In his view a sentence cannot be qualified as perfect or imperfect because of the perfectio vocis alone, for, according to Bacon, this perfection would only have regard to the correct and perfect arrangement of the grammatical accidentia at the level of the utterance and would thus be insufficient. Apart from vocal perfection, there must also be a perfection of meaning, a perfectio intellectus that is proportionate to the vocal component of the sentence. This perfectio presupposes the perfectio vocis. Bacon calls this intellectus that is proportioned to the vox, the vocal component of the sentence, the 'intellectus primus'. It results from the modi significandi.

Apart from this intellectus primus, or first meaning, Bacon discerns another intellectus in the sentence, the intellectus secundus, that does not result from the modi significandi but from the significata, the significates of the parts of speech used. The perfection of this intellectus, or meaning, does not need congruity or perfection at the vocal level in order to occur. It is only with the perfectio vocis of this intellectus, viz. the intellectus secundus, that Bacon admits that an appropriate (competens) distinction may be made.

So it appears that Bacon considers the perfection of the sentence at three levels, in agreement with the three levels he discerns in meaningful speech:

1. the perfectio vocis, viz. the perfection that concerns the vocal component;

2. the perfectio of the intellectus primus that has regard to the modi significandi and that cannot occur in a sentence without the perfectio vocis;

3. the perfectio of the intellectus secundus that concerns the significate of the words used and is not necessarily linked with the congruitas and perfectio vocis.[35]

In Bacon's view a sentence is said to be perfect on account of the perfection of the second intellectus. However, the problem that arises now will be obvious, for if a sentence is said to be perfect because of the perfection of the second meaning, the door is opened to all those kinds of sentences that are ungrammatical but interpretable, e.g., 'dominum venit' instead of 'dominus venit', in other words, to all those sentences to which the modern notion of meaningfulness would apply, both the grammatical and ungrammatical ones. This view could also result in an absolute predominance of that semantic component of the sentence, the significates, and degrade grammar, even as the science of the modi significandi.[36]

Bacon's solution is that it is not only — 'non absolute' in his Latin — the perfection of the second intellectus that brings about the oratio perfecta. The presence of the perfection of the first intellectus, and therefore of the utterance too, is also a necessary condition in order to achieve a perfect sentence. However, this latter perfection must be actually present, or, if it is absent, there has to be an excuse for its absence.[37] This requirement of the presence of the perfectio intellectus primi or of an excuse for its absence, enables Bacon to exclude all those incongruous sentences that are not reckoned to be figurative constructions. So it is possible for Bacon to accept the figurative sentence 'urbem quam statuo vestra est' but, at the same time, to reject the — incongruous — sentence 'dominum venit' as being an oratio imperfecta.[38]

Another problem that arises now concerns competence. Traditionally the significata belong to the domain of the logician, whereas the grammarian occupies himself with the world of modi significandi. However, Bacon's solution introduces the grammarian into the area of the significates. Bacon argues that attention to the same subject-matter on the part of several disciplines is not problematic at all, since the point of view under which the significata are considered is different.[39] Regrettably, he does not specify what this difference is. Of course, we could suppose that it is because the logician deals with the significates from the point of view of truth and falsity, whereas the grammarian looks for the presence of suppositum and appositum. But it would be interesting to know whether Bacon would assign the judgement about nugatory sentences to the grammarian or to the logician. Although he touches on this matter further on, in the discussion of appositive constructions,[40] I could not detect a definite opinion on this in his Summa.

4. Roger Bacon's Position in the Development of
the Theory of Double Intellectus:
An Orientation

There is serious evidence that the theory of the double intellectus did
not originate with Bacon himself. We find it already present, be it in a
slightly different way, in the commentary on Priscianus minor by master
Jordanus.[41]   This work, which is one of the earliest witnesses to the
increasing influence of the Aristotelian concept of science in grammar,[42] was
composed at Paris in the first half of the thirteenth century and, in all
probability, around 1230. Whether this master Jordanus is to be identified
with the famous master Jordanus of Saxony, the second head of the
Dominican Order, is a question that I have to leave undecided here, although
arguments have been adduced against this identification.[43]

Prompted by Priscian's remark that every construction has to be referred
to the intellectus vocis, Jordanus introduced a distinction in Priscian's
intellectus vocis between intellectus taken for the significatum or the res
significata and intellectus regarded as the modus significandi of the word, a
distinction which, according to Jordanus, corresponds with that in the
significative utterance (vox) between the sign and the modus significandi of
the vox.[44] In Jordanus' view, Priscian's observation concerns the intellectus
vocis taken for modus significandi: a proper construction has to be referred
to the vox not as sign but in regard to its modi significandi-component. The
intellectus vocis as the significatum or res significata must be left out of
consideration here, since that aspect of the vox belongs to the domain of
truth and falsity, whereas the modi significandi concern the domain of
congruity and incongruity.[45] This implies that the criterion for congruity or
incongruity has been associated with the intellectus vocis conceived as the
modus significandi. Jordanus' problem, however, was how to apply Priscian's
statement in the case of figurative speech. It was commonly accepted that
such constructions were incongruous; most grammarians even held that these
constructions were burdened with a simple incongruity. On the other hand, it
is argued that figurative speech was used by wise men in order to express
their intentions in a more convenient way than they could with proper
constructions.[46] This would mean that figurative speech is more convenient
than proper speech, an argument we have already met in Bacon's Summa.

The dilemma with which Jordanus was faced is obvious. He has to conform to Priscian's rule, mentioned above, which applies to every construction, figurative constructions included. But in the case of figurative speech it cannot be the intellectus vocis, taken for the modus significandi, to which the construction must be referred, since the characteristic feature of figurative speech is the very conflict between the sentence expressed and its obligatory syntactic structure, which depends on the modi significandi. On the other hand, in the previous section Jordanus had argued that the intellectus vocis, taken there for the res significata or the significatum, must be left out of consideration in this discussion. In order to escape this grammatical Scylla and Charybdis, Jordanus adduces the distinction in the intellectus vocis between the intellectus primus and the intellectus secundarius. The first is the modus significandi or the combination of the modus significandi with the principal significate (aggregatum ex modo significandi cum principali significato). Referred to this intellectus, figurative speech — by which Jordanus evidently understood only Bacon's first category of figurative speech -- is simply incongruous. The intellectus secundus is, then, the meaning that the utterance can hold secondarily: it is the meaning intended by the speaker. Referred to this intellectus, figurative speech is congruous, but, Jordanus emphasizes, it is a congruity in a certain respect (secundum quid).[47]

Another grammatical work dating from the first half of the thirteenth century in which we meet the theory of the double intellectus, is Robert Kilwardby's commentary on Priscianus minor, which it is commonly accepted that he wrote in Paris during his regency in arts before he entered the Dominican Order, so between 1237 and 1245.[48] In his comment on the statement of Priscian, which we have already often mentioned, about the reference of every construction to the intellectus vocis, Kilwardby deals with figurative constructions and their relationship to the intellectus vocis.[49] He starts by making the now familiar distinction of intellectus vocis between an intellectus primus, based on the modi significandi of the words, and an intellectus secundus, based on their significates. According to Kilwardby, a construction ordinarily has to be referred to both the intellectus primus and the intellectus secundus, but a figurative construction only to the second intellectus.

Next Kilwardby broaches the question whether a figurative construction is simply congruous or incongruous. In a long discussion, which in many respects corresponds almost literally to Bacon's treatment, Kilwardby arrives at the same distinction with regard to figurative speech that we have seen in Roger Bacon's Summa. Those sentences that have an impropriety in their surface structure are simply incongruous but congruous secundum quid; those that have an impropriety regarding the meaning intended by the speaker are simply congruous but incongruous secundum quid.

Another point of discussion concerns the relationship between congruitas or perfectio secundum vocem and congruitas or perfectio secundum intellectum. According to Kilwardby, there is a vocal incongruity or imperfection in some sentences, athough they are congruous or perfect secundum intellectum, e.g., 'urbem quam statuo, vestra est'; whereas others are vocally congruous but imperfect in meaning, e.g., 'homo albus', a topic also touched on by Bacon. The question is posed now whether the distinction between congruitas and perfectio secundum vocem and congruitas and perfectio secundum intellectum or sensum would be a correct one. Kilwardby's answer shows a striking resemblance to Bacon's discussion once more. He speaks about the perfectio vocis, the perfectio of the intellectus primus and too of the intellectus secundus. It is also argued that the perfection of the first intellectus is proportionate to the congruity or the perfection of the vox and that it is the perfection of the second intellectus, and not the perfection of the first intellectus, that applies to figurative constructions. His conclusion is that a correct distinction may be made between the perfectio vocis and the perfectio of the intellectus secundus.

At the end of this part of the discussion, Kilwardby briefly repeats his doctrine and clearly shows that he accepts three levels of language: first, he says, there is the vox; next, the intellectus primus originating from the modi significandi -- these, the vox and the intellectus primus, are equal as to perfection and imperfection, congruity and incongruity -- apart from these two, there is the intellectus secundus originating from the significates of the words. Finally, Kilwardby appends a question whether arguments can be given for a priority of perfectio over congruitas. He feels inclined to discuss this matter because it is often touched on in the introductory sections to the grammatical sophisms.

The similarity, verbal as well as doctrinal, between Bacon and Kilwardby in this discussion appears to be so striking that fortuitous agreement must be ruled out. However, the question whether Kilwardby used Bacon or Bacon Kilwardby or both had a common source at their disposal, is hard to answer without a much wider knowledge of the texts which still remain unpublished in manuscript. Kilwardby's remark about the introductory sections to the grammatical sophisms may be considered an indication for giving priority to Bacon, whose Summa has been rightly characterized by Jan Pinborg as a collection of grammatical sophisms. On the other hand, we must bear in mind that the traditional chronology and a comparison of their discussions point to the reverse order.

5. Final Remarks

After this analysis and initial placing of Bacon's theory of the double intellectus in the history of linguistic thought, I should like to make the following points by way of general conclusions from this brief inquiry:

It emerges that the theory of the double intellectus developed within the doctrine of the congruitas and perfectio of figurative constructions in the first half of the thirteenth century.

According to Kilwardby and Bacon, the (congruitas and) perfectio of the first intellectus belongs to the level of the modi significandi. One must look for the difference between these two notions in the condition that in order to achieve perfectio a suppositum and an appositum are necessary.

The perfectio of the second intellectus belongs to the level of the significata and might be compared with the perfectio absoluta mentioned by William de Bonkes.[50] Unlike Kilwardby, Bacon does not speak of congruitas on the level of the second intellectus. The presence of both suppositum and appositum is also a necessary condition for perfectio on this level.

As to how far nonsense or meaninglessness is an impediment to perfectio on the level of the significata, i.e., on that of the intellectus secundus, this is not quite clear in Bacon's Summa. The same is the case with regard to the question, to whom the judgement about nugatory speech pertains, viz. whether to the grammarian or to the logician.

In order to achieve an oratio perfecta, in principle both perfectiones are required. The perfectio of the second intellectus is a conditio sine qua non, but the perfectio of the first intellectus may be lacking if and only if there exists an excuse for its absence. The only category of incongruous but perfect speech is thus that of figurative speech, which belongs to the domain of wise men.

The question what excuse or excuses may be adduced in the case of particular figurative constructions is dealt with by Bacon in his section De figurativis locutionibus in speciali.

As is clearly proved in some of the studies mentioned above,[51] the mediaeval discussions of congruity and perfection display a close resemblance to those in modern linguistics of the notions of grammaticality, acceptability and meaningfulness. However, we must recognise that there was no agreement about the exact interpretation of the notions at issue among the mediaeval grammarians and that the same holds true for their twentieth-century colleagues and the corresponding notions in modern linguistic theory.

To my mind, the presence of a theory of double intellectus in the Notulae of master Jordanus, be it in a somewhat rudimentary form, and, in a more elaborate way, in the Commentum of Robert Kilwardby raises the surmise that this theory could form part of the Parisian grammatical tradition. The conformity between Kilwardby and Bacon in this respect may be a serious indication that Bacon's Summa belongs to the same tradition and that Bacon wrote this work in Paris. However, master Jordanus, Robert Kilwardby and Roger Bacon are surely not the only mediaeval grammarians who incorporated this theory of double intellectus in their doctrine of figurative speech. It is referred to, inter alia, in the Lectura super minori volumine of the still mysterious master Rubertus Anglicus in MS Firenze, Biblioteca Nazionale Centrale, Conv. soppr. D.2.45, fol. 18[r],[52] and in the Expositio on Priscianus minor by a certain Arnoldus,[53] but a serious survey cannot be given until more texts are available in edited form. So the answer to the question whether this theory is typical of the Paris tradition or not, must be left open at present.

Notes

[1] It should be noted that Dr. Sten Ebbesen has recently published a study of great interest dealing with twelfth-century writers on these topics: 'The Present King of France Wears Hypothetical Shoes with Categorical Laces. Twelfth-Century Writers on Well-Formedness', Medioevo 7 (1981) 91-113. Unfortunately, this issue of the journal did not appear until August 1983. I refer to this article as 'Ebbesen, 1981'.

2 See, e.g., Jan Pinborg, Die Entwicklung der Sprachtheorie im Mittelalter (BGPTM 42.2; Münster i. W - Copenhagen, 1967); G.L. Bursill-Hall, Speculative Grammars of the Middle Ages. The doctrine of 'partes orationis' of the 'modistae' (Approaches to Semiotics 11; The Hague-Paris, 1971); John A. Trentman, 'Speculative Grammar and Transformational Grammar: A comparison of philosophical presuppositions' in H. Parret ed., History of Linguistic Thought and Contemporary Linguistics (Berlin-New York, 1976), pp. 279-301; L.G. Kelly, 'De modis generandi: points of contact between Noam Chomsky and Thomas of Erfurt', Folia linguistica: Acta Societatis Linguisticae Europaeae 5 (1971) 225-52; idem, ed., Pseudo-Albertus Magnus, Quaestiones Alberti de modis significandi (Amsterdam, 1977), introduction, pp. xxxi-xxxiii.

3 Osmund Lewry, 'The Oxford Condemnations of 1277 in Grammar and Logic' in H.A.G. Braakhuis, C.H. Kneepkens, L.M. de Rijk eds., English Logic and Semantics from the End of the Twelfth Century to the Time of Ockham and Burleigh: Acts of the 4th European Symposium on Mediaeval Logic and Semantics, Leiden-Nijmegen, 23-27 April 1979 (Artistarium Supplementa 1; Nijmegen, 1981), pp. 235-78, especially pp. 236-40.

4 Ibid., pp. 236, 239.

5 Cf. the explanation master Guido, a glossator in the Glosule-tradition, gives of this notion in the first lines of his gloss-commentary on Priscianus minor, MS London, BL Burney 239, fol. 3ra: 'Per congruum notatur quod recte casus cum casu, tempus cum tempore, persona cum persona iungatur, et ita in ceteris.' For this commentary see C.H. Kneepkens, 'Master Guido and his View on Government: On Twelfth Century Linguistic Thought', Vivarium 16 (1978) 108-41.

6 For the text of Petrus Helias see James E. Tolson ed., 'The Summa of Petrus Helias on Priscianus minor' with an introduction by Margaret Gibson, CIMAGL 27-28 (1978), especially pp. 1-3. Ebbesen, 1981, pp. 93-94, gives a comprehensive analysis of Peter's view.

7 Alberic's view is referred to in a commentary on the Perihermeneias; cf. L.M. de Rijk, Logica Modernorum 2.1 (Wijsgerige Teksten en Studies 16; Assen, 1967), p. 218. For John of Salisbury see C.C.J. Webb ed., Ioannis Saresberiensis episcopi Carnotensis Metalogicon libri IIII, lib. 1, cap. 15 (Oxford, 1929), pp. 34 et seq.

[8] Cf. Noam Chomsky, Syntactic Structures (Janua linguarum 4; The Hague, 1957), p. 15.

[9] Ed. Tolson, p.1 (20-21): 'Congrua tamen est sensu hec ordinatio, quia habet auditor quid ex ea rationabiliter intelligat.'

[10] Ibid., (24-25): '...et ubicumque congruit sensus quamvis vox non congruat figura est, et talis constructio recipitur a grammaticis.'

[11] For this grammarian and his work see R.W. Hunt, 'Absoluta: The Summa of Petrus Hispanus on Priscianus minor', Historiographia linguistica 2 (1975) 1-22; reprinted in R.W. Hunt, The History of Grammar in the Middle Ages: Collected Papers ed. G.L. Bursill-Hall (Amsterdam Studies in the Theory and History of Linguistic Science, Series 3, Studies in the History of Linguistics, Vol. 5; Amsterdam, 1980), pp. 95-116; additions and corrections ed. M.T. Gibson and S.P. Hall, Bodleian Library Record 11.1 (1982), pp. 13-14.

[12] Priscianus, Inst. gram. 17.187: 'Omnis enim constructio, quam Graeci σύνταξιν vocant, ad intellectum vocis est reddenda ('referenda' is the variant reading which often occurs in the writings of the mediaeval grammarians).'

[13] I give a text based on the MSS Wien, ÖN 2498 and London, BL Royal 2.D.xxx, which, as far as I can see at present, belong to different branches of the textual tradition: 'Primum igitur quid sit constructio et que eius species sint, exponemus. Constructio tripliciter attenditur: uel actus construentis quem in lectione exercemus, uel passio construendorum que dictionibus attribuitur, cum dictionem dictioni transitiue uel intransitiue construi dicimus, uel oratio constructa, hoc est ex dictionibus composita. Hec autem sic describitur: constructio est congrua dictionum ordinatio. Congrua ad intellectum refertur, non ad uocem. Omnis enim constructio, quam Greci sintasim uocant, ad intellectum referenda est. Sola igitur uocis congruitas non facit constructionem, nisi etiam ex ipsa uoce aliquis ad auditorem descendat intellectus. Itaque "tu es homo qui es asinus" et "quidlibet est rationale quod ipsum est" et "lapis non diligit filium suum" secundum uocem bene dicitur, idest secundum accidentium constructionem, simpliciter autem non est dicendum. Quod enim quidam obiciunt homine supra tectum sedente bonam esse grammaticam "homo qui sedet supra tectum", cadente autem minime, satis pueriliter instant. In puerorum tamen

dictaminibus non que ad intellectum, sed que ad uocem sunt, leuitatis causa considerantur.

Queritur cur hee constructiones, que adiectiuum secunde impositionis ut uniuersalis, categoricus, substantiuo prime construuntur, non recipiantur, ut "homo ypotheticus habet cappam affirmatiuam." Quoniam adiectiuum secunde impositionis per se nichil habens ex adiuncto querit significationem. Ideoque nisi tale sit substantiuum, a quo possit aliquid contrahere, euanescit eorum significatio ad eorum coniunctionem; quod in omnibus prime positionis substantiuis et quibusdam secunde aperte perspicitur.

Queritur cur similiter adiectiuum prime cum substantiuo secunde male construatur ut "propositio est alba." Quia utrumque suam habens per se a neutro significationem mutatur. Ideoque manet utriusque intellectus totale quiddam efficiens, non incongruum quidem, sed falsum. Itaque recta ratio construendi non minus rei quam uocis soloecismum excludit.'

[14] See R.W. Hunt, 'Studies on Priscian in the Twelfth Century, II. The School of Ralph of Beauvais', Mediaeval and Renaissance Studies 2 (1950) 1-56; repr. in idem, The History of Grammar (v.s. n. 11), pp. 39-94; add. and corr., Bodleian Library Record 11.1 (1982) 12-13.

[15] MS Oxford, Bodl. Laud lat. 67, fol. 56vb: 'Item queritur si una res ad alias possit comparari per superlatiuum, et eadem ad easdem per comparatiuum, ut "Socrates est fortissimus istorum quibus ipse est fortior." Magister: Congrua est gramatica, sed falsa locutio. Congrua est quia superlatiuum genitiuo plurali construitur, et comparatiuum ablatiuo. Falsa est quia eadem res uere non potest ostendi esse de numero aliquorum et eis esse diuersa; quod fit illa locutione. Tamen Magister Petrus Helias et sui sequances, ⟨quia incongrua,⟩ quia iudicant inconuenientem locutionem, si sit falsi positiua. Sed secundum hoc inconuenienter dicitur "iste est fortior se." Nos dicimus quia congrua. Gramaticus enim non debet attendere nisi congruam dictionum iuncturam, et si sit in accidentibus quibus oportet, debet iudicare congruam. Hoc autem inuenitur ibi "iste est fortissimus istorum quibus est fortior." Probamus autem sic esse congruam. Conuenienter coniungitur hic genitiuus istorum huic superlatiuo fortissimus et hic ablatiuus quibus huic comparatiuo fortior; ergo conuenienter dicitur "iste est fortissimus, etc."' This part of the gloss has also been printed in the study by Dr. Hunt, 'The School of Ralph of Beauvais' (v.s. n. 14), p. 54, repr. p. 92. Dr. Hunt, however, does

not indicate an omission immediately after the word 'sequaces' but after 'positiua'.

16 Priscianus, Inst. gram. 2.15.

17 I quote from master Guido's gloss-commentary (v.s. n.5): 'Est autem perfecta oratio siue constructio, in qua plures dictiones congrue posite insimul faciunt perfectum sensum, ut sic possimus constructionem diffinire: constructio est congrua ordinatio dictionum perfectum sensum generans quantum in ipsa est....Sed quia sunt quedam orationes que inperfectos sensus habent, ut hec "homo albus" ad illarum remotionem additur perfectum sensum generans. Quia uero sunt quedam perfecte orationes, quibus tamen auditis auditoris animus adhuc aliquid expectat sicut ista "Socrates legit": expectat adhuc aliquid auditor uel gramaticam uel rethoricam uel aliquid huiusmodi sibi responderi, ideo additur quantum in ipsa est. Sufficit enim orationi, ut ipsa in se perfecta sit, etsi auditor non uideatur.'

18 William of Conches, Glosule super minorem, MS Paris, BN lat. 15130, fol. 85ra: 'Quidam tamen dicunt quod in istis de perfecta oratione agitur, inde quod constructionem esse orationem putant decepti, quia Priscianus de constructione et ordinatione dictionum se in eis tractaturum proponit. Nos uero dicimus quod quemadmodum coniunctio domus neque est pars domus neque est domus, ita constructio dictionum neque est pars orationis neque oratio.'

19 Cf. ed. Tolson, pp. 2-3 (68-80), 15 (30-32).

20 Cf. ibid., p. 154 (58 et seq.).

21 See also Ebbesen, 1981, pp. 93-94 (v.s. n.1).

22 R. Steele ed., Summa gramatica Magistri Rogeri Bacon (Opera hactenus inedita Rogeri Baconi 15 [Oxford, 1940], pp. 1-190).

23 Ibid., introduction, p. x: 'It is obviously a set of lectures delivered during Bacon's regent mastership in one of the compulsory courses on Priscian's de Constructione....'

24 Pinborg, Die Entwicklung (v.s. n.2), pp. 28, n. 30 and 52, n. 105.

[25] Ed. Steele, pp. 13-14, 14-17, 17-27 respectively.

[26] Ibid., p. 15 (10 et seq.).

[27] Verg., Aen. 3.2-3.

[28] Ed. Steele, pp. 14 (20)-17 (3).

[29] Ibid., pp. 17 (4)-27 (16).

[30] Prisc., Inst. gram. 17, 187 (v.s. n. 11).

[31] Ed. Steele, p. 18 (1-4).

[32] Ibid., (10-12).

[33] Ibid, (16 et seq.)

[34] Ibid., p. 19 (21 et seq.).

[35] Ibid., p. 20 (1 et seq.).

[36] The Ps-Kilwardby, in whose commentary on the Maior I did not meet the theory of the double intellectus, refers in this context to sentences like 'homo videt asinus.' Cf. K.M. Fredborg, N.J. Green-Pedersen, Lauge Nielsen and Jan Pinborg eds., 'The Commentary on "Priscianus Maior" Ascribed to Robert Kilwardby', CIMAGL 15 (1975) 1-146, especially p. 99.

[37] Ed. Steele, p. 25 (1-15).

[38] Ibid., (23-29).

[39] Ibid., (16-22).

[40] Ibid., p. 44 (3 et seq.).

[41] Mary Sirridge ed., 'Notulae super Priscianum minorem magistri Jordani', partial edition and introduction, CIMAGL 36 (1980).

42 Cf. Pinborg, Die Entwicklung (v.s. n.2), p. 25.

43 Father P. Osmund Lewry was so kind as to call my attention to the Note additionnelle appended by R.-A. Gauthier to his article, 'Notes sur les débuts (1225-1240) du premier "averroisme"', Revue des sciences philoso- phiques et théologiques 66 (1982) 321-74, ibid., pp. 367-373. Père Gauthier argues on the grounds of quotations from Aristotle's works that this master Jordanus must have written his Notule not earlier than the 1240s, so that an identification with the well-known Jordanus of Saxony must be excluded.

44 Ed. Sirridge, pp. 64-65.

45 Ibid.

46 Ibid., p. 66.

47 Ibid.

48 Cf. D.A. Callus, 'The "Tabulae super Originalia Patrum" of Robert Kilwardby O.P.' in Studia mediaevalia in honorem admodum reverendi patris Raymundi Josephi Martin O.P. (Bruges, 1948), pp. 243-70, ibid., p. 247.

49 For the text of this section of Robert Kilwardby's Commentum see the appendix below, pp. 135-143.

50 For this master and his view on the perfectio absoluta see Lewry, 'The Oxford Condemnations...' (v.s. n.3), p. 237.

51 V.s. nn. 1 and 2.

52 Cf. G.L. Bursill-Hall, A Census of Mediaeval Latin Grammatical Manuscripts (Grammatica speculativa 4; Stuttgart-Bad Canstatt, 1981), no. 91.5.1. The text runs as follows (fol. 18^r): 'Queritur de hac oratione: Omnis constructio quam Grece synthasim uocant, ad intellectum uocis referenda est, utrum ad intellectum uocis uel proferentis. Et quod non sit referenda ad aliquem istorum, probatio: Non ad intellectum proferentis, quia propter nostrum negare uel affirmare non mutatur aliquid in re. Ad intellectum uocis contingit referri dupliciter: aut ad intellectum qui est significatio, aut consignificatio. Non qui est significatio, quia si sic, eque bene dicitur "lapis

est alba" quemadmodum "Petrus est alba." Nec ad intellectum qui est consignificatio, quia si sic, eque bene diceretur "pars in frustra secant." Hec autem omnia sunt incongrua etc.

Dicendum quod constructio habet referri ad intellectum, idest ad modos significandi, quod quidem modus significandi comprehendit utrumque modum, scilicet significandi et consignificandi. Et ideo non habet referri tantum ad alterum eorum, sicut obiciebatur.'

In the lower margin the same hand has written: 'Omnis constructio, etc. ad intellectum uocis reddenda est. Ita nota quod intellectus uocis ut sintasim faciat, est duplex: primus est modus significandi (another hand added: 'per quem male dicitur "Petrus currunt") que est consignificatio per accidencia quo ad uocem. Secundus est modus significandi rei ipsius uocis (another hand: 'per quem male dicitur "omnis Petrus" et similia) que dicitur significatio....'

53 I quote from MS München, Clm 561 (cf. Bursill-Hall, A Census, no. 176.12.1), fol. 93vb: 'Nota quod constructio potest referri ad intellectum uocis dupliciter: Vno modo ad intellectum eius primarium, quem intellectum ipsa uox pretendit de sua impositione et ad talem intellectum uocis refertur constructio congrua. Alio modo ad intellectum uocis secundarium, quem intellectum ipsa uox non pretendit prima facie a parte uocis, sed magis a parte rei uel significationis. Ad talem intellectum uocis autem (2 ut MS) frequenter habet referri constructio figuratiua.'

Robert Kilwardby, In Priscianum minorem
(MS Oxford, Corpus Christi College D 119, fols.
84va - 85rb, with specified corrections from
MS Vatican, Chigi L.V.159, fols. 55vb-56va)
⟨DE CONSTRUCTIONE FIGURATIVA⟩

(f. 84va)...Adhuc. Si omnis constructio pertinet ad intellectum uocis, potior erit constructio que magis fit per intellectum uocis; sed figuratiua constructio magis fit secundum intellectum uocis quam propria constructio; ergo potior erit constructio figuratiua quam propria; quod falsum est.

Ad hec. Dicendum quod intellectum uocis ad quem referenda est constructio, est duplex, scilicet primus et secundus. Primus intellectus est qui primo cadit in apprehensione, scilicet qui consistit ex modis significandi dictionum. Secundus qui secundo comprehenditur, scilicet qui consistit ex significatis dictionum.

Et ad utrumque uocis intellectum referenda est constructio. Sed constructio propria refertur ad intellectum primum, figuratiua autem ad secundum.

Et sic patet responsio ad obiecta. Non enim oportet quod constructio propria sit penes significata neque potior sit figuratiua quam propria. Verumptamen sciendum quod hec conclusio concedi potest uno modo. Est enim quedam constructio potior quo ad plures et hec est propria, quia non est <fas> (a Oxf., om. Vat.) loqui communiter nisi proprie; et quedam est potior quo ad sapientes et autentice loquentes et hec est figuratiua, quando intentionem suam complete exprimere nequeunt per sermonem proprium. Sed quamuis huiusmodi constructio sit potior quo ad eos, non tamen sequitur quod sit simpliciter potior.

Sed quia hoc habet dubitationem, queritur utrum constructio figuratiua simpliciter dici debeat incongrua uel simpliciter congrua. Omnis enim oratio uel talis uel talis est simpliciter, quamuis participet oppositum secundum quid. Aliter enim non esset gramatica oratio.[a]

Videtur autem quod sit simpliciter congrua, cum omnis constructio quam Greci etc.

Adhuc. Cum sermo sapientis in quantum huiusmodi maxime congruus sit et perfectus, erit figurativa oratio maxime congrua et perfecta, cum non pertineat loqui figuratiue nisi ad solos sapientes.[b]

Adhuc. Conuenientior est oratio que conuenientius representat (f. 84[vb]) intentionem proferentis; sed figuratiua oratio multotiens hoc conuenientius facit quam propria.[c]

Ad oppositum. Locutio disposita non secundum regulas gramaticas, sed opposito modo, simpliciter incongrua est. Sed talis est figuratiua, ut 'turba ruunt' etc. Quare figuratiua locutio est simpliciter incongrua.[d]

Adhuc. Constructio intransitiua secundum gramaticam ydemptitatem exigit substantie et accidentium. Quare si componatur sub diuersitate eorum, erit incongrua. Sed sic est hic 'turba ruunt' et in (om. Oxf.) consimilibus. Quare tales orationes sunt simpliciter incongrue.

Adhuc. Oratio simpliciter congrua est de usu communiter loquentium; sed oratio figuratiua non est de usu eorum; ergo non est simpliciter congrua, quia simpliciter incongrua.[e] Sed dicet aliquis quod huiusmodi oratio est partim congrua et partim incongrua et non simpliciter sic aut sic, quia quantum habet de inproprietate, et de incongruitate; et quantum de ratione excusante, tantum de congruitate.

Sed contra. Soloecismus et scema sunt eadem inproprietas secundum substantiam, sicut dicit Donatus; ergo cum inproprietas soloecismi simpliciter sit incongrua, et inproprietas figure ei respondentis similiter erit.[f]

Adhuc. Cum fieri secundum regulas gramatice et non fieri secundum eas nichil medium habeant, et oratio facta secundum regulas gramatice et sola dicatur simpliciter congrua, oratio autem facta contra regulas sit simpliciter incongrua et sola, manifestum inter congruam simpliciter et simpliciter incongruam nichil medium. Et ita nulla erit partim congrua et partim incongrua.[g]

Adhuc. Penes debitam dispositionem dictionum in modis significandi est simpliciter proprietas et solum sic. Quare cum non est debita dispositio in illis, erit simpliciter inproprietas et incongrua ordinatio. Et hoc contingit in figuratiuis orationibus.

Adhuc. Si oratio figuratiua neque sit simpliciter congrua neque simpliciter incongrua et tamen est oratio gramatica, erit aliqua oratio gramatica neque congrua neque incongrua.

Adhuc. Congruitas uel incongruitas simpliciter omnino resultat ex principiis intraneis dictionum constructarum, sed ratio excusandi inproprietatem extra est ex parte construentis. Quare propter ipsam nichilominus dicetur simpliciter incongrua, cum sit (si Oxf.) dissonantia inter principia intranea.[h]

Ex hiis uidetur quod oratio figuratiua simpliciter incongrua dici debeat, quamuis secundum quid congrua uel propria.

Et dicendum quod oratio figuratiua aut facit inproprietatem quantum ad intellectum significatum aut quantum ad intellectum intentum. Si quantum ad intellectum significatum absolute loquendo, talis est oratio incongrua, quamuis rationem habeat. Et ita secundum quid sit congrua, scilicet secundum intellectum proferentis. Cuiusmodi est hec 'urbem quem statuo uestra est', que quantum ad intellectum significatum est incongrua et quantum ad intellectum intentum congrua.[i]

Si (sed Oxf., est Vat.) facit inproprietatem tantum quo ad intellectum intentum, est simpliciter congrua, sed secundum quid incongrua, ut hec 'una Eurusque Nothusque ruunt', que omnino congrua est secundum intellectum significatum. Tamen non representat omnino intellectum intentum. Et ideo quo ad proferentem incongrua est, sed simpliciter congrua.[j]

De oratione autem figuratiua primo modo dicta concludunt rationes inducte ad partem secundam questionis et omnino concedende sunt.

Ad rationes autem prime partis respondendum:
Ad primam quod omnis constructio propria et inpropria refertur ad intellectum uocis, ut predictum est. Vnde nichil prohibet orationem esse simpliciter incongruam, dico figuratiuam, et tamen constructionem referri ad intellectum uocis, dummodo referatur ad intellectum secundum. Sed congruitas refertur ad intellectum primum.

Ad secundam dicendum quod sermo sapientis maxime congruus est et perfectus uel simpliciter uel quo ad intentionem eius enuntiandum. Non tamen semper maxime congruus est. Habet enim sapiens autoritatem inproprie loqui propter necessitatem. (f. 85[ra]) Et ideo non est omnis sermo eius simpliciter congruus.[k]

Ad tertiam dicendum quod magis congrua est oratio que magis congrue representat intentionem proferentis uel simpliciter uel quo ad intentionem proferentis, sed non semper simpliciter magis congrua, sed multotiens minus congrua secundum regulas gramatice.[l]

Consequenter restat querere de distinctione quam assignat Priscianus postea in littera. Intendit enim quod oratio potest esse congrua uel perfecta secundum sensum aut secundum intellectum, incongrua tamen uel inperfecta secundum uocem uel econuerso. Verbi gratia. Quando in accidentibus penes que construuntur dictiones est inconcinnitas, tunc est inperfectio siue incongruitas in uoce, ut hic 'urbem quam statuo, uestra est.' Est tamen congruitas et perfectio quo ad sensum. Econuerso autem contingit, quando oratio non indicat affectum plenum, congrua tamen est, ut hic 'tu qui sedes' uel 'homo albus'. Huiusmodi enim oratio inperfecta est quo ad sensum et tamen congrua. Similiter uidetur posse dici de constructionibus figuratiuis que non habent inproprietatem nisi quo ad intellectum intentum a proferente. Tales enim congrue sunt quo ad uocem, sed aliquo modo incongrue uel inperfecte quo ad sensum uel intellectum. Sic igitur patet intentio distinctionis.

Sed quia communis distinctio est in multis gramaticis orationibus, queritur utrum distinctio sit bona necne.

Et uidetur quod non. Videtur enim quod ad perfectionem uocis sequatur necessario perfectio intellectus: tum quia signum proportionatur significato, et ideo si unum illorum perfectum, et reliquum;[m] tum quia uoces sunt note passionum que sunt in anima, et ideo se habent ad modum illarum passionum secundum perfectionem et inperfectionem, secundum congruitatem et incongruitatem.[n]

Adhuc. Videtur quod deficiente perfectione secundum uocem, deficiat perfectio secundum intellectum: tum quia uox primum est in apprehensione et deinde intellectus, et ita perfectio uocis prima est et precedens ad perfectionem intellectus, sed deficiente primo, deficit et secundum;[o] tum quia perfectio siue congruitas in uoce est finaliter ad perfectionem et congruitatem intellectus representandam, sed deficiente eo quod est ad finem, necesse est non esse finem.[p]

Ex hiis ergo uidetur quod posita perfectione apud uocem, ponitur et apud intellectum; et ipsa destructa, destruitur. Quare non bene distinguitur una istarum perfectionum ab alia.

Eodem modo arguitur econuerso ex eisdem mediis.[q] Si enim signum et significatum proportionalia sunt et si uoces sunt passionum etc., uidetur quod si sit uel non sit perfectio secundum intellectum, erit uel non erit et secundum uocem.

Adhuc. Si perfectio intellectus posterius apprehenditur et sic sicut finis

ad quem est perfectio representanda, non est perfectio intellectus nec est
perfectio (representanda...perfectio om. per hom. Oxf.) uocis.

Ex hiis uidetur quod distinctio non competat.

Sed contra. Perfectio et congruitas uocis inuenitur sine perfectione et
congruitate intellectus, et econuerso, perfectio intellectus sine perfectione
uocis; ergo inter has perfectiones siue congruitates est bona distinctio; quod
concedendum est.

Ad obiecta ergo sciendum quod perfectio siue congruitas uocis est cum
accidentia uocis fuerint concinna et debito modo disposita apud uocem.[r]
Perfectio autem et congruitas intellectus duplex est: una que consistit penes
modos significandi et intelligendi, quando concinne se habent scilicet; alia que
consistit penes ipsa significata, que sunt sub modis significandi aut
intelligendi significata.

Prima perfectio siue congruitas intellectus est in sermone omnino
congruo. Et ipsa proportionalis est perfectioni siue congruitati que est in
uoce, sicut significatum signo. Et illa omnino conuertentiam habet cum
perfectione siue (f. 85[rb]) congruitate que est ex parte uocis, et ad illam
representandam immediate ordinatur et precedit illam in apprehensione. Vnde
considerando ad hanc perfectionem siue congruitatem intellectus, uerum
concludunt omnia obiecta, scilicet quod si est uocis perfectio uel non, est et
intellectus et econuerso.[s]

Sed hec perfectio siue congruitas non est nisi in sermone simpliciter
constructo; secunda autem perfectio siue congruitas (non...congruitas om. per
hom. Oxf.) intellectus, scilicet que pertinet ad significata tantum, pertinet ad
sermonem figuratiuam. Et hec perfectio bene potest esse sine perfectione uel
congruitate uocis, sicut hic 'pars infrustra secant.' Et hec non est
conproportionalis illi que est ex parte uocis, nec ordinatur congruitas uocis
aut perfectio uocis ad hanc representandam nisi per accidens et ex
consequenti, quia hec pertinet ad secundum intellectum uocis.[t]

Sed inter secundum intellectum et uocem ipsam cadit simpliciter (primus
Vat.) intellectus medius, cuius perfectio omnino equalis est perfectioni siue
congruitati uocis. De hac igitur congruitate siue perfectione que est apud
intellectum secundum, non concludunt obiecta. Sed inter hanc et perfectionem siue congruitatem uocis datur distinctio, et bene, ut ostensum est.

Ad intelligendum igitur distinctionem diligenter nota quod primo est uox et deinde intellectus primus contextus ex modis significandi, et ista duo equalia sunt secundum perfectionem et inperfectionem, congruitatem et incongruitatem. Et inter hec non datur hec distinctio. Tertio est intellectus secundus contextus ex ipsis significationibus. Et iste intellectus dissonat ab hiis qui (que Oxf.) precesserunt secundum perfectionem et congruitatem, sicut patet in figuratiuis locutionibus. Et inter istum intellectum et uocem distinguitur.

Et quia iam dictum est de congruitate et perfectione orationis gramatice, consequenter queritur (om. Oxf.) utra istarum conditionum precedit aliam. Hoc enim sepe tangitur in introductione sophismatum gramaticorum.

Et uidetur quod perfectio sit prior congruitate, quia perfectio finaliter intenditur, sicut patet per diffinitionem orationis, que est: congrua dictionum ordinatio congruam perfectamque sententiam demonstrans.[u] Et finis est primum omnium eorum, que sunt ad finem in motu.

Adhuc. Totum naturaliter prius est sua parte. Sed perfectio est sicut totum ad congruitatem eo quod ad congruitatem requiritur ex parte uocis conformitas, ad perfectionem exigitur et uocum et intellectum completio.

Adhuc. Dignissimum in omni re est sua perfectio; quare et (om. Oxf.) naturaliter primum; quare perfectio orationis (primum...orationis om. per hom. Oxf.) primum et dignissimum in illa.

Sed contra (om. Oxf.). Congruitas ex parte uocis principaliter est, perfectio ex parte intellectus. Sed prior est uox quam intellectus. Et dico apud philosophum sermocinalem, quia prior est in apprehensione. Quare congruitas precedit.

Adhuc. Prius est illud e quo non conuertitur consequentia. Sed sequitur: si est perfecta, et congrua. Sed non conuertitur. Hec enim 'homo qui currit' congrua est, sed inperfecta. Ergo congruitas prior est.

Et dicendum quod 'prius' dicitur hic dupliciter, scilicet aut secundum intentionem aut secundum executionem. Secundum intentionem est idem primum quod est ultimum in executione siue in apprehensione. Et sic est (om. Oxf.) perfectio orationis primum in illa, sicut ostendunt orationes ad primam

partem.   Primum secundum executionem est quod ordinatur ad finem intentum.
Et sic est congruitas prior quam perfectio orationis simpliciter.   Est enim
prior quam perfectio in apprehensione et etiam in generatione orationis.   Et
sic concludunt uerum rationes ad secundum partem inducte.

Apparatus fontium

a Cf. Roger Bacon, Summa gramatica, ed. Steele, p. 13 (1 et seq.).

b Ibid., p. 14 (9-12).

c Ibid., (13-16).

d Ibid., (7-9).

e Ibid., p. 13 (3-7).

f Ibid., (14-17).

g Ibid., p. 14 (1-6).

h Ibid., p. 13 (18-22).

i Ibid., p. 15 (10-15).

j Ibid., (15-25).

k Ibid., (26-31).

l Ibid., pp. 15 (32)-16 (2).

m Ibid., p. 18 (5-8).

n Ibid., (9-12).

o Ibid., (13-15).

p Ibid., (16-18).

q Ibid., (19).

r Ibid., p. 19 (8-9, 25-27).

s Ibid., pp. 19 (21)-20 (8).

t Ibid., p. 20 (9-18).

u Prisc., Inst. gram. 2.15.

5

Roger Bacon on the Compounded and Divided Sense

Georgette Sinkler
Cornell University

The first and most ambitious account of the fallacies in general is found in Aristotle's <u>Sophistici elenchi</u>. There we find a list of what Aristotle considers <u>the</u> thirteen types of fallacy. We find as well a few examples of and cryptic remarks about each type. Despite, or perhaps because of, the brevity of the remarks, the rediscovery of this work in the early part of the twelfth century (ca. 1120)[1] stimulated a great deal of activity[2] in the form of commentaries and related treatises. Fairly early on, two of the fallacies in particular -- namely, the fallacies of composition and division -- proved to be more interesting and useful than the others, both logically and philosophically. For instance, a recognition of these fallacies helped medieval logicians and theologians to solve certain problems having to do with divine foreknowledge and human freedom, and certain semantic and syntactic distinctions which resulted from the analysis of these fallacies enabled the medievals to clarify various epistemological and modal issues connected with what we might broadly describe as the logic of propositional attitudes.

Medieval logicians through about the first quarter of the fourteenth century spent much time in trying to elaborate and refine Aristotle's account of the fallacies of composition and division. Since these fallacies were seen as fallacies of ambiguity with respect to composition and division in expressions, the discussions of these fallacies center, for the most part and quite naturally, on three issues: what composition and division are (that is, what the source of the ambiguity in the expression is); which sense of the expressions is the compounded sense and which the divided; and why people persistently fall victim to fallacious arguments involving these types of

The <u>Rise of British Logic</u>, ed. P. Osmund Lewry, O.P., Papers in Mediaeval Studies 7 (Toronto: Pontifical Institute of Mediaeval Studies, 1985), pp. 145-171. © P.I.M.S., 1985.

ambiguity. Although there are numerous treatments of composition and division prior to the early fourteenth century,[3] I have chosen to discuss the treatment of Roger Bacon (d. 1292/4), because it is, along with Lambert of Auxerre's (fl. 1250), the most systematic and rewarding of the treatments I have seen so far.

Lambert of Auxerre's discussion of composition and division occurs in his Logica, written around 1250;[4] Roger Bacon's discussion occurs in his Sumule dialectices, written around the same time.[5] The two treatises develop their accounts of composition and division, to varying degrees, in terms of 'determination' (which I shall be discussing later). Roger's discussion seems to me to result from his attempt to improve on Lambert's account of the nature of the compounded/divided ambiguity by working out that account in more detail. And this I take to be some evidence that Roger's Sumule dialectices was written after Lambert's Logica. I have several reasons for thinking that there is such a relationship between the two accounts of composition and division. First, there is much more detail in the Sumule than in the Logica about the nature of the compounded/divided ambiguity in terms of determination -- Roger devoting approximately three times more space to it than Lambert does (about one thousand words as compared with about three hundred). Second, Roger, unlike Lambert, argues that there is no third mode of composition and division,[6] and illustrates the second mode of composition and the second mode of division with examples that Lambert takes as illustrative of a third mode of composition and of a third mode of division. Third, Roger is fairly clearly referring to Lambert when he argues that there is no third mode of composition: the formulation of the third mode which Robert assails is the very formulation that Lambert uses, and the example that prompts the assault is one which Lambert includes in his third mode and which Roger includes in the second mode. And, finally, although Lambert's account of composition and division in terms of determination seems to have been an innovation in one respect,[7] he apparently does not believe that all the modes of composition and division can be characterized in terms of determination, whereas Roger apparently does. For Lambert does not describe the modes of composition and division in terms of determination. Rather, the notion of determination appears suddenly in Lambert's listing of examples of the second and third modes of division only. And an explanation of determination does not occur until the very end of his discussion of composition and division. He says,

In the interest of clarity regarding what has been remarked [in this discussion of composition and division], notice that it can be inferred that in paralogisms of composition...and also division, sometimes one determinant and two determinables or two determinants and one determinable are laid down. [8]

Roger, on the other hand, speaks of determination in connection with the second modes of composition and of division,[9] and implies that the first modes of composition and of division can also be described in terms of determination.[10]

Before presenting Roger's account of the source of the compounded/divided ambiguity in terms of determination, I must say something about what Roger takes composition and division (or the fallacies of composition and division)[11] to be in general. I must emphasize that it is Roger's account of composition which I shall say something about, since the theories developed during the Middle Ages regarding composition and division are by no means unified or consistent with one another. 'Composition', Roger says, 'is the conjunction of things that should be disjoined; i.e., of things that deserve to be divided.'[12] I take Roger to mean that composition occurs when an expression which is ambiguous because of the capacity for the words or groups of words in it to be compounded (taken together) or divided (separated) expresses something false when these words are compounded, and true when they are divided. That is, I take the 'should' or 'deserve' in Roger's statement to imply that that construal of the words in the expression will result in a true expression. My understanding of Roger on this point is confirmed by a consideration of the following two examples of composition he provides:

(A) For a sitting person to walk is possible.[13]
    Sedentem ambulare est possibile.
(B) Whoever know the alphabet now has learned it.
    Quicumque scit litteras nunc didicit illas.

When the phrase 'sitting person' and the word 'walk' are compounded, the sense of (A) is that a person can sit and walk at one and the same time — which is not only false, but impossible; when the phrase 'sitting person' and the word 'walk' are divided, the sense is that a person who is now sitting has the capacity to walk at some other time — which is ordinarily true. In

(B) when the word 'now' and the phrase 'has learned' are compounded, the sense is that all those people who know the alphabet have learned the alphabet now — which is false (since one of them, as Roger points out, may have learned it ten years ago)[14]; when the word 'now' is divided from the phrase 'has learned' and compounded with the word 'knows', the sense is that all those people who now know the alphabet have learned it -- which is true.

Roger also tells us that 'division is a deception produced in an utterance or in the understanding coming about in virtue of the division of things that should be conjoined.'[15] I take Roger to mean that division occurs when an expression which is ambiguous with respect to composition and division expresses something false when the words that constitute it are divided, and something true when those words are compounded. Once again, my understanding of Roger on this point is confirmed by a consideration of his examples:

(C) Five are two and three.
    Quinque sunt duo et tria.
(D) I made you a servile being free.
    Ego te posui servum entem liberum.

When the word 'two' and the word 'three' are divided, the sense of (C) is that five are two, and five are three — which is false: when the word 'two' and the word 'three' are compounded, the sense is that five are two and three taken together — which is true. In (D) when the word 'being' is divided from the word 'servile' and compounded with the word 'free', the sense is that I have made you, a free being, a slave — which according to Roger is false if the discourse is directed to a slave;[16] when the word 'being' and the word 'servile' are compounded, the sense is that I have made you, a servile being, free -- which according to Roger is true (if and only if, I suppose, the discourse is directed to a slave whom you have freed).

One might wonder at this point why part of the description of composition and division involves truth and falsity in the stipulated way when it looks as if the truth-value of the expression in either of its senses is sometimes context-dependent -- the more so given Roger's context-dependent exposition of (D). One might also wonder why (B) is not or could not be classified as an example of division instead of an example of composition, and vice versa concerning (D). What is to prevent us from describing (B), for instance, in the following way: when the word 'now' and the word 'knows' are compounded, the sense of the expression is true, and when the word 'now' is divided from the word 'knows' and compounded with the phrase 'has learned', the sense of the expression is false? Such questions can only be answered on the basis of modes of composition and division, to which I now turn.

The modes of composition and division can be understood as the classifications of the different linguistic contexts in which composition and division arise. Although Aristotle does not classify examples of (the fallacies of) composition and division into modes or types, throughout the scholastic period (ca. 1130-1530) those who write treatises dealing in whole or in part with composition and division do attempt such a classification -- ranging from Peter of Spain's two modes to the thirteen distinguished in <u>Fallacie Londinenses.</u> These modes pick out the different linguistic contexts in which composition and division occur, and the classifications into modes seem to be attempts to point toward what it is in an expression that is responsible for the ambiguity. From all appearance, however, before Roger no medieval logician succeeds in identifying any feature common to all the modes. That is, none succeeds in getting at what they take to be the heart of the fallacy — laying bare that one feature, or those features, explaining the ambiguity in each type of expression that is called ambiguous with respect to composition and division. According to Roger, the one common feature is this: the words in an expression ambiguous in this way have the potential to be <u>determined</u> in more than one way. Now although Roger actually describes only one of the modes of division in terms of determination, he speaks, as I pointed out earlier, of determination in connection with all of the modes of composition and of division that he recognizes. For this reason, the modes as actually given by Roger should be translatable into the language of determination. In what follows, I shall attempt to carry out such a translation. For by so doing we shall be in a better position to assess the merits of Roger's view that determination is the source of the compounded/divided ambiguity.

As the following two tables indicate, Roger recognizes two modes of composition, and two modes of division. The formulations with unprimed numerals are Roger's, and those with primed numerals are mine. Also, the examples listed under each mode are examples used by Roger.

Mode 1 of composition can be described in terms of determination in the following way: In an expression containing one determinant and one determinable, the determinable can be determined by the determinant or not determined by the determinant. Determinants (<u>determinaciones</u>) are expressions that can determine other expressions, and determinables (<u>determinabiles</u>) are expressions that can be determined by other expressions. The act of determining is the genus of which the linguistic operation of modifying is a species. For instance, the modifying of verbs by adverbs or of nouns by adjectives are species of determination. Thus, the root of the compounded/divided ambiguity is the fact that sometimes one linguistic expression can either determine or not determine another linguistic expression.

Expressions that exemplify Mode 1 of composition are ones in which there is one determinable together with a determinant which can either determine or not determine that determinable. Consider the familiar example of Mode 1: 'For a sitting person to walk is possible.' You know what the two senses of the expression are. But how is it to be analyzed in terms of determination? It is, I think, correct to say that 'walk' is the determinant which can either determine or not determine 'sitting person' <u>with respect to the modal word</u> 'possible'. When 'walk' determines 'sitting person', what is being spoken of is someone who has the potential for both sitting and walking at the same time; when 'walk' does not determine 'sitting person', what is being spoken of is someone who is sitting but has the potential for walking at some future time. And from even this one example, we can see that determination is not to be identified with adverbial or adjectival modification.

TABLE 1

Modes of Composition

Mode 1) When something is compounded with one thing, and when it is divided [from that thing] it is not compounded with another thing

'Et sunt duo modi secundum

1')* In an expression containing one determinant and one determinable, the determinable can be determined by the determinant or not be determined by the determinant

* The formulations with primed numerals are my versions of the modes.

hunc locum; primus, quando
aliquid componitur cum uno
et cum dividitur non componitur cum alio....'
(S, 335)

Examples:
     a) For a sitting person to walk is possible.[+]
       Sedentem ambulare est possible.
     b) What one alone can carry several can carry.
       Quod unum solum potest ferre plura potest ferre.

Mode 2) When some word is com-   2') In an expression contain-
pounded with one thing,   ing one determinant and
and when it is divided   two determinables, the de-
it can be compounded   terminant can determine
with another thing   one determinable, and when
                                it is divided from that
'Secundus modus est   determinable the determi-
quando aliqua diccio   nant can determine the
componitur cum uno et   other determinable
cum dividitur potest
cum alio componi....'
(S, 335)

Examples:
     a) Whoever knows the alphabet now has learned it.
       Quicumque scit litteras nunc didicit illas.
     b) With an eye you have seen this man beaten.
       Oculo vidisti hunc percussum.

[+] I translate the infinitive/accusative construction in this non-standard
way because Roger thinks that we can differentiate between the two senses
of an expression ambiguous with respect to composition and division by
employing a continuous or a discontinuous pronunciation, repectively. A
discontinuous pronunciation, however, cannot be obtained when one uses the
standard translation 'that a sitting person walk is possible.'

TABLE 2

Modes of Division

Mode 1) Where something is divided from one thing and is not compounded with another

'Primus est modus quando aliquid dividitur ab uno et non componitur cum alio....'
(S, 336)

1')* In an expression containing one determinant and one determinable, the determinable is divided from the determinant, but can be determined by the determinant

Examples:
a) Five are two and three.
   Quinque sunt duo et tria.
b) Every proposition or its contradictory is true.
   Omnis proposicio vel eius contradictoria est vera.
c) What is false is true if the Antichrist is.
   Falsum est verum si Antichristus est.

Mode 2) When some determinant is falsely divided from one thing and compounded with another thing laid down in the expression

'Secundus modus est quando aliqua determinacio dividitur falso ab uno et componitur cum alio posito in oracione.'(S,337)

2') In an expression containing one determinant and two determinables, the determinant is falsely divided from one determinable and can determine the other determinable

Examples:
a) I made you a servile being free.
   Ego te posui servum entem liberum.
b) God ceases now to be.
   Deus desinit nunc esse.
c) Forty of men a hundred divine Achilles left behind.
   Quadraginta virorum centum reliquit dives Achilles.

Mode 1 of division, on the other hand, can be described in terms of determination in this way: In an expression containing one determinant and one determinable, the determinable is divided from the determinant but can be determined by the determinant. We might wonder why the example 'For a sitting person to walk is possible' is not or could not be an example of Mode 1 of the division. Cannot we say that 'sitting person' is the determinable which can be divided from the determinant 'walk' and can also be determined by 'walk'? No -- or at least we cannot when the truth-values of the expression are taken into account. For, we are told, when the compounded sense of an expression is false and the divided sense is true, then we are dealing with a mode of composition; when the compounded sense is true and the divided sense is false, a mode of division. Accordingly, the expression 'For a sitting person to walk is possible' is an example of Mode 1 of composition and not of Mode 1 of division. It appears, then (in respect to the first question), that the desire to categorize examples of certain types of ambiguous expressions may have motivated certain medieval logicians like Roger to focus on truth-values. But a recognition of this possible motivation does nothing to alleviate the problems generated by an account that depends on truth-values. In addition to the fact that the truth-values of many contingent, context-dependent sentences are theoretically unknowable or at least are not known to us, there is the fact that not even all non-contingent sentences or ambiguous expressions examined in the light of a particular context will have different truth-values for both senses. For instance, in question 24 of his Super libros Elenchorum, Duns Scotus says that the expression 'video hominem magnum baculum tenentem' is ambiguous with respect to composition and division, and yet 'in each sense the proposition can be true, supposing that a possible hypothesis is laid down.'[17] That is 'magnum' can determine 'hominem' or it can determine 'baculum'. In the first case, the sense is 'I see a big man holding a stick'; in the second case, 'I see a man holding a big stick.' Both senses can be true if, say, what I see is a big man holding a big stick. Are such expressions examples neither of composition nor of division, even though compounded and divided senses can be distinguished?[18] This view would trivialize the distinction.

Now consider Mode 2 of composition. In terms of determination it can be described in the following way: In an expression containing one determinant and two determinables, the determinant can determine one determinable, and when it is divided from that determinable the determinant can determine the other determinable. An example of this mode is 'Whoever knows the alphabet now has learned it.' Again, you know what the two senses of this expression are. And in this case 'now' is the determinant which can determine either 'has learned' or 'knows'.

Finally, Mode 2 of division can be described in terms of determination in the following way: In an expression containing one determinant and two determinables, the determinant is falsely divided from one determinable and can determine the other determinable. An example of this mode is 'I made you a servile being free,' the two senses of which you are already familiar with. In this case, 'being' is the determinant which can determine either 'free' or 'servile'.

Two questions need to be asked at this point. First, what exactly is a determinant and what exactly is a determinable? Second, which acts of determining, with regard to some given string of words, are to be considered compounded and which divided? Or, to put this second question in another way, which acts of determining give rise to the compounded sense and which to the divided sense? In answer to the first question, a determinant qua determinant, Roger says, is dependent on or leans on something else, and requires something else to complete its dependence.[19] I take this to mean -- in the case of expressions that have more than one determinant or determinable -- that a determinant is a word or group of words that can function as a subject or as a predicate in a sentence only when conjoined with something else. This can be easily seen in the case of determinants that are adjectives or adverbs: in order to function in a sentence, adjectives depend on nouns, and adverbs on verbs. A determinant in such cases, then, cannot stand alone and function as an essential unit in a sentence.

A determinable qua determinable, on the other hand, is independent, fixed, and free-standing (per se stans).[20] In the case of expressions that have more than one determinant or determinable, I take this to mean that a determinable is a word or group of words that, unlike a determinant, can function as a subject or as a predicate in a sentence. And, just as one might expect, this 'fundamental character' of a determinable to be independent makes it the prime candidate for the role of that on which a determinant depends or leans. Roger says that a determinable 'can determine the dependence and the inclination of the determinant.'[21] In short, a determinant depends on a determinable in order to be complete. In the case of expressions that have more than one determinant or determinable, this seems to mean that a determinant depends on a determinable in order to function grammatically. When a determinant in such cases determines a determinable, the determinant is transformed: it forms part of a linguistic unit that can function as a subject or a predicate in a sentence.

Consider again the example 'Whoever knows the alphabet now has learned it.' If the determinant 'now' is to function in the expression, it must determine a determinable -- in this case either 'has learned' or 'knows'. That is, the determinant 'now' depends for completion either on the determinable 'has learned' or the determinable 'knows'. And insofar as it depends on either of them, it will determine one of them.

It should be pointed out that the concept of dependence was important to the speculative grammarians of the late thirteenth to early fourteenth centuries,[22] and that this concept was one of the distinctive features of speculative grammar. Very broadly speaking, speculative grammar is grammatical theory that tries to account for grammatical categories 'e.g. nouns, verbs, cases, and tenses) in terms of general, non-definitional properties of the objects signified. It is believed to have begun developing around 1270[23] -- apparently after Roger's Sumule dialectices was written. With the aid of the concept of dependence, the speculative grammarians, or Modistae, were able to deduce the whole system of possible Latin grammatical constructions.[24] Jan Pinborg believes that 'the notion of dependency seems to have been intuitional for the Modistae.'[25] He says that 'no purely linguistic rules are formulated in modistic grammar which help in deciding which of two semantic features is dependent on the other.'[26] Now it might be true that treatises currently taken to be part of the modistic literature do not discuss linguistic rules that help in deciding which of two semantic features is dependent on the other. But Roger spends approximately one third of his chapter discussing rules of this sort. As it turns out, the answer to the second question -- which acts of determining with regard to a given expression give rise to the compounded sense and which to the divided sense -- is that the compounded sense of the expression is the sense that results when a determinant agrees with a determinable in connection with some special nature, or when what is naturally better suited[27] to be compounded is compounded; and that the divided sense is the sense that results when what agrees in connection with some special nature is divided, or when what is naturally better suited to be compounded is divided. When Roger discusses what constitutes the naturally better suited arrangement of words, he states rules as well as the grammatical and metaphysical considerations that underlie these rules.   And it is in connection with these rules that determination and the related notion of dependence are taken up.   In the remainder of the paper, then, I will lay out and discuss these rules.

In order to avoid possible confusion, I should say at this point that there is a difference between composition and division on the one hand, and the compounded sense and the divided sense on the other.   'Composition' and 'division' are names for types of ambiguity in expressions, whereas the compounded and divided senses are two possible senses of such ambiguous expressions.

Roger discusses three types of cases in which rules regarding determination are relevant: one in which a determinant occurs between two determinables, one in which a determinant occurs before the two determinables, and one in which a determinant occurs after the two determinables. In what follows I will discuss only the rules that Roger lays down in connection with the first of these cases; namely, the one in which a determinant occurs between two determinables.   This discussion can be followed most easily by reference to Table 3.

When a determinant occurs between two determinables, it either agrees with one and only one of those determinables in connection with some special nature or it does not.   The example that Roger gives of the case in which a determinant agrees with one and only one of the determinables is this: 'You cannot truly deny that Cerion is a donkey' (Tu non potest vere negare Cerion esse asinum).   The determinant in this case is the adverb 'truly' (vere), and the determinables are the verbs 'can' (potes) and 'deny' (negare).   'Truly' agrees with 'can' in connection with some special nature.   For that reason, when 'truly' determines 'can', the expression is compounded, and the sense is that you are not truly able to deny that Cerion is a donkey.   When 'truly' does not determine 'can', but determines 'deny' — that with which it does not agree in connection with some special nature — the expression is divided, and the sense is that you are not able to deny truly that Cerion is a donkey.

Roger claims that all affirming and denying adverbs, such as 'truly' and 'falsely', agree 'more naturally with the indicative mood than with other moods, because "truly" designates an affirmation in some way and

TABLE 3

The compounded sense of an expression ambiguous with respect to composition
and division when the determinant is between two determinables

The determinant agrees with one determinable in connection with some special nature	The determinant does not agree with either determinable in connection with some special nature

[Rule 1:] The determinant agrees with one determinable in connection with some special nature

Example:
You cannot truly deny that Cerion is a donkey.
Tu non potes vere negare Cerion esse asinum

If the determinant is adjectival

[Rule 2:] If the determinant is a pure determinant, it is better suited to be compounded with the preceding determinable, because a [pure?] determinant qua [pure?] determinant is subsequent to and depends on a determinable

Example:
You saw with a stick this man beaten.
Vidisti baculo hunc percussum.

[Rule 3:] When both determinables are substantives, the determinant is better suited to be compounded with the more independent, fixed, and freestanding of the determinables

Example:
God ceases now to be.
Deus desinit nunc esse.

[Rule 4:] When neither of the substantive determinables is more independent, etc., the determinant is better suited to be compounded with the determinable following it

Example:
Whatever lives always is.
Quicquid vivit semper est.

[Rule 5:] When only one of the determinables is a substantive, the determinant is better suited to be compounded with that determinable

Example:
I see a good musical man.
Video hominem bonum musicum.

[Rule 6:] When both determinables are adjectives, the determinant is better suited to be compounded with the one which is substantive (if either is such)

(No example given)

[Rule 7:] When both determinables are pure adjectives, the determinant is better suited to be compounded with the first determinable, because the determinant has more of the fundamental character [of a determinant] when it follows the adjective

(No example given)

"falsely" a negation.'[28]   Although Roger's explanation for this particular
special nature will strike us as either not particularly good, or as no
explanation at all, the implication is that a determinant agrees with one
determinable in connection with some special nature when the determinant
and one determinable are linguistically more compatible than are the
determinant and the other determinable.   There is some reason for thinking
that, in general, special natures have something to do with discoverable rules
of syntax, since in this instance Priscian is the authority Roger cites[29] to
support the claim about what agrees with what by virtue of a special nature,
and since Priscian's approach to grammar is to describe in a more or less
systematic way the linguistic habits of the classical authors.   What these
special natures are, then, seems to find formulation in rules -- whether the
natures reflect something about the orderly arrangement of things in the
world or an imposed order which stems from arbitrary choices made by the
founding fathers of Latin literature.   Though Roger says nothing on this
point, one thing seems clear: the only way of knowing whether a particular
expression ambiguous with respect to composition and division contains words
or groups of words that do in fact agree in connection with some special
nature is to be well-trained in grammar or to have particularly precise
grammatical intuitions — intuitions acquired by years of reading and writing.

When a determinant occurs between two determinables and does not
agree in connection with some special nature with either determinable, then
we must consider the nature of the determinant or the determinable, and
what they are naturally better suited to be construed with.   And what a
determinant is better suited to be construed with depends, to some extent, on
whether the determinant is 'pure' or 'adjectival'.   When the determinant is
'pure', it is better suited to be construed with the preceding determinable
because a determinant qua determinant is 'subsequent to and depends on a
determinable.'[30]   By 'pure determinant' Roger seems to mean nothing more
than 'non-adjectival determinant'.[31]   The example that he gives for this case
is the following: 'You saw with a stick this man beaten' (Vidisti baculo hunc
percussum).   The determinant is the prepositional phrase 'with a stick'
(baculo), and the determinables are the verb 'you saw' (vidisti) and the
participle 'beaten' (percussum).   Because the determinant 'with a stick' is
used adverbially and not adjectivally, and the determinable 'you saw' precedes
it, 'with a stick' is better suited to be compounded with 'you saw'.   When
these are compounded, the expression is compounded and the sense is that
you see a man being beaten, and the instrument of your seeing is a stick.

When 'with a stick' is divided from 'you saw', however, and compounded with 'beaten', the expression is divided and the sense is that you see a man being beaten, and the instrument of his beating is a stick.

The reasons for these rules will become clearer, I think, as we consider the rest of the examples:

When a determinant occurs between two determinables, does not agree with either determinable in connection with some special nature, and is not a 'pure' determinant, then it is 'adjectival' and we must consider the nature of the determinables. There are three possibilities: (1) both determinables are substantives; (2) both determinables are adjectives; and (3) one determinable is an adjective, the other a substantive. By a substantive, Roger seems to have in mind any linguistic expression that has meaning in its own right (categorematic expressions) or can have meaning in its own right (expressions used categorematically): a noun, a pronoun, a participle, or a verb.

When both determinables are substantives, either one of the determinables is more independent, fixed, and free-standing than the other determinable, or neither determinable is more independent, fixed, and free-standing than the other. If one determinable is more independent, fixed, and free-standing than the other, then the determinant is better suited to be compounded with it, because, as you recall, a determinant is dependent on something else, requiring something else to complete its dependence. Roger says that 'we must consider regarding the determinables which of them has more of the fundamental character of a determinable.... And if a determinant determines such a determinable, the expression will be compounded.'[32] And it stands to reason that the determinable will provide firmer support for the determinant than will the determinable that possesses less of this fundamental character. Thus, in the example 'God ceases now to be' (Deus desinit nunc esse), the determinant 'now' (nunc) is better suited to be compounded with the determinable 'to be' (esse) than with the determinable 'ceases' (desinit), because, Roger tells us, the infinitive is more independent, fixed, and free-standing than the other verb forms. When 'now' and 'to be' are compounded, the expression is compounded and the sense is that at time t_n God ceases to exist. The expression is divided, however, when 'now' is divided from 'to be' and compounded with 'ceases'. The sense in that case is that God ceases at time t_n to exist, but God exists at time t_{n+1}.

We have already seen that the fundamental character of a determinable is to be independent, fixed, and free-standing. But how are we to tell which determinable has more of this fundamental character? Roger says that in addition to the infinitive (compared with the other verb forms), the following two sorts of determinables possess more of the character of a determinable: a whole (compared with a part), and a substantive (compared with an adjective).[33] What Roger seems to believe is that there is an ontological ordering that carries over from the things in the world to those things as expressed in language. That a whole or something considered in its entirety should be on firmer ontological footing than any of its parts taken singly, or that a substance should be on firmer ontological footing than anything that could be considered one of its characteristics, properties, or attributes,[34] is understandable and plausible enough -- at least from an Aristotelian point of view -- and needs no explanation or defense here. But what about Roger's contention, in connection with the example under Rule 3, that the determinable that is an infinite verb is more firmly grounded (i.e., more independent, fixed, and free-standing) than the determinable that is another verb form? Since the primary function of an infinitive might be seen as that of expressing a type of activity without reference to person, number, time, or mood, it is not intuitively difficult or far-fetched to think of it as being the block upon which the other verb forms are built, as expressing the essence or core of the verb. I take this to be what Roger has in mind when he says that the infinitive 'marks out the activity of the verb (_signat rem verbi_)[35] by the mode of standing and having been fixed although its inclination (which is its mode) is indefinite (_infinita_).'[36]

We can see, then, that the ontological status that Roger attributes to infinitives relative to the other forms is not without some intuitive basis. The ontological ordering in this case, however, seems to be entirely within the realm of language, and has to do as well with the conditions under which one can form a grammatical utterance. I cannot produce a grammatical utterance without a verb in the appropriate form -- that is, if there is no verb indicating person, mood, number, and tense. And yet there is no verb which does not at least indicate or express an activity of some sort. Therefore, the infinitive relative to the other verb forms is 'more fixed and independent and free-standing.'

An example of an expression in which one of the determinables possesses more of the character of a determinable insofar as it is a substantive and the other determinable an adjective is 'I see a good musical man' (<u>video</u> <u>hominem</u> <u>bonum</u> <u>musicum</u>)[37] -- an example under Rule 5 used by Roger in connection with the case in which one determinable is a substantive and the other is an adjective. The two determinables are 'man' (<u>hominem</u>) and 'musical' (<u>musicum</u>). 'Man' is a substantive, 'musical' an adjective (even though in Latin it can be used substantively as 'musical male'). Thus, the compounded sense is the sense resulting when the adjectival determinant 'good' (<u>bonum</u>) is construed with 'man': I see a good man who is a musician. The divided sense results when 'good' is divided from 'man' and construed with 'musical': I see a man who is a good musician.

Now when both determinables are substantive, but neither of them is more independent, fixed, and free-standing, Roger says that the determinant is better suited to be compounded with the determinable following it, 'since, as Priscian maintains, adjectives are more suitably put before substantives than put after...[and] adverbs...are the adjectives of verbs.'[38] Roger goes on to say that 'this can be confirmed because accidents work especially toward the cognition of the subject, as Aristotle says....and therefore adjectives ought to be placed before.'[39] One of the examples Roger gives is 'Whatever lives always is' (<u>quicquid</u> <u>vivit</u> <u>semper</u> <u>est</u>). The determinant is the adverb 'always' (<u>semper</u>) and the determinables are 'lives' (<u>vivit</u>) and 'is' (<u>est</u>). Neither the verb 'lives' nor the verb 'is' is more independent, fixed and free-standing than the other, so 'always' is better suited to be compounded with 'is', since in the expression 'is' comes after 'always'.

Finally, when both determinables are adjectives, the determinant is better suited to be compounded with the determinable that is substantive (if either is substantive); otherwise, the determinant is better suited to be compounded with the determinable that comes before it, because the determinant 'has more of the fundamental character [of a determinant] when it follows the adjective.'[40] Roger does not give examples for either of these cases.

If I am right in what I have said so far then one can see where the difference lies between those cases in which a determinant and a determinable are to be combined in connection with a special nature (Rule 1), and those cases in which this is not so; for instance, those cases in which a determinant and determinable are naturally better suited to be combined because that determinable is more independent, fixed, and free-standing than the other determinable (Rules 3 and 4). The difference lies in the fact that the special nature cases have to do with discoverable grammatical rules that may be to some degree arbitrary, whereas those cases in which there is no agreement in connection with a special nature do not have to do with discoverable grammatical rules. For instance, the fixed-and-independent-determinable cases have to do not with grammatical rules but with metaphysical priorities.

But, someone might ask, how can you maintain this, given that Roger appeals to grammatical rules found in Priscian in both cases -- that is, in the case in which a determinant _agrees_ with one determinable in connection with a special nature (Rule 1), and in the case in which the determinant does not agree (Rule 5)? I can maintain it, I believe, by pointing out that when Roger speaks of the case in which a determinant agrees with a determinable in connection with some special nature, he appeals to rules having to do with an order imposed on grammatical constructions and stemming from arbitrary choices made by the best Latin authors. The rule that those things that have the nature of an affirmation and a negation agree more with an indicative than with another mood does not seem to be anything but arbitrary. What in the nature of things in the world could account for affirmatives agreeing more naturally with a verb in the indicative rather than in, say, the subjunctive mood?

On the other hand, when Roger speaks of those cases in which a determinant _does not agree_ with a determinable in connection with some special nature, he can and usually does appeal to an ontological ordering that carries over from things in the world to those things as expressed in language. We saw this in Roger's explanation of the rules concerning the case in which both determinables are substantive: first, when Roger described which determinable had more of the fundamental character of a determinable (Rule 3); and second, when Roger not only cited a descriptive grammatical rule from Priscian in support of the rule that a determinant is better suited to be compounded with the determinable following it when neither substantive determinable is more independent, fixed, and free-standing, but also cited a bit of metaphysical doctrine from Aristotle (Rule 4). Furthermore, Rules 5 and 6 are metaphysically accounted for by what Roger says about which sorts of determinables possess more of the fundamental character of a determinable. And finally, although Roger does not attempt to support Rules 2 and 7, which have to do with the determinant _qua_ determinant being subsequent to a determinable, it is not difficult to see what metaphysical consideration is available to him: namely, that whatever has a dependent nature (as a determinant does) is ontologically posterior to whatever has an independent nature (as a determinable does). For, as Roger says, a determinant depends on a determinable in order to be complete. And surely that which depends on something else can be thought in some sense to come after that something else.

This theory of determination, for all its innovative character, has problems. In addition to the difficulties associated with whether reference to truth-values can adequately distinguish composition from division, there is another difficulty which I take to be more serious. It can be seen most clearly if we consider examples (a), (b), and (c) of Mode 1 of division (Table 2). We can distinguish readily enough the two senses of these expressions: 'Five are two and three' can have either the sense 'five are two, and five are three', or 'five are two and three taken together'; 'Every proposition or its contradictory is true' can have either the sense 'every proposition is true, or the contradictory of every proposition is true', or 'for every proposition either it or its contradictory is true'; and finally, 'What is false is true if the Antichrist is' can have either the sense 'that which is true if the Antichrist exists is false' (in this case the sentence is a categorical with a conditioned subject), or 'that which is false is true, if the Antichrist exists' (in this case the sentence is a conditional). But how are these sorts of examples to be described in terms of determination? What is the determinant and what is the determinable in these cases? For the first example, can we say that 'two' is the determinable and 'three' the determinant, or vice versa? Can we say that the one word determines the other with respect to the conjunction 'and'? Perhaps, but only, it seems, if we emphasize the notion of dependence. 'Three' could, I suppose, be viewed as dependent on 'two' in the sense that three could not exist if two did not exist, or in the sense that three is epistemically posterior to two. But if it is the conjunction 'and' that is in some sense responsible for the ambiguity in this case (just as it is the modal word 'possible' that is in some sense responsible for the ambiguity in example [a] of Mode 1 of composition), then it is hard to see how we can identify the determinant and the determinable on the basis of dependency. Consider, for example, the expression 'These men are Socrates and Plato',[41] which can be understood as 'these men are Socrates, and these men are Plato', or 'these men are Socrates and Plato taken together.' Presumably, no one could seriously maintain that a relationship of dependence obtains between Socrates and Plato, or between their names.

One might suppose that example (a), 'Five are two and three', is explainable in terms of scope-ambiguity. For instance, one might say that 'five' can fall within the scope of 'and' or outside the scope of 'and'. That is, 'five' falls within the scope of 'and' in the divided-sense reading 'five are two and five are three', but 'five' falls outside the scope of 'and' in the compounded-sense reading 'five are (two and three).' In this case, 'five' is the determinable, 'and' the determinant. But this interpretation of the example is not helpful for two reasons. First, since 'and' is not the same operator in both readings, the ambiguity is not a scope-ambiguity. In the divided-sense reading 'and' is used as an operator for propositional conjunction; in the compounded-sense reading 'and' is used as an operator for arithmetical summation, where the arguments are numbers and not propositions. Second, on this interpretation, the number of determinables changes. When 'and' does not determine 'five', there is one determinable; namely, 'five'. On the other hand, when 'and' determines 'five' (i.e., when 'five' falls within the scope of 'and'), it also determines 'two' and 'three' (i.e., 'two' and 'three' also fall within the scope of 'and'). Yet if 'and' determines 'five', 'two', and 'three', there are three determinables in the divided sense, and not one. Concerning Mode 1 of division, however, Roger says that one thing is divided from one thing and is not compounded with anything else: '...aliquid dividitur ab uno et non componitur cum alio....' This attempt to accommodate examples (a), (b), and (c) under Mode 1 of division is also unsuccessful.

I do not see, then, how these examples can be described in terms of determination when they are considered under Mode 1 of division. And although it is conceivable that these examples, and others like them, can be described in terms of determination under Mode 2, say, or perhaps under some altogether different mode, I doubt that this can be done in anything but an ad hoc manner. Thus, it is at the very least doubtful that all of the examples standardly included among composition and division can be accommodated by determination.

I take this to be the fatal flaw in the theory of determination as an account of the source of the compounded/divided ambiguity. The hypothesis that logicians after Roger also saw it as flawed gains some slight support from the fact that within forty years of the writing of the Sumule dialectices there seems to be a return to speaking of determination as Peter of Spain spoke of it; namely, only in connection with what Roger would classify as Mode 1 of composition, Mode 2 of composition, and Mode 2 of division, and with no attempt to explain the nature of determination. This is the practice, for example, of the unknown author of a set of questions on the Sophistici elenchi, edited by Sten Ebbesen in 1977 and dated by him as having been written between 1270 and 1280,[42] and it is the practice of Duns Scotus as well, whose questions on the Sophistici elenchi have been dated by Ebbesen to around 1290.[43]

Although Roger does not, I think, succeed in pin-pointing the source of the compounded/divided ambiguity, he does at least attempt to pin-point it -- something that, despite its being crucial to a full understanding of the ambiguity, I have seen no one except Roger attempt prior to the early fourteenth century. In addition, what Roger's account of the compounded/divided ambiguity suggests is that there is a systematic indeterminacy in language; that certain ambiguities exist because the grammatical rules that are in operation simply do not require one and only one reading of each expression. But since one is aware of this indeterminacy, one can proceed in either of two ways: (1) accept the indeterminacy, and master the operative grammatical rules; (2) attempt to rid the language of its flexibility either by creating new and stronger grammatical rules, or by stipulating that the operative rules (taking into consideration as well the contexts in which the sentences appear) really do decide the sense one way or the other. It is my view that the second of these two routes won out, having been the one taken by William Heytesbury, who from the early part of the fourteenth century established the tradition for the discussion of composition and division.

Notes

[1] See Bernard G. Dod, 'Aristoteles latinus' in N. Kretzmann, A. Kenny and J. Pinborg eds., The Cambridge History of Later Medieval Philosophy (Cambridge, 1982), p. 46.

[2] See ibid., p. 69.

[3] Such treatments can be found in the following anonymous twelfth-century treatises edited by L.M. de Rijk, Logica Modernorum, 2 vols in 3 (Wijsgerige Teksten en Studies 6 and 16; Assen, 1962, 1967): Glose in Aristotilis Sophisticos elencos (1.187-255); Summa Sophisticorum elencorum

(1.257-458); Fallacie Vindobonenses (1.491-543); Dialectica Monacensis 5 (2.2, pp. 556-604); Fallacie Parvipontane (1.545-609); Fallacie Londinenses (2.2, pp. 639-78); and Tractatus Anagnini 6 (2.2, pp. 327-32). Such treatments can also be found in Martin Grabmann ed., 'Die Introductiones in logicam des Wilhelm von Shyreswood (†nach 1267)', Sitzungsberichte der Bayerischen Akademie der Wissenschaften, Philosophisch-historische Abteilung, Jahrgang 1937, Heft 10 (Munich, 1937), pp. 85-104; repr. idem, Gesammelte Akademie-abhandlungen 2 (Veroffentlichungen des Grabmann-Institutes NF 25/II; Paderborn-Munich-Vienna-Zurich, 1979), pp. 1339-58; L.M. de Rijk ed., Peter of Spain (Petrus Hispanus Portugaliensis), Tractatus, tract. 7 (Wijsgerige Teksten en Studies 22; Assen, 1972), pp. 89-184; S. Thomae Aquinatis De fallaciis ('ad quosdam nobiles artistas') in Opera omnia ed. Leonina 43 (Rome, 1976), pp. 401-18; Vincentius Bellovacensis, Speculum doctrinale, lib. 3, cap. 90-98, in Vincentii Burgundi Bibliotheca mundi seu Speculi maioris 2 (Douai, 1624; repr. Graz, 1965), cols. 275-80; S. Ebbesen et al. eds., Simon of Faversham, Quaestiones super libro Elenchorum (Studies and Texts 60; Toronto, 1984); Ioannis Duns Scoti Super libros Elenchorum Aristotelis in Opera omnia, editio nova juxta editionem Waddingi 2 (Paris, 1891), pp. 1-80); Raymundus Lullus, Logica nova, dist. 5, cap. 17-33 (Palma de Mallorca, 1744; repr. Frankfurt, 1971), pp. 94-113.

4 See Franco Alessio ed., Lamberto d'Auxerre, Logica (Summa Lamberti) (Pubblicazioni della Facoltà di Lettere e Filosofia dell' Università di Milano 59, Sezione a cura dell'Istituto di Storia della Filosofia 19; Florence, 1971), pp. xxx-xxxi. Hereafter, references to this edition will be indicated in the following manner: A, page number.

5 See Robert Steele ed., Rogeri Bacon Sumule dialectices (Opera hactenus inedita Rogeri Baconi 15; Oxford, 1940), p. xiv. Hereafter, references to this edition will be indicated in the following manner: S, page number.

6 S, 336.

7 Lambert is not the first to use terms deriving from 'determinare' in discussing various examples of composition and division. For instance, the unknown author of Fallacie Parvipontane, the unknown author of Tractatus Anagnini, and Peter of Spain in the Tractatus use such terms. It is Lambert, however, who takes determination to be important enough to warrant some

explanation of its nature and its role in compounded/divided ambiguity.   He seems to be the first to do this.

[8] A, 165.   Also, if Lambert believed that determination characterizes the first mode of composition and the first mode of division, presumably he would have said in addition to what he does say, 'Sometimes one determinant and one determinable are laid down.'   He does not say this, although Roger Bacon does (S, 337).

[9] See S, 335, 337.

[10] S, 337.

[11] As far as I can see, 'composition' and 'fallacy of composition', and 'division' and 'fallacy of division' are not carefully distinguished by Roger. Compare these two passages: (a) 'Sequitur de fallacia composicionis; et est composicio disjungendorum conjunccio....' (S, 334); (b) 'Sequitur de fallacio divisionis; et est fallacia divisionis decepcio proveniens ex conjungendorum divisione....' (S, 336).

[12] S, 334.

[13] I translate the infinitive/accusative construction in this non-standard way because Roger thinks that we can differentiate between the two senses of an expression ambiguous with respect to composition and division by employing a continuous or a discontinuous pronunciation, respectively (See S, 337, for instance).   A discontinuous pronunciation, however, cannot be obtained when one uses the standard translation 'that a sitting person walk is possible.'

[14] S, 335.

[15] S, 336.   Regarding my omission of 'fallacia' in the text of the paper, see n. 11.

[16] Roger's exact words are, 'Similter "ego posui te servum entem liberum"; si dirigatur sermo ad servum ("servum" Steele) et dividatur hoc participium "entem" ab eo quod est "servum", falsum est, cum oracio componatur, sic est vera.' (S, 337).

17 In a rebuttal of a third opinion concerning the question, Scotus says, 'Sed convenit reperire compositionem, et divisionem, sine falsitate alterius sensus, ut patet per exemplum: <u>Video</u> <u>hominem</u> <u>magnum</u> <u>baculum</u> <u>tenentem</u>, hic est compositio, et divisio, eo quod haec determinatio nominalis <u>magnum</u> potest determinare <u>hominem</u>, vel <u>baculum</u>, et in utroque sensu potest esse propositio vera, posito casu possibili.' (Scotus, <u>Super</u> <u>libros</u> <u>Elenchos</u>, q. 24; <u>Opera</u> <u>omnia</u> 2.38ᵃ).

18 Although Roger apparently failed to see the difficulties in this regard, Scotus, who comes after him, does not. In q. 25 he says, 'Ad quaestionem dicendum, quod compositio potest dupliciter considerari, aut in se, et absolute, aut prout pertinet ad finem Sophisticae. Si primo modo consideratur, non est necesse in compositione sensum compositum esse falsum, quia ad potentialem multiplicitatem non requiritur, nisi quod materialia sub diverso modo proferendi diversa significent. Quod autem illa materialia sint vera, vel falsa, vel in alio sensu vera, et alio falsa, hoc accidit potentiali multiplicitati. Si consideratur secundo modo, sic necesse est sensum compositum in compositione esse falsum. Nam opponens sophistice, intendit respondentem ducere ad metam, sed hoc non facit, nisi faciat ipsum opinari falsum esse verum, propter similitudinem falsi ad verum. Et propter hoc Aristoteles determinans de locis Sophisticis....' (ibid., p. 40).

19 '...quia determinacio est dependens et inclinans ad aliud, exigens aliud finiens suam dependenciam.' (S̲, 338).

20 '...racio autem determinabilis est ut sit stans et fixum et independens....' (S̲, 340). '...aut igitur unum determinabile magis est finitum et independens et per se stans qua<m> aliud aut non....' (S̲, 338).

21 '...ut dependenciam et inclinacionem determinacionis possit determinare....' (S̲, 340).

22 See Jan Pinborg, 'Speculative Grammar' in Kretzmann <u>et al.</u> eds., <u>The</u> <u>Cambridge</u> <u>History</u> <u>of</u> <u>Later</u> <u>Medieval</u> <u>Philosophy</u>, pp. 259-60.

23 Ibid., pp. 254-56.

24 Ibid., p. 260.

25 Ibid., p. 259.

26 Ibid.

27 When Roger speaks of certain words or groups of words in an expression as more naturally suited to be, apt to be, or deserving of being combined, he does not take himself to be pointing out a device that will enable us to disambiguate expressions ambiguous with respect to composition and division. In other words, there is no reason to believe, and every reason not to believe, that he thinks that there is no ambiguity once we see which words in an expression are better suited to be joined together. There is still another way to construe the words which grammar, for all that, does in fact allow.

28 S, 338.

29 Priscian is often cited — at least from the middle of the thirteenth century -- in connection with composition and division when attempts are made to give reasons why one combination of the words produces the compounded sense.

30 '...determinacio in quantum tale posterius est et dependet a determinabili....' (S, 338).

31 'Non-adjectival' as used in this sentence should be taken rather broadly, since 'adjective' seems to have a fairly broad meaning for Roger, who says at one point (following Priscian) that adverbs are the adjectives of verbs: '...et eciam de adverbiis, que sunt adjectiva verborum....' (S, 339).

32 Roger says this when he is discussing cases in which a determinant is not between the two determinables: 'Et tunc consideranda est ad ipsa determinabilia quod eorum habet majorem racionem determinabilis...et si determinet determinacio tale determinabile erit oracio composita....' (S, 340).

33 Ibid.

34 At one point Roger says, 'magis natum est su<b>stantivum terminare dependenciam adjectivi quam adjectivum... (S, 339); and he says that this is so 'sive adjectivum purum sive su<b>stantivum sit.'

[35] I feel justified in translating 'rem verbi' in this way (given the context) because of a remark made by Sten Ebbesen, 'Ancient Scholastic Logic as the Source of Medieval Scholastic Logic' in Kretzmann et al. eds., The Cambridge History of Later Medieval Philosophy, p. 110: 'For instance, verbal forms other than the infinitive not only signify an "activity" (Greek "pragma", mistranslated into Latin as res) but also consignify some definite mood, number, and the like, these "accidents"...being specified by morphological devices.' But even if 'rem verbi' is translated more literally as 'the actual thing belonging to the verb', I believe that Roger can still be understood to mean what I take him to mean.

[36] 'Cujusmodi est infinitus modus respecto aliorum modorum, quia signat rem verbi per modum stantis et fixi, quamvis inclinacio ejus que est modus sit infinita....' (S, 338).

[37] This expression cannot be translated into English with the Latin word order preserved.

[38] S, 339.

[39] Ibid.

[40] '...quia majorem racionem habet cum sequatur adjectivum.' (ibid.).

[41] This example is used by Ockham, F. del Punta ed., Guillelmi de Ockham Expositio super libros Elenchorum, lib. 1, cap. 3, § 6, Guillelmi de Ockham Opera philosophica 3 (St. Bonaventure, 1979), p. 40; but it is not used there for the same purpose for which I use it.

[42] See Sten Ebbesen ed., Incertorum auctorum quaestiones super Sophisticos elenchos (Corpus philosophorum Danicorum Medii Aevi 7; Copenhagen, 1977), p. XXXIV. The author of these questions describes the modes of composition and division in q. 64 and q. 827. What Roger describes in terms of determination and as Mode 1 of division, this author does not describe in terms of determination, but in terms of what can copulate between terms or between propositions: '...primus [modus divisionis] provenit ex eo quod aliqua coniunctio potest copulare inter terminos vel inter propositiones coniungendo vel dividendo, ut patet....' (q. 64; p. 148 [13-15]; 'Secundus modus [in compositione et divisione] est quando coniunctio aliqua

potest coniungere inter terminos vel inter propositiones, ut hic "quinque sunt duo et tria".' (q. 827; p. 332 [148-50]. Like Peter of Spain, the author of these questions uses the word 'determinatio' when he describes what Roger describes as Mode 2 of division, Mode 2 of composition, and Mode 1 of composition (examples like [b] under Roger's Mode 1 of composition, but not examples like [a]).

It should be pointed out that in q. 69 (p. 161 [18]) the word 'determinatione' (changed to 'dispositione' in q. 831; p. 345 [28] -- the corresponding question in the author's revised version of the Quaestiones) occurs in connection with what the author takes to be Avicenna's views on why 'quinque sunt duo et tria' is false in the sense of composition. But it is clear both that these views are not shared by the author and that 'determinatione' is not being used in the Latin Avicenna in the broad sense in which Roger uses it. Rather, it is being used in the narrow sense of grammatical modification. The author of these questions does not adjudicate q. 69 by saying that 'three' ('two') is the determinant of 'two' ('three').

The author's discussion of this question — whether 'quinque sunt duo et tria' is true in the sense of composition — is strikingly similar to Simon of Faversham's discussion of this question in Ebbesen et al, eds., Quaestiones super libro Elenchorum, Quaestiones novae, q. 15, pp. 139-42.

[43] See Sten Ebbesen, 'Suprasegmental Phonemes in Ancient and Medieval Logic' in H.A.G. Braakhuis, C.H. Kneepkens, L.M. de Rijk eds., English Logic and Semantics from the End of the Twelfth Century to the Time of Ockham and Burleigh: Acts of the 4th European Symposium on Mediaeval Logic and Semantics, Leiden-Nijmegen, 23-27 April 1979. (Artistarium Supplementa 1; Nijmegen, 1981), pp. 331-59.

Duns Scotus mentions determination in q. 24 (Opera omnia 2.38[a]), q. 32 (2.47[b]), and q. 33 (2.48[a]) in connection with the following two examples: 'video hominem magnum baculum tenentem' and 'quod unum solum potest ferre plura potest ferre.' He does not mention determination in the questions dealing with the example 'sedentem ambulare est possibile.' From all appearances, Scotus takes determination to be nothing broader than adverbial and adjectival modification.

6

Thomas Sutton's Commentary on the Categories
according to MS Oxford, Merton College 289

Alessandro D. Conti
University of Pisa

The first item in MS Oxford, Merton College 289 (=Q),[1] fols. 1r-31v, is a commentary on Aristotle's Categories, preserved there without ascription, but if we compare this text with W. Seńko's description of the commentary on the Categories extant in MS Wrocław, University Library IV.Q.3,[2] with an ascription to Thomas Sutton,[3] we can readily see that they are two copies of the same work. MS Merton College 289 thus contains a second, until now unrecognized, copy of Sutton's commentary on the Categories. My purpose here is to give a short account of this work, based on the Oxford manuscript, trying to place it within the historical and doctrinal context of commentaries on that text.

1. According to Mr. Seńko,[4] this commentary could have been written by Sutton before the year 1282. This is a conjecture, and we can only fix the *terminus post quem* of composition with certainty to the year 1270, when Thomas Aquinas wrote the First Part of the Second Part of his Summa Theologiae,[5] a short passage from which is silently incorporated into Sutton's commentary in speaking of quality.[6]

Notwithstanding this obvious dependence on Aqinas, the main source of the work appears to be the commentary on the Categories of Simplicius.[7] In fact, many times Simplicius is mentioned by name and quoted verbatim as an auctoritas,[8] and, with regard to teaching, Sutton accepts Simplicius' basically nominalist interpretation of the Categories. The same judgment may be made, but to a lesser degree, in regard to Boethius, whose commentary on

The Rise of British Logic, ed. P. Osmund Lewry, O.P., Papers in Mediaeval Studies 7 (Toronto: Pontifical Institute of Mediaeval Studies, 1985), pp. 173-213. © P.I.M.S., 1985.

the Categories substantially agrees with that of Simplicius in the general evaluation of the treatise and in the explanation of many particular points.

On the other hand, no explicit mention is made of contemporary authors, whose positions on the Categories are not directly discussed by Sutton. However, this does not mean that his commentary is merely a simple repetition of the views of Simplicius and Boethius: in fact, it is possible to recognize in it personal conceptions and problems and solutions proper to medieval exposition of the text, as in the case of the table of categories and the handling of substance, quantity, relation and quality. For a better understanding of Sutton's theory of categories, it could, thus, be useful to compare it both with Simplicius' interpretation of the Categories and that which was standard in the Middle Ages at the time of Sutton.

2. The main goal of Simplicius' exposition of the categories was to show the possibility of a reconciliation and integration between the philosophies of Plato and Aristotle.[9] In order to achieve this task, like Porphyry, Simplicius assumed: (a) a sharp division in spheres and procedures between logic and metaphysics, the former having as its concern demonstration and language, the latter beings as they are in the real order; and (b) a difference of fields of interest between Plato and Aristotle, the former being interested in metaphysics and theology, the latter in logic and natural philosophy.[10] The consequence of this for the interpretation of the categories was that the skopòs of the book was identified as dealing with non-compounded utterances in their capacity for being significant.[11] In this way, it was possible to reconcile with the Platonic position some Aristotelian statements that, in fact, have the opposite sense. This is the case with the primacy of the individual substance in relation to the universal.[12] According to Simplicius,[13] in the Categories individual substances are called 'primary' and universals 'secondary' because from a logical point of view, what is individual is first, as it is the first to fall under our knowledge and to receive a name; but naturally, from a metaphysical point of view, what is universal comes before the individual in virtue of its more stable and higher mode of existence.

Other capital points of Simplicius' interpretation are the following: (i) the theory of the categories is the foundation of logic, as the non-compounded utterances with which the Categories deals are the basic constituents of demonstration; (ii) the table of categories has also an ontological value, because the same ten basic kinds of reality can be distinguished in the sensible world; (iii) the ten highest genera are the first principles of that sensible world; (iv) the categories have a similar internal structure based on genera, differences and species; (v) the division into categories can be reduced to the division into substance and accidents;[14] (vi) there are at least three types of universals, separate universals, material universals and mental universals; (vii) the relationships between genera and species, universals and individuals, are dynamic and not static, since that which is more universal produces that which is less; (viii) the constitutive principle of the category of pros ti is the schesis (relation), an accidental form that is inherent and joins two distinct entities making them relatives and mutually dependent in virtue of some aspect of their nature; (ix) the four species of quality are related to their genus as to a focus (they are pros hen legomena), and descend from it according to different modalities.

3. The Neoplatonic interpretation of the Categories, of which the commentary of Simplicius is the finest expression, was transmitted, not without some simplification, through the mediation of Boethius' commentary to the thinkers of the Middle Ages and influenced them in more than one respect. Nevertheless, there are some very important points of disagreement between the Neoplatonists and the medievals in their reading of the work, especially with regard to its subject. In fact, according to most authors of the thirteenth century (e.g., Johannes Pagus, Nicholas of Paris, Gerard of Nogent,[15] Albert the Great[16] and Simon of Faversham[17]), the Categories deals with ens dicibile incomplexum ordinabile in genere and not with voces precisely as they are significant.[18]

I am not able to indicate with certainty the reasons for such a change from a nominalist to a realist point of view in the evaluation of this Aristotelian treatise. I can only advance some suggestion that might explain the shift: (i) the Arab thinkers, who had a certain influence on the medievals, introduced a conception of logic quite different from that of the Neoplatonists which Boethius knew; (ii) because of the very success of the Neoplatonic enterprise in reconciling and integrating the philosophies of Plato and Aristotle and because of the lack of direct knowledge of the Platonic corpus,[19] the medievals could not be aware of all the differences between the two Greek philosophers, and so had no impetus to deprive the Categories of metaphysical implications; (iii) the importance of the role of the proper subject of a science in giving it status, unity and distinction,[20] required a more unified and higher subject for the science of the categories than utterances precisely as significant.

An important consequence of seeing *ens* *dicibile* *incomplexum* *ordinabile* *in* *genere* as the subject-matter of the *Categories* was the new value attributed to the theory of equivocity, univocity and denomination in the first chapter. The theory is considered by Albert the Great,[21] for example, as having also a metaphysical side -- something unknown to Simplicius and Boethius -- inasmuch as the theory of equivocity explains the relationship between being (*ens*) and the ten highest genera; the theory of univocity explains the internal relations among the items of each categorial field; that of denomination the relationship that links the genera of accidents to the genus of substance. In this way, what according to the Neoplatonists was a theory about the relations between terms and things, became principally a theory about certain particular relations between different kinds of entities in the real order.[22]

Other differences in the doctrine of the categories between Neoplatonist and medieval thinkers are the following: (i) The medievals had theological preoccupations obviously lacking to the Neoplatonists; thus, the medievals usually try to clarify the relationship between God and the ten highest genera by discussing the possibility of placing God within the categorial field of substance; they are also particularly interested in the problem of the kinds and degrees of reality of relations and relatives that play an important role in speculation about the Trinity. (ii) The medievals do in a certain way maintain the Neoplatonic multiplication of universals, inasmuch as they usually admit the existence of universals *ante* *rem*, *in* *re* and *post* *rem*,[23] but, under the influence of Arabic thinkers and particularly of Avicenna, the universals are now conceived as essences or common natures in themselves prior to any division into universality and individuality. Thus, the common theory of that period about the existence of universals -- upheld, for example, by Albert the Great, Thomas Aquinas and Giles of Rome -- asserted that things are universals *in* *potentia* and become universals in act (*actu*) only by virtue of an act of intellection of the human mind. (iii) The relationships between universals and individuals, and of universals among themselves, become static, while they were dynamic with the Neoplatonists, for medieval philosophers consider genera as parts in relation to species, and these in turn as parts in relation to individuals, rather than causes producing them.

What is unchanged, by contrast, is the doctrine of the metaphysical status of the ten categories as supreme genera. Nobody in this period calls in question the ontological value of the table of the categories, the status of the ten supreme genera as first principles of reality; all agree that the categories are similarly structured and that accident functions as a meta-genus.

4. The novelty and peculiarity of Thomas Sutton by comparison with both Simplicius' and the common medieval approach to the _Categories_ lies in his use of an instrument of modern logic like the theory of supposition in solving particular problems of the text, and in his greater sensitivity to the logico-linguistic questions. This is particularly evident in the prologue to his commentary, where Sutton introduces a little digression on the theory of supposition and its usefulness in distinguishing logic from grammar. Otherwise, when he is dealing with the major topics of the _Categories_, he adopts an eclectic position: following Simplicius (and Boethius) on the question of the subject of the book; sharing the traditional position on the question of the metaphysical status of differences, the list of categories and the supreme genera; and following Thomas Aquinas on relation and quality. [24] In view of this, we shall concentrate our attention mainly on certain aspects of the prologue and on the question of the subject-matter of the _Categories_, as they are the elements characterizing Sutton's personal views.

4.1 Although he does not discuss the common position of his time on the question of the subject of the book, it is hard to believe that he did not know it. We may assume that he follows Simplicius and Boethius on this matter, not because of his ignorance of common opinion, but from deliberate choice. In fact, many times, in different parts of the commentary, Sutton gives us the reasons for his choice. They are of two kinds: one is extra-textual and the other textual. The extra-textual reason can be summarized as follows: logic deals with the syllogism and second intentions inasmuch as they are attributable to first intentions; but both the syllogism and second intentions are utterances, the former compounded utterances, the latter simple utterances; whence, the _Categories_ too, being a text of logic, must treat of utterances, and specifically of non-compounded utterances, which are the basic components of the syllogism, just as the _Categories_ is the basic and introductory book among those constituting logic. [25] In conclusion, then, to admit that the _Categories_ is directly concerned with things would be to destroy the homogeneity and unity of logic as a science.

There are also four important pieces of textual evidence adduced by Sutton in favour of a nominalist interpretation of the book: (i) In the second chapter, Aristotle gives a fourfold division of things into universal substance, individual substance, universal accident and individual accident; but universality and individuality, even when they are grounded in things, derive their reality from the modes of signification of terms. If the division were concerned with things inasmuch as they are things, and not inasmuch as they are receptive of second intentions and are signified by terms, it would be sufficient to divide things into substance and accident alone.[26] (ii) In the fourth chapter, when he introduces the table of the categories, Aristotle says that it is a division of what is said (eorum quae dicuntur) — and certainly it is utterances that are said and not things -- and that each one of the items of the division signifies either as a substance or as a quantity, etc. — and only utterances can signify, things being rather the signified.[27] (iii) This latter consideration also holds for an important passage in the fifth chapter, where Aristotle asserts that the individual substance signifies hoc aliquid and the universal only quale quid: because it is terms alone that can signify, it is evident that in this passage Aristotle refers to the names of individual and universal substances.[28] (iv) Finally, in chapter seven, in dealing with relatives, Aristotle many times explicitly refers to terms.[29] Therefore, the obvious conclusion from an analysis of the text is, according to Sutton, that the Categories is concerned with non-compounded utterances and more particularly with the decem primae voces decem prima genera rerum significantes.

But this does not mean that the treatise does not deal with things in any sense. In fact, the book is concerned with utterances of first imposition, which directly refer to and have supposition for things, and it is not possible to deal with such terms without at the same time dealing with the things signified themselves. So Sutton can conclude that 'multa dicta Aristotelis verificantur in hoc libro pro rebus ipsis et non pro vocibus.'[30] In this way, he tries to reconcile his nominalist reading of the treatise with the many parts of the text clearly devoted to ontology and physics.

4.2 To maintain that logic deals with utterance, entails the problem of carefully distinguishing logic from grammar, which is also concerned with utterances. To say that the business of grammar is to establish the congruitas of speech, while that of logic is to establish the correctness of syllogistic demonstration, would not be sufficient. In view of this, Sutton introduces a distinction based on the different supposition of subject-terms in statements pertaining to grammar and to logic. While the subject-terms of sentences concerned with grammatical matters are in material supposition, the subject-terms of logical sentences are in simple supposition. In fact, these are respectively the kinds of supposition allowed by the terms of second imposition used by grammar and logic. Terms like 'verbum' and 'nomen', which signify the modes of signification on the part of the terms signifying ('significant modos significandi ex parte nominum significantium'), can only have as subject a term in material supposition; while terms like 'species' and 'genus', which signify the modes of signifying on the part of the thing signified ('ex parte rei significatae'), can only have as subject a term in simple supposition.[31]

In this way, the distinction between logic and grammar is situated in that reference to reality peculiar to logic but lacking in grammar. Like Simplicius and Boethius, Sutton links logic and metaphysics, because simple supposition, which he sees as characteristic of logical speech, implies a reference to those universal things with which metaphysics is also concerned. This connection between logic and metaphysics introduces into a nominalist context that principle of isomorphism of language and reality which was the main presupposition of every realist interpretation of the _Categories_ and which is obviously in contrast with his nominalist reading of the book. On the other hand, this principle is consonant with Sutton's interpretation of many particular points of the treatise, such as the table of categories and the account of substance, quantity, relation and quality, and it is in line with the statement in the prologue that many parts of the treatise are about things and not utterances. So, in conclusion, the implicit assumption of this principle of the isomorphism of language and reality is one of the clearest manifestations of the ambiguity that pervades Sutton's interpretation.[32]

4.3 The keystone of Sutton's realist reading of many points of the treatise lies in his judgment about the value of the table of the categories in chapter four. On his reading, the division into categories is a division of things existing _extra animam_: in reality itself there are ten different kinds of things, each irreducible to the others.[33] He will often come back to this subject: for example when, in commenting on the seventh chapter, he maintains that certain kinds of relationship, like paternity and slavery, have a real existence.[34] The Dominican master argues there that relations and relatives are also _res_ existing _extra animam_ because the ten supreme genera and everything belonging to the categorical fields are realities of this kind.

Like other authors of the thirteenth century, Sutton also gives us a justification of the _sufficientia praedicamentorum_. The majority of thinkers of that period (e.g. Albert the Great,[35] Simon of Faversham[36] and Henry of Ghent[37]) based their method of finding the ten categories on the differences of essences and modes of being (_modi essendi_), and divided the nine categories of accidents into two main groups, in the first of which (that of the accidents of inherence properly so called) they placed quantity and quality alone. Sutton, on the other hand, following the method and grouping employed by Thomas Aquinas in his commentary on the _Metaphysics_ (book 5, _lectio_ 9), finds the basis of the ten categories in their different _modi praedicandi_ and also places relation in the first group of accidents with quantity and quality.[38]

4.3.1 Another important question closely connected with the treatment of the table of categories is that of which entities fall within the various categorical fields, whether only simple accidental forms or also the compound entities caused by simple accidental forms when they inhere in substances: _quanta_, _relativa_, and _qualia_. Sutton, like all the commentators on the _Categories_ till that time, does not directly discuss this problem, but throughout his commentary, in speaking of quantity, relation and quality, he seems to admit that both kinds of accidents, simple forms and compound, fall within the categorical fields _in the same way_. Such a position raises two difficulties for the doctrine of the categories, which, regrettably, Sutton does not treat: (i) it reduces the distinction among the categorial fields, as the accidental compounds are realities less distinct one from the other than the simple accidental forms; and (ii) it presupposes that within each categorial field there are two different groups of entities, simple and compound, each irreducible to the other, and so, in a certain way, two different supreme genera.

4.4 Much of Sutton's interpretation of the Aristotelian treatise is very little marked by his personal position, as the English master substantially agrees with the common reading of the doctrine of the categories adopted in the thirteenth century and, on particular points, follows the interpretation of Simplicius or that of Boethius. Thus, for example, in dealing with the problem of the nature of substantial difference, Sutton,[39] like Boethius, claims that substantial differences are something in between substance and quality, because like primary substances they are not _in_ a subject but unlike secondary substances they are not essentially predicated _of_ the individual substances. Also, in dealing with relatives, he does not wholly embrace the theory of Simplicius,[40] according to which relation is an accidental form that inheres in two distinct subjects at the time, but, like all the authors of his time,[41] he seems to think that a relation inheres only in one substance and _refers_ to the other. However, he agrees with the Neoplatonist commentators in defending the reality of relation and its distinction from the _fundamentum_ (that is the accidental form by which it inheres in substance).

5. As far as I know, Sutton's commentary represents one of the few attempts in the thirteenth century to use the instruments of the _logica modernorum_ in the context of the doctrine of the categories and one of the few to give a nominalist interpretation to the treatise. But, as we have seen, the attempt partially fails in achieving its goal, because Sutton, trying to be faithful to Aristotle, accepts on many points of the text the common medieval reading which is realist. In this way, there is a conflict between his general evaluation of the _Categories_ and his interpretation of particular doctrines (like the table of categories, the doctrine of substance, quantity, etc.), especially in his explanation of the peculiar properties of each category. Furthermore, in spite of his nominalist evaluation of the treatise, Sutton does not say anything about the significance of the doctrine of the categories for the analysis of language. His interpretation thus leads to the paradox that Aristotle, while wishing to treat non-compounded utterances precisely as significant, in effect develops a set of ontological and physical theories.

In order to have a coherent nominalist interpretation and exposition of the _Categories_, we must wait for Ockham, who in detaching himself from the real Aristotelian intention will consider the division into ten categories to be a division of terms alone and not of things too and will translate statements on the ontological and physical status of substances, quantities, etc., into rules for the correct use of terms. In this fashion, the level of language in the _Categories_ is raised a step, the necessary presupposition of any coherently nominalist interpretation of the text.

Notes

[1] For the description of this manuscript see H.O. Coxe, _Catalogus codicum manuscriptorum qui in collegiis aulisque Oxoniensibus hodie_

adservantur 1 (Oxford, 1852), pp. 114-15; and F.M. Powicke, The Medieval Books of Merton College (Oxford, 1931), p.153, no. 515.

2 Władysław Seńko, 'Le commentaire de Thomas Sutton sur le Catégories d'Aristote dans le ms. IV Q 3 de la Bibliothèque de l'Université de Wrocław', Mediaevalia philosophica Polonorum 4 (1959) 35-38.

3 On Thomas Sutton's life and works and for bibliography see Johannes Schneider ed., Thomas von Sutton, Quaestiones ordinarie (Bayerische Akademie der Wissenschaften, Veröffentlichungen der Kommission für die Herausgabe ungedruckter Texte aus der mitteralterlichen Geisteswelt 3; Munich, 1977), pp. 15*-267*; W.Seńko, 'Trzy studia nad spuscizną i poglądami Tomasza Suttona dotyczącymi problemu istoty i istnienia', Studia mediewistyczne 11 (1970) 111-52; BRUO 3.1824-25.

4 Seńko, 'Trzy studia...', p. 119.

5 Cf. James A. Weisheipl, Friar Thomas d'Aquino, His Life, Thought and Works (Garden City, N.Y., 1974), pp. 221-22.

6 Cf. Thomas Sutton, In Categorias, Q fol. 23rb; Thomas Aquinas, Summa theologiae I-II. q. 49, a. 2.

7 Cf. Sten Ebbesen, 'Hoc aliquid - quale quid and the Signification of Appellatives', ΦΙΛΟΣΟΦΙΑ 5-6 (1975-76) 373, where this use of Simplicius is already noted.

8 Cf. Sutton, In Cat., Q fols. 3rb, 5va, 6va, 9ra, 12va, 17ra, 20va, 20vb, 21ra, 21rb, 22vb, 23ra, 23rb, 23vb, 29vb.

9 On this topic see A.C. Lloyd, 'Neoplatonic logic and Aristotelian logic', Phroneses 1 (1955-56), 58-59.

10 Cf. Karl Kalbfleisch ed., Simplicii in Aristotelis Categorias commentarium (Commentaria in Aristotelem Graeca 8; Berlin, 1907), pp. 6 (27-30), 7 (29-32).

11 Cf. ibid., pp. 9 (4)-13 (26).

12 Cf. Aristotle, Categoriae 5, 2a11–3a7.

13 Cf. Simplicius, In Cat., pp. 80 (17)–82 (22).

14 In this way accident is conceived as a meta-genus to which the nine categories apart from substance are subordinate.

15 Cf. Patrick Osmund Lewry, 'Robert Kilwardby's Writings on the Logia vetus studied with regard to their teaching and method' (unpublished Oxford Univ. D.Phil. thesis, 1978), p. 91.

16 Alberti Magni Liber de praedicamentis, tract. 1, cap. 1, in A. Borgnet ed., B. Alberti Magni Opera omnia 1 (Paris, 1890), p. 150a (P. Jammy ed., Lyons, 1751, vol. 1, p. 95); cf. ibid., cap. 7, p. 163b (Jammy, p. 103).

17 Quaestiones super libro Praedicamentorum, q. 1, in P. Mazzarella ed., Magistri Simonis Anglici sive de Faverisham Opera omnia 1 (Pubblicazioni dell'Istituto Universitario de Magistero di Catania, Serie filosofica, Testi critici 1; Padua, 1957), pp. 72–74.

18 This same interpretation was maintained in the fourteenth century by Walter Burley, In Categorias, prooemium, Expositio super artem veterem (Venice, 1509), fol. 17va.

19 On this subject see Raymond Klibansky, The Continuity of the Platonic Tradition during the Middle Ages (London, 1939).

20 See Sten Ebbesen and Jan Pinborg, 'Bartholomew of Bruges and His Sophisma on the Nature of Logic', CIMAGL 39 (1981) viii–ix.

21 Alberti Magni Liber de praedicamentis, tract. 1, cap. 2, ed. Borgnet, 1.151–52 (ed. Jammy, 1.96–97).

22 Walter Burley also followed this theory; cf. In Cat., cap. de aequivocis, ed. cit., fol. 18vb.

23 Cf., for example, Clemens Stroick ed., Alberti Magni De anima 1, tract. 1, cap. 4, in Alberti Magni Opera omnia 7.1 (Münster i.W, 1968), p. 8 (81–90).

24 Cf. Sutton, In Cat., Q fols. 19^{va-b}, 20^{va-b}, 23rb, and Thomas Aquinas, Summa theologiae I, q. 13, a. 7; q. 42, a. 1; I-II, q. 49, a. 2.

25 Cf. Sutton, In Cat., Q fol. 3va.

26 Ibid., fol. 5^{va-b}.

27 Ibid., fol. 6va.

28 Ibid., fol. 11^{ra-va}.

29 Ibid., fols. 16va-22va, passim.

30 Ibid., fol. 3va.

31 Ibid., fol. 2rb.

32 Sutton also uses the theory of supposition for solving, in an elegant way, the old problem of giving an answer to the question, why one cannot infer from 'homo est animal' and 'animal est genus' that 'homo est genus', a common topic in the explanation of Categories 3. He says quite simply that this conclusion does not follow from the premises because the middle-term 'animal' has different suppositions, personal in the first case, simple in the second (Q fol. 2rb).

33 Cf. Sutton, In Cat., Q fols. 7ra, 19va.

34 Ibid., fol. 19va.

35 Alberti Magni Liber de praedicamentis, tract. 1, cap. 7, ed. Borgnet 1.165-65 (ed. Jammy, 1.103).

36 Quaestiones super libro praedicamentorum, qq. 1, 12, 13, 20, ed. Mazzarella, 1.73, 83-84, 86-87, 93.

37 On the sufficientia praedicamentorum in Henry of Ghent see Jean Paulus, Henri de Gand: Essai sur les tendences de sa métaphysique (Études de philosophie médiévale 25; Paris, 1938), pp. 152-63.

[38] Sutton, In Cat., Q fol. 7ra.

[39] Ibid., fol. 10^{va-b}.

[40] On Simplicius' theory of relatives see A.D. Conti, 'La teoria della relazione nei commentatori neoplatonici delle Categorie di Aristotele', Rivista critica di storia della filosofia 38 (1983) 259-83.

[41] Cf., for example, Alberti Magni Liber de praedicamentis, tract. 4, cap. 10, ed. Borgnet 1.241 (ed. Jammy 1.153); Simonis de Faverisham Quaestiones super libro Praedicamentorum, q. 43, ed. Mazzarella, 1.137-48.

TEXTS*

Thomas Sutton, In Categorias
(MS Oxford, Merton Cllege 289, fols. 1vb -30ra, extracts)

<Prologus>

(1vb) Secundo queritur utrum logica sit de intentionibus secundis vel de intentionibus primis. ...

(2ra) ... Responsio. Dicendum quod logica est de intentionibus secundis quae sunt communes et applicabiles primis intentionibus, sicut dicit Avicenna quod logica est de secundis intentionibus adiunctis <primis>.

Ad cuius intellectum videndum est quae sunt primae intentiones et quae secundae. Sicut autem dicit Boethius in principio commenti super Praedicamenta, rebus in propria natura manentibus, solum genus humanum exstitit quod eis nomina posset imponere. Unde factum est ut sigillatim omnia prosecutus animus humanus singulis vo`ca´bula rebus aptaret. Et hoc quidem corpus subsistens vocavit hominem, illud vero lapidem, aliud vero lignum. Mensuram vero corporis aliam bipedalem, aliam tripedalem vocavit. Sensibile autem visus hoc vocavit album, illud vero nigrum. Et sic de speciebus uniuscuiusque predicamenti. Quia vero vidit quod species diversae unius praedicamenti conveniunt in aliquo communi, ut homo, equus, leo et huiusmodi conveniunt in natura sensitiva, imposuit illi communi nomen, quo tota multitudo habentium naturam sensitivam vocaretur, scilicet hoc nomen 'animal'. Et eodem modo imposita <sunt> nomina generum superiorum usque[1] ad genus supremum, quod est substantia. Simili autem modo processit ad imponendum nomina tam generalia quam specialia in aliis novem praedicamentis, quae quidem nomina significant genera et species in illis praedicamentis. Ista igitur nomina quae sic significant res decem generum sunt nomina primae impositionis, propter hoc quod prima intentio impositoris fuit nomina rebus imponere quae erant sensibiles et magis manifestae. De istis autem rebus sic significatis sunt speciales scientiae reales, ... Invenit etiam impositor quaedam esse[2] communia non solum rebus unius praedicamenti, sed rebus omnium praedicamentorum, et illis communibus imposuit nomina quae vocamus transcendentia, quia in communitate excedunt omnia[3] alia nomina. Huiusmodi sunt: 'ens', 'unum', 'multum', 'accidens', 'potentia', 'principium', 'causa', 'contrarium' et huiusmodi. Et ista etiam nomina, quia sunt in potentia rebus, sunt primae impositionis. De istis autem communibus non potuit esse aliqua scientia specialis, sed metaphysica, quae est communis scientia, tractat de istis.

Post impositionem vero omnium praedicamentorum nominum significantium res, reversus est impositor ad imponendum vocabula praedictis nominibus. Sicut enim multae res conveniunt in aliquo communi, et propter hoc illi communi imponebatur nomen quod dicitur de illis multis rebus, ita videtur quod multa nomina conveniunt <in> uno modo significandi, et alia vocabula conveniunt in alio, + ad significandum alia nomina rerum imposuit nomina rerum, sed nomina nominum seu vocabulorum +. Illa vero vocabula quae significant sine tempore vocavit communi vocabulo 'nomen'; quae autem significant cum tempore alio vocabulo appellavit, scilicet 'verbum'; quod autem praedicatur de pluribus 'universale'; quod autem de uno solo 'singulare' vel 'individuum', et sic de aliis. Et ista dicuntur nomina secundae impositionis, quia eorum impositio[4] (2rb) fuit posterior quam impositio nominum quae res significant. Dicuntur etiam secundae intentiones vel propter illam causam vel quia non significant veras res, sed ea quae esse debile habent, quae dicuntur intentiones, sicut species coloris in medio dicitur non habere esse reale, sed esse intentionale. Et quia istae secundae intentiones sunt communes nominibus primae impositionis, quaedam generalibus et quaedam specialibus, quibus[dam] utuntur in scientiis realibus, ideo de istis <est> scientia communis quae est logica. Non enim potuit uti specialibus terminis, de quibus[5] est scientia specialis, nec etiam terminis transcendentibus, de quibus tractat metaphysica; et ideo necessario habet tractare de secundis intentionibus, quae sunt nomina nominum primae impositionis, ex quibus fiunt syllogismi in scientiis realibus. ...

Sed inter nomina secundarum intentionum consideranda est quaedam differentia. Quaedam enim eorum dicuntur de nominibus primae impositionis, sed non pro rebus significatis, sed pro nominibus significantibus, ut cum dicitur 'homo est nomen', 'currit est verbum'. Quaedam vero dicuntur de nominibus primae impositionis, sed non pro ipsis nominibus significantibus, sed pro rebus significatis, ut cum dicitur 'homo est species', 'animal est genus'. Non enim est hoc nomen 'homo' species,[6] neque hoc nomen 'animal' genus, sed res significata sic abstracta <ab> individuis per hoc nomen 'homo' est species, et res significata abstracta[7] a speciebus per hoc nomen 'animal' est genus. Quaedam enim nomina secundarum intentionum dicuntur de nominibus primae impositionis, et quandoque pro nominibus ipsis significantibus, quandoque pro rebus significatis. Cum enim dicitur 'canis est aequivocum' accipitur 'aequivocum' pro nomine aequivoco, cum autem dicitur "aequivoca dicuntur quorum nomen solum commune est, ratio `autem´ secundum illud nomen diversa", res dicuntur aequivocae. Similiter autem 'universale' et 'singulare' dicuntur tam de rebus quam de nominibus. Sunt enim quidam termini universales ut 'homo', 'animal'; quidam vero singulares, ut 'Socrates', 'Plato'. Rerum etiam quaedam sunt universales, quaedam singulares, ut dicit Aristoteles, I Perihermenias. Huius autem diversitatis ratio est quia quaedam nomina secundarum intentionum significant modos significandi ex parte nominum significantium, ut 'nomen', 'verbum', 'adiectivum', 'sostantivum', 'appellativum' et huiusmodi; et omnia talia accipiuntur pro vocabulis primae impositionis significantibus, et non pro rebus significatis. Alia vero nomina significant modos significandi vocabulorum, sed non ex parte vocis significantis, sed ex parte rei significatae, ut 'genus', 'species', 'differentia', 'proprium' et 'accidens', 'definitio' et 'definitum', et huiusmodi; et ideo ista dicuntur de rebus significatis per nomina primae impositionis. Et ex ista diversitate consequitur quaedam diversitas terminorum quantum ad suppositionem. Unde enim nomen primae impositionis subicitur in oratione et praedicatur de ipso nomen secundae impositionis importans modum aliquem significandi vel aliquid aliud[8] quod se tenet ex parte nominis significantis, et non ex parte rei significatae, ut cum dicitur 'homo est nomen' vel 'homo est disyllabum', subiectum habet suppositionem materialem. Et dicitur suppositio materialis quando terminus stat pro voce sua et non pro re quam significat. Et ex hoc contingit fallacia ex variatione suppositionis terminorum: 'homo est disyllabum; Socrates est homo; ergo Socrates est disyllabum'. Est enim hic fallacia figurae dictionis ex variata (2va) suppositione, quia in prima 'homo' habet suppositionem materialem pro[9] ipsa voce, in secunda habet suppositionem formalem, et stat pro re significata. Quando vero nomen primae impositionis subicitur et praedicatur nomen secundae intentionis quod significat aliquam rationem quae convenit rei significatae — ut cum dicitur 'homo est species', 'animal est genus' — tunc subiectum habet suppositionem formalem, quia non stat materialiter pro voce, sed formaliter pro re significata. Non tamen supponit suum significatum pro aliquo suo supposito, et ideo non habet suppositionem personalem, sed simplicem. Et secundum istam diversitatem provenit quandoque fallacia figurae dictionis, ut hic: 'animal est genus; homo et animal; ergo homo est genus'. In prima enim 'animal' habet suppositionem simplicem, in secunda personalem; et ita variatur suppositio.

<Prooemium expositionis super **Praedicamenta**>

(2va) ...Visis istis generalibus de logica quaerenda sunt quaedam specialiter circa librum **Praedicamentorum**. Sunt autem in principio tria quaerenda: primo, utrum scientia praedicamentorum pertineat ad logicam; secundo, utrum sit de vocibus aut de rebus; <tertio>, utrum sit una scientia....

(3ra) Ad secundum sic proceditur. Videtur quod iste liber sit de rebus et non de vocibus. Substantia, quantitas, qualitas et alia praedicamenta sunt res significatae per voces primae impositionis; sed de decem praedicamentis est iste liber; igitur est de rebus et non de vocibus.

Praeterea, Aristoteles volens descendere[10] ad ea de quibus determinat, praemittit istam divisionem: "eorum quae sunt haec quidem de subiecto quodam dicuntur, in subiecto vero nullo <sunt", etc.>. Manifestum est autem quod haec divisio est entis quod est vera res in sua contenta, et non est divisio vocis. Hic igitur determinat de rebus, non autem de vocibus.

Praeterea, dicta Aristotelis in hoc libro non possunt verificari de vocibus, sed de rebus; puta quod substantia non est in subiecto, et quantitas alia est continua alia discreta, et sic de aliis. Sed dicta sua sunt vera de illis quae hic determinantur; igitur liber iste non est de vocibus <***> sed iste liber non est [per] grammatice sed syllogistice, igitur non est de vocibus, sed de rebus.

Praeterea, iste liber principaliter ordinatur ad demonstrationem sicut ad finem; in demonstratione autem concluditur passio de subiecto per medium quod est causa; ista autem sunt res. Igitur iste liber est de rebus.

Praeterea, ubi non determinatur de vocibus nisi propter docere et addiscere res, ibi non est principalis intentio de vocibus, sed de rebus — ut patet de scientia naturali et de scientiis mathematicis — sed logica non considerat voces nisi quia non potest doceri et addisci nisi per voces docentis et addiscentis — si enim aliter posset doceri non curaret de vocibus—; igitur principalis intentio logici non est (3rb) de vocibus, sed tantum de rebus, et per accidens de vocibus.

Contra: Boethius dicit quod Aristoteles agit hic de primis ˙decem´ vocibus decem genera prima rerum significantibus, in eo quod significantes sunt.

Responsio. Dicendum quod quidam posuerunt hunc librum esse de rebus, quae per voces significantur. Alii autem dixerunt ipsum esse de nominibus, ipsas res significantibus. Alii autem neque de nominibus significantibus neque de rebus significatis, sed de conceptibus simplicibus. Et omnes istae tres opiniones allegant pro se verba Aristotelis. Qui enim ponunt istum librum esse de vocibus significativis rerum confirmant dictum per illud quod Aristoteles dicit: "eorum quae dicuntur haec quidem cum complexione dicuntur". Et iterum, subdividens alterum membrum in decem voces, dicit: "eorum quae[11] secundum nullam complexionem dicuntur" <etc.>, "singula igitur horum quae dicta sunt, ipsa quidem secundum se in nulla affirmatione dicuntur; <ex> complexione autem horum ad invicem affirmatio fit". Quia igitur complexa et incomplexa non sunt res, sed voces, neque etiam res significat, sed vox, neque [in] affirmatio fit <ex> complexione rerum, sed vocum, manifestum est quod Aristoteles loquitur de vocibus incomplexis, significantibus decem praedicamenta. Alii vero qui ponunt hunc librum esse de rebus allegant pro se Aristotelem — ut patuit in opponendo. Similiter vero qui dicunt librum esse de simplicibus conceptibus adducunt pro se Aristotelem, qui dividit ea quae dicuntur in dicta secundum complexionem et in dicta sine complexione. Quae autem dicuntur sunt conceptus rerum, non res ipsae.

Simplicius autem dicit quod omnes isti in parte verum dicunt, propter quod omnes Aristotelem pro teste habent. Unusquisque tamen eorum in parte

attingit intentionem libri. Non enim est iste liber de vocibus nudis, neque de
entibus in quantum entia, neque de conceptibus solum, sed est de vocibus
simplicibus in quantum significant res mediantibus simplicibus conceptibus.
Ubi enim determinatur de dictionibus secundum quod significant <res>, necesse
est res significatas admitti[12] et etiam conceptus simplices mediantibus quibus
res significantur per voces. Voces enim primo significant conceptus animae
et secundario ipsas res; et ideo non potest tradi cognitio vocum significantium
in quantum significantes sunt nisi simul tradatur cognitio rerum quae
significantur. Similiter, quia hic non determinat de rebus praedicamentorum
nisi in quantum significantur per voces, ideo non est hic intentio libri
determinare solum de rebus secundum quod res. Sed cum hic est intentio de
vocibus significantibus, quae res significant, prout illae voces et res sunt
necessariae ad ratiocinandum <***>. De conceptibus autem secundum quod
conceptus sunt, eorum cognitio pertinet ad librum De anima, cum conceptus
sint operationes animae, et non pertinet eorum cognitio ad logicum, nisi
secundum quod voces significant conceptus et mediantibus ipsis significant res,
quarum sunt conceptus. Propter quod Simplicius, comprehendens praecise
intentionem libri, dicit quod intentio in hoc libro est docere de simplicibus[13]
et primis et generalibus vocibus secundum quod significativae sunt entium
quae sunt decem prima genera. Condoce<n>tur autem et res a vocibus
significatae et conceptus secundum quos significantur res per voces.

Et notandum est quod dicit quod voces significativae docentur, res autem
et conceptus condocentur, ad insinuandum quod iste liber magis proprie dicitur
sermocinalis, tamquam de sermone, quam realis, tamquam de rebus; sicut
autem tota logica est scientia sermocinalis. Ad cuius evidentiam considerandum
dum est quod quamvis homo possit per se invenire aliquas veritates, non
tamen est possibile quod aliquis per se inveniat aliquam scientia totam vel
pro maiori parte. Unde Commentator dicit quod nullus per se potest invenire
artes operativas aut speculativas in maiori parte, quia non complentur nisi per
iuvamentum[14] prioris ad sequentem, et nisi prior fuisset non esset sequens.
Et isto modo per longa tempora (3va) scientiae fuerunt inventa per hoc quod
prior aliquid invenit et docuit sequentem, et sequens aliquid addidit et docuit
posteriorem. Et ideo dicit Aristoteles quod iustum est reddere gratias non
solum illis qui bene dixerunt, cum quibus communicamus[15] in opinionibus, sed
etiam illis qui superficialiter enuntiaverunt, quia illi intellectum excitaverunt.
Propter hoc igitur necesse est dictam scientiam acquiri per doctrinam, qua
magister proponit discipulo principia et conclusiones sequentes secundum
debitum ordinem, deducendo a principiis notis ad conclusiones ignotas.

Quaedam quidem deductio est ratiocinatio in voce sive argumentatio; quia igitur argumentatio exterior per vocem est necessaria in qualibet scientia, ars argumentandi per sermonem debuit tradi in aliqua scientia, et non in aliqua scientia particulari, cum ista ars sit communis cuilibet scientiae.   Oportuit igitur esse scientiam communem quae esset de argumentatione exteriori sive de syllogismo, quae est potissima[16] species argumentandi; et haec est logica. Est igitur logica non solum rationalis scientia, a 'logos' quod est ratio, sed sermocinalis, a 'logos' quod est sermo.   Unde tota logica est de sermone complexo vel incomplexo, ...

Liber igitur Praedicamentorum, cum sit pars logicae, est de decem primis vocibus decem prima genera rerum significantibus -- ut dicit Boethius -- ut significantes sunt, et ut sunt praedicabiles et subicibiles, et prout aliae intentiones secundae eis conveniunt in ordine ad syllogismum.

His visis respondendum est ad argumenta. Ad primum dicendum quod verum est quod substantia, quantitas et caetera praedicamenta sunt res, sed istae res sunt significatae per voces primae impositionis, quibus conveniunt nomina secundae intentionis.   Sunt enim termini universales ex quibus formantur enunciationes in ordine ad syllogismum.   Et sic determinatur hic de praedicamentis, prout sunt partes syllogismi, et non tantum prout res sunt, sed prout significantur per voces.

Ad secundum patet per hoc idem <quod> non potest determinari de vocibus significativis rerum in quantum significativae sunt nisi simul dicantur multa de rebus significatis; et ideo non solum dividit voces, quae dicuntur, sed etiam entia, quae significantur.

Ad tertium dicendum quod quia determinat hic de praedicamentis prout significantur per voces primae impositionis, quae immediate significant res et supponunt pro rebus, ideo multa dicta Aristotelis verificantur in hoc libro pro rebus ipsis et non <pro> vocibus, quia voces primae impositionis non supponunt pro vocibus, sed pro rebus.   In sequentibus vero libris determinat de syllogismo et suis partibus non prout significantur per voces primae impositionis, sed per nomina secundarum intentionum, quae supponunt pro vocibus primae impositionis complexis; ut in libro Perihermenias <de> enuntiatione, affirmatione, negatione et huiusmodi, in libro Priorum de syllogismo variato per diversas figuras et per diversos modos.   Quia nomina secundarum intentionum non significant immediate res, sed voces significati-

vas[17] primae impositionis dant intelligere et pro ipsis supponunt, ideo dicta
Aristotelis in libris sequentibus verificantur pro nominibus primae impositionis
et non pro rebus significatis, sicut in hoc libro, qui determinat de nominibus
decem generum, quae sunt primae impositionis.   Unde in definitionibus
nominum secundarum intentionum ponitur vox; oratio enim est vox significativa, et similiter enuntiatio una est vox quae unum de uno significat.
Syllogismus <etiam> est oratio, et per consequens vox.   Patet igitur quod
multa <dicta> Aristotelis in logica verificantur pro vocibus significativis,
quamvis alia verificantur pro rebus prout per voces significantur in ordine ad
syllogismum.   Unde sequitur quod magis proprie dicitur logica esse de vocibus
significativis quam de rebus; et etiam iste liber Praedicamentorum est de
vocibus significativis, quamvis possit dici quod sit de (3vb) rebus prout per
voces significantur.

Ad quartum dicendum quod aliter est grammatica de vocibus et aliter
logica.   Grammatica enim docet quae dictiones sunt simplices et quae
compositae, quae primitivae et quae derivativae, et tales diversitates
pertinentes ad modum loquendi congrue; considerat etiam accidentia quae sunt
modi significandi, per quos partes orationis congrue convertuntur ad invicem.
Sed logica est de voce significativa, supponendo omnia ista a grammatico et
determinando de ea prout pertinet ad syllogismum; puta, quae est oratio
affirmativa, quae negativa, quae universalis, quae particularis, et quae sunt
contrariae et quae contradictoriae, et huiusmodi.   Et non est inconveniens de
voce esse diversas scientias, secundum diversas considerationes et proprietates
ipsius.

Ad quintum dicendum quod demonstrationis tres sunt termini: subiectum,
passio et medium, quod est causa.   Cum autem dicimus passionem concludi de
subiecto per medium, intelligimus quod una extremitas syllogismi concludi<tur>
de alia per medium.   Unde quamvis passio, subiectum et medium sint res
prout significantur per ista nomina primae impositionis, sunt tamen in
proposito voces significantes, quia accipiuntur pro tribus terminis syllogismi
demonstrativi.

Ad sextum dicendum quod non propter hoc determinat logica de voce
significativa vel sermone quia non potest sine sermone doceri vel addisci, sed
quia est scientia communis.   Ideo habet determinare de oratione et voce
prolata, et de suis partibus, quia talis <o>ratio est necessaria in omni
scientia; et ideo de illa est communis <scientia> quae est logica.   Sicut

grammatica, quae est scientia communis, determinat de congruitate sermonis, quae est necessaria in qualibet scientia.   Sicut enim in qualibet scientia requiritur quod homines congrue loquantur, ita requiritur in qualibet scientia quod recte ratiocinentur.   Communia autem in communi scientia determinari debent, sicut in metaphysica de ente et de his communibus quae sunt entis in quantum ens. ...

<Utrum scientia praedicamentorum sit una scientia>

Responsio.   Dicendum quod ista scientia de praedicamentis est una. Quando enim multa considerantur sub una ratione communi, de illis multis est scientia una; sicut visus est una potentia, quamvis multa vident, scilicet homines, asinos,[18] et lapides[19] et alia corpora, quae omnia conveniunt in una ratione (4ra) communi, quod est obiectum visus.   Conveniunt[20] autem praedicamenta in hoc quod significantur per dictionem incomplexam, quae est terminus in syllogismo.   Et sub hac ratione determinatur hic de praedicamentis, prout scilicet quodlibet eorum significatur per dictionem quae potest esse pars syllogismi.   Quia igitur sub una ratione formali determinatur de omnibus, ideo est una scientia.

Ad primum igitur dicendum quod haec scientia non est de vocibus et rebus tamquam diversis materiis, sed tamquam de una materia.   Non enim de vocibus ut voces sunt, nec de rebus ut res sunt, sed de vocibus prout significant res et de rebus prout significantur per voces.   Et ideo salvatur unitas scientiae.

Ad secundum dicendum quod decem praedicamenta sunt multa genera. Conveniunt tamen in una ratione communi, quae constituit unum genus, subiectum unius scientiae — ut dictum est.

Ad tertium <dicendum> quod decem primis generibus nihil reale est commune secundum univocationem quod sit primae intentionis.   Est tamen eis aliquid commune secundae intentionis, et secundum univocationem, quia quodlibet eorum est genus.   Et isto modo est eis commune significari per vocem incomplexam in ordine ad syllogismum.   Et haec est una ratio formalis per quam hic determinatur de praedicamentis; et propter hanc rationem unam haec scientia est una.

Ad quartum dicendum <quod> decem praedicamenta conveniunt in quodam communi, quod est intentionale. Nec oportet quod unitas intentionis accipiatur ab aliqua unitate rei, sed ab unitate secundum proportionem. Sic enim quodlibet praedicamentorum dicitur esse genus, quia sicut substantia praedicatur in quid de speciebus suis, ita quodlibet aliorum praedicatur in quid de speciebus sub se contentis. Et ita sicut <substantia> dicitur genus, ita et quodlibet aliorum, et eodem[21] modo. Dicendum quod significari per vocem incomplexam in ordine ad syllogismum `est´ una ratio intentionalis communis omnibus praedicamentis.

Ad quintum dicendum quod decem praedicamentis quaedam sunt communia quae sunt primae impositionis, et quaedam quae sunt secundae intentionis. Communia primae impositionis sunt ens et ea quae sunt entis; et sic de decem praedicamentis determinat metaphysica, quae est de ente in quantum ens ut de subiecto. Communia vero secundae intentionis sunt universale, dicibile, genus generalissimum, genus, significatum per vocem incomplexam, ordinabile in syllogismo et huiusmodi. Et quantum ad ista communia non tractat metaphysica de decem praedicamentis, sed logica. Et necesse fuit de decem praedicamentis determinare in logica quia decem praedicamenta omnes res in se continent; syllogismus autem est de omnibus rebus. Per hoc igitur quod habemus hanc scientiam praedicamentorum, habemus cognitionem cunctarum rerum quae pertinent ad logicam, quae est de syllogismo; et per <hoc quod> determinatur de decem vocibus decem praedicamenta significantibus in ordine ad syllogismum, habemus significationem cunctarum vocum res praedicamentorum significantium quantum pertinet ad logicum negotium.

<De subiecto et praedicato>

(5[va]) ...Dubitatur autem hic tripliciter. Et primo de hoc quod dicunt Boethius et Simplicius quod ista divisio est minima[22]; videtur enim quod posset fieri in pauciora, quia divisio entis in substantiam et accidens omnia entia comprehendit, et tamen est in pauciora quam divisio hic posita, sicut duo sunt pauciora quam quattuor. Ista igitur divisio non est in pauciora.

Ad hoc dicendum quod ista divisio est in pauciora quantum ad praesens spectat.[23] Hic enim agitur de praedicamentis non solum secundum quod sunt entia, sed ut <eis> conveniunt intentiones secundae quae sunt praedicari vel non-praedicari, esse-in vel non-esse-in, prout per voces significantur. Quamvis autem omne ens sit substantia vel accidens, tamen utrumque istorum significatur per vocem universaliter vel particulariter ... Prout enim substantia significatur universaliter est unum membrum, prout autem significatur singulariter est aliud membrum; similiter prout accidens significatur universaliter est tertium membrum divisionis, et prout significatur singulariter est quartum membrum. Et[24] ideo non potest divisio entis pauciora quam in quattuor coartari. Patet igitur quod divisio entis <in substantiam et accidens> non est sufficiens quo ad logicum, quia logicus considerat (5vb) significationes vocum; igitur tam substantia quam accidens dupliciter significatur, scilicet universaliter et singulariter, ut homo et hic homo, grammatica et haec grammatica.

<De ordine praedicati ad subiectum>

(6ra) ... Secundo cum dicit: "quando alterum de altero", ponit duas regulas de his quae dicuntur de subiecto. Secundam ponit ibi: "diversorum generum", etc.

Prima est haec: quando alterum de altero praedicatur ut de subiecto, quaecumque dicuntur de eo quod praedicatur omnia dicentur de subiecto. Et exemplificat: "ut homo praedicatur de quodam homine, animal vero praedicatur de homine, igitur et de quodam homine animal praedicatur. Quidam enim homo et homo est et animal".

Sciendum est autem quod per istam regulam exponitur dici de subiecto, quod superius non exposuit, sed solum esse in subiecto. Est autem[25] dici de subiecto univoce praedicari, scilicet secundum nomen et rationem; et hoc est praedicari substantialiter. Si enim sit praedicatio secundum accidens non oportet `id´[26] quod dicitur de praedicato dici de subiecto. Si enim homo est albus, et albus est color, non sequitur ex hoc quod homo `sit´ color. Requiritur etiam ad dici de subiecto quod praedicatum sit universale respectu subiecti. Si enim animal rationale mortale dicitur de homine, quamvis dicatur de eo in quid, non tamen dicitur de eo ut de subiecto, quia non est praedicatum alterum a subiecto tamquam universale, sed idem cum eo. Definitio est idem cum definito, et propter hoc dixit Aristoteles: "quando alterum de altero praedicatur", ad removendum eiusdem de se.

Sed adhuc obiciunt quidam contra regulam. Nam animal dicitur de homine ut de subiecto, quia in quid et tamquam universale; genus autem dicitur de animali; non tamen vere dicitur genus de homine. Non igitur quaecumque dicuntur de praedicato dicuntur de subiecto.

Ad hoc dicendum quod genus quamvis praedicetur non tamen ut de subiecto, [et] quia non praedicatur de eo in [in] eo quod quid, sed secundum accidens. Regula autem intelligenda est quod quaecumque praedicatur de praedicato ut de subiecto illud dicitur de subiecto ut de subiecto; ut tota regula intelligatur uniformiter de dici de altero ut de subiecto. Et sic[27] patet quod per regulam istam docetur quod de quocumque subiecto dicitur aliquid, illud quod dicitur et illud de quo dicitur pertinent ad idem praedicamentum. Si enim animal dicitur de homine ut de subiecto, et animal reducitur ad substantiam, oportet quod homo ad substantiam reducatur. Singularia enim, quae sunt imprehensibilia[28] propter suam infinitatem, reducuntur ad decem praedicamenta per sua superiora, quae de ipsis dicuntur ut de subiectis. Quod enim Socrates sit substantia scimus per hoc, quod de ipso dicitur homo ut de subiecto, et de homine animal, et sic per multa superiora procedendo usque ad substantiam.

<De numero praedicamentorum>

(7ra) ...Ad evidentiam huius sufficientiae sciendum est quod praedicamenta dicuntur a praedicando, quia secundum diversos modos praedicandi distinguuntur praedicamenta. Est autem triplex modus praedicandi aliquid de aliquo. Unde quidam modus <est> quando praedicatur de subiecto illud quod pertinet ad eius essentiam, ut cum dico: 'Sortes est homo' vel 'homo est animal'; secundum talem <modum> accipitur praedicamentum substantiae. Alius modus praedicandi est quando praedicatur de substantia aliqua illud quod non est de essentia eius, sed est accidens inhaerens ei. Et hoc potest esse tripliciter. Quia vel inhaeret ei ex parte materiae, et omne tale accidens habet extensionem in suis partibus, et per hoc est mensura substantiae intrinseca, ut cum dico 'lignum est bipedale vel tripedale'; et omne tale est de praedicamento quantitatis. Vel est accidens inhaerens ex parte formae ut color vel figura, quae fundatur super quantitatem[29]; et sic est praedicamentum qualitatis. Vel respectus ad alterum, et non aliquid absolutum inhaerens; et sic praedicamentum relationis. Cum enim dico 'homo est pater' non praedicatur de homine aliquid absolutum, sed respectus qui est ad aliquid extrinsecum. Tertius vero modus praedicandi est quando praedicatum denominat subiectum ab aliquo extrinseco. Et hoc potest esse dupliciter, scilicet vel communiter vel specialiter. ...

<De substantia>

(7vb) Circa primum duo facit: primo ponit descriptionem primae substantiae, secundo describit substantias secundas, ibi: "secundae autem substantiae dicuntur" etc.

Circa primum considerandum est quod sicut ab eo[dem] quod est esse dicitur essentia, ita ab eo quod <est> subsistere vel substare dicitur substantia. Quod autem subsistit et substat, illud per se exsistit, et non est in alio et etiam aliis suponitur. Neque materia per se exsistit, neque forma, sed compositum ex utroque; et ideo compositum ex materia et forma propriissime dicitur substantia, quia ipsi convenit per se exsistere et aliis substare. Principaliter autem et maxime convenit hoc substantiis [et] individuis, quia illae non solum subiciunt accidentibus, sed etiam substantiis universalibus, quae de ipsis praedicantur.   Et ideo substantiae singulares dicuntur primae substantiae, quia primo et principaliter convenit eis ratio substandi. Substantiae autem universales, quia per substantias singulares substant, dicuntur secundae substantiae. Ponit igitur descriptionem primae substantiae dicens quod substantia quae proprie et principaliter et maxime dicitur substantia est illa quae neque de subiecto dicitur neque de subiecto est, ut aliquis homo singularis vel aliquis equus. [Quia] Socrates enim quia non est in subiecto est substantia, et quia non dicitur de subiecto est principaliter et maxime substantia. Prius enim Socrates substat accidentibus: quia Socrates est homo, ideo homo posterius subicitur ipsis. Socrates etiam subicitur homini et animali, et non e converso.

(8vb) Dubitationes sunt circa litteram, sed praetermissae sunt ne interrumpe<re>tur expositio litterae. Prima dubitatio <est> de divisione substantiae in primam substantiam et secundam, quam innuit Aristoteles describendo tam substantiam primam quam secundam. Videtur quod divisio non sit conveniens. Nam divisio substantiae in sua contenta non debet esse per differentias alterius generis; sed primum et secundum sunt de genere relationis, quia ordinem important; ergo inconvenienter dividitur substantia per primum et secundum. ...

Responsio. Hic sunt duae opiniones. Quidam enim dicunt quod haec divisio substantiae in primam substantiam et secundam est divisio analogi in suas significationes, de quibus dicitur per prius et posterius. Cum igitur substantia dicitur[30] ab actu substandi, illud quod maxime substat primo et principaliter dicitur substantia. Maxime autem substat subiectum primum, quod est substantia individua; et ideo bene[31] vocatur prima substantia. Substat enim non solum accidentibus, sed etiam speciebus et generibus de praedicamento substantiae.   Species autem et genera de praedicamento substantiae substant accidentibus secundo loco et paucioribus quam primae substantiae; et ideo per posterius dicuntur substantiae; et haec[32] merito vocantur secundae substantiae. Ostenditur autem hoc per signum: in V° namque Metaphysicae distinguit Philosophus substantiam in quattuor modos, quorum primus est quod substantia dicitur [quod] quae non dicitur de aliquo subiecto, sed alia de ipsa -- et haec est prima substantia -- et reducit alios tres modos in unum, scilicet in secundas substantias. Et similiter in VII° Metaphysicae ponit quattuor modos substantiae, ubi etiam istos (9ra) duos modos ponit, scilicet subiectum primum quod hic vocat substantiam primam, et universale, quod est genus et species, quod hic vocat substantiam secundam; et ad istos duos modos alii duo reducuntur. Illae autem divisiones substantiae quas ponit in Metaphysica sunt divisiones, analogi in sua significata, sicut et aliae divisiones nominum quas[33] Philosophus distinguit in V⁰ Metaphysicae.

Hoc idem ostendit per rationem, quae magis movet eos: quandocumque divisum praedicatur de dividentibus secundum prius et posterius, ita quod illud a quo sumitur ratio nominis divisi primo convenit uni dividenti et secundario alteri, illud divisum praedicatur analogice de dividentibus. Verbi gratia, ens praedicatur de substantia, et quantitate et aliis praedicamentis per prius et posterius, ita quod esse, a quo sumitur nomen 'entis', primo convenit substantiae et per posterius aliis. Ideo ens praedicatur de eis non univoce, sed analogice; et divisio entis in praedicamenta est analogi. Substantia autem accipitur ab actu substandi, et maxime dicitur de prima substantia, quae maxime substat, et secundario de secunda substantia, quae paucioribus substat. Ergo substantia praedicatur per prius et posterius de prima substantia et secunda; non univoce sed analogice.

Alia est opinio quam ponit Boethius et ʿetiamʾ Simplicius quod substantia dicitur univoce de substantia prima et substantia secunda.   <Divisio enim substantiae in substantiam primam et secunda> est divisio generis quasi[34] in suas species.   Et ista opinio videtur mihi verior.   Hic enim dividitur substantia prout est genus <et prout> est praedicabile; sic enim determinat hic de substantia, ponens species eius et proprietates -- et huiusmodi[35] modum tenet de aliis praedicamentis.   Consequenter dividit ipsa in species et ponit eorum proprietates. Manifestum est autem quod substantia prout est genus praedicatur univoce de substantiis primis et de substantiis secundis, cum tam substantiae primae quam secundae directe contineantur sub substantia; et ita substantia dicitur de eis ut de subiectis. Oportet igitur quod dicatur de eis secundum nomen et rationem — quod est univoce praedicari.

Nec est contra istam opinionem quod Philosophus in Metaphysica distinguit substantiam sicut et alia nomina analoga; ibi enim distinguit substantiam in diversos modos, quorum quidam non sunt directe in ordine praedicamenti substantiae, ut in formam rei, et etiam in essentiam, et etiam in quemdam modum non verum, prout a Platonicis numerus dicitur substantia rerum et puncta dicuntur substantiae lineae. Unde patet quod ista distinctio substantiae in alios modos multum differt ab ista divisione substantiae in primam et secundam, quae sunt directe in genere substantiae secundum veritatem. Unde propter hoc non sequitur, si illa distinctio substantiae posita in Metaphysica sit secundum analogiam, quod ista hic posita sit talis. Similiter non debet movere ad ponendum hanc divisionem esse analogi quod prima substantia maxime substat et maxime dicitur substantia, non autem secunda substantia, quae paucioribus substat. Hoc enim non est propter analogiam nominis 'substantia' in significando primam substantiam et secundam per prius et posterius, sed propter hoc quod prima substantia est causa per quam secuna substantia substat et et[36] dicitur substantia. Quia enim prior est causa quam effectus, ideo, quando causa et effectus conveniunt in nomine, illud nomen magis praedicatur de causa quam de effectu. Sicut ignis est magis calidus quam ea quae calefiunt per ignem; semper enim propter quod unumquodque et illud magis — ut dicitur in I⁰ Posteriorum. Et ideo principia sunt magis cognita quam conclusiones, quae sunt cognitae per principia; et tamen univoce dicuntur cognita principia et conclusiones, sicut ignis et alia calida univoce dicuntur calida.... Patet igitur quod prima substantia, ex hoc quod est causa generibus et speciebus ut[37] sint substantiae, maxime (9rb) est substantia. Et, cum substantia dicitur univoce de istis tamquam de per se contentis, et propter naturam univocationis,[38] assimilatur ista divisio divisioni generis in suas species, quamvis prima substantia et substantia non sint species realiter distinctae.

Ad primum igitur dicendum quod primum et secundum important hic ordinem non realem, sed ordinem rationis; et ideo non sunt de genere relationis. Est autem attendendum quod non dividit Aristoteles substantias per differentias reales oppositas, ut per corporeum et incorporeum, quia

substantiae incorporeae non sunt nobis manifestae ut per eas possint
proprietates substantiae manifestari; sed divisio substantiae in primam
substantiam et secundam comprehendit omnes substantias, et utrumque
dividentium comprehendit substantias sensibiles, quae sunt nobis notae ⟨et⟩
per quas manifestantur convenienter proprietates substantiae....

(10va) ... Dubitatur autem hic de differentia, quam dicit esse aliam a
substantia, utrum differentia substantialis sit substantia. Videtur enim quod
sit substantia: omne quod est vel est substantia, vel accidens; differentia
substantialis non est accidens, cum non sit in subiecto, sicut Aristoteles
affirmat; ergo est substantia....

Aliter dicit Boethius quod differentia non est substantia neque accidens,
sed est quoddam medium inter substantiam et qualitatem.

Contra: decem praedicamenta sunt decem genera, quia continent omnes
res quae sunt extra animam; sed differentiae substantiales sunt verae res
extra animam, quia veras res constituunt; ergo vel sunt substantiae vel
accidentia.

Responsio.[39] Dicendum est quod praedicamenta distinguuntur secundum
diversos modos praedicandi quibus res praedicantur de substantia aliqua. Nam
substantiae praedicantur in quid, quia cum quaeritur de substantia aliqua quid
est, bene respondetur 'homo' vel 'lapis'. Quantitas autem praedicat mensuram
substantiae; cum enim quaeritur de substantia quanta est, respondetur
'bicubita' vel 'tricubita'. Quaedam vero significant qualis est substantia; et
ista sunt de genere qualitatis. Oportet autem quod omnis res, in quocumque
genere fuerit, habeat qualitatem sibi essentialem per quam constituatur in
specie determinata sui generis, et per quam differat essentialiter ab aliis.
Ista autem qualitas est differentia cuiuscumque praedicamenti, quae ideo
dicitur qualitas (10vb) quia per ipsam, respondetur ad quaestionem factam per
'quale'. Ut si quaeratur quale animal est homo, respondetur quod bipes vel
rationalis; et qualis figura est circulus, respondetur quod sine angulo; et
qualis linea est diameter, respondetur quod recta. Ideo in omni genere
differentia praedicatur in quale, et quantum ad hoc participant praedicamentum qualitatis; secundum autem quod constituunt speciem proprii generis
pertinent ad proprium genus. Quia igitur differentiae substantiales non
praedicantur in quid de substantiis, sicut praedicantur species et genera, ideo
non proprie dicuntur substantiae, quia proprium est rerum illius generis

praedicari in quid. Quia cum differentiae substantiales constituunt species de genere substantiae, ideo non sunt accidentia nec in subiecto; sed quia praedicantur in quale, ideo participant naturam qualitatis, quae est praedicamentum cuius res praedicantur in quale de substantia, secundum propriam rationem illius generis, quia omnes res illius generis sunt qualitates substantiae. Et per hoc respondendum est ad argumenta.

Ad primum dicendum quod omne quod est vel est substantia, vel accidens, vel medium participans utriusque....

(11ra) ... Sciendum autem est quod in propositione aliqua potest attendi sola unitate absque hoc quod attendatur ex parte praedicati proprius modus praedicandi et ex parte subiecti proprius modus subiecti. Et isto modo praedicatur prima substantia de se ipsa. Haec enim est vera 'Socrates est Socrates'. Et sic loquendo dicit Porphyrius quod individuum praedicatur de uno solo; sic etiam potest praedicari de specie, ut 'homo est Socrates'; sic et praedicatur subiectum de accidente, ut 'album est lignum'. Alio modo in praedicatione alicuius de aliquo attenditur non solum unitas, sed etiam proprietas praedicationis ex parte praedicati et proprietas subiecti communis ex parte subiecti. Quia autem praedicatum comparatur ad subiectum sicut forma ad materiam -- nam praedicatum est pars formalis propositionis, subiectum vero pars materialis -- ideo tunc^{40} aliquid praedicatur proprie de aliquo quando praedicatum habet rationem formae respectu subiecti, sive in constituendo ipsum substantialiter, sicut superius est de constitutione inferioris, sive inhaerendo ei accidentaliter, sicut accidens inhaeret subiecto. Secundum istam proprietatem praedicationis a prima substantia nulla est praedicatio -- sicut hic dicitur -- quia prima substantia non habet rationem formae respectu alicuius, sed habet rationem subiecti respectu omnium aliorum. Et ideo bene describitur quod neque de subiecto dicitur neque in subiecto est. Quia enim non dicitur de subiecto, <ideo non praedicatur essentialiter, quia autem non est in subiecto>, ideo non praedicatur accidentaliter; et sic nulla est praedicatio a prima substantia, neque essentialis neque accidentalis. Similiter etiam nec subiectum praedicatur, de propria praedicatione, de accidente. Et ideo dicitur in I^o Posteriorum quod haec praedicatio est secundum ˋseˊ 'lignum est album' quia praedicatur quod aptum natum est praedicari de illo subiecto, et subicitur quod aptum natum est subici tali praedicato. Haec autem praedicatio est secundum accidens 'album est lignum'; non enim subicitur album ratione sui ipsius, sed ratione ligni cui accidit album. Similiter quamvis vere praedicetur idem de se vel autem inferius de superiori, tamen non est praedicatio propria et secundum se. Unde in isto libro non concedit Aristoteles talem praedicationem, sed excludit[41] eam. Talis <enim> praedicatio non est in demonstrationibus syllogisticis,[42] ad quas principaliter ordinatur liber iste. Et sic patet quod non est repugnantia inter Aristotelem dicentem quod a prima substantia nulla est praedicatio et Porphyrium dicentem quod individuum, ut Socrates, praedicatur de uno solo....

(11[rb]) Circa proprietatem duo facit: primo ostendit eam convenire[43] substantiis primis; secundo ostendit eam convenire subtantiis secundis, ibi: "secundis vero substantiis" etc.

Circa primum est sciendum quod ista proprietas substantiae est de eius significatione. Omne enim praedicamentum habet suam propriam significationem; nam quantitas significat quantum, qualitas vero quale [quale], relatio vero ad aliquid. Propria vero significatio substantiae est[44] esse hoc aliquid. Et haec est proprietas quam ponit dicens: "omnis substantia videtur hoc aliquid significare". Dicit autem "videtur", quia aliorum opinio fuit quod omnis substantia hoc aliquid significat. Et dicitur fuisse opinio Platonis, qui posuit omnes substantias per se exsistentes tam universales quam particulares. Et in primis substantiis, quae sunt individua, non est dubitabile, sed manifeste verum quod hoc aliquid significant omnes substantiae individuae. Ex hoc enim quod prima[45] substantia est individuum, quod est unum numero per materiam, ita quod non est plura in numerando, est demonstrabile et significat hoc; ex hoc autem quod est substantia per formam substantialem, et non est accidens nec differentia, significat aliquid. Et ita significat hoc aliquid. Et non tantum significat aliquid vel quid, nec tantum significat hoc, sed utrumque importat, et hoc et aliquid. Patet igitur quod haec proprietas, quae est significare hoc aliquid, convenit primis substantiis et non convenit aliis substantiis nec accidentibus.

Secundo, cum dicit: "in secundis vero substantiis", ostendit dictam proprietatem non convenire substantiis secundis. Et ita non convenit omni substantiae, quamvis conveniat soli. Et primo ostendit hoc, secundo ostendit dictum suum, ibi: "non simpliciter autem" etc.

Dicit igitur quod in secundis substantiis videtur secundum quandam apparentiam quod significant hoc aliquid propter figuram appellationis, id est: propter similitudinem nominationis earum ad primas substantias. Quando enim

aliquis proferit 'hominem' vel 'animal' non significat rem aliam a prima
substantia; cum enim dicitur 'homo currit', significatur quod aliquis homo
particularis currit.   Et similes sunt secundae substantiae primis substantiis
quantum ad significationem.   Et ideo videntur secundae substantiae significare
hoc aliquid sicut primae substantiae.   Non tamen est verum quod significent
hoc aliquid prout praetenditur,[46] sed magis significa<n>t quale quid; homo
enim vel animal non est unum suppositum vel individuum quemadmodum prima
substantia est unum individuum, sed homo dicitur de pluribus in quae dividitur,
et similiter animal.   Et non[47] est homo demonstrabile, ut possit dici hoc
aliquid; 'homo' enim non magis indicat Sortem vel Platonem vel alium
particularem hominem.   Neque enim subsistit per se, nec demonstratur per se;
sed demonstrat[48] individuum velut Sortem, dicendo quod tale quid est quale
Sortes.   Et ideo significat quale quid, et non significat hoc aliquid quod est
demonstratum.

Secundo cum dicit: "non simpliciter autem quale" etc., exponit quod
dixerat secundas substantias significare quale quid, et dicit quod 'homo' vel
'animal' non significat quale simpliciter, id est: quale sine additione, sicut
'album' significat quale.   'Album' enim nihil aliud significat quam qualitatem,
et ideo significat quale sine aliquo addito.   Genus autem et species de
praedicamento substantiae determinant qualitatem circa substantiam, et ita
non significant[ur] quale, sed cum quali significant quid.   Differentia namque
substantialis adveniens generi constituit speciem; species igitur ex hoc quod
constituitur ex differentia significat quale, ex hoc autem quod constituitur ex
genere significat quid.   Et ita non significat quale simpliciter, sed quale quid.
Homo igitur et animal significant quale quid. ...

Est autem hic duplex dubitatio.   Primo de hoc quod dicit substantiam
significare.   Substantia enim est res; res autem non significant, sed
significantur; non igitur substantia significat: neque quale quid, neque hoc
aliquid.

Ad hoc dicitur quod cum dicitur "significare" accipitur (11ᵛᵃ) 'substantia'
pro voce significante substantiam, non autem pro re ipsa secundum se.   Et
sic[49] dicitur accipi materialiter sicut cum dicit<ur> 'substantia est nomen'.
Et quod sic accipitur quandoque in ista doctrina contingit ex hoc quod hic
non determinatur de substantia et aliis praedicamentis prout sunt res
absolutae, sed prout significantur per voces.

Secunda dubitatio: utrum substantiae secundae significent quale quid.
Videtur quod non.   Superius dictum est quod differentiae non sunt substantiae,[50] quia differentiae significant quale; si igitur genus et species
significant quale, sequitur quod non sunt substantiae.

Praeterea, prima substantia includit in se quicquid importatur nomine
speciei et nomine generis, quia quodlibet superius est de intellectu inferioris;
si igitur species et genus significant quale, propter differentias quas
includunt, eodem <modo> primae substantiae, quae easdem differentias omnes
includunt, significant quale.

Ad primum istorum dicendum quod differentiae non solum significant
qualitatem substantialem, sed habent modum praedicandi in quale, et ita
deficiunt a manerie praedicandi substantiae, scilicet in quid; et ideo non sunt
substantiae, sed qualitates substantiales.   Sed genus et species, licet
significent quale ratione differentiarum quas includunt, tamen non significant
per modum qualis, et ideo non praedicantur in quale, sed in quid, et sunt
substantiae.   Unde licet corporeum non sit substantia, tamen corpus, quod est
genus, est substantia.

Ad secundum 'dicendum quod Socrates, licet determinate importet
differentias quas continent sua superiora, non tamen nomen 'Sortis'
principaliter imponebatur propter illas differentias significandas, sed ad
significandum individuum illud demonstrabile;[51] et ideo dicitur significare
`hoc´ aliquid, non quale quid, quod significantur per genus et speciem, quibus
nomina imponuntur ad significandum qualitatem circa substantiam, non tamen
per modum qualitatis.   Et ex hoc contingit esse deceptionem secundum
figuram dictionis quando proceditur ab eo quod est quale quid ad hoc aliquid,
ut a specie ad individuum.   Ut hic: 'Sortes est alter ab homine; Sortes est
homo; igitur est alter a se'.   Similiter est fallacia quando proceditur ab eo
quod est hoc aliquid ad quale quid; ut hic: 'quod ego sum, tu non es; homo
sum; ergo tu non es homo'.

<De quantitate>

(13[rb]) ... Circa quae dicta sunt, sunt dubitationes.   Et primo quaeritur
utrum quantitas sit genus. ...

(13va) ... Responsio. Dicendo quod quantitas est genus generalissimum, quia, cum quantitas sit divisibilis in partes eiusdem rationis, secundum illam rationem dicitur de omnibus contentis inferioribus, quae sunt speciales quantitates, ⟨quae⟩ secundum illam rationem praedicantur denominative de substantia. Iste autem modum praedicandi convenit omni quantitati et nulli alteri; et ideo quantitas est genus omnium quantitatum specialium, distinctum ab aliis praedicamentis. ...

Hic autem distinguit species quantitatis secundum diversas rationes mensurae, et ideo etiam locum ponitur alia species a superiori, quia habet aliam rationem mensurae.

⟨De relatione⟩

(17ra) ... Sciendum est quod quaedam sunt nomina relativa quae sunt imposita ad significandum ipsas habitudines ⸍relativas⸌ ut 'dominus', 'servus', 'pater' et 'filius', et huiusmodi. Et ⟨haec⟩ vocantur relativa secundum esse. Et omnia talia non possunt esse alterius praedicamenti quam praedicamenti ad aliquid, quia nihil aliud significant nisi ipsam relationem. Alia vero sunt nomina quae sunt imposita ad significandum res absoluti generis quas consequuntur quaedam habitudines, ut 'movens' et 'motum', 'caput' et 'capitatum', 'ala', et 'alatum'. ⟨Et haec vocantur relative secundum dici. Et omnia talia⟩ sunt ad aliquid propter habitudines quas important, et sunt in alio praedicamento propter rem illius generis ad quam significandum sunt imposita. Et huiusmodi relativa secundum dici sunt scientia et virtus. Hoc nomen 'scientia' impositum est ad significandum certam cognitionem rei, ... Et quia talis cognitio qualificat animam, ideo scientia est in genere qualitatis; sed quia talis cognitio mensuratur quantum ad suum esse et quantum ad suam veritatem ex re cognita ex qua dependet, ideo consequitur ipsam cognitionem habitudo ad rem scitam, et secundum hoc quod hoc nomen 'scientia' significat illam habitudinem est ad aliquid.

(19rb) ...Circa istud capitulum quaeruntur quaedam. Et primo quaeritur utrum relatio sit ens extra animam vel ens rationis.

Arguitur quod sit ens rationis. .....

(19va) Oppositum arguitur. Ens per se extra animam dividitur in decem praedicamenta; sed decem praedicamentorum unum est relatio; igitur relatio est ens extra animam.

Responsio. Dicendum est quod omnes relationes quae sunt in genere praedicamentali sunt vel res extra animam, ut paternitas, filiatio, vel [sunt] habitus animae qui referuntur ad rem extra animam.

Ad cuius evidentiam sciendum est quod, sicut dicit Commentator XII° Metaphysicae, relatio est debilius esse quam alia praedicamenta, et ideo putaverunt quidam philosophi relationem esse de secundis intentionibus, quae non habent esse nisi in anima, sicut sunt intentio generis et speciei. Hoc autem non potest esse verum [52]. Quod enim non est res exsistens, sed in sola consideratione intellectus, non potest poni in aliquo praedicamento, quia ens rationis dividitur contra ens divisum in decem praedicamenta, ut patet in V^{o} Metaphysicae. Si igitur relatio non esset in rebus extra animam, ad aliquid non esset unum genus praedicamentorum.[53]

Praeterea, perfectio et bonum (19vb) quae sunt in rebus extra animam non solum attenduntur secundum illud quod est abstractum[54] in rebus, sed etiam secundum ordinem unius rei ad aliam, sicut in exercitu bonum exercitus consistit in ordine partium. Huic enim ordini comparat Philosophus ordinem universi XII° Metaphysicae; ordo enim rerum est[55] relatio earum. Oportet igitur in rebus esse quasdam relationes secundum quas una ordinatur ad alteram.

Ulterius autem sciendum quod sicut extra animam una res habet ordinem seu relationem ad aliam, ita intellectus quandoque concipit unam rem in ordine ad aliam[56], quamvis in rebus ipsis intellectis non sit ordo ille, sed in sola consideratione intellectus. Et talis ordo est relatio rationis, et non est realis. Et hoc contingit quattuor modis.

Uno modo quando relatio quae intelligitur non habet in re aliquid supra quod fundatur, sicut dextrum quod dicitur de columna determinatam positionem secundum nullam[57] virtutem in una eius parte exsistentem per quam dicatur dextra. Sicut est in animali, in quo sunt positiones secundum diversas virtutes diversarum partium; et ideo ibi sunt relationes reales. In columna vero et in aliis inanimatis sunt relationes rationis, quia non habent praedictas virtutes inter extrema relationis.

<Secundo modo> quando[58] accipit<ur> unum tamquam duo, sicut est relatio identitatis, quando aliquid dicitur idem sibi. Relatio enim realis requirit[59] extrema distincta.

Tertio modo quando significatur relatio entis ad non ens, ut cum dicitur quod nos sumus priores illis qui futuri sunt. Non enim potest esse relatio realis alicuius ad non ens, quia relatio realis exigit utrumque extremorum in actu; et ideo ista prioritas non est relatio secundum rem, sed solum secundum rationem.

Quarto modo est relatio rationis quando ponitur relatio relationis ad aliquid. Relatio enim per se ipsam refertur et non per aliam relationem; et ideo paternitas non comparatur ad subiectum per aliam relationem mediam, sed per se ipsam; nec etiam ad terminum[60]. ...

Istos duos ultimos modos ponit Avicenna in sua Metaphysica; duo primi modi sunt extracti ex verbis Aristotelis.

<De qualitate>

(22[va]) Dubitatur de ista descriptione.[61] Videtur enim quod inconvenienter sit assignata.

Primo quia idem non potest notificare se ipsum. ...

Secundo quia sicut per qualitatem dicimur quales, ita per quantitatem dicimur (22[vb]) quanti, et per substantialitatem dicimur substantiae; sed substantiam et quantitatem non sic describit, nec alia praedicamenta; igitur qualitatem non debuit sic describere. ...

Responsio. Dicendum est quod descriptionis duplex est modus. Uno modo descriptio est ita manifesta quod est concessa[62] ab omnibus, ut cum dicitur 'bonum est quo accipit<ur> utilitatem habere' vel 'anima est qua est vivere'; et talis descriptio vocatur enthymemat`ic´a. Alio modo est descriptio quae indicat substantiam rei, et vocatur substantialis, ut cum dicitur 'bonum est virtus vel pertinens <ad> virtutem' vel 'anima est substantia per se mobilis'. Et tali descriptioni non omnes consentiunt, sed contradicunt ei illi qui sunt alterius opinionis. In primis autem introductionibus utendum est descriptionibus quibus omnes assentiunt; illae enim sunt magis notae et ad primum auditum magis idoneae. Substantialibus autem utendum est in prima philosophia, quae speculatur ens in quantum ens. Et ideo Aristoteles substantialem rationem qualitatis tradidit in Metaphysica; hic autem ponit rationem eius enthymematicam[63] — sicut dicit Porphyrius et[64] Simplicius in commento praedicto[65].

Ad primum igitur dicendum quod licet quale dicatur a qualitate tamquam posterius secundum naturam, tamen notius quo ad nos est quale et evidentius quam qualitas[66]; quale enim est sensibile, qualitas autem, ut in abstracto accipitur, est intelligibile. Sicut igitur homo est notior humanitate, ita et quale notius est qualitate quo ad nos. ...

Ad secundum dicendum, secundum Simplicium, quod differentia accepta secundum partitionem formae in quocumque genere facit proprium characterem et determinationem ad speciem. ...Et ideo alia genera participant[67] particularem modum qualitatis secundum quod in eis fit denominatio a formis participatis per differentias determinantes ad speciem. Differentia ponitur in quale in omni praedicamento, secundum quod habet modum qualitatis. Et sic proprium est qualitatis quod secundum eam dicantur qualia. Modus autem substantiae vel qualitatis vel alterius generis non sic se extendit ad omnia genera ut secundum participationem formae fiat denominatio suo modo in omni genere; et ideo non sic describimus alia genera.

<De oppositis>

(29vb) ...Dicendum quod bonum non potest contrariari bono, quia bonum fit uno modo tantum; et ideo si contrarietur bono, contrarietur sibi ipsi. Malum autem est multipharia, et secundum excessum (30ra) mensurae et secundum defectum; et ideo malum quod est defectus est contrarium malo quod est excessus. Unde non est simile de bono et malo, quod sicut bonum non contrariatur bono ita malum non sit contrarium malo.

Deinde, cum dicit: "amplius contrariis", non necesse est si unum[68] sit in actu quod reliquum sit. Et hoc manifestat per exempla; si enim omnes sint sani, sanitas quidem erit, sed aegritudo, quae est suum contrarium, non erit similiter. Si omnes sunt albi, albedo quidem erit, sed nigredo non erit.

Aliam vero particulam huius proprietatis ponit, dicens quod in eodem individuo non est possibile, si unum contrariorum sit, reliquum <simul esse>. Ut si Socratem esse sanum contrarium est ad illud quod est Socratem aegrotare, cum non sit possibile ambo contraria inesse simul eidem, non[69] est possibile, cum alterum contrariorum sit, reliquum <esse>. Quando enim est Socrates sanus, non est Socrates aeger.

Videtur autem falsum quod hic dicit quod si unum contrariorum sit non necesse est alterum esse, quia in II° De caelo et mundo dicit quod si terra est necesse est ignem esse; et hoc ostendit per hoc quod contrariorum si unum est necesse est esse et reliquum. Igitur vel sua probatio ibi non valet, vel hic dicit falsum.

Ad hoc dicendum quod in libro De caelo loquitur de substantiis quae sunt partes essentiales individui, habentes contrarias qualitates, scilicet de elementis quattuor, quae secundum quattuor combinationes primarum qualitatum contrariarum constituuntur; et qua ratione unum eorum et reliquum. Sic hic loquitur de qualitatibus contrariis, quae contingenter insunt individuis, quae non sunt partes essentiales individui; et isto modo potest unum contrariorum esse altero non exsistente.

Deinde, cum dicit: "palam vero est" etc., ponit tertiam proprietatem contrariorum, ut doce<a>t in quibus nata sunt fieri. Contraria nata sunt fieri circa idem. Idem[70] autem dicitur tripliciter, scilicet idem genere, [et] idem specie, idem numero. Dicit manifestum esse quod contraria nata sunt fieri circa idem specie vel genere. Et hoc manifestat per exempla; aegritudo enim et sanitas, quae sunt contraria, nata sunt fieri in corpore animalis, quod quidem corpus est species corporis -- et ita habent fieri circa idem specie. Albedo vero et nigredo sunt in corpore simpliciter, quod est genus -- et ita sunt in eodem secundum genus. Iustitia autem et in iustitia sunt in anima;<***> et ita sunt in eodem secundum speciem.

Sciendum autem quod non dixit contraria esse nata fieri circa idem numero, cum [tam] in capitulo de substantia dixerit quod substantia, cum sit una et eadem numero, susceptibilis est contrariorum. Videtur igitur Aristoteles insufficienter dicere in quibus nata sunt fieri contraria. Sed sciendum est quod hic vult dicere in quibus nata sunt contraria esse simul; et propter hoc non fuit opponendum circa idem numero, quia non possunt simul esse in eodem secundum numerum, sed in eodem specie vel genere. Vel potest dici quod, quia hoc dictum est in capitulo de substantia, quod hoc est proprium substantiae quod cum sit una et eadem numero est susceptibilis contrariorum, quod ibi expresse est dictum est hic praetermissum tamquam manifestum.

* I employ the following sigla:

`...´ words added by the scribe in the margin or between the lines

<...> words added by the editor

[...] words which should be deleted

<***> probable lacuna in the text

1 usque: lectio dubia

2 esse: lectio incerta

3 omnia: alia ms

4 impositio: spat. vac. 3 fere litt. ms

5 quibus: qua ms

6 species: spat. vac. 2 fere litt. ms

7 significata abstracta: significatae abstractae ms

8 aliud: spat. vac. 10 fere litt. ms

9 pro: per ms

10 descendere: decendere ms

11 quae: dicuntur add. et del. scriba

12 admitti: lectio dubia

13 simplicibus: simplicis ms

14 iuvamentum: lectio dubia

15 communicamus: communicant ms

16 potissima: p^{9}q^c ms

17 voces significativas: significativas voces ms

18 asinos: asini ms

19 lapides: lapis ms

20 conveniunt: sic scriba correxit ex communia

21 eodem: sic scriba correxit ex eorundem

22 minima: m̄tāta ms

23 spectat: māḡm ms

24 et: spat. vac. 3 fere litt. ms

25 autem: de add. et del. scriba

26 id: vel illud

27 sic: sic scriba correxit ex ut

28 imprehensibilia: lectio incerta

29 quantitatem: qualitatem ms

30 dicitur: dividitur ms

31 bene: vocatur add. et del. scriba

32 haec: vel hae

33 quas: quae ms

34 quasi: <u>lectio incerta</u>

35 huiusmodi: habent <u>ms</u>

36 et: ut <u>ms</u>

37 ut: sicut <u>add. et del. scriba</u>

38 naturam univocationis: <u>lectio dubia</u>

39 responsio: respondeo <u>ms</u>

40 tunc: <u>lectio incerta</u>

41 excludit: <u>lectio dubia</u>

42 syllogisticis: <u>lectio dubia</u>

43 convenire: aliis <u>add. et del. scriba</u>

44 est: vel (?) <u>ms</u>

45 prima: prima <u>add. et del. scriba</u>

46 praetenditur: <u>lectio valde dubia</u>

47 non: ideo <u>ms</u>

48 demonstrat: demonstrans <u>ms</u>

49 sic: dicitur <u>add. et del. scriba</u>

50 substantiae: <u>sic scriba correxit ex differentiae</u>

51 demonstrabile: determinabile (?) <u>ms</u>

52 verum: v^{ta} <u>ms</u>

53 praedicamentorum: praedicamenti <u>ms</u>

54 abstractum: lectio valde dubia

55 est: res add. et del. ms

56 aliam: ita intellectus quandoque add. et del. ms

57 nullam: partem add. et del. ms

58 quando: ex coniectura, prae macula legere non possum

59 requirit: reliquit ms

60 terminum: lectio dubia

61 descriptione: scilicet de descriptione qualitatis

62 concessa: consessa ms

63 enthymematicam: lectio dubia

64 et: spat. vac. 3 fere litt. ms

65 praedicto: forte pro praedicamentorum

66 qualitas: qualis ms

67 participant: lectio dubia

68 unum: subintellige contrariorum

69 non: Socratem add.et del. ms

70 idem: illud ms

7

Some Thirteenth-Century Existential Disputes:
Their Identification and Its Status

Desmond Paul Henry
University of Manchester

A survey of some of the papers published as a result of earlier meetings of
the European Symposia on Medieval Logic naturally raises questions as to the
logical location, so to speak, of the subject-matter of the disputes on
existence connected with the 1277 Oxford condemnation, for example. Thus
it is possible to edit, recount, and compare the theses of Kilwardby, Bacon,
and so forth, as is done so excellently in the proceedings recorded in English
Logic and Semantics.[1] So far we are at the level of what Boethius of
Dacia, himself a participant in thirteenth-century disputes, calls the 'modus
narrativus'.[2] But it is possible to go further, and to attempt to locate this
narrative more precisely, relative to the co-ordinates provided by our
contemporary logic. This, in other words, would be an attempt to view the
interconnection and significance of the material in terms of the modus
demonstrativus towards which Boethius of Dacia himself strove.[3] However, it
is highly desirable that the methods and concepts applied in the course of
this exploitation of the demonstrative mode are sufficiently sympathetic to
ensure that the material in question is not being cast in a totally alien
mould. In what follows I hope to show that far from being alien, the
progress of the analyses presented concretely re-creates, in a contemporary
form, precisely that progress from metaphysic, through the modi essendi and
intelligendi to the modi significandi, which was proposed by Boethius of Dacia
himself.

This analytic exercise is going to involve seeing our contemporary logical
language as what Lejewski calls the 'categorial language', because it shows

The Rise of British Logic, ed. P. Osmund Lewry, O.P., Papers in Mediaeval
Studies 7 (Toronto: Pontifical Institute of Mediaeval Studies, 1985), pp. 215-
233. © P.I.M.S., 1985.

forth, by means of its generalised translations, the parts of speech or semantic categories which are in question, and which can be made explicit in terms of Ajdukiewicz's categorial indices.[4]   Under such circumstances we are presenting the present-day correlate of that 'mental grammar'[5] or of that rational grammar of speculative grammarians (e.g., Boethius of Dacia), both of which figure in thirteenth-century linguistic studies. Likewise a similar

> move to connect all valid semantical distinctions with linguistic features
> of proper language (virtus sermonis) is characteristic of 14th century
> English logic. It is accompanied by a move to define some linguistic
> features even in cases where they are not customary in normal Latin
> usage.[6]

The method of working by reference to a logical language, itself regarded as a categorial language in the sense of Lejewski, is therefore by no means remote from the ways of working employed in the period to which it is to be applied.

Let us now hence attempt to converge on the location of some of the existential puzzles which exercised not only well-known figures such as Bacon and Kilwardby, but also Bonkes and other viri obscuri mentioned in P. Osmund Lewry's illuminating paper.[7]   These puzzles primarily concerned definitionally-associated indefinites such as 'Homo est animal', but also had to do with inferences from the negation of a simple sentence as in the case of the move from 'Asinus non est homo' to the correspondingly negatively-termed 'Asinus est non-homo' and vice versa.   The case of the negations is covered by item 10 of the Kilwardby 1277 Oxford condemnations: 'quod ex negativa de predicato finito sequitur affirmativa de predicato infinito sine constancia subiecti.'[8]   The constancia subiecti that Kilwardby's condemnation implies is indeed reqired if the inference is to hold. Ockham gave the general solution to puzzles of this sort when he dealt with connotatives.[9]   He realised that as well as the negative sentence an existential component is also required as the equivalent of such a negatively-termed sentence.[10]   This in turn presupposes a Lesniewski-style definitional frame[11] which has important consequences for logic in general, as I attempted to show in my own contribution to the Fourth Symposium.[12]   In particular, the presence of the existential component which ensures the constancia subiecti also serves to avoid a version of Russell's Paradox such as the one that is outlined in Quine's 'New Foundations.'[13]

Thus far, these remarks are for the most part mere reminders of things covered in the acts of our previous meetings. But before proceeding to the analysis of other problems which also concerned English logicians of the same period we may first situate the ground covered in the light of the principles of logical grammar as outlined by C. Lejewski.[14] As already noted, the logical language that shows forth the parts of speech or semantic categories involved in our analysis is called the 'categorial language'. This language makes visible, by its form, the logical grammar of the deep structure of the solution. Thus the equivalence, common to both Ockham and Lesniewski, that shows that relation between propositional and nominal negation would be expressed in the categorial language as:

.1 [ab]: a εN (b).$\equiv$.a ε a. $\sim$(a ε b)

For all a and b (a) is (non-b) if and only if

(a) is (a) and it's not that (a) is (b)[15]

In connection with .1 it may be pointed out that the primitive term of the axiom system presupposed is '....ε....' (rendered in system-English as '( ) is ( )'). At this point we may also begin to make explicit, in the manner of Lejewski's 'Syntax and Semantics of Ordinary Language', the logical grammar involved. Thus given that that primitive term is a functor that forms a proposition out of two names, we may use 's' to denote propositions and 'n' to denote names, and then go on to display the semantic category of that primitive by means of the categorial index '$s/(n\ n)$'. This shows that here we have a functor (i.e. an incomplete expression) that forms a proposition (see the 's' to the left of the oblique stroke) from two names (as indicated by the '$(n\ n)$' to the right of the oblique stroke). This characterisation need not entail any general 'two-name theory of predication', as the further remarks and my forthcoming That Most Subtle Question (§ 2.7) both tend to show. Again, the main functor of .1 (i.e., '....$\equiv$....', '....if and only if....') is one that forms a proposition from two propositions, so that $s/(s\ s)$ is its categorial index. Continuing this elementary exercise in logical grammar, we may also perceive that .1 contains both a functor of negation that forms a proposition from a single proposition, i.e., '$\sim$( )' ('it's not that....'), so that s/s is its index, as well as a functor of negation that forms a name from a name, i.e., 'N( )' ('non-....'), so that n/n is its index.

Now as Lejewski's introduction to this technique shows, there can be various categorial languages, with various senses of 'name' (for instance), and accordingly there are various possible types of nominal quantification. Awareness of these possibilities offers a whole range of alternative areas within which medieval discussions may be precisely located. For present purposes the categorial language which we assume is that of Lesniewski's Ontology. We have in effect just seen how, relative to that language, puzzles concerning the logical location of questions concerning 'constancy of subject' in negation are resoluble with comparative ease and brevity. One is, however, on ground that is somewhat more unfamiliar when the location of the difficulties surrounding the indefinite 'Homo est animal' is attempted. The difficulties themselves, however, are obvious enough. Why, for instance, should William of Sherwood look on 'Homo currit' as an indefinite amounting to a particular proposition when the apparently similar 'Homo est animal' is seen by him as the universal 'Every man is animal' for inferential puroses?[16] Again, there is diversity of opinion as to whether 'Homo est animal' (and similar cases) imply existence. This in turn leads to questions about 'Omnis homo est' and 'Caesar est homo': are they true if there are no men?[17]

In fact the materials for rational decisions on these and kindred matters are obviously about the place in the medieval period. All that remains to be done is to organise their use in an intelligible and linguistically efficient fashion. Thus Peter of Cornwall reminds us that 'esse habitu est esse essentiarum, esse actu est esse entis; sed essentiae dicuntur res incompletae respectu entium, et solum entia dicuntur completa....'[18] Here he is implying that statements concerning quiddities or esse essentiae, such as the 'Homo est animal' mentioned above, have incompleteness (i.e. functors) as their terms, and this accords exactly with present-day analyses of such quidditative discourse.[19] The functors in question, being verb-like, have s/n as their categorial index. And whereas the primitive '.... ε....' (or '( ) is ( )') has s/(n n) as its index, the copula of 'Homo est animal' in a definitional context has s/(s/n s/n) as its index. This can be brought out by the use of '{ } is { }' in a systematised English version. Such functorially-termed discourse is one pole of a contrast made prominent by Anselm of Canterbury,[20] and quite apart from its fulfilling the requirements of quidditative discourse in general,[21] it receives interesting independent discussion from the point of view of early medieval logical grammar.[22] We were hence not doing anything particularly unmedieval when we distinguished between functors the index of which is s/(s/n s/n) which (as this index shows) form propositions from two proposition-forming functors (i.e., verbs[23]) and those more familiar functors having the index s/(n n), i.e. which form a proposition from two names. Among the copulas covered by the first of these two groups of proposition-forming '....is....' functors we have those that found the not necessarily existential esse essentiae or quidditative discourse already mentioned,[24] whereas among those covered by the second may be found <u>esse</u> <u>existentiae</u>, in the sense that reference to existents tends to figure among their truth-conditions, and certainly does so in the primitive '....is....' encountered above.

As becomes evident from texts edited by Pinborg and Ebbesen,[25] some of which will be brought to bear on these questions in due course, the distinction between these two forms of <u>esse</u> is plainly common in the thirteenth-fourteenth century. It corresponds to certain versions of the distinctions between <u>ens</u> <u>ut</u> <u>nomen</u> and <u>ens</u> <u>ut</u> <u>participium</u>. However, the present-tense form of the nominally-termed '( ) is ( )' (of '....est....') borrowed from natural language need not trap us into requiring the incorporation of a literal present-existence requirement into its truth-conditions. We are thus simply released from Bacon's rabid insistence that a word loses its meaning when it comes about that it refers to nothing actually and presently existing, as in the case of 'Caesar', shortly to be recorded.

From this point onwards, in the light of the few simple conventions outlined above, the controversy around the question of <u>constancia</u> <u>subiecti</u> may be seen as reflecting a quite irrational insistence on the part of each protagonist that their proposed definitions or linguistic conventions are the only possible ones. Certainly the ferocious Bacon is only announcing, in a convoluted sort of way, his own lack of semantic sophistication when he attacks those who hold that an indefinite in quidditative discourse (such as the 'Homo est animal' introduced above) can be true if its names are empty (i.e., refer to nothing):

...they prove that a word cannot	...probant quod vox non potest
fall away from its meaning, and	cadere a sua significatione,
underpin this on the basis of	sed hoc supponunt tamquam
an infinity of things which they	rationem infinitorum quae
imagine to be most true when in	existimant verissima cum
fact they are most false, such	sint falsissima, ut quod
as the <u>man</u> is <u>animal</u> when	homo est animal nullo
neither exists, and that Caesar	existente, et quod Caesar
is a man....and other	est homo....et alia
innumberable erroneous doctrines;	innumerabilia erronea,
thus from the aforementioned	sicut ex praecedenti
argument carried to its most false	ratione sua falsissima
pitch, namely that a name signifies	quod nomen significat

something common to both being and	aliquid commune enti et
non-being, they drag out an	non-enti eliciunt
almost infinite pack of lies.	mendacia paene infinita.[26]

The very minimum required to release us from all this controversy is the intemporal '....is....', for example, which is certainly envisaged by the Worcester manuscript and by Bonkes.[27]   True, they seem to attach the intemporality to quidditative discourse only, i.e. to discourse centred around the '{ } is { }' which is among the functor-flanked functors having the s/(s/n s/n) index. Such a restriction is quite unnecessary. The name-flanked '( ) is ( )', comprising the systematised English version of the original primitive term for Lesniewski's Ontology, can be just as intemporal, even though in this particular instance it is not a non-existential name-flanked functor.

Let us grant, then, that an indefinite can be true in what Peter of Spain called 'natural matter' and at the level of what we call 'quidditative' discourse, without having to have any presently-existential entailment, or indeed any existential entailment. The definitions I have provided elsewhere ensure this non-existentiality.[28]   We can hence certainly agree with a position that Bacon attacks, namely that when a name signifies its subject-matter at the level of esse essentiae, i.e., at the s/(s/n s/n) level, then this is not a matter of actual being (esse actuale) but of what is common to present, past and future: 'nomen significat rem <suam> sub esse essentiae quae non est esse actuale, sed commune praesenti, praeterito et futuro.'[29] (It is assumed that the intemporal can be considered to be thus common, at least for present purposes). Even passages that deny the truth of certain quidditative indefinites such as the one with which we are concerned can show up the nature of their misapprehension of the case, e.g.:

...if man does not exist in the	...si homo non sit universaliter,
universal sense, then 'Man is	haec erit falsa: 'Homo est
animal' is false because in per	animal'. Et ratio huius est:
se predication of the first type	In propositione per se primo modo
the predicate holds of the subject	praedicatum inest subiecto
on account of the essence of the	per essentiam
subject, and this in such a fashion	subiecti, ita quod
that the essence of the subject is	essentia subiecti
the cause of the inherence of the	causa est inhaerentiae
predicate in the subject.	praedicati ad subiectum.
And it is obvious that on the	Et manifestum est, quod

destruction of the cause the	destructa causa
effect is destroyed. If,	destruitur effectus. Si
therefore, the essence of man	ergo essentia hominis
is destroyed, then since this is	destructa est, cum haec sit
the cause of the inherence	causa inhaerentiae
of animal in man, the inherence	animalis ad hominem, destruetur
of animal in man is also	inhaerentia animalis ad
destroyed.	hominem.[30]

Leaving aside the inappropriate causal thread, the trouble here is obvious enough. Man in the universal sense does 'exist', since the following is true:

.2   Cl ⟦ man ⟧   ε   Cl ⟦ man ⟧
     {being man} is {being man}[31]

Plainly no sense can be given to any assertion that the essence of man (in respect of the beingness of man displayed in this last expression) can be 'destroyed'; this would involve nominal-level predicates inappropriate to the terms of this expression. Indeed, in the same vein, one could say that destruction itself cannot be destroyed. As a counter-argument puts it, a man can perish, but man cannot: 'quamvis homo corrumpatur ipso non existente quantum ad esse quod accidat sibi, non tamen quantum ad essentiam suam.'[32]

Another objection to the truth of 'Man is animal' if no men exist relies on the well-known alleged priority of the 'Whether it is' question to the quidditative (or 'What is it?') question:

...the proposition 'Man is	...ista propositio 'homo est
animal' derives from the	animal' est sumpta a
quidditative question, for the	questione quid est, quoniam si
reply to 'What is man?' is	queratur quid est homo, respon-
'Animal'. Hence it presupposes	detur animal. Ergo supponit
'(a) man exists' which derives	istam 'homo est', quia sumpta est
from the 'Whether it is' question.	a questione si est.
But the proposition '(a) man is'	Sed hec propositio 'homo est'
is straightforwardly false	falsa est simpliciter
given that there are no men,	nullo homine existente.
and hence so also is	Ergo et hec:
'Man is animal'.	'homo est animal'.[33]

To this Kilwardby -- if it is Kilwardby -- replies by invoking the mediation of intellectus to maintain the truth of the indefinite proposition now in question, i.e., 'Man is animal':

As Aristotle suggests towards the beginning of De interpretatione 1, 'utterances are marks or signs of things understood, but understandings are signs of things.' Hence an utterance is a sign of a thing only through the understanding. As, therefore, it is possible for the understanding or semblance of any thing to remain in the mind and be signified by the utterance even though the thing be destroyed, it is obvious that should no man exist it is possible for the understanding or semblance thereof to abide in the mind and to be signified by the utterance....On this basis I contend that the same relation holds between man actually signified qua thing to animal signified qua thing as holds between that understanding or semblance of man which is signified by the name 'man' and the understanding or semblance of animal which is signified by the name 'animal'. But the relation of inherence that holds between man as an actual thing and animal as an actual thing is on the level of the nature, for 'Man is animal' is in natural subject-matter. Hence likewise the inherence of the under-

Sicut innuit Aristoteles in primo Peryarmenias principio 'voces sunt note sive signa intellectuum, intellectus vero sunt signa rerum'. Unde vox non est signum rei nisi per intellectum. Cum igitur possibile sit qualibet <re> destructa intellectum eius sive speciem in anima remanere et significari per vocem, manifestum quod nullo homine existente possibile est intellectum eius vel speciem in anima remanere et significari per vocem....Tunc arguo: que est comparatio hominis actualiter significati ut res ad animal ut res significatum, eadem est comparatio intellectus sive speciei hominis significati per vocem ad intellectum sive speciem animalis significatum per vocem. Sed naturalis est inherentia hominis ut res actu ad animal ut res actu, hec enim est in naturali materia 'homo est animal'. Ergo similiter est naturalis

standing or semblance of <u>man</u> as
signified by the utterance in the
⟨understanding or⟩ semblance of
<u>animal</u> signified by the utterance
is natural. Hence the proposition
that predicates the one of the
other, as when 'Man is <u>animal</u>'
is asserted, is true. Hence 'Man
is <u>animal</u>' is true <u>per se</u>
even though no man
exists....

inherentia intellectus sive
speciei hominis significati
per vocem ad speciem
animalis significatum per
vocem. Ergo enuntiatio
enuntians unum de
altero erit vera, ut cum
dicitur 'homo est animal'. Ergo
hec est vera simpliciter 'homo est
animal', nullo homine
existente....[34]

Now although this passage can obviously be analysed legitimately at the quidditative level if attention is paid to the points expressed in terms of <u>natura</u> and its corresponding <u>intellectus,</u> there is an unfortunate alternation of 'semblance' (<u>species</u>) with 'intellectus' which opens up the possibility of a perverse thesis according to which the preservation of truth in 'Man is <u>animal</u>' (there being no men) is dependent upon the presence in the mind of a 'semblance' for which the terms now in question can stand. This would open the way to some feeble-minded 'way of ideas' according to which truth is preserved in such cases by making the terms of quidditative-level propositions stand for mental entities <u>qua</u> entities, and not <u>qua</u> vehicles of <u>intellectus.</u>

Under these circumstances, i.e., in the absence of stress on the essential role of the <u>content</u> of the <u>intellectus,</u> the status of which can be functorially expressed at the quidditative level, the way is open for criticism from the Pseudo-Boethius of Dacia such as the following, which is dealing with the question as to whether 'Caesar is a man' can likewise hold if there is no Caesar:

...if (Caesar) remains in the mind he
can do so only under the guise of his
semblance; but that a thing has a
semblance is accidental to the thing
...and should Caesar abide merely
insofar as some accident of his is
concerned, this is of no service in
sustaining a true predication
of him,

...si maneat in anima
non tamen potest manere in
anima nisi per suam speciem,
species autem est accidens rei
...si Caesar maneat
quantum ad aliquod eius accidens, illud tamen accidens non
sufficit ad verificandum
hominem de ipso,

for Caesar is not one of his   quia Caesar non est suum
accidents.   accidens.[35]

The point that is being made here is clear enough. It merely just happens to
be the case that Caesar is thought of, and one can hardly found what
presumably is some sort of perpetual truth upon such a remote contingency.

A similar objection is raised by the Anonymous of MS Uppsala C.604:

...the logician decides on the   ...logicus iudicat
per se nature of propositions   perseitatem in propositionibus
based on the understanding   considerando ad rationes
of things. But this   intelligendi. Hoc enim
would seem not to be so,   non videtur esse verum,
because a proposition should not   quia propositio aliqua non debet
be said to be per se in the   dici per se
primary mode just on account of   primo modo ex eo
what has a merely accidental con-   quod accidit
nection with the subject-matter   subiecto
of the proposition. It just so   propositionis illius.
happens to be the case that such a   Ratio autem
consideration based on the under-   intelligendi talis
standing of things leads to the   per quam simul homine
understanding of animal as soon   intellecto intelligitur animal
as man is understood. Hence   accidit homini. Ergo
it is not by means of considera-   per talem rationem
tions based on the understanding   intelligendi
of things that the logician   non debet
should judge the proposition   logicus iudicare istam
'Man is animal' to be   esse per se: homo
per se in the primary mode.   est animal.[36]

Recollecting that this last expression refers to quidditative-level
discourse, the reply that the same manuscript supplies and which is now
reproduced, could scarcely be bettered:

...it does indeed merely happen   ...licet ratio
to be the case accidentally   intelligendi talis,
in respect of man as man   per quam homine

in the absolute sense that
considerations based on understandings lead to _animal_ being
understood when _man_ is understood; likewise it just happens
to be the case that being man
as man comes to be understood.
Nevertheless it is not accidental
in respect of the proposition
insofar as it is the object
of the logician's consideration
in respect of the subject of the
proposition of logic. For
the object of the logician's
thought is the fixed exigency
of the mode of understanding
insofar as it is appropriately
attributed to _man_, and hence
it is on this basis that he asserts that 'Man is _animal_'
is a _per se_ proposition.

intellecto
animal intelligitur,
accidat homini
unde homo est absolute,
sicut etiam
esse homini unde homo
est accidat intelligi,
tamen non accidit
propositioni ut
consideratur
a logico
et ut subiectum
propositionis logicae.
Considerat enim logicus
determinatum (?) respectum
modi intelligendi,
quia appropriate debetur
homini et ideo
ratione istius dicit
illam esse per se
'homo est animal'.[37]

Now although by this stage the situation has been brought well under control, in that its accidental elements have been expelled, yet there is another and more important qualification added. Beyond the logician, the producer and classifier of propositions based on the content of understandings, lies the metaphysician, whose interest is centred upon the quiddity which lies behind the whole process:

...the logician does not take note
of the _per se_ status of propositions in the most fundamental
fashion. He who does this is said
to be a practitioner of First
Philosophy. His task is to
explain the basis of what
the logician is saying when he
classifies a proposition as
per se in the first mode. For

...logicus non eo modo considerat
perseitatem in propositionibus
quomodo verius considerari
potest. Sed qui hoc modo considerat, dicitur esse primus
philosophus. Nam ipse habet
reddere causam eius,
quod dicit logicus, cum
assignat propositionem aliquam
esse per se primo modo.

as the logician makes the following
assertion: 'The proposition "Man
is animal" is per se because
when man is understood then
animal is understood.' But the
reason why, when man is understood, animal is understood,
has to be accounted for
by the metaphysician. The reason
behind it is because animal is
included in the quiddity of man.

Dicit enim logicus, quod haec
est per se: homo est animal, quia
homine intellecto
intelligitur animal.
Sed causa huius,
quare homine intellecto
intelligitur animal,
debet concedi
a metaphysico. Nam hoc
ideo est, quia animal includitur
in 'quod-quid-est' hominis.[38]

Thus is confirmed the fundamental nature of quidditative-level discourse
relative to intellectus discourse. This relation, here propounded in a
thirteenth-century form, has been a constant preoccupation at least since it
was clearly enunciated by Anselm of Canterbury in his De grammatico.[39]
When we come to review the whole scene in the light of Boethius of Dacia's
sequence from metaphysics, through modi intelligendi to modi significandi, the
present passage will afford precious confirmation of the interpretation of that
sequence that is going to be proposed.

There still remain, however, further discussions of the existence-question
in respect of indefinites as it occurs in the work thought to be by Kilwardby
from which quotations have been drawn above. Thus there occurs an
interesting corollary on being and existing which accords well with the
analyses proposed:

...'Man is a being, therefore a
man exists' does not follow, for
in the same way as 'Man is
animal' is true because of
the way in which understandings
hang together, so also, I assert,
is 'Man is a being' true
because of the way in which the
understanding of man and being
go together. Hence I say that
'being' in that proposition does
not have actual being as its

...non sequitur 'homo est ens,
ergo homo est', quia
sicut ista est vera 'homo
est animal' propter
convenientiam intellectuum,
similiter dico quod
ista est vera 'homo est ens'
propter convenientiam intellectuum
entis et hominis.
Unde dico quod
ibi 'ens'
non sumitur pro

significate, but rather its understanding. Hence 'Man is a being hence a man exists' does not follow.	significato entis actu, sed pro intellectu ipsius. Et ideo non sequitur 'homo est ens, ergo homo est'.[40]

Here it is quite properly being denied that the following is true:

.3   Cl⟦ man ⟧ ε   ⟦ V ⟧.⊃. ex (man)

If {being man} is {being included in being} then there
exists at least one (man)

Another way of expressing the position would be to say that, in the first
place, the following is a thesis of our ontology:

.4   [a]: a ε a. ⊃ . ex(a)

For all a if (a) is (a), then there exists at least
one a

In contrast, it is not the case that

.5   [a]: Cl⟦ a ⟧ ε Cl⟦ a ⟧. ⊃ . ex(a)

For all a if {being a} is {being a}, then there exists
at least one a

The position then is that if 'Man is a being' (the expression at issue in the
passage above) is taken to be the same as, or derivable from '{being man} is
{being man}', an instance of the antecedent of .5, then in view of the
untruth of .5, the existence of a man does not follow from that instance, in
spite of the superficial analogy with .4.

Hitherto, for the purpose of keeping the discussion contained in this
paper as uncomplicated as possible, the nullo homine existente clause of the
question concerning the indefinite 'Man is animal' has been taken to allow
'man' to have the status of an empty name. But there could obviously be a
difference between this case and that of 'chimera', for example, in that it is
taken for granted that the latter never named anything, whereas the
possibility that there were men but at some later time there are none seems
implicit in the medieval discussion around the case of man, as when Boethius
of Dacia says: 'Homine...corrupto non est essentia hominis plus quam erat

ante suam generationem....'41   In this sort of case, if the nominal level of discourse is taken to be intemporal, as is our primitive '.... ε....', according to the possibility envisaged by Boethius of Dacia himself,42 then in spite of the present non-existence of man, the name 'man' is not an empty name. Thus in an anonymous question on the Posterior Analytics we have:

When they say that 'Caesar is Caesar, hence Caesar is a man' does not follow, then they assert a falsehood. For he was a man earlier, as they admit. Hence he is a man. The proof of this is that that which is related in the same way to many things follows directly from any one of them. But 'man' is related in the same way to men past, present, and future.	Quod etiam dicunt, quod non sequitur 'Caesar est Caesar. Ergo Caesar est homo' falsum dicunt, quia fuit homo praeteritus, ut ipsi dicunt. Ergo est homo. Probatio, quia quod indifferenter se habet ad aliqua plura, simpliciter sequitur ad quodlibet ipsorum. Sed homo indifferenter se habet ad hominem praesentem, praeteritum et futurum.43

This is at any rate construable as yielding 'Caesar is a man' as an intemporal truth.   Adoption of such intemporality then postpones worries concerning the reference of terms having no present reference, but entails the use of a theory of time (chronology) after one's mereology (theory of part and whole) for the purpose of sorting out present existents from past existents, and vice versa.   Thus 'Caesar is a man and Caesar is wholly earlier than Charlemagne' would ensure temporal priority of Caesar relative to Charlemagne.   The intemporal '....is....' which is emerging in the last-quoted passage probably derives form the separation from time of names, which had been effected by Aristotle in De interpretatione.

That, for the moment, will suffice as a set of reminders of the way in which a categorial language may be used for analytic purposes.   Reflection on the process shows that the medieval discourse has been relativised to a set of contemporary logical systems, these being seen as constituting the categorial language, and hence as facilitating the reading off of the logical grammar (in terms of categorial indices) of the deep structure of the propositions undergoing investigation. The question arises: how does this whole procedure stand relatively to the medieval linguistic disciplines?   Is it so foreign to them as to represent the imposition of an alien form upon the material, screening it from us, rather than elucidating?

There are many ways in which an answer could be given to this question, and which would reassure us as to the sympathetic nature of the approach suggested. However, for the present it suffices to call attention to Boethius of Dacia's remarkable conspectus of the situation of his own rational speculative grammar. The relation of that grammar to metaphysics is such as to reassure us that the process exemplified above is by no means foreign to the medieval scene of the time. Thus in question 1 of his <u>Modi significandi</u> this Boethius describes the movement from metaphysics, with its <u>modi essendi,</u> to the <u>modi intelligendi,</u> and finally to the <u>modi significandi</u> of speculative grammar. Indeed, at the beginning of this process, as he says, the grammarian is a philosopher, and only when the <u>modi significandi</u> are being contrived does he begin to become a grammarian.[44] If it is granted that the presupposed Lesniewski systems (e.g., Ontology, Mereology) are the present-day counterparts of Aristotelian medieval metaphysics,[45] then the Boethian process, beginning with metaphysics and ending in <u>modi significandi,</u> is clearly being reproduced, at least in some of its aspects, in the analytic process exemplified above. This applies particularly if, as has been possible throughout, the categorial indices are used to identify the semantical categories figuring in the analyses in question. At any rate, the identity of some of his <u>modi significandi</u> with the constructions depictable by the categorial indices, is certainly entailed by what he has to say in q. 41 of his work on the subject of these <u>modi.</u>[46] Again, for example, the statement of the diversity of <u>modi essendi</u> picked out by common and proper nouns, a diversity that founds corresponding <u>modi significandi,</u> is stateable in terms of the many-link functors available in our presupposed ontology.[47] These and other examples tend to confirm the continuity and sympathy of the present-day enterprise exemplified above with the medieval project advocated by Boethius of Dacia.

Notes

[1] H.A.G. Braakhuis, C.H. Kneepkens, L.M. de Rijk eds., <u>English Logic and Semantics from the End of the Twelfth Century to the Time of Ockham and Burleigh: Acts of the 4th European Symposium on Mediaeval Logic and Semantics, Leiden-Nijmegen, 23-27 Apris 1979</u> (Artistarium Supplementa 1; Nijmegen, 1981).

2 J. Pinborg and H. Roos eds., Boethii Daci Modi significandi, q. 9 (Corpus philosophorum Danicorum Medii Aevi 4; Copenhagen, 1969), p. 39; cf. D.P. Henry, That Most Subtle Question: The Metaphysical Bearing of Medieval and Contemporary Linguistic Disciplines (Manchester, 1984), § 1.2; idem, 'Two Medieval Critics of Traditional Grammar', Historiographia linguistica 7 (1980) 85-107, ibid., pp. 85-87.

3 Modi significandi, q. 9; ed. cit., p. 39.

4 See Czesław Lejewski, 'Syntax and Semantics of Ordinary Language', The Aristotelian Society, Supplementary Volume 49 (1975) 127-46; Henry, Quaestio subtilissima, § 0.5.

5 See Osmund Lewry, 'The Oxford Condemnations of 1277 in Grammar and Logic' in English Logic and Semantics (v.s. n.1), pp. 235-78, ibid. p. 252.

6 See Jan Pinborg, 'Walter Burley on Exclusives' in English Logic and Semantics, pp. 305-29, ibid., p. 319.

7 Lewry, 'The Oxford Condemnations of 1277...' (v.s. n. 5).

8 Ibid., p. 277, n. 148.

9 See D.P. Henry, 'Suppositio and Significatio in English Logic' in English Logic and Semantics, pp. 361-85, ibid., p. 365.

10 P. Boehner, G. Gál, S. Brown eds., Guillelmi de Ockham Summa logicae, pars 2, cap. 12 (Guillelmi de Ockham Opera philosophica 1; St. Bonaventure, N.Y., 1974), p. 283 (10-28); see too Henry, 'Suppositio and Significatio...', p. 365; idem, That Most Subtle Question, § 2.65.

11 See Henry, 'Suppositio and Significatio...', p. 363; idem, Medieval Logic and Metaphysics (London, 1972), pp. 36 (.2), 74(.3).

12 Henry, 'Suppositio and Significatio...'; cf. also idem, That Most Subtle Question, § 2.6.

13 W.V.O. Quine, From a Logical Point of View (Cambridge, Mass., 1953); cf. Henry, That Most Subtle Question, § 2.641; idem, Medieval Logic and

Metaphysics, p. 46.

14 Lejewski, 'Syntax and Semantics...'.

15 Here and hereunder a strict and non-strict version of the propositions in question will be provided. In the strict version the conventions and definitions outlined in Henry, Medieval Logic and Metaphysics, part 2, and idem, That Most Subtle Question, § 6, will be adopted, whereas the systematised English version also given will retain the category-evincing brackets adopted in Henry, Medieval Logic and Metaphysics, part 1, § 3.

16 Norman Kretzmann transl. and ed., William of Sherwood's Introduction to Logic (Minneapolis, Minn., 1966), p. 30, n. 36.

17 See Lewry, 'The Oxford Condemnations...', pp. 246-47.

18 Ibid., pp. 269-70, n. 114.

19 See Lejewski, 'Syntax and Semantics...'; idem, 'Proper Names', The Aristotelian Society, Supplementary Volume 31 (1957. 229-56, ibid., pp. 248-50; Henry, Medieval Logic and Metaphysics, p. 43; idem, That Most Subtle Question, §§ 3, 4.

20 See Henry, 'Suppositio and Significatio...', p. 379; idem, Medieval Logic and Metaphysics, part 3, § 2.

21 See Henry, That Most Subtle Question, § 4.

22 See C.H. Kneepkens, '"Legere est agere": the first quaestio of the first Quaestiones-Collection in the MS Oxford CCC 250', Historiographia linguistica 7 (1980) 109-30, ibid. 48.4.13; D.P. Henry, 'Two Medieval Critics...' (v.s., n. 2), p. 102.

23 Cf. Henry, Medieval Logic and Metaphysics, p. 43.

24 See Lewry, 'The Oxford Condemnations...', pp. 269-70.

25 Sten Ebbesen and Jan Pinborg, 'Studies in the Logical Writings attributed to Boethius of Dacia', CIMAGL 3 (1970).

26 Ibid., pp. 41–42.

27 As described and quoted in Lewry, 'The Oxford Condemnations...', pp. 246–47; cf. ibid., p. 269, n. 108.

28 Henry, Medieval Logic and Metaphysics, pp. 42–43.

29 Ebbesen and Pinborg, 'Studies...', p. 41.

30 Ibid., p. 36; cf. pp. 14–15.

31 Cf. Henry, Medieval Logic and Metaphysics, p. 44 (.22).

32 Ebbesen and Pinborg, 'Studies...', pp. 36–37. It may be noted that the per se predication of the first type mentioned in the last-quoted passage, is an allusion to discourse at the quidditative level, of which expression .2 is a simple example.   As Aquinas puts it: 'Primus...modus dicendi per se est, quando id, quod attribuitur alicui, pertinet ad formam eius' (In Aristotelis libros Posteriorum analyticorum expositio 1, lectio 10; ed. R.M. Spiazzi, ed. 2a (Turin, 1964), p. 180, § 84).

33 Ebbesen and Pinborg, 'Studies...', p. 38 (7–11).

34 Ibid., pp. 38 (45)–39 (59).

35 Ibid., p. 32 (13–18); cf. Sten Ebbesen ed., Incertorum auctorum Quaestiones super Sophisticos elenchos, q. 92 (Corpus philosophorum Danicorum Medii Aevi 7; Copenhagen, 1977), pp. 209–19.

36 H. Roos, 'Drei Sophismata zum Formproblem in der Hs. Uppsala C 604', CIMAGL 24 (1978) 16–54, ibid., p. 48.

37 Ibid.

38 Ibid.

39 See Henry, That Most Subtle Question, § 4.41.

40 Ebbesen and Pinborg, 'Studies...', p. 40.

41 Ibid., p. 14 (44-45).

42 Boethii Daci Modi significandi, q. 84; ed. cit., pp. 200-201.

43 Ebbesen and Pinborg, 'Studies...', p. 25 (18-22).

44 Boethii Daci Modi significandi, q. 1; ed. cit., pp. 6-8; cf. Henry, That Most Subtle Question, § 1.1.

45 As has been argued in D.P. Henry, 'Medieval Metaphysics and Contemporary Logical Language' in Sprache und Erkenntnis im Mittelalter (Miscellanea Mediaevalia 13/1; Berlin, 1981), pp. 343-51; cf. idem, That Most Subtle Question, § 2.2.

46 Cf. Henry, That Most Subtle Question, § 0.54301.

47 Cf. ibid., § 2.752.

8

The Mertonians' Metalinguistic Science and the Insolubilia

Francesco Bottin
University of Padua

1. In the medieval treatises on the insolubilia a profound change is evident in the early decades of the fourteenth century, a change which occurred concomitantly with the appearance of the 'calculatorial techniques' of the Mertonians. This was also a change, as I have discovered, in the theoretical value and function that was assigned to these treatises in the conceptions of logic and science at this period.

In general, we may note above all a transition, which can be quite clearly verified, from the early texts on insolubilia of the thirteenth century to the tracts of the fourteenth century. In the insolubilia literature of the earlier period we find an investigation of the paradoxes, based essentially on the Aristotelico-Augustinian theory of signs, the results of which prove to be one of the critical components making an integral contribution to 'the rebuilding of grammatical theories from the view-point of dialectic.'[1] However, in the texts of the fourteenth century we find a different approach taken by the Mertonians, which proved decisive in their quest for an investigation of the logico-calculatorial nature of the semantical problems implied in the paradoxes.

In what follows, I wish to bring together only the more important aspects of this change in the texts, already noted by scholars.

2. One characteristic common to the early treatises can be arrived at, as I have hinted above, by an attentive analysis of the logical and grammatical

The Rise of British Logic, ed. P. Osmund Lewry, O.P., Papers in Mediaeval Studies 7 (Toronto: Pontifical Institute of Mediaeval Studies, 1985), pp. 235-248. © P.I.M.S., 1985.

situations which give rise to paradox, adopting a semiotic point of view. The
Augustinian notion of signum, rightly understood as (i) a res that (ii) has the
function of being the vehicle for signifying something else,[2] serves as the
basis for further developments in the conception of linguistic theory in the
Middle Ages. According to this conception one cannot imagine a signum
which does not signify something different from the specific res that it is
itself. When these notions were introduced into medieval logic during the
twelfth and thirteenth centuries, they determined profoundly the understanding of the nature of linguistic signs. Of course, these doctrines, in the hands
of earlier medieval logicians, constituted directly the fundamental principles
by which one had to accept or reject the complex casus of the insoluble
sentences, something which appears to have been very difficult from a
semantical and linguistic point of view.

It is widely recognized that one can find in the early texts the origin of
the threefold division of the radices insolubilium, namely, ex actibus hominis,
ex proprietatibus vocis and ex essentia ipsius enuntiabilis. This division
concisely expresses the conception that language is constituted with a
threefold aspect: a phonological aspect, a linguistic aspect and a signifying
aspect. Paradox can be hidden in each of these aspects. Moreover,
according to this conception, the actus hominis and the proprietates vocis
constituted the signa by which a particular significate is expressed.

In addition and in regard to these same doctrines, the author of
Insolubilia Monacensia holds that it is preferable to begin with the oral or
written expression in the solution of such paradoxes, but this treatment is
according to the ordo percipiendi, not the ordo naturalis. In fact, the
meaning always precedes the external manifestation by a speaker.[3]
Sometimes the authors of this period seem to be sufficiently aware of the
fact that 'omnia insolubilia reduci ad illam radicem que dicta est tertia',
namely that all insoluble situations can be reduced to that kind of insolubile
that depends 'ex substantia alicuius quod debet significari', so that they often
hold that 'una sola radix est insolubilium.'[4] However, they limit the focus of
their inquiry mainly to the solution of the first two roots of paradox, i.e., to
the actus hominis and proprietates vocis.[5]

In accordance with these assumptions the anonymous author of the
Insolubilia Monacensia offers a solution to the antinomies by some appropriate
distinctions that are peculiar to the dictio, oral or written, with the purpose

of discriminating a correct self-reference from an incorrect one. He holds that a _dictio_ is constituted by what he calls an 'assertio' and a 'prolatio'. This distinction seems to be similar to that usually involved in the definition of a _dictio_ as a _vox_ with a particular _ratio significandi._ Therefore, one might hold that he is himself speaking falsely only in the sense of producing an _assertio,_ i.e., only in the sense of articulating sounds. But self-reference is impossible if we assume the term 'dictio' to be a significant expression.[6]

In a similar fashion, in the case of the _insolubilia scripta_ one must distinguish the sense of 'scribere', which can be taken to mean simply _figuras protrahere_, from the sense of 'scribere' that can be understood more precisely as _figuras repraesentare._ Only in the second sense do the marks drawn on paper carry meaning.[7]

The authors of the earlier tracts on _insolubilia_ advance similar considerations with regard to the paradoxes having their origin in a mistaken application of the _proprietates vocis,_ i.e., _significatio, suppositio_ and _appellatio._ For, in these cases one must assert that the self-reference is incorrect from the principle:

> ....quando aliquod officium includitur in aliquo enuntiabili cum hac dictione '_falsum_' respectu alicuius vocis, id officium non potest esse in illa voce respectu totalis.'[8]

More precisely, the anonymous author of the _Insolubilia Monacensia_ maintains that the formation of a sentence is linked to an exact set of rules and, in particular, to a rule that says that a sentence must always have a subject and a predicate. He holds firmly to the consequence of the more general rule that precedes, which says that one cannot use a term as a linguistic sign and attribute to it a specific function, while simultaneously negating the very same function. For example, one cannot attribute to a term the function of being the subject or predicate and at the same time negate it in this way:

> ...si appellatio negetur ab aliqua voce respectu subiectionis, illa vox non potest esse subiectus in aliqua propositione.
> ...si appellatio negetur ab aliqua voce respectu predicationis, id non potest esse predicatus in aliqua propositione.[9]

For this reason, utterances of the kind 'propositio non appellata a suo subiecto', 'propositio non appellata a suo predicato', do not lead to the formation of linguistically correct propositiones:

...cum tales voces non possint esse subiectus vel predicatus, illa propositio non habet subiectum et predicatum, et ita non est propositio.[10]

These principles and all the distinctions set forth above are justified by having recourse to the doctrine by which the authors of the speculative grammars determine as linguistic signs the dictio, the propositio and the enuntiabile.[11]

In the analysis of the insoluble sentences, carried out with the special insights of a theory of signs, one may readily conclude that the proposed conditions for the correct formation of the propositio, and of the other elementary parts of the oratio, are not correctly fulfilled and for that reason they allow for self-reference. In this way, too, the congruitas and modus significandi of the linguistic expressions are more useful for the correct solution of self-reference than the veritas itself of the propositio. Thus, the solutions presented in the earlier tracts to the occasions of paradox in language are primarily based on the principles of cassatio and restrictio. These principles, however, are applied to precisely the same constitution of the different components of the linguistic expressions as signs, whether they are dictiones, propositiones or enuntiabilia.

In similar fashion, the anonymous author of the Insolubilia erroneously attributed to Shyreswood expounds the solutions of those who hold the theory of casatio and restrictio, which he will accept at least in part, and emphasizes the difficulty in admitting the correctness of a self-referential situation, given his conception of the relations between the different components of a linguistic sign. For example, in the same tract it is asserted that a part may not have supposition for the whole: 'quia pars tunc supponeret pro toto, et hoc est inconveniens...opponere verbum sermoni.'[12] This passage is to be taken in the sense that the level at which the verbum is constituted as a linguistic sign may be differentiated from that of the sermo. Likewise, the author insists on denying the assumption that one can make a meaningful self-reference at the phonological level:

...nullus potest videre se videre nisi videat aliquid aliud, nec audire se audire nisi audiat aliud.   ...Ergo qui nichil aliud dicit non potest dicere....[13]

In another passage he makes an express reference to the Augustinian definition of signum in order to deny the linguistic correctness of the paradoxical sentences:

> ...cum hec oratio sit quoddam significatum, et significatum est quod se offert sensui, aliud derelinquens intellectui, tunc ipsa significat de alio, et non de se.   Et hoc est quod dicebant quod instrumenta dicendi non subserviunt sue dictioni.[14]

In the same tract the author seems weakly to endorse the doctrine of the restringentes according to which 'omnis sermo imponitur ad aliud significandum, sicut naturaliter signum aliud a se significat.'[15]   These specifications are also drawn from the Augustinian definition of 'signum'. Thus, the Anonymous nevertheless criticizes the solutions of the cassantes and the restringentes in an attempt to construct his own solution, while he continues to treat the insolubilia in a manner not dissimilar from that of the preceding authors.   To those who maintain the cassatio and restrictio and deny that a part can stand for a whole, he observes that one loaf on display in front of an oven as a sign can rightly stand for all the bread from that oven:

> ...quamvis ipse panis ostendendo se significat totum et in illo toto seipsum, non tamen significat se ibi ut ipse fuit signum totius sed ut ipse in se est res aliqua....[16]

In the thinking of this author the loaf, inasmuch as it is a thing (res), can be employed in the double function of (i) 'significare de se', and (ii) 'significare aliud a se': '...bene accidit quandoque idem significare seipsum et esse nomen sui ipsius...nec est inconveniens aliquando signum et significatum esse idem.'[17]

Here once again, the Anonymous specifies the position of the restringentes, saying that it is correct only in the case of signa obtained by imposition (per impositionem).   The same principle cannot be used for natural signs (signa naturalia).   Only when one brings to bear the meaning of something else, will it be necessary that 'signum aliud a se significat';[18] in other cases this is not so.

His own solution, constructed on the basis of the Aristotelian distinction secundum quid/simpliciter, is obtained by applying the rule of the restringentes that is retained only in via solutionis. In fact, one must still specify the different senses in which one can take the self-referential sentences by distinguishing the twofold function of a linguistic sign, i.e., significare de se and significare aliud a se. But this is an operation incumbent upon anyone who wants to solve the paradox, because,

> ...quantum est ex parte huius dictionis falsum, in se considerate, indifferenter stat pro hoc vel pro aliis, sed hoc secundum quid tantum, et sic dicens hanc simpliciter mentitur, secundum quid autem verus.[19]

In this way, a correct conception of the double nature of the sign also remains as the basis in a solution obtained through the distinction secundum quid/simpliciter.

3. The Mertonians not only found the solution of the earlier authors to be unsatisfactory and misleading, but they also made frequent reference to them with great scorn. Unfortunately, we do not know with certainty to which tracts Walter Burley, Thomas Bradwardine, Richard Kilvington, Roger Swyneshead and many others referred when they opposed their own way of solving insoluble sentences to the antiquus modus respondendi.[20] However, this is not very crucial for my purpose, because the Mertonians did not simply limit themselves to making reproaches against specific solutions, but they directly condemned this very way of treating and solving insolubilia of the preceding authors. In fact, the Mertonians found unacceptable attempts at solving paradoxes in language primarily on the basis of working with signa or external expressions of what is at the heart of the occurrence of paradox, analyzed by means of the rules of a general theory of signs alone. The claim that paradoxical sentences are incorrect from the point of view of congruitas and modus significandi was found by the Mertonians to be linguistically inadmissible.

Here one can see that the Mertonians felt that they themselves were working toward the same goal and were quite aware of the fact that they had shifted the inquiry from a theory of signs to a more refined level of a theory of meaning. For this reason, Thomas Bradwardine launched invective against the cassantes and restringentes, calling them 'nimis asinarii':[21] having perceived that the paradox was hidden essentially in the tertia radix, i.e., 'ex essentia ipsius enuntiabilis', he found that they did not elaborate a theory which adequately resolved it.   They ended, according to the thinking of Bradwardine, by simply denying the legitimacy of self-reference, either from a linguistic or a grammatical point of view.

The Mertonians, even with their differing solutions, agreed about the treatment of the core of paradox on a metalinguistic level. For this purpose they had to have reached a special linguistic level that would not only be free from ambiguities and contradictions but would also permit one to 'speak of' or 'make reference to' the significates of the inferior level.

Unfortunately, it is necesary to delve into the medieval tracts in order to present the different attempts to propose a metalinguistic analysis of the paradoxes instead of looking for a doctrine explicitly set out for this purpose. To be sure, the most important line of inquiry to follow in order to comprehend the use of the metalinguistic level is grounded in the Mertonians' insistence on speaking of different levels of signifying. Above all, we find in this mode the distinction between a significatio primaria or principalis and a secondary way of signifying. In particular, Bradwardine in his tract distinguished a significatio principalis from that which he called 'significatio ex consequenti', i.e., a way of signifying derived from the former. Now we must remember that for Bradwardine the insolubilia are false not because they signify something false principaliter but because they always signify, at the same time, the truth of one and the same statement. This is asserted in the following conclusio, which is rigorously demonstrated in the tract of this medieval logician:

> ...si aliqua propositio significat se non esse veram vel se esse falsam ipsa (ipsam Roure) significat se esse veram et est falsa....[22]

His own solution tends to reinforce the level of the significatio principalis, that is to say, the level at which 'primo repraesentat idem intellectui, aut...significat idem',[23] in the sense that he has to introduce (explicitly for insoluble sentences and implicitly for any kind of sentence)[24] another level, distinct from that of signifying principaliter. On this second level each sentence signifies that it is itself true, i.e., it affirms its own truth. And so we find the resulting levels of signification are of three kinds: (i) signifies metalinguistically that each sentence is true; (ii) signifies or does not signify principaliter, as is the case; (iii) signifies ex consequenti, i.e., it conveys a significate derived from (ii) and which is often in contrast to (ii) by means of an arbitrary imposition of meaning on the sentence. As anyone can see, only level (i) remains immune from the change of truth-value that is usually found in self-referential sentences. The property 'firmness' (based on the assumption that all sentences are primarily true), attributed by him to level (i), allows for a solution of paradoxes, as is demonstrated by Bradwardine with adapted calculationes.

In similar fashion, the solution of Roger Swyneshead is based on the distinction of different levels of signifying conveyed by the sentences, i.e., the distinction between signifying principaliter sicut est and signifying aliqualiter est. By the former the author means an adequate description of the state of things through a sentence; by the latter, such an ambiguous description that one cannot decide whether the sentence in question is true or false. From his point of view, the two ways of signifying seem to be considered to be inconsistent in the same sentence, because, without question, he defines the second way of signifying as that which is characteristic of a sentence that is 'pertinens ad inferendum se ipsam non significare principaliter sicut est....'[25] In connection with this distinction he also sets out a definition of an insoluble sentence: for him, an insoluble sentence is precisely a sentence 'significans principaliter sicut est vel aliter quam est, pertinens ad inferendum se ipsam fore falsam.'[26]

Roger Swyneshead, in order to re-establish the initial conception of the two ways of signifying of the sentences, broken by the insolubilia, had to introduce in the second suppositio a principle according to which 'Omnis propositio falsificans se (i.e., any insoluble sentence) est propositio falsa.'[27] It is worth noting that this principle is not found at the semantical level, that is to say, among the necessary rules for discriminating true sentences from false ones, but rather at the meta-semantic level, that is to say, as a meta-rule designed to govern the correct use of the semantic rules. For example, if the sentence 'Δ' (='Socrates dicit falsum') is stated in the object-language, and the general rules for determining the truth or falsity of such a sentence are, (i) sentence 'Δ' is true if and only if the case is as Socrates says it is, (ii) sentence 'Δ' is false if and only if the case is not as Socrates says it is, then the second suppositio constitutes a meta-rule, which means that rules (i) and (ii) function only in the case of sentences which do not falsify themselves.

These distinctions concerning the levels of signification are of importance in understanding the route the Mertonians followed in their solutions of the paradoxes, but there are also other doctrines in their tracts which enable us to see quite clearly that in general they tried to resolve semantic antinomies by distinguishing the language about which one speaks from that by which one speaks. These attempts indicate to us that the Mertonians were looking for a distinction analogous to that of the object-language and meta-language distinction.

But in truth, on this subject the Mertonian authors must have found some interesting observations in the works of their predecessors, authors whom they had already condemned for other reasons. The Anonymous of the Tractatus Sorbonensis alter looked for a distinction between 'id de quo fit sermo' and 'sermo factus de illo' and concluded that 'nichil in veritate facit sermonem nisi de eo quod est prius....' The priority posited by this author is, first of all, a temporal priority ('eorum que sunt idem specie, contingit unum esse prius altero tempore')[29] and then, more generally, a priority of nature (prius natura), in the sense of something being more simple than the whole sentence ('subiectum est simplicius, et sic prius secundum naturam oratione facta de eo').[30]

The doctrine offering a solution of the paradoxes per transcasum, presented by Walter Burley as very close to that of his own opinion, enunciated a more straightforward distinction between the 'tempus in quo dico aliquid' and the 'tempus pro quo dico aliquid'. This temporal distinction is fundamental in the mind of its author for resolving paradoxes:

> ...si dico me dicere falsum, dico hoc pro tempore precedente; et quia in tempore precedente nihil dixi, ideo, in dicendo me dicere falsum, dico falsum, quia dico aliter quam est in re....[31]

The Mertonians held very diverse attitudes about these distinctions between the part and the whole, the moment of utterance and time of reference. In fact, either they rejected them because they considered them completely arbitrary (see, for example the criticism of Bradwardine, directed against the principle of the restringentes according to which the part cannot stand for the whole[32]) or they regarded them as insufficient for solving paradox (for example, the criticism of temporal distinctions by Burley and Bradwardine[33]); and finally, when they accepted them, they understood them

in a completely different sense, so that, for example, the rule of the
restringentes was considered valid by some medieval authors only while it
determined a relation between terms of first and second intention.[34]

More generally, Bradwardine appears to have appealed to the arbitrari-
ness of linguistic conventions in order to assert the claim that it is
impossible to prevent self-reference by means of purely grammatical rules or
on the basis of distinctions obtained from the theory of signs, since it is
always possible to have an impositio ad placitum for whatever sentence is
used in a self-referential sense. Bradwardine preferred other formulations of
the different levels into which language can be analyzed in order to avoid
paradoxes. In particular, Bradwardine introduced an attitude, widely adopted
among the Mertonians after him, toward the use of the letters of the
alphabet, for example 'A', 'B', 'C', etc., as singular names of sentences.[35] He
defends the correctness of such a substitution, maintaining that 'ille voces
(i.e. 'A','B', 'C', etc.) sunt ad placitum et hoc potest quilibet experiri.' By
assigning, for instance, the name 'A' to the sentence 'B est falsum' and the
name 'B' to the sentence 'A est verum', we can construct a formulation of
the paradox (set out below) where the substitution can be continued
indefinitely, giving rise to an indefinite series of linguistic levels:

  1. 'B est falsum.'
  2. '"A est verum." est falsum.' (by substitution of the
                                    sentence of which 'B' is
                                    the name in 1)
  3. '""B est falsum.' est verum." est falsum.' (by substitution of
                                    the sentence of which 'A' is
                                    the name in 2)
and so on.[36]

The most evident conclusion that we can draw from the new formulation
— at this point quite remote from the communis modus loquendi -- is that
the Mertonians were well aware of the fact that it is not sufficient to make
a distinction only between two stages of a single linguistic level in order to
resolve the paradoxes (i.e., the stages of asserere and proferre, of figuras
protrahere and figuras repraesentare), or between levels differing only in
temporal frame (for example, the level of the tempus in quo loquitur and the
level of the tempus pro quo loquitur, and so on), because the antinomial
situation is very likely to be perpetuated at all stages and at all levels of

language if one does not exercise the requisite precautions. In other words, the naïve claim of the so-called 'antiqui' that paradox would be eliminated by simply operating at the level of the construction of a sermo as a particular way of relating linguistic signs, is replaced in the tracts of the Mertonians by the artificial set of a linguistic level that, by its own nature, cannot be liable to falsifying self-reference. This is precisely the point at which the Mertonians generally made their distinctions of linguistic levels.

4. This new approach worked out by the Mertonians in regard to insolubilia leads us to an understanding of the function of these treatises within their scientific framework. If we recognize, as many scholars have held, that 'The metalinguistic analysis of conceptions and problems by way of terms and propositions was a recommended and most fruitful technique in later medieval natural philosophy',[37] and thus was a common characteristic of science in the Later Middle Ages, we may readily see how a guiding role emerged for the treatises on insolubilia, one that served as the source and principle of development for a new frame of mind.

Notes

I must thank Professor Philip Drew, currently studying in the Centro per la storia della tradizione aristotelica nel Veneto, Padua, for his invaluable assistance in providing a first translation of my paper into English, of which this is an edited version. I, of course, am responsible for any conceptual or doctrinal errors in the text.

[1] L.M. de Rijk, Logica modernorum: A Contribution to the History of Early Terminist Logic 2.1 (Wijsgerige Teksten en Studies 16; Assen, 1967), p.120.

[2] See B. Darrell Jackson, 'The Theory of Signs in St. Augustine's De doctrina christiana', Revue des études Augustiniennes 15 (1969) 9-49; A. Maierù, 'Signum dans la culture médiévale' in Sprache und Erkenntnis im Mittelalter 1 (Miscellanea Mediaevalia 13/1; Berlin-New York, 1981), pp. 51-72.

[3] Insolubilia Monacensia ed. L.M. de Rijk, 'Some notes on the mediaeval tract De insolubilibus, with the edition of a tract dating from the end of the

twelfth century', _Vivarium_ 4 (1966) 83-115 (edition, pp. 104-15); ibid., p. 105 (16-18).

4 _Insolubilia Parisiensia_ (MS Paris, BN lat. 11412), passages in De Rijk, 'Some notes...', pp. 93-98; ibid., pp. 95-96.

5 Of course, the authors of the earlier tracts on _insolubilia_ tried also to solve the _insolubilia_ of the _tertia radix_, even though they discussed this kind of paradox in a manner not dissimilar from the two preceding kinds. See _Ins. Mon._, p. 115 (4-17); _Ins. Par._, p. 95.

6 See _Ins. Mons._, p. 106 (3-10).

7 Ibid., p. 114 (9-14).

8 Ibid., p. 112 (32-34).

9 Ibid., p. 113 (3-6).

10 Ibid., (12-14).

11 See Jan Pinborg, 'Speculative Grammar' in Norman Kretzmann, Anthony Kenny, Jan Pinborg eds., _The Cambridge History of Later Medieval Philosophy_ (Cambridge, 1982), p. 257.

12 'Insolubilia _Guilelmi Shyreswood_ (?)' ed. M.L. Roure, 'La problématique des propositions insolubles au XIIIe siècle et au début du XIVe, suivie de l'édition des traités de W. Shyreswood, W. Burleigh et Th. Bradwardine', _Archives d'histoire doctrinale et littéraire du Moyen Âge_ 37 (1970) 205-326 (edition, pp. 248-61); ibid., p. 249,   1.03.

13 Ibid., p. 250,   1.06.

14 Ibid., p. 252,   3.05.

15 Ibid., p. 253,   4.09.

16 Ibid., p. 252,   4.05.

[17] Ibid.,   4.06.

[18] Ibid., p. 253,   4.09.

[19] Ibid., p. 260,   11.02.

[20] See Insolubilia Walteri Burlei, ed. Roure, 'La problématique...', pp. 262-84; ibid., p. 271,   3.01. See too Insolubilia Thomae de Bradwardine, ed. Roure, 'La problématique...', pp. 285-326; ibid., p. 288,   3.04: '...hoc non est nisi figmentum illorum qui ad insolubilia nesciunt aliter respondere.'; cf. ibid., p. 295,   5.06; Richard Kilvington, Insolubilia ed. F. Bottin, 'L'opinio de insolubilibus di Richard Kilmyngton', Rivista critica di storia della filosofia 28 (1973) 408-21; ibid., p. 415: '...ista solutio...fundatur super antiquum modum arguendi in insolubilibus'; Roger Swyneshead, Insolubilia ed. Paul Vincent Spade, 'Roger Swyneshead's Insolubilia: edition and comments', Archives d'histoire doctrinale et littéraire du Moyen Âge 46 (1979) 177-220; ibid., p. 196,   47: '...illa causa nulla est nisi fatuorum protervientium qui ad insolubile aliter nesciunt respondere nisi possibile fore impossibile sustinere.'

[21] Bradwardine, Insolubilia, p. 295,   5.06.

[22] Ibid., p. 298,   6.05.

[23] Ibid., p. 302,   7.025.

[24] See Paul Vincent Spade, 'Insolubilia and Bradwardine's Theory of Signification', Medioevo 7 (1981) 115-34; ibid., p. 131.

[25] Swyneshead, Insolubilia, p. 181,   3.

[26] Ibid., p. 182,   5.

[27] Ibid., p. 186,   18.

[28] Tractatus Sorbonensis alter ed. H.A.G. Braakhuis, 'The second tract on insolubilia found in Paris, B.N. Lat. 16.617: An edition of the text with an analysis of its content', Vivarium 5 (1967) 111-45 (edition, pp. 131-45); ibid., p. 139 (3-4).

29 Ibid., p. 138 (1-2).

30 Ibid., pp. 137 (1)-138 (1).

31 Burley, Insolubilia, p. 270,   2.07.

32 See ibid.,   2.05; Bradwardine, Insolubilia, pp. 287-89,   3.00-3.07.

33 See Burley, Insolubilia, p. 271,   2.08: '...volo loqui precise de isto tempore in quo tu dicis te dicere falsum et quero: in illo tempore aut dicis verum aut falsum. Si in illo tempore dicis falsum et in illo tempore non dicis nisi te dicere falsum, ergo in illo tempore te dicere falsum est falsum, et ultra: ergo in illo tempore te dicere falsum non est verum, ergo non dicis falsum, ergo in illo tempore dicis falsum, in illo tempore non dicis falsum. Si detur quod in illo tempore dicis verum, ergo in illo tempore est tuum dictum verum, et tuum dictum est te dicere falsum, ergo si in illo tempore dicis verum, in illo tempore dicis falsum.'; Bradwardine, Insolubilia, p. 295,   5.041: '...ista autem positio faciliter improbatur, quia licet esset conveniens quantum ad solutionem predicti sophismatis, tamen non est generalis ad alia, quia non potest aptari nisi ad insolubilia fundata in actu dicendi. Ergo non sufficit.'

34 See F. Bottin, Le antinomie semantiche nella logica medievale (Padua, 1976), pp. 173-75.

35 See ibid., pp. 168-70.

36 See Bradwardine, Insolubilia, p. 292,   4.06; Kilvington, p. 419.

37 John E. Murdoch, 'Scientia mediantibus vocibus: Metalinguistic Analysis in Late Medieval Natural Philosophy' in Sprache und Erkenntniss 1.73-106; ibid., p. 106.

9

William Heytesbury on 'Necessity'

Ria van der Lecq
University of Utrecht

1. This paper is an attempt to clarify Heytesbury's doctrine of necessity and contingency. I shall try to achieve this end by means of an analysis of the relevant parts of the sophism 'anima Antichristi necessario erit'. My intention is to interpret this text from the point of view of somebody who has read Simo Knuuttila's paper 'Time and Modality in Scholasticism.'[1] But first I shall say something about the history of the sophism.

2. Examples concerning Antichrist occur for the first time in logical texts at the end of the twelfth century.[2] The question was whether Antichrist would be a human being (and, consequently, would have a soul) or a supernatural being.

The sophism is also discussed by William of Sherwood. According to him the proposition 'anima Antichrist necessario erit' may be interpreted in two ways:

(1) the modal operator is a determination of the composition — here the sense is that the proposition 'anima Antichristi erit' is necessary —

(2) the mode determines the action of the verb as such — then the meaning is: necessary being goes together with the soul of Antichrist.

The composite sense (1) could be rewritten as '"Antichrist will have a soul" is necessary',[3] which is false, because it is not certain whether Antichrist

---

The Rise of British Logic, ed. P. Osmund Lewry, O.P., Papers in Mediaeval Studies 7 (Toronto: Pontifical Institute of Mediaeval Studies, 1985), pp. 249-263. © P.I.M.S., 1985.

will be a man or not. The divided sense (2) should be read as follows: every soul has necessary (i.e., eternal) being, therefore also the soul of Antichrist will necessarily be, when it will be.

Another work that discusses the sophism is a **sophistaria**-tract dating from the second half of the thirteenth century. It is ascribed to Walter Burley. This is his solution:

> Potest ergo hoc quod dico 'necessario' determinare primam compositionem; et sic est falsa; et est sensus 'anima Antichristi necessario erit' idest: necessario ducetur de non esse ad esse; quod est falsum, immo hoc est contingens, quia potest duci et non duci. Si autem determinet aliam compositionem sic dicitur determinare predicatum; et tunc est vera; et est sensus 'anima Antichristi necessario erit' idest: habebit esse necessarium; et sic est vera: anima Antichristi habebit <esse> immutabile. Unde primo modo importatur per hoc quod dico 'necessario' necessaria ordinatio exitus anime Antichristi de non esse ad esse; secundo vero modo continuitas sive incorruptibilitas ipsius anime in esse.[4]

Thus, like Sherwood this author distinguishes two ways according to which the sentence may be understood. In the composite sense the sentence is false, because the coming-into-existence of the soul of Antichrist is not necessary. In the divided sense the sentence is true, because then it means: whenever the soul of Antichrist will be, it will be incorruptible. So in the composite sense 'necessarily' seems to be equivalent to 'incorruptible' and 'eternal'.

The author adds the following remark about the truth of propositions about the future:

> Ad illud quod querit de veritate propositionum de futuro, dicendum quod quedam propositiones future sunt contingentes, sed omnes de preterito sunt necessarie, quia esse futurorum contingentium est esse in potentia, que permutabilis est et se habens ad opposita; unde potest fieri et non fieri. Sed quod factum est, non potest non fieri. Unde preterita sunt intransmutabilia. Et ideo eorum veritas est sua necessitas.[5]

Thus, it is argued that every proposition about the past is necessary, and some propositions about the future are contingent. If a proposition about the past is true, then it is necessarily true, because whatever has happened, cannot cease to have happened. This is the traditional Aristotelian conception of necessity as omnitemporal being of omnitemporal truth. According to this theory a proposition about a past event is necessary because afterwards it will always be true to say that this event has happened, although the proposition could have been false before. As to the proposition 'anima Antichristi erit', this proposition is contingent, but as soon as the soul has come into existence, it will have necessary being, because it will be incorruptible and eternal. The divided sense of the sophism should be understood in this way.

3. In a recent paper, entitled 'Time and Modality in Scholasticism', Simo Knuuttila studies the fate of the Aristotelian theory of modality in the Middle Ages.[6] It may be useful to summarize the content of this paper as far as it is relevant to my purpose.

Let us take the proposition 'possibile est album esse nigrum.' In ancient and medieval discussions this proposition is usually considered false if we interpret it in the composite sense: it is possible that something is black and white at the same time. The proposition may be true if it is understood in the divided sense: then it means that something that is black now can be white at another moment. So, the difference between the two interpretations lies in the moment of actualisation of the possibility. According to Knuuttila (who follows the theory of Jaakko Hintikka) an important role is played by the so-called 'principle of plenitude', that is the principle that no genuine possibility can remain for ever unrealized. If this principle is applied to future events, it means that what can be actual at a certain moment, has to be actual at that moment:

$$M\underset{t_1}{p} \longrightarrow N\underset{t_1}{p}$$

This theory is based on Hintikka's interpretation of the famous sentence in Aristotle's De interpretatione 9 (19a23-24): 'What is, necessarily is, when it is; and what is not, necessarily is not, when it is not.' On this interpretation Aristotle intends to say that every temporally definite proposition is necessarily true, if it is true, because the truth-value cannot change. However, if the temporal specification is removed, the proposition is not necessarily true, because then the truth-value may change, depending on the

moment of utterance of the sentence. So, the proposition 'there will be a
sea-battle on the 24th of July 1983' is necessarily true, if true, whereas
'there will be a sea-battle tomorrow' is not necessarily (not always) true,
because a proposition of this kind may refer to different events depending on
the moment the sentence is uttered. In other words: a proposition about a
future event is necessarily true if it contains a temporal specification, but
not necessarily true if there is no such specification.

Elsewhere[7] I have argued that in my opinion this interpretation of
Aristotle's sentence cannot be maintained, but since this does not affect the
main issue of Hintikka's theory I shall not discuss it here any further. I also
believe that the principle of plenitude is not integrally linked with Aristotle's
theory of modality. But what matters is that in the Aristotelian conception
of modality a proposition is necessarily true if it is always true, and not
necessarily true (contingent) if it is sometimes true and sometimes false.
Possible being is equivalent to sometime-being (i.e., contingent being) and
necessary being is equivalent to omnitemporal being, and what never is, is
impossible. This implies that a proposition about the past is necessarily true
because it is and will always be true. This is exactly what is expressed in
the sophistaria-text quoted above.

Knuuttila asserts that the Aristotelian (diachronic) theory of modality
stands firm in the works of, among others, Boethius, Abailard and Thomas
Aquinas. Duns Scotus, however, developed a new modal theory which may be
rightly compared with a 'possible worlds'-theory in modern philosophy. Let us
consider again the proposition 'possibile est album esse nigrum.' According to
Scotus the divided sense of this proposition should be understood as follows:
something that is white now, could have been black at this same moment. In
the Scotist (synchronic) view contingency means that, when something is the
case, the opposite state of affairs could have been actualized instead.
Knuuttila concludes his paper by saying: 'The break with the Aristotelian
theory of modality is a general feature of the fourteenth century modal
logic.'[8]

Now it is time to consider Heytesbury's sophism. Let us see whether
Knuuttila's thesis holds for Heytesbury's conception of necessity.

4. The text that has been printed as an appendix to this article has been
taken from the Abbreviation of Heytesbury's Sophismata and is based on the

MSS Venezia, Padri Redentoristi 519, fols. 11^V-15^r and Città del Vaticano, Bibl. Apost. Vaticana, Vat. lat. 3056, fols. 8^V-11^V.[9] I have chosen the parts most relevant for our purpose, viz. the first and last arguments.

In the first argument it is supposed that Antichrist does not exist now but will exist contingently, in the sense that it is not determined whether he (or she or it) will be or not. Apparently the subject of 'erit' is 'Antichristus', but I am inclined to think that 'anima' would make better sense as subject since, as has been remarked above, the question was whether Antichrist would have a soul or not.[10]

First it is supposed that moment a is the first moment Antichrist (and his soul) will be. Then it is argued that after a the soul will necessarily be; therefore after a it will not be able not to be ('post a non poterit non esse' [10-11]), because after a it will be eternal and incorruptible. So here 'necessary' is considered to be equivalent to

(1) eternal, and

(2) not possible that not.

Then Heytesbury argues that the soul of Antichrist will not be necessarily but rather contingently; nor in a, nor after a will it necessarily be. The author concedes that something eternal may not be ('aliquod eternum potest non esse' [16-17]). Is this an indication of a Scotist conception of necessity? It would seem that Heytesbury rejects the equivalence of 'necessity' and 'omnitemporality', which, as we have seen, is a feature of the Aristotelian theory of modality, but I think a conclusion like this has yet to be justified. Let us consider the next sentence: 'Non aliquod quod est eternum, sed aliquid quod potest esse eternum potest non esse' (17-18). It now becomes clear what he means: something may be eternal when it exists, in the sense that it cannot cease to be. However, it is also possible that it will not exist at all, but as soon as it has come into existence it cannot cease to exist.

Well, says the opponent, since something eternal may not be, it should be concluded that it will not be (19-20). This seems to be the principle of plenitude applied to future events: if it is a genuine possibility that something will exist, then this possibility cannot remain for ever unrealized, and if it is possible for something not to exist, then it is impossible that it will exist. It is clear that the principle is denied by Heytesbury. In the longer version of the text it is expressed as follows: 'non sequitur "aliquod

eternum potest non esse; ergo possibile est quod aliquod eternum non erit.'"11
The antecedent is true, but the consequent is impossible.

Our interpretation of lines 17-18 is confirmed by lines 27-29. There it is
conceded that: 'aliquod eternum potest non esse, et tamen omne eternum est
tale quod non potest non esse' (something that is eternal, when it is, may not
be, although every eternal thing is such that it cannot not be). An eternal
object that already exists cannot cease to be, otherwise it would not be
eternal. It is clear that, according to Heytesbury, the propositions before
and after the words 'et tamen' are both true. Let us see what happens if
we interpret it in a synchronic way. From the foregoing remarks it is clear
that 'aliquod eternum' (27-28) has to refer to something that does not yet
exist. Until the moment that this object exists it is still possible that it will
not exist at that moment. The second part of the sentence, viz., 'omne
eternum est tale quod non potest non esse' (28-29), would be false on a
synchronic interpretation, since then it would mean that every eternal object
exists in every possible world. Well, in the actual world there is at least
one eternal object that does not exist, viz., the soul of Antichrist, as is
assumed at the beginning of the sophism. Moreover, if this soul were to
exist, it would exist contingently, that is, it would not exist in every possible
world. Therefore the synchronic interpretation should be rejected here.

In line 36 the term 'inevitable' is introduced. It is argued that 'the soul
of Antichrist will inevitably be after a, therefore after a it will not be able
not to be' (36-37). Heytesbury denies the antecedent, because it means that
it is impossible to prevent it from being after a, which is false (43-44).
There then follows a difficult passage. It is said that the following
consequence is not valid: 'after a it will be inevitable that the soul will be;
therefore after a it will inevitably be' ('post a erit inevitabile illam fore;
ergo post a illa inevitabiliter erit' [45-46]). Likewise it does not follow:
'after a it will be necessary that this soul will be, therefore after a it will
necessarily be' ('post a erit necessarium illam fore; ergo post a illa
necessario erit' [46-47]). Let us consider the corresponding text of the long
version:

Et ad argumentum, quando arguitur quod continue post a erit inevitabile
ipsam fore, ergo post a ipsa inevitabiliter erit, negatur consequentia.
Sicut non sequitur 'post a erit necessarium ipsam esse, ergo post a ipsa
necessario erit', quia licet in a erit ita quod ipsa necessario erit', post a

tamen modo non est ita quod ipsa necessario erit post a.[12]

So there is a difference between the proposition 'in a erit ita quod ipsa necessario erit', which is true, and 'post a est ita quod ipsa necessario erit post a', which is false. Now the reasoning becomes more clear. Although at moment a it will be the case that this soul will necessarily be, that does not imply that this soul will necessarily-be-after-a. Its being will be necessary, not its being-after-a.

Similar reasoning can be found at the beginning of the sixth argument, to which I shall now pass. The sixth argument assumes that Antichrist already exists ('ponatur quod Antichristus iam sit' [53-54]). In that case, Heytesbury argues, it is true to say that at some moment in the future his soul will necessarily be (58-59). However, it is not true to say that the soul of Antichrist will necessarily be at that moment (59-60). It is clear that the difference lies in the position of 'in illo instanti'. In the first proposition it falls outside the scope of 'necessario', whereas in the second case it falls within the scope of 'necessario'. The point is that the soul's being will be necessary, not its being-at-that-moment. The difference is stressed by the author in the following way: the first proposition means that at this moment the soul will not be able not to be; the second proposition means that this soul will not be able not-to-be-at-that-moment (71-73). The first proposition ('in hoc instanti non erit potens ad non esse' [71-72] is interesting because it may be understood in two ways: it is true on the Aristotelian (diachronic) theory, since then it means that at this moment the soul will not be able not to be, because it is eternal and, consequently, cannot cease to exist; on the synchronic theory, however, I suppose the proposition would signify that at some moment in the future the non-existence of the soul will not be an alternative possibiliby (a counterfactual). Understood in this second way the proposition would be false because, as is said at the beginning of the sophism, the coming into existence of Antichrist is a contingent event: it could have happened at another moment or not at all. Now Heytesbury seems to affirm this proposition. So, if my interpretation is right, this passage gives us some reason to think that Heytesbury is adhering to the traditional Aristotelian model of modality, since he affirms a proposition that would be false on a synchronic interpretation.

In lines 99-100 it is assumed that Antichrist has already existed for a long time before the present moment. Then it follows that his soul has

necessarily been ('illa anima necessario fuit' [100]).   But then an opponent
argues: 'In nullo instanti ipsa necessario fuit, quia quocumque instanti dato in
illo illa potuit non fuisse, quia illa adhuc potuit fuisse futura' (101-102).
Thus, since it could have been the case that this soul did not (yet) exist, it
is not true to say that it has necessarily been.   This is an argument
belonging to the synchronic model of modality: the non-existence of the soul
is considered to be an alternative state of affairs to its existence.
Heytesbury, however, does not agree with this argument.   Whenever the soul
has been, he says, it has been necessarily.   He concedes that from the first
moment it came into existence, it has been necessarily, because neither could
it not not be nor did it have the potency not to be ('quia tunc illa non
potuit non esse nec fuit potens ad non esse' [105-106].   So there are two
reasons why this soul has been necessarily ever since it has come into
existence:

(1) It could not be, and
(2) It was not able not to be.

What is the difference?   The second reason is clear.   It has been stated
before: the soul of Antichrist will not necessarily be, but when it is, it is
eternal and, consequently, cannot cease to be.   The first reason is quite in
agreement with the Aristotelian theory of modality as it is interpreted, for
example, by John Buridan.[13]   On this interpretation Aristotle distinguishes
two kinds of necessity: (1) something is necessary _simpliciter_ if it is, has
always been and will always be; (2) another kind of necessity is applied to
things and events in the past, and in this sense a past or present event is
necessary because afterwards the proposition that says that it has happened
will always be true.   Thus, as soon as the soul of Antichrist exists, the
proposition that says that it exists will always be true.

In the longer version it is put in the following way:

> Sed forte adhuc arguitur contra propositionem prius concessam, scilicet
> quod hec anima fuit necessario, quia non videtur aliqua ratio propter
> quam debet ista concedi nisi quia necesse est quod hec anima fuit.   Sed
> hec responsio non sufficit, quia consimiliter contingit arguere quod tu
> necessario fuisti quia necesse est quod tu fuisti.   Et sic posset probari
> quod necessario fuisti in ecclesia vel cucurristi in bello monte, etc., quia
> sic forte necesse est quod sic fecisti.   Ergo necessario sic fecisti.   Ideo

pro isto dicitur ut prius quod ista non est causa nec ratio quare ista anima necessario fuit. Sed hec est ratio istius, quia ista anima fuit quando non potuit non esse. Et in quolibet instanti in quo ista fuit ista non potuit non esse. Ideo etc. Sed sic non contingit arguere de esse tui in ecclesia. Fuisti enim in ecclesia quando potuisti non esse in ecclesia. Et cucurristi in bello monte quando potuisti non currere. Ideo etc.[14]

So it is argued that the proposition 'hec anima fuit necessario' is not only true because it is necessary that this soul existed. In this sense a proposition like 'you have been in the church' is also necessarily true, if it is true. This is not sufficient in our case. The other reason why this proposition is true is that this soul cannot cease to exist, when it exists. However, when you were in the church you had the possibility not to be in the church, not at the same time, but at another moment.

In the diachronic theory it is possible for something to be contingent and necessary at the same time. Suppose you were in the church, then it is necessary that you were in the church, because the proposition 'tu fuisti in ecclesia' will always be true. But the event is also contingent because you had the possibility not to be in the church, that is, to leave it.

This, then, is my interpretation of some relevant passages from Heytesbury's sophisma 'anima Antichristi necessario erit.' If my interpretation of this text is correct, it leads emphatically to the conclusion that Knuuttila's thesis that a break with the Aristotelian theory of modality is a general feature of fourteenth-century modal logic cannot be admitted as far as Heytesbury is concerned. It has already been shown that the thesis does not hold either for Buridan or for Ockham.[15] This makes it highly improbable that it should be maintained at all.

Notes

1 In Simo Knuuttila ed., Reforging the Great Chain of Being: Studies of the History of Modal Theory (Synthese Historical Library 21; Dordrecht-Boston-London, 1981), pp. 163-257.

2 See, for example, Fallacie Parvipontane ed., L.M. de Rijk, Logica

modernorum 1 (Wijsgerige Teksten en Studies 6; Assen, 1962), pp. 551-609, esp. p. 569 (33).

3 See Norman Kretzmann transl. and ed., _William of Sherwood's Introduction to Logic_ (Minneapolis, Minn., 1966), p. 42, n. 66.

4 This text is a transcription from MS Toledo, Biblioteca del Cabildo 94-26, by Professor De Rijk, who is preparing an edition of the _sophistaria_-tracts; ibid., fols. 67rb-68ra.

5 Ibid., fol. 68rb.

6 See above, n. 1.

7 See Ria van der Lecq, _Johannes Buridanus, Questiones longe super librum Perihermeneias_. Edited with an introduction (Artistarium 4; Nijmegen, 1983), pp. XXXIX-LI.

8 Knuuttila, 'Time and Modality in Scholasticism', p. 238.

9 See below, pp. 259-263. Line references are indicated here by bracketed numbers.

10 The longer version, printed with the _Tractatus Gulielmi Hentisberi de sensu composito et diviso_ (Bonetus Locatellus; Venice, 1494), fol. 99rb, reads 'quando ipsa erit', but 'quando' instead of 'an...vel non' does not seem to be an improvement.

11 Ibid., fol. 99va.

12 Ibid., fol. 99vb.

13 _Questiones longe super librum Perihermeneias_ 1.12; ed. Van der Lecq, pp. 54-56.

14 Ed. Venice, 1494, fol. 104ra.

15 For Buridan, see Van der Lecq, _Johannes Buridanus, Questiones longe_, pp. XXVIII-XXXIX; for Ockham, see A. Vos, _Kennis en Noodzakelijkheid. Een_

kritische analyse van het absolute evidentialisme in wijsbegeerte en theologie
(Kampen, 1981), pp. 87-98, 273-75.

Text

Abbreviatio sophismatis Guillelmi Heytesbury
'ANIMA ANTICHRISTI NECESSARIO ERIT', args. 1 & 6
(MSS Venezia, Padri Redentoristi 519, fols. 11^V-15^r;
Città del Vaticano, Bibl. Apost. Vat., Vat. lat. 3056,
5   fols. 8^V-11^V)

Ponatur quod Antichristus nunc non sit, sed quod ipse contingenter post
hoc erit ita quod non sit determinatum an erit vel non. Et vocetur primum
instans illius temporis a. Tunc arguitur sic: aliquando anima Antichristi
necessario erit; igitur sophisma. Antecedens sic: quia in a instanti anima
10 Antichristi necessario erit, igitur post a non poterit non esse, igitur etc.
Consequentia patet. Et antecedens sic probatur, quia post a ipsa erit
perpetua et incorruptibilis. Igitur tunc non poterit non esse, quia si sic,
sequitur quod aliquod eternum poterit non esse.

Ad illud respondeo negando sophisma in illo casu et concedo quod anima
15 Antichristi contingenter erit et nego quod in a vel post a necessario erit. Et
ulterius nego quod post a illa non poterit non esse. Et concedo quod aliquod
eternum potest non esse. Non aliquid quod est eternum, sed aliquid quod
potest esse eternum potest non esse.

Et si dicitur: ex quo aliquod eternum potest non esse, ponatur quod
20 aliquod eternum non erit, dicitur negando casum, sicud non sequitur 'album
potest esse nigrum; ponatur ergo quod album sit nigrum'.

⟨...⟩

Item. Si aliquod eternum poterit non esse, vel illud est vel non est. Si
illud eternum non est, ergo aliquod eternum non est. Consequens inpossibile;
25 ideo etc. Si illud eternum est, tunc aliquid quod est eternum potest non esse
quod fuit negatum.

Ad primum respondeo negando consequentiam. Unde concedo quod aliquod

eternum potest non esse, et tamen omne eternum est tale quod non potest
non esse. Sicud aliquis homo potest esse Antichristus, et tamen quilibet homo
30 est talis qui non potest esse Antichristus. Similiter aliquis homo potest
generari, et tamen quilibet homo est talis qui non potest generari de novo.

Ad secundum cum queritur si aliquod eternum potest non esse istud est
vel illud non est, dico quod non est. Et tunc non sequitur: 'illud eternum
non est, igitur aliquod eternum non est', quia arguitur ab inferiori ad suum
35 superius per accidens negatione postposita sine medio.

Sed aliquando arguitur sic: anima Antichristi erit inevitabiliter post a,
ergo post a non poterit non esse. Antecendens patet, quia post a erit
inevitabile ipsam fore.

Similiter: in a ipsa incipiet esse necessario post a, quia in a erit ita
40 quod incipit esse necessario post a.

Similiter: post a instanti illa erit eterna. Et tunc erit ita quod non
poterit non esse; ergo post a illa non poterit non esse, etc.

Ad hoc respondetur negando quod anima Antichristi inevitabiliter erit
post a, quia illa significat quod inpossibile est evitare quin illa erit post a.
45 Et tunc non sequitur: 'post a erit inevitabile illam fore; ergo post a illa
inevitabiliter erit'. Sicud non sequitur: 'post a erit necessarium illam fore,
ergo post a illa necessario erit', quia prima significat quod post a erit ita
quod illa inevitabiliter erit. Ideo caveas bene de illis terminis 'erit ita'!

Ad secundum. Non sequitur: 'in a incipiet esse ita quod illa omnino
50 necessario erit post a; ergo in a instanti illa incipiet esse necessario post a'.

Ad aliud. Concedo quod anima erit eterna et ultra non sequitur quod
illa necessario erit.

SEXTO principaliter ad sophisma arguitur sic. Et ponatur quod
Antichristus iam sit. Tunc arguitur sic. Antichristus est; ergo anima
55 Antichristi necessario erit. Et tunc ultra illa anima necessario erit; ergo in
aliquo instanti. Et per consequens necesse est quod illa anima erit in
quolibet instanti futuro.

Ad istam respondetur dicendo quod in quolibet instanti futuro illa anima
necessario erit et quod in illo instanti illa anima necessario erit. Sed non
60 necessario erit in illo instanti.   Sicud non sequitur 'in hoc instanti Deus
necessario est; ergo necessario est in hoc instanti'.

Iterum. Ad aliud nego in sensu diviso quod illa anima necessario erit in
quolibet instanti futuro. Sed concedo in sensu composito, quod necesse est
quod illa anima erit in quolibet instanti futuro, sicud patet per expositionem.
65 Et non sequitur quod necesse est quod illa anima erit in illo instanti futuro
quocumque determinato. Sicud non sequitur 'necesse est quod omnis homo sit;
b est homo; ergo necesse est quod b sit'.

Iterum. Nota differentiam inter illa duo: 'in hoc instanti illa anima
necessario erit' et 'necessario erit illa anima in hoc instanti'. Sed tamen
70 idem est dicere: 'in hoc loco illa anima necessario erit' et 'illa anima
necessario erit in hoc loco'. Prima propositio significat quod in hoc instanti
non erit potens ad non esse, sed secunda significat quod illa anima non erit
potens non esse in hoc instanti. Sed sic non est de isto termino 'in hoc
loco' quando preponitur et quando postponitur.

75   Similiter arguitur sic. Si illa anima necessario erit in aliquo instanti,
ergo in aliquo necessario erit in aliquo instanti. Ponatur quod in a instanti.
Tunc in a instanti non necessario erit in aliquo instanti quod erit a nec in
aliquo quod non erit a. Ergo non necessario erit in aliquo instanti.

Similiter fiat argumentum de presenti. Et sit a nunc instans presens.
80 Tunc in a instanti illa anima non necessario est in a instanti nec in a
instanti nec in aliquo instanti quod non est a. Ergo non necessario est in
aliquo instanti.

Iterum. Ita respondeo et concedo quod illa anima necessario erit in
aliquo instanti. Et tunc non seqitur: 'illa anima necessario erit in aliquo
85 instanti; et non necessario erit in a instanti; ergo necessario erit in aliquo
instanti quod non erit a.' Similiter non sequitur: 'necesse est quod alterum
istorum sit verum si ista sunt, demonstrando duo contradictoria contingentia;
et necesse est quod hoc sit verum demonstrando unum istorum; ergo necesse
est quod hoc sit verum demonstrando alterum illorum.

90   Ulterius concedo disiunctivam quod: 'illa anima necessario est in a

instanti vel in aliquo instanti quod non est a'. Sed divisive nego, scilicet
quod 'illa anima necessario est in a instanti vel illa anima necessario est in
aliquo instanti quod non est a.' Sicud necesse est quod rex sedet vel quod
nullus rex sedet disiunctim. Sed tamen nego quod necesse est quod rex sedet
95 vel necesse est quod nullus rex sedet.

In aliis modis enim est turpissimus modus arguendi, quia non sequitur 'scis
alterum istorum contradictorium esse verum, sed non scis hoc esse verum;
ergo scis hoc esse verum'.

Iterum. Aliter arguitur. Pono quod Antichristus fuit per magnum tempus
100 ante hoc. Tunc sequitur quod illa anima necessario fuit.

Sed contra. In nullo instanti ipsa necessario fuit, quia quocumque
instanti dato in illo illa potuit non fuisse, quia illa adhuc potuit fuisse futura.

Ad ista respondeo dicendo quod quandocumque hec anima fuit illa
necessario fuit. Ymmo concedo quod in primo instanti in quo illa fuit illa
105 necessario fuit, quia tunc illa non potuit non esse nec fuit potens ad non
esse. Ideo in illo illa necessario fuit. Sed tunc nego quod illa necessario
fuit in illo instanti, quia magna est differentia. Sed concedo quod necesse
est quod illa fuit in isto instanti.

Et nota bene quod non sequitur de preterito 'necesse est quod illa fuit in
110 illo instanti, ergo illa anima necessario fuit in illo instanti'. Sed de futuro
bene sequitur 'necesse erit illam animam esse in illo instanti, ergo illa anima
necessario erit in illo instanti.' Unde concedendum est quod necesse est
aliquid esse quod non necesse est esse in sensu composito, quia necesse et
aliquod contingens ad utrumlibet esse quod non necesse est esse.

115   Iterum. Supposito quod tu fuisti in ecclesia beate Marie. Tunc
proponitur numquam: necessario fuisti in ecclesia quia necesse est quod tu
fuisti in ecclesia.

Ad istam respondeo negando quod tu necessario fuisti in ecclesia beate
Marie, quia quando tu fuisti in illa tu habuisti potentiam non essendi in illa.
120 Unde si iam sedeas, tunc in illo instanti non necessario sedes. Ymmo
concedo: in hoc instanti potes non sedere. Et si arguitur sic: 'in hoc instanti
sedes et in hoc instanti potes non sedere; ergo simul potes sedere et non

sedere', dicitur quod consequentia non valet.

     Sed si arguitur contra illam responsionem sic: quod in isto sequitur quod:
125 in hoc instanti futuro eris episcopus quia in hoc instanti eris futurus
episcopus, supposito quod numquam posterius eris episcopus. Similiter sequitur
quod tu es episcopus quia tu es futurus episcopus. Patet consequentia per
assimile: in hoc instanti tu potes sedere quia in hoc instanti tu es potens
sedere.

130   Ad istam respondeo dicendo quod ista consequentia non valet: 'in hoc
instanti eris futurus episcopus, ergo in hoc instanti eris episcopus'. Sed
tamen bene sequitur 'in hoc instanti tu es potens sedere, ergo in hoc instanti
tu potes sedere'. Sed tamen non 'in quocumque instanti hoc erit futurum,
hoc erit'. Sed 'in quocumque instanti hoc poterit esse hoc erit potens esse'.
135 Ideo etc.

10

La signification d'objets imaginaires
dans quelques textes anglais du XIVe siècle
(Guillaume Heytesbury, Henry Hopton)

Joël Biard
C.N.R.S., Paris

La possibilité de <u>signifier</u> des objets <u>imaginaires</u> est un élément qui me paraît
de la première importance dans l'évolution de la sémantique médiévale vers
une théorie générale de la référence. Cette possibilité est attestée chez
certains auteurs parisiens à partir de Marsile d'Inghen, mais il semble qu'elle
apparaisse, ou à tout le moins que les conditions de son développement soient
créées d'abord chez des auteurs anglais.

Un texte allant dans ce sens est le <u>De veritate et falsitate propositionis</u>
imprimé avec les oeuvres de Guillaume Heytesbury dans l'édition incunable de
1494 mais dû, selon L.M. de Rijk, à Henry Hopton, dont on a trace à Oxford
dans les années 1350 et 1360.[1] Mais j'évoquerai également Guillaume
Heytesbury lui-même, car ce n'est pas par une simple contingence éditoriale
que l'on rapprocha de ses textes le <u>De veritate et falsitate propositionis</u>
malgré deux ou trois décennies d'écart; si certains aspects sont plus ou moins
développés d'un côté ou de l'autre, le contenu doctrinal semble assez voisin.
Certes, Guillaume Heytesbury ne propose pas explicitement de théorie
complète et systématique de la signification des termes. Ses préoccupations,
sa démarche et même le type d'oeuvre qu'il élabore sont à cet egard assez
différents de ceux de quelqu'un comme Guillaume d'Ockham. A tel point qu'il
paraît risqué de vouloir unifier ces deux auteurs dans une même tradition
doctrinale, malgré leur proximité à la fois géographique et chronologique --
une dizaine d'année seulement séparent les <u>Regule solvendi sophismata</u> de la
<u>Summa logicae</u>. Quoi qu'il en soit, on ne peut essayer de reconstituer ce que

<u>The Rise of British Logic</u>, ed. P. Osmund Lewry, O.P., Papers in Mediaeval
Studies 7 (Toronto: Pontifical Institute of Mediaeval Studies, 1985), pp. 265-
283. © P.I.M.S., 1985.

Heytesbury entend par signification d'un terme, qu'en rassemblant des éléments épars dans les Regule ou les Sophismata. Dans ces conditions, la possibilité de signifier des objets imaginaires n'est pas aussi clairement affirmee qu'elle l'est dans le De veritate et falsitate propositionis. Cependant, non seulement elle s'accorde avec les principes logico-sémantiques présupposés et avec la démarche épistémologique d'ensemble mise en oeuvre, mais elle semble même requise par eux. Ce n'est donc pas un hasard si ultérieurement, en un passage au moins, Gaétan de Thiene fait appel aux thèses exposées dans le De veritate et falsitate propositionis pour gloser les Sophismata.

Le problème afférent à la possibilité de signifier des objets imaginaires présente un certain enjeu historique qui ne peut être apprécié qu'à la condition de garder présents à l'esprit quelques traits marquants de la tradition logique oxonienne, dans la deuxième moitié du XIIIe et au début du XIVe siècle.

L'usage à la fois répandu et controversé de cette expression de 'logique oxonienne' appelle quelques précisions et requiert des précautions. D'une part, ce n'est ici qu'une désignation commode pour circonscrire quelques idées dont je vais énoncer les lignes directrices et dont j'estime qu'elles apparaissent, se développent et prennent une importance particulière à Oxford, avant de se propager à Paris. D'autre part, je n'ai ici en vue que des thèses qui s'affirment pleinement à partir de Roger Bacon et je laisse donc de côté les debats qui ont pu les précéder et les préparer.

L'un de ces éléments consiste à considerer l'objet réel, extérieur à l'esprit, et non pas le concept, comme le signifié propre du mot. Certes, il faut se garder de tout schématisme excessif. Cette thèse n'est pas au XIIIe siècle le propre des logiciens anglais. D'un côté, ce n'est pas la position de Guillaume de Sherwood[2] ni celle du Commentaire sur Priscien Majeur attribué (faussement) à Robert Kilwardby.[3] D'un autre côté, surtout, l'idée fut également formulée à Paris, par example par Siger de Brabant.[4] Mais ce fut sous une forme assez différente car on n'y entend pas par res la même chose qu'à Oxford: ce peut être une nature universelle. A Oxford, cette thèse prend un sens particulier puisque c'est l'objet réel dans son individualité qui est signifié. C'est donc d'une manière différente que se pose non seulement la question de la signification du concept universel, mais encore celle du rapport aux déterminations temporelles. Après des premières indications dans la Logica 'Cum sit nostra'[5] et la prise de position très nette de Roger Bacon,[6] l'idée selon laquelle un mot signifie un objet réel est reprise par Jean Duns Scot[7] et amplifiée par Guillaume d'Ockham.[8] L'importance de cette thèse est bien connue: elle permet en particulier de considérer le concept lui-même comme un signe.

Le second élément consiste à faire de la désignation d'objets présents le principe même de la relation signifiante. Ici encore, Roger Bacon joue un rôle décisif en niant que la signification d'objets présents soit univoque à la signification d'objets non-présents et en estimant que les noms signifient d'abord exclusivement des êtres actuellement existants:

> ...videtur sustineri satis probabiliter terminum solum esse communem enti, qui quidem entibus tantum inponebatur, et eciam non erit communis non-entibus nisi <ubi> fit nova inposicio, et tunc erit talis terminus equivocans ad entes et ad non-entes....[9]

Sans aller aussi loin que Roger Bacon, tout auteur qui, dans sa théorie de la supposition, privilégie l'ampliation sur la restriction — démarche qui est celle de la Logica 'Cum sit nostra' et de Guillaume de Sherwood même si ce dernier admet par ailleurs un esse habituale [10] — accorde de ce fait un privilège au présent, à l'encontre de ceux qui mettent au premier plan une signification intemporelle. On peut ajouter, dans le même ordre d'idées, que les débats qui precèdent et entourent l'oeuvre de Roger Bacon à propos de l'esse habituale, à propos du rapport entre signification et référence à des objets présents, s'insèrent dans une problématique qui, pour admettre diverses réponses, n'en suppose pas moins un fonds commun, lequel met au premier plan la dénotation alors que la tradition parisienne du XIIIe siècle fait plutôt de la signification une connotation intemporelle, distinguée de la référence présente ou appellation. Dans la perspective oxonienne, on n'évite pas le problème de l'univocité ou de l'équivocité entre la signification d'objets présents et celle d'objets non-présents.[11]

Guillaume d'Ockham recueille cette tradition. Même si pour lui la signification et la supposition sont univoques vis-à-vis des objets présents et des objets non-présents ou seulement possibles, toute sa démarche revient à faire reposer l'ensemble de la construction linguistique sur la désignation d'objets présents: il redéfinit en effet la signification comme supposition possible, il privilégie incontestablement la supposition personelle et il définit la supposition elle-même au moyen de la deixis, de la monstration d'objet.[12]

Guillaume Heytesbury n'est pas non plus étranger à ces tendances. Selon lui, un terme, dans son usage normal, standard, nomme des objets réels individuels. Il suffit pour s'en convaincre d'examiner brièvement le sophisme XVII: 'Omnes apostoli sunt duodecim.' Sa résolution passe par la distinction de deux sens du terme 'omnes', selon qu'il est pris collectivement ou distributivement (divisive). Au sens distributif, la phrase signifierait quelque chose comme 'quiconque est apôtre de Dieu est douze', ce qui à l'évidence est faux. Le sens collectif peut quant à lui donner lieu à un doute et susciter une discussion. Il équivaut en effet à: 'Illi qui sunt omnes apostoli dei sunt duodecim.'[13] C'est-à-dire, en fin de compte: il y a douze individus qui sont les apôtres de Dieu'. La question est alors de savoir qui doit être appelé 'apôtre de Dieu'. On pourrait supposer que Dieu reconnaisse comme ses apôtres, en raison de leur fonction qui consiste à être ses représentants sur terre, le pape, les cardinaux, etc. La dénotation serait alors subordonnée à une signification intemporelle. Et dans ce cas, la phrase serait fausse. Mais en réalité le nom d'apostolat (nomen apostolatus), c'est-à-dire aussi bien la nature ou la fonction connotée par le terme d'apôtre, convient principalement à ceux qui, à l'origine, ont suivi le Christ en personne pour exercer la tâche d'envoyées de Dieu. Eux seuls peuvent être appelés 'apôtres': '...et ipsi apostoli dei nominantur.'[14] De l'ensemble de ce développement, il ressort clairement que dans tous les cas, des individus réels (présents ou passés) sont visés. De là résulte l'absurdité de l'énoncé pris au sens distributif. Mais l'analyse du sens collectif permet d'aller plus loin: on se demande quels individus peuvent recevoir cette dénomination. Assurement, il faut pour ce faire énoncer des caractères permettant de décider si le nom convient ou ne convient pas à tel ou tel individu. Mais il ne s'agit par de lier un terme à une signification abstraite ou intemporelle; l'essentiel semble de délimiter en extension un ensemble d'objets individuels que le terme pourra nommer.

Le même sophisme soulève en outre la question de la portée existentielle de la copule, d'une manière qui confirme l'insertion de Guillaume Heytesbury dans la tradition oxonienne. Car il apparaît qu'au sens strict l'énoncé est toujours faux, dans la mesure où aucun apôtre n'existe actuellement:

Ideo, simpliciter loquendo iuxta communem modum loquendi de apostolis, negandum est sophisma in utroque sensu quia nullus illorum apostolorum est.[15]

Cette précision reprend une objection énoncée antérieurement:

Similiter, si omnes apostoli dei sunt duodecim, ergo omnes apostoli dei sunt. Sed arguitur quod non, quia nec Petrus est, nec Paulus, et sic de singulis, ergo etc. Antecedens sic arguitur: quilibet illorum erat occisus pro fide Christi et sustinendo fidem vel salutem moriebatur, ergo etc.[16]

Cela prouve bien que c'est l'existence actuelle qui est en cause. Certes, Heytesbury ne s'en tient pas à cette conception restrictive de la signification et il tient l'énoncé en question pour vrai dès lors que le syncatégorème est pris collectivement:

Si tamen ponitur gratia exempli quod modo forent duodecim apostoli dei et non plures, tunc accipiendo istum terminum 'omnes' collective, est sophisma concedendum.[17]

Encore faut-il voir ce qui a permis de surmonter l'objection précédemment énoncée. Et il me semble que c'est précisément la limitation, dans ce cas particulier, du domaine de référence à douze individus passés, tous morts, qui évite toute équivocité entre le passé et le présent, lors même que l'on parle du passé au présent. Si ce n'était pas le cas, si par exemple je disais 'les cardinaux sont douze', seul le présent se trouverait concerné par mon assertion et la phrase serait fausse s'il se trouvait que certains d'entre eux soient morts. Si tel est bien le raisonnement qui sous-tend les conclusions de Guillaume Heytesbury, il n'ignore pas toutes les questions débattues à Oxford dans la deuxième moitié du siècle précédent, dont témoignent les textes de Roger Bacon. A partir du moment où la signification repose sur la dénotation d'objets réels, elle ne peut plus être intemporelle et la référence à des objets présents jouit inevitablement d'un certain privilège, même si par ailleurs on prévoit des procédures pour étendre la signification et/ou la référence en acte dans un contexte propositionnel à des objets non-présents.

La théorie de l'ampliation, on le sait, a pour fonction d'énoncer les conditions d'après lesquelles la référence de tel ou tel terme est étendue au-delà des seuls objets présents. L'ampliation dépend de la place du mot dans la proposition, du temps du verbe et de la présence éventuelle de certains

termes -- un syncatégorème ou un verbe intentionnel, par example. Dans
cette perspective, un pas décisif est franchi lorsque l'on admet que certains
verbes étendent le champ de référence des termes, non seulement à des
objets qui n'existent pas actuellement (passés ou futurs) ou à des objets
possibles (donc qui peuvent exister ou ne pas exister), mais également à des
objets qui ne peuvent pas exister et dont il est par conséquent impossible
qu'ils soient désignés au présent. C'est ce que soutient de manière
particulièrement nette le De veritate et falsitate propositionis, à propos des
verbes 'significare' et 'intelligere'.

Ce texte ne propose pas explicitement de définition générale de la
signification. À fortiori, on n'y trouve pas de théorie complète, élaborée sur
la base d'éléments de sémiologie, comme c'est par example le cas chez
Guillaume d'Ockham. Les démarches sont différentes. Mais quelques
indications montrent que l'auteur s'en tient à la presentation habituelle qui
fonde la signification sur l'intellection. Plus précisément, il semble assimiler
'signifier' et 'comprendre':

...ad significare sequitur intelligere et per consequens quicquid per
aliquod intelligitur per ipsum significatur.[18]

Un tel énoncé laisse toute une marge d'interprétation; il peut être le point
de recoupement de conceptions sémiologiques par ailleurs diverses.
Cependant, le rapprochement de ces deux notions, ainsi formulé, ne saurait
conduire à faire de l'intellection l'objet de la signification: l'équivalence est
au contraire celle de deux actes visant un même troisième terme, la chose.

Dans ces conditions, la question incontournable est celle d'une
délimitation du domaine d'objets auquel peuvent s'appliquer ces termes, car
personne ne soutient qu'il est constitué des seuls objets présents. Or le
verbe 'signifier' est précisément tenu pour un verbe ampliatif, qui étend la
référence des termes gouvernées jusqu'à ce qui n'existe pas. Dans le passage
du De veritate et falsitate propositionis qui traite de cette question, l'exposé
des arguments est assez complique, alternant le pour et le contre sans
ménager le lecteur. Finalement, l'auteur se détermine de la manière
suivante: '...iste terminus "significat" est terminus ampliativus equaliter ad
non-entia sicut ad entia.'[19] Mais pour saisir toute la portée de cette thèse,
il faut revenir sur l'argumentation qui la justifie -- présentée sous forme
d'arguments contra par l'auteur, qui a commencé par rapporter l'opinion

opposée:

> ...iste terminus 'significat' est verbum ampliativum. Ergo terminus communis supponens respectu huius supponit indifferenter pro illo quod est et quod potest significare et pro illo quod non est aliquid, quod potest significare.[20]

On peut remarquer que dans ce texte la relation de supposition elle-même s'applique à quelque chose (aliquid) qui n'existe pas.[21] Il n'est pas question cependant — comme nous l'a montré l'étude du sophisme 'Omnes apostoli sunt duodecim' -- de confondre sous tous points de vue les objets existants et non-existants. L'auteur insiste seulement sur le fait que la signification couvre ces deux registres:

> Isti duo termini 'intelligere' et significare' sunt termini equalis ambitus. Ergo eque ampliativum est unum sicut reliquum. Sed 'intelligere' est ampliativum ad non-entia que non possunt esse sicut ad entia que possunt esse, ergo et 'significare' eodem modo.[22]

Avec cette citation, une étape supplémentaire est franchie. Certains de ces non-entia qui peuvent être objets de signification ne peuvent pas exister; autrement dit, il ne s'agit pas seulement d'objets passés, futurs ou possibles, mais impossibles. L'exemple donné est d'ailleurs significatif: il s'agit de s'interroger '...de modo significandi et significato terminorum significantium solum res imaginabiles, sicut iste terminus "chymera".'[23] Le terme 'chimère' sert d'exemple tout au long de la discussion. L'opinion critiquée repose sur le fait que la chimère n'étant rien, un tel terme s'il signifie -- sans quoi ce ne serait pas un mot -- signifie une chimère et par conséquent ne signifie rien. Tout en refusant cette argumentation, l'auteur adopte une position qui n'a rien à voir avec celle développée, par example, par Jean Buridan, pour qui à travers le terme 'chimère' c'est toujours une pluralité d'objets réels incompossibles qui est signifiée. Ici au contraire, le terme renvoie, selon une expression plusieurs fois reprise, à une res imaginabilis.

Une telle position pourrait certes s'autoriser de quelques précédents. Le Pseudo-Robert Kilwardby admet que des objets imaginaires tels que la chimère, le bouc-cerf, la montagne d'or, etc., peuvent être signifiés.[24] Mais la problématique est toute différente: l'objet premier de la signification étant le concept, tout ce qui peut être concu et/ou imaginé peut devenir l'objet de la signification d'un terme conventionnel.

Cela soulève plus de problèmes lorsque la chose existante est érigée en objet premier de signification. Il est vrai que Roger Bacon, tout préoccupé de souligner la liberté qui caractérise selon lui l'acte d'imposition, estime qu'un mot peut se voir attribuer n'importe quelle signification, y compris imaginaire.[25] Cela ne l'empêche pas de défendre, comme on l'a vu, l'équivocité de la signification des objets non-existants par rapport à celle des objets existants, et le primat théorique de cette dernière puisqu'en tout nom est conçu l'être. Ces divers aspects de la doctrine baconnienne ne se concilent que dans la mesure où la signification et l'intellection se trouvent dissociées. On peut certes signifier directement ce qui est imaginé mais on ne peut sous peine d'erreur le concevoir positivement: 'Licet intellectus conciperet haec per viam positionis non tamen hoc faceret de se, sed per imaginationis et fantasiae errorem.'[26]

La position d'une res imaginabilis ne va donc pas de soi dans le contexte de la sémiologie oxonienne, et peut-être plus largement dans la logique terministe. Il suffit pour s'en convaincre de rappeler comment elle devint l'objet d'âpres débats à Paris, du milieu du XIVe siècle jusqu'au début du XVIe siècle. Une brève excursion hors du champ géographique et chronologique de notre recherche va permettre de mesurer les enjeux de la discussion.

Il est en effet frappant de voir Jean Mair, qui recueille et en quelque sorte résume tout le nominalisme parisien, évoquer la question en des terms semblables à ceux que nous venons de rencontrer. En premier lieu, il note l'existence de divergences: 'Dubitatur an sit ampliatio ad ymaginabilia.'[27] Il rapelle la position de Buridan qui refuse une telle ampliation. Puis il ajoute: 'Alia est positio communis quod aliqui termini ampliant ad quinque, ut "cognosco", "intelligo", "ymaginor".'[28] Le mot 'quinque' désigne ce que l'on nomme habituellement les cinq déterminations temporelles, bien que cette expression soit en toute rigueur inappropriée: 'Quinque sunt differentie temporales: est, fuit, erit, potest esse et ymaginatur.'[29] Cette ampliation qui s'étend à un cinquième domaine d'objets, les objets imaginables, concerne, entre autres, le verbe 'signifier': 'Terminus sequens "significat" vel hoc complexum "supponit pro", "verificatur pro", ampliatur ad quinque differentias temporum.'[30] Une telle position, ici qualifiée de 'commune', semble avoir été introduite à l'Université de Paris par Marsile d'Inghen.[31] Mais ce n'était ni celle de Buridan ni celle d'Albert de Saxe. Celui-ci s'en tient à quatre déterminations temporelles, de telle sort que le terme 'chimère' ne signifie rien d'autre que des objets réels ou possibles.[32] Il reste ainsi, sur ce point, fidèle à Buridan qui estime qu'aucune ampliation ne peut porter au-delà du possible, car seul le possible est concevable et signifiable.

La possibilité de signifier des objets imaginaires ne va donc pas de soi. Mais il est d'autant plus surprenant de voir certains anglais adopter la position qui sera celle de Marsile d'Inghen et de ses successeurs que cela semble contrevenir à l'habitude oxonienne consistant à faire de la relation aux objets présents la base de toute signification. D'ailleurs, Guillaume d'Ockham estime qu'un terme comme 'chimère' ou 'vide' ne signifie aucun objet, fût-il qualifié d'imaginaire. En aucun sens on ne peut dire 'chimera est aliquid.'[33] La signification se définit en termes de supposition possibles et l'idée de suppléer une chimère est tout à fait étrangère à Guillaume d'Ockham. Pour que cette idee prenne sens, il faut admettre explicitement des objets imaginaires-impossibles.

Au XIIIe siècle et au debut du XIVe, la grande opposition en matière de théorie de la signification passe entre ceux qui admettent une signification intemporelle (position liée la plupart du temps à l'acceptation de natures universelles) et ceux qui, tels Roger Bacon ou Guilllaume d'Ockham, voulant ancrer la signification dans la référence aux objets du monde réel, accordent d'une manière ou d'une autre un privilège aux objets présents. Sur la base de ce primat de l'objet présent, on pense au moyen des concepts de supposition et d'ampliation les variations extensionelles de la références et son élargissement aux objets actuellement non-existants. Mais tant qu'on s'en tient aux quatre déterminations temporelles que sont le présent, le passé, le futur et le possible, la désignation d'objets présents peut rester le modèle sur lequel est pensée toute relation signifiante -- le possible risquant alors de n'être que la recollection des trois dimensions temporelles au sens propre.[34] Il ne peut plus en aller de même lorsque l'on accepte des objets imaginaires qui, pour ne pas se confondre avec le quatrième domaine, sont inévitablement impossibles. Les réticences implicites de Guillaume d'Ockham, reprises et explicitées à Paris par Buridan et Albert de Saxe, se fondent sur cette manière d'aborder les problèmes de signification, liée au premier chef, du moins dans une première etape, à la tradition oxonienne et en particulier au fait de placer à la base de toute étude de la signification l'idée du signe comme substitut d'objet(s) réel(s).

Affirmer la possibilité de signifier des objets imaginaires ne rompt pas avec ces principes pour renouer avec la position consistant à faire du concept l'objet propre de la signification. Elle n'en implique pas moins un véritable saut puisque de certains 'objets', il n'est possible à aucun moment de dire 'ceci est un x' en les designant réelement. C'est pourquoi cette thèse revêt une certaine importance pour l'histoire de la sémantique médiévale.

Les conséquences et/ou les enjeux sont à situer sur deux plans: épistémologiques et sémiologique.

L'aspect épistémologique nous permet de revenir à Heytesbury. Je rapelle simplement quelques données bien connues. On sait que Guillaume Heytesbury donne, par ses _Sophismata_ et ses _Regule solvendi sophismata_ une impulsion nouvelle à l'étude de problèmes concernant par example le début ou la fin d'un processus physique, ou bien l'intensité d'une qualité.[35] De ce qui caractérise sa demarche, deux traits nous concernent ici.[36] D'abord, les problèmes physiques sont traités dans le cadre d'une analyse linguistique.[37] Ensuite, Heytesbury semble moins soucieux de simplifier et de schématiser les problèmes (à l'instar de son compatriote Guillaume d'Ockham) que de les compliquer en épuisant toutes les hypothèses, en multipliant variantes et variations, en énumérant tous les cas possibles. Heytesbury ne pense pas en physicien au sens moderne, au sens où l'expérience devrait confirmer une hypothèse voire permettre de trancher entre les hypothèses; il étudie plutôt, par une démarche purement logique, tous les cas possibles _secundum imaginationem_.

Précisons ce dernier point par un example. Dans le sophisme XVIII, '_Infinita sunt finita_', l'auteur fait l'hypothèse que quelqu'un compte de 1 à 6 pendant la première moitié d'une heure, puis de 6 à 12 pendant le quart d'heure suivant, puis de 12 à 18 pendant le huitième d'heure suivant, et ainsi de suite. Auquel cas, avant la fin de l'heure, on obtiendrait un nombre infini. Cette hypothèse est tout à fait impossible, irréalisable expérimentalement. C'est néanmoins sur cette base que l'auteur formule un certain nombre de thèses sur l'infini.[38] Il est parfaitement conscient de cette situation: 'Qui casus, licet sit impossibilis simpliciter, tamen est imaginabilis satis....'[39] Plus avant dans les _Sophismata_, il explicite cette démarche:

Et ideo gratia disputationis potest admitti totus casus tanquam imaginabilis, et non tanquam possibilis...Unde notum est quod multa sunt imaginabilia quae non sunt possibilia, sicut vacuum esse, et hominem esse immortalem, et sic de talibus... (162^{ra-va})...

Unde breviter quilibet casus qui non claudit contradictionem formaliter seu tale impossibile quod non bene potest imaginari, sicut hominem esse asinum vel huiusmodi, satis potest admitti gratia disputationis.[40]

Tout ne peut donc pas être admis, même à titre de réalité imaginaire. Mais la limite semble être simplement la contradiction formelle.[41] La possibilité physique et a fortiori la vraisemblance ne sont aucunement pertinentes.[42] Comme J.E. Murdoch l'a fait remarquer, la plupart du temps, dans les sophismes du XIVe siècle, l'ingéniosité s'exerce surtout à la construction de 'cas' de plus en plus complexes, plutôt qu'elle n'apparaît dans la formulation du sophisme lui-même. A cela il faut ajouter que de nombreux objets étudiés au moyen de sophismes physiques, tels que le temps ou le mouvement, sont tenus pour des êtres purement imaginaires: dans la nature des choses selon Heytesbury, il n'y a rien qui soit un instant, ni même temps ou mouvement.[43] Par là, on mesure aisément l'importance de la démarche secundum imaginationem.

Sans doute une telle démarche sera-t-elle ultérieurement adoptée et pratiquée par des penseurs qui ne partagent pas forcément toutes les thèses sémantiques évoquées plus haut. Mais étant donné le moment et le contexte où elle apparaît, il me semble possible de la mettre en rapport avec la thèse selon laquelle on peut signifier des objets imaginaires. Ainsi, le rôle de l'imagination, conçue comme production de cas hypothétiques de plus en plus complexes et libérés des données empiriques immédiates, peut être un facteur d'explication de l'élargissement et de la transformation que subit la théorie oxonienne de la signification.

Sur le plan proprement sémiologique, en effet, la position qu'exprime de manière développée le De veritate et falsitate propositionis mais dont on trouve des prémisses dans les textes de Heytesbury, constitue l'amorce d'une voie particulièrement intéressante qui, comme nous l'avons vu, sera adoptée après une large discussion par les nominalistes parisiens. Cette voie dépasse et transforme la thèse qui consiste à prendre la désignation d'objets présents comme le modèle de la relation signifiante. Mais elle n'en revient pas à une théorie de la signification purement conceptuelle. Guillaume Heytesbury lui-même reconnaît que tout terme signifie en propre des choses, des res; ces choses doivent même être conçues comme des individus que les termes ont pour fonction de nommer. Mais il refuse toute inférence de l'objet pensable à l'objet réel, existant: '...non sequitur: iste terminus "deus" significat deum et deum esse est deum ens, ergo iste terminus "deus" significat deum esse.'[44] Cela revient à contredire la thèse baconienne: '...in omni nomine intelligitur ens.'[45] Une explication de ce changement, c'est sans aucun doute la possibilité de signifier des objets non-existants ou plus, qui ne peuvent pas exister. Les attendus implicites des textes de Guillaume Heytesbury sont bien ceux que développe un peu plus tard Henry Hopton.

L'intérêt de cette position est de constituer une tentative pour concilier deux exigences qui, si on les poussait chacune à la limite, deviendraient peut-être contradictoires: d'une part, maintenir la référence aux objets (individuels) comme pierre de touche de toute signification; d'autre part, élargir au maximum les variations autour de ce modèle sans détruire le modèle lui-même. En effet, la position sémiologique de base, telle qu'elle est synthétisée et systématisée par Guillaume d'Ockham, fait preuve d'une fécondité certaine. Mais elle rencontre aussi des limites, exigeant par exemple que l'on tienne pour fausse une phrase comme '"chimère" signifie une chimère.'

Le propos d'un auteur comme Heytesbury n'est pas d'élaborer une théories systématique de la signification.[46] Mais quand l'évolution du nominalisme parisien amènera certains penseurs à soulever des problèmes logico-sémantiques de plus en plus complexes et à développer une théorie de la signification dans laquelle le souci de complétude primera sur celui de simplicité, ils retrouveront ou reprendront cette idée selon laquelle des termes peuvent signifier des objets qui non seulement n'existent pas mais même ne peuvent pas exister, plus encore peuvent suppléer ces objets dans des propositions.

Sans doute, au terme de cet exposé, bien des questions historiques restent en suspens. Il m'a semble que le rapprochement des Regule et des Sophismata de Guillaume Heytesbury, d'une part, et du De veritate et falsitate propositionis d'autre part, était fondé. Le dernier éclaire les premiers, dans lesquels transparaissent des positions en matière de théorie de la signification qui ne sont pas toujours pleinement explicitées et developpées. Mais peut-être faudrait-il, pour légitimer définitivement ce rapprochement, aller plus loin dans la comparasion. En outre, la même transformation des thèses sémantiques, la même élargissement de la dénotation à des objets imaginaires, s'effectue à Paris, sous l'impulsion, semble-t-il, de Marsile d'Inghen. Le problème étant posé dans les même termes, la question surgit de savoir comment s'est opéré le transfert d'un côté à l'autre de la Manche. Tout ce que l'on peut dire, malgré certaines imprécisions concernant les dates,[47] c'est que la transmission semble bien s'être faite d'Oxford vers Paris.[48] On peut donc estimer que c'est dans le milieu anglais, postérieure-ment à Guillaume d'Ockham, que cette position se développe, d'autant plus qu'elle est parfaitement cohérente avec la démarche épistémologique inaugurée par Heytesbury. Dans ce cas, Heytesbury hériterait, à certains égards, d'une tradition déjà solidement établie, celle de la sémantique oxonienne. Mais tout imprégné qu'il puisse être de cette logique et de la sémiologie qu'elle implique, ses préoccupations sont bien différentes de celles de Guillaume d'Ockham. Elles ont donc pu l'amener à transformer certaines thèses sémantiques, faisant naître des idées que d'autres, ailleurs et un peu plus tard, intégreront à une théorie générale de la référence.

Notes

[1] Sur l'attribution du De veritate et falsitate propositionis à Henry Hopton, cf. L.M. de Rijk éd., Some 14th Century Tracts on the Probationes Terminorum (Artistarium 3; Nijmegen, 1982), introduction, p. *39*. Sur Henry Hopton lui-même, cf. aussi Emden, A Biographical Register of the University of Oxford to A.D. 1500, 2 (Oxford, 1958), p. 960.

[2] Cf. M. Grabmann, 'Die Introductiones in logicam des Wilhelm von Shyreswood (+ nach 1267)', Sitzungsberichte der Bayerischen Akademie der Wissenschaften, Philosophisch-historische Abteilung, Jahrgang 1937, Heft 10 (Munich, 1937) 5, p. 74 (16-17); idem, Gesammelte Akademieabhandlungen 2 (Veröffentlichungen des Grabmann-Institutes, Neue Folge 25/2; Paderborn-Munich-Vienne-Zürich, 1979), p. 1328 (16-17).

[3] K.M. Fredborg, N.J. Green-Pedersen, L. Nielsen & J. Pinborg éd., 'The Commentary on "Priscianus Maior" Ascribed to Robert Kilwardby: Selected texts', 2.1.9., CIMAGL 15 (1975), 71: '...vox instituitur primo et per se ad significandum intellectum mentis.'

[4] Cf. C.A. Graiff éd., Siger de Brabant, Questions sur la Metaphysique

(Philosophes médiévaux 1; Louvain, 1948), lib. 4, q. 16, p. 220 (18-19):
'...nomina non significant intellectum rei, sed sunt signa rerum.' Cf. aussi B.
Bazán éd., Siger de Brabant. Ecrits de logique. de morale et de physique
(Philosophes médiévaux 14; Louvain-Paris, 1974), Quaestiones logicales, p. 62.

5 Editée par L.M. de Rijk, Logica modernorum 2.2 (Wijsgerige Teksten en
Studies 16; Assen, 1967); cf. ibid., p. 446 (30-31): '...significare est rem suam
sub principali ratione ipsius instituentis designare.'

6 Après avoir fait état d'un grand débat sur cette question, Roger Bacon
estime pour sa part que la signification porte sur la chose; K.M. Fredborg, L.
Nielsen et J. Pinborg éd., 'An Unedited Part of Roger Bacon's "Opus Maius",
"De Signis"', Traditio 34 (1978), 133 (De signis 5.163): '...certum est inquirenti
quod facta impositione soli rei extra animam, impossibile est ⟨quod⟩ vox
significet speciem rei tamquam rei signum datum ab anima et significativum
ad placitum, quia vox significativa ad placitum non significat nisi per
impositionem et institutionem. Sed concessum est vocem soli rei imponi et
non speciei.'

7 Cf. Ordinatio, lib. 1, dist. 27, q. 1, ad 2; éd. C. Balić, Ioannis Duns
Scoti Opera omnia 6 (Citée Vaticane, 1963), p. 97 (4-5): '...illud quod signatur
per vocem proprie, est res.'

8 Cf. Summa logicae, pars 1, cap. 1; éd. Ph. Boehner. G. Gál et S.
Brown, Guillelmi de Ockham Opera philosophica 1 (St. Bonaventure, N.Y.,
1974), p. 8 (29-30): '...voces imponuntur ad significandum illa eadem quae per
conceptus mentis significatur....'

9 Sumule dialectices magistri Rogeri Bacon éd. R. Steele, Opera hactenus
inedita Rogeri Baconi 15 (Oxford, 1940), p. 287 (5-9).

10 Cf. Introductiones in logicam 5; éd. Grabmann (1937), p. 85 (16-19),
(1979), p. 1339 (16-19): '...si proprie valimus loqui, dicimus, quod terminus de
se supponit pro presentibus et si supponat pro aliis, hoc erit ratione sui
adiuncti scilicet verbi ampliandi vel verbi preteriti vel futuri temporis.' Cf.
H.A.G. Braakhuis, 'The Views of William of Sherwood on Some Semantical
Topics and Their Relation to Those of Roger Bacon', Vivarium 15 (1977) 111-
42.

11 C'est ce dont temoignent par example les textes commentés ici-même par P.O. Lewry, 'Oxford Logic 1250-1275: Nicholas and Peter of Cornwall of Past and Future Realities' (v.s., pp. 19-62.)   Pour un aperçu de la tradition parisienne, cf. A. de Libera, 'The Oxford and Paris traditions in logic', in N. Kretzmann, A. Kenny et J. Pinborg éd., The Cambridge History of Later Medieval Philosophy (Cambridge, 1982), pp. 174-87.

12 Sur ce dernier point cf. Summa logicae, pars 1, cap. 63, pp. 193-95. Il est vrai que l'usage du pronom démonstratif n'est pas limité par Guillaume d'Ockham aux seuls objets présents.   Il n'empêche qu'on peut difficilement délier le pronom démonstratif de toute désignation actuelle, qui seule permet de lui donner sens; l'expression fréquemment employée par l'auteur, 'pronomine demonstrante ipsum' (cf. ibid., pp. 193 [13], 194 [16-17, 20]) souligne d'ailleurs le geste de désignation.   Si l'argument paraît à seul insuffisant (le déictique pouvant être consideré comme embrayant le discours sur l'actualité du locuteur autant ou plus que sur celle de l'objet visé), il trouve cependant une confirmation dans d'autres aspects de la théorie ockhamiste: d'une part, l'analyse de la signification qui part du présent pour élargir ensuite au passé, futur ou possible (cf. ibid., pars 1, cap. 33, p. 95); d'autre part, celle des conditions de vérité où là encore ce sont les énoncés au présent, avec 'est' qui permettent de définir les conditions de vérité des phrases passées, futures, etc. (cf. ibid., pars 2, cap. 7, pp. 260-72).

13 Sophisma XVII, in Tractatus Gulielmi Hentisberi de sensu composito et diviso. Regule eiusdem. cum Sophismatibus (Bonetus Locatellus; Venise, 1494), fol. 129rb.

14 Ibid.

15 Ibid.

16 Ibid.

17 Ibid.

18 Hopton, De veritate et falsitate propositionis (Venise, 1494), fol. 186ra.   Cf. A. Maierù, 'Il problema della verità nelle opere de Guglielmo Heytesbury', Studi medievali (serie 3) 7.1 (1966) 40-74; voir spécialement p. 57 et sqq.

[19] Hopton, De veritate et falsitate propositionis (Venise, 1494), fol. 187vb.

[20] Ibid., fol. 186rb.

[21] Gaétan de Thiene précisera dans son commentaire, à propos du sophisme XXV, 'Omne verum et deum esse differunt': 'Dicunt quidam quod in ista propositione "chimera est" ly "chimera" supponit pro eo quod est; sed ex hoc non sequitur quod chimera est, quia iste terminus "supponit" usque ad imaginabilia ampliat terminum se sequentem et rectum a parte post.' (Venise, 1494, fol. 146ra).   Toutefois, Guillaume Heytesbury lui-même semble plus prudent: dans 'aliquid est chimera', 'aliquid' ne suppose pour rien (ibid., fol, 145rb).

[22] Hopton, De ver. et fals. prop. (Venise, 1494), fol. 186rb.

[23] Ibid.

[24] Fredborg et al. éd., 'The Commentary on "Priscianus Maior"...', 2.1.7, p. 68.

[25] Fredborg et al. éd., 'An Unedited Part of Roger Bacon's "Opus Maius", "De Signis"', 2.2.19, pp. 87-88.

[26] Ibid., 2.2.20, p. 88; c'est moi qui ai souligné.

[27] Johannis Maioris Scoti Libri quos in artibus in Collegio Montis Acuti Parisius regentando compilavit (Paris, 1506), fol. 115ra.

[28] Ibid., fol. 115^{ra-rb}.

[29] Ibid., fol. 111vb.

[30] Ibid., fols. 114vb-115ra.

[31] Cf. Tractatus de proprietatibus terminorum éd. E.P. Bos, Marsilius of Inghen, Treatises on the Properties of Terms (Univ. de Leyde, Ph. D. thèse, 1980), p. 96, et Quaestiones super Peri Hermeneias, ibid., pp. 176-77.

[32] Cf. Gulielmus de Occham, Expositio aurea...super Artem veterem cum questionibus Alberti parvi de Saxonia (Benedictus Hector: Bologne, 1496; Ridgewood, N.J., 1964), q. 2 de nomine, fol. 94rb: '...hoc verbum "significat" ampliat ly "aliquid" ad supponendum pro eo quod est vel fuit vel erit vel potest esse....'; et ibid., fol. 94va: '...hoc nomen "chimera" non solum aliquid significat, verum etiam aliquid quod est; patet hoc, quia significat caudam piscis et ventrem mulieris et caput virgini....' (guillemets ajoutees).

[33] Cf. Summa logicae, pars 2, cap. 12, p. 284.

[34] Au XIVe siècle cependant, il est des auteurs tels Pierre de Mantoue (E.P. Bos l'a montré ici même dans sa communication, 'Peter of Mantua and his Rejection of Ampliatio and Restrictio', v.i., pp. 381-399) qui vont tenter de détacher le possible de toute référence à l'actualité (présente, passée ou future). Mais en renforçant et en élargissant ainsi la détermination du possible, il exclut la signification d'objets impossibles.

[35] Cf. C. Wilson, William Heytesbury and the Rise of Mathematical Physics (Publications in Medieval Science 3; Madison, Wis., 1956).

[36] Un troisième élément est de la première importance historique mais ne nous concerne pas ici; les rudiments de mathématisation; cf. Wilson, op. cit., et J.E. Murdoch, 'Mathematics and Sophisms in Late Medieval Natural Philosophy and Science' dans Les Genres Littéraires dans les Sources Théologiques et Philosophiques Médiévales: Actes du Colloque international de Louvain-la-Neuve, 25-27 mai 1981 (Publications de l'Institut d'Études Médiévales, 2e série, vol. 5; Louvain-la-Neuve, 1982), pp. 85-100. Dans cet article, Murdoch souligne également le rôle de l'imagination dans la démarche de Heytesbury (ou de Swineshead), sur lequel je me propose de revenir.

[37] Cf. J.E. Murdoch, 'Scientia mediantibus vocibus: Metalinguistic Analysis in Late Medieval Natural Philosophy', dans Sprache und Erkenntnis im Mittelalter 1 (Miscellanea mediaevalia 13/1; Berlin-New York, 1981), pp. 73-106, et idem, 'Propositional Analysis in 14th-Century Natural Philosophy: A case study', Synthese 40 (1979) 117-46.

[38] L'analyse en est faite par E. Sylla dans 'William Heytesbury on the Sophism "Infinita sunt finita"', Sprache und Erkenntnis im Mittelalter 2 (Miscellanea mediaevalia 13/2; Berlin-New York, 1981), pp. 628-36.

39 Heytesbury, Sophisma XVIII (Venise, 1494), fol. 132ra.

40 Heytesbury, Sophisma XXXI, 'Necesse est aliquid condensari si aliquid rarefiat' (Venise, 1494), fols. 161vb, 162va.

41 Cf. fol. 133ra, dans le sophisme XVIII, 'Infinita sunt finita': '...primus casus est imaginabilis licet non sit possibilis de facto, sed secundus casus est impossibilis tam de facto quam etiam de imaginatione, quia ex isto sequitur formaliter quod Sor numerabit infinitas unitates et tamen nec subito nec successive. Sequitur enim in isto casu, ut iam argutum est, quod non prius numerabit unam unitatem quam omnes unitates et Sor non infinities (?) numerabit omnes, nec in aliquo instanti numerabit aliquam, quod est mere impossibile.' Une distinction semblable se recontrait déjà chez Guillaume d'Ockham au subjet de la positio impossibilis dans son chapitre sur l'obligation. Si dans la discussion, l'impossible peut faire l'objet d'une position, la proposition impossible ne doit pas être admise lorsqu'elle inclut une contradiction ou implique que l'on en infère une proposition contradictoire (cf. Summa logicae, pars 3.3, cap. 42, p. 739).

42 Rappelons ce cas amusant, déjà signale par Wilson (William Heytesbury, p. 23) et qui montre bien que la vraisemblance n'est nullement de mise: dans le sophisme V, 'Omnis homo qui est albus currit', Heytesbury établit que dans le cas où l'on convient d'appeler 'blanc' celui dont la surface extérieure de la moitié supérieure est blanche, Socrate peut fort bien être blanc et Platon noir bien que la proportion de la surface extérieure de Platon qui est blanche soit plus grande que celle de Socrate. C'est le cas si la figure de Socrate est blanche et que le reste de sa peau est noire et si la figure de Platon est noire tandis que le reste de sa peau est blanche.

43 Cf. Heytesbury, De incipit et desinit (Venise, 1494), fol. 26ra.

44 Heytesbury, sophisme XXV, 'Omne verum et deum esse differunt' (Venise, 1494), fol. 144va. Cf. aussi Hopton, De ver. et fals. prop. (Venise, 1494), fol. 183va, où l'opinion selon laquelle 'Deum esse est deum et...Sor esse est Sor' est critiquée.

45 Bacon, Summule dialectices éd. Steele, p. 279 (33-34).

46 On en trouve peut-être un indice lexicographique dans le fait signalé

par A Maierù (Terminologia logica della tarda scolastica [Lessico Intellettuale Europeo 8; Rome, 1972], p. 489) que Heytesbury utilise peu le terme 'significatio', même s'il emploie beaucoup 'significare'.

[47] Les Tractatus se situent sans doute dans la période parisienne de Marsile d'Inghen, soit entre 1359 et 1379 environ. Les textes d'Henry Hopton sont plus difficiles à situer; mais celui-ci est mentionné comme membre du University College en 1357, puis du Queen's College en 1361, et il y est encore en 1367.

[48] Heytesbury est connu à Paris dès le milieu du XIVe siècle. Grégoire de Rimini l'évoque, pour une autre question, dans son Commentaire des Sentences; cf. A.D. Trapp et V. Marcolino éd., Gregorii Ariminensis O.E.S.A. Lectura super primum et secundum Sententiarum 1 (Spätmittelalter und Reformation Texte und Untersuchungen 6; Berlin-New York, 1981), prol., q. 1, art. 3, dub., p. 33.

11

Early British Treatises on Consequences

N.J. Green-Pedersen
University of Copenhagen

From around 1300 and throughout the fourteenth century we meet a considerable number of works entitled De consequentiis (On consequences). It is remarkable, however, that the overwhelming majority of these texts is of British origin. We know very few such texts from Paris: the earliest seems to be that of Jean Buridan (ca. 1335), and besides this work we apparently possess only the treatise by Marsilius of Inghen (1360s?). Of course, we may also count the relevant chapters in Albert of Saxony's Perutilis logica, but that seems to be all — so far at least. From this we should certainly not infer that the Parisian logicians did not have a doctrine of consequences, for they evidently did, yet they obviously felt little need for a particular genre of literature in which they could expound it.

In contrast, the British literature of this genre is rather numerous in the fourteenth century. Hitherto, more than fifteen such works have been found, and in addition a number of British manuals of logic contain chapters that set out the doctrine of consequences in a manner quite similar to that of the separate treatises. Further, we possess commentaries on several of the treatises on consequences, at least two of which were composed in the fourteenth century (commentary i on Sutton [no. 5] and the commentary on Martinus [no. 9]). Apparently, however, the majority of these commentaries is of German origin and belongs to the fifteenth century, which means that we may leave them out of account here. In an appendix I have arranged in an approximately chronological order a list of the treatises on consequences and the commentaries on them of which I am aware.[1] The reader will readily see that we possess works from almost every part of the century.

The Rise of British Logic, ed. P. Osmund Lewry, O.P., Papers in Mediaeval Studies 7 (Toronto: Pontifical Institute of Mediaeval Studies, 1985), pp. 285-307. © P.I.M.S., 1985.

At first glance, this rich literature seems to testify to a great interest in the theory of consequences. In a way this is true, of course, yet, upon closer inspection, we can hardly avoid some disappointment. First, these texts show very little development; indeed, it is often difficult to tell if a work belongs to the beginning or the end of the fourteenth century. Another characteristic of these tracts is that they remain on a rather elementary level in their treatment of the problems. Further, the treatises are of a practical character; they appear to be manuals designed for use rather than theoretical reflections. None of the British works attains a degree of sophistication which compares with that we find in Jean Buridan's or Marsilius of Inghen's texts.

One feature which plainly illustrates this nature of our works is the fact that they do not care much about defining a consequence or discussing and determining what a consequence is. Frequently the texts will open with the statement that a consequence is a connexion (aggregatum) of an antecedent and a consequent and a sign of the consequence (nota consequentiae) holding between them.[2] Another common explanation is that a consequence is a relation (habitudo) between an antecedent and a consequent.[3] These two brief statements are practically all that we find if we look for express attempts at defining a consequence.

Yet all the authors proceed to determine more precisely what a consequence is in an indirect manner with the help of rules for consequences from which we may recognize whether any consequence — chosen at random — is valid (bona) or not. The earliest authors, and a few later ones, apply these rules indiscriminately to all valid consequences.[4] The majority of our works, however, first distinguish between material and formal consequences. The discussion of the material consequence is then quickly concluded with an explanation that the rules for material consequences are two: that from the impossible anything follows; and that the necessary follows from anything.[5] Richard Lavenham adds that a material consequence is one that holds only because of its terms (gratia terminorum). This is the only description of the material consequence which the unknown author Rodolphus gives.[6] After the material consequence has thus been put aside our authors proceed to describe what a formal consequence is with the help of their list of rules.

This kind of treatment of the material consequence can only be taken to mean that the material consequence is not considered a consequence in the strict or full sense of that term.   Furthermore, it is remarkable in this connection how rarely our tracts introduce the distinction between absolute (simplex) and as-of-now (ut nunc) consequences.[7]   If this distinction is made at all, it is never compared to the one between formal and material consequences, nor even mentioned in the same sections of our texts.

Anyway, our authors go on to assert that we may recognize with regard to any consequence whether it is valid and formal (bona et formalis) with the help of a set of rules.   Now, it is often difficult -- if not impossible -- to see whether our authors intend this assertion to refer to all the rules enumerated in their treatises or only to those contained in the opening chapters.   The latter seems to be the case with such authors as Walter Burley, William of Sutton, Martinus Anglicus and the anonymous compiler of the Oxford-consequences.   These works, at least, single out the rules listed in the first chapter as being of a more basic character than those in the following chapters.   Evidence for this interpretation is the fact that our authors in the following chapters frequently derive other rules from those mentioned in the first chapter, or at least they adduce these as support for later rules.[8]   Be that as it may, it seems certain that our authors adhere to the view that the concept of consequence should be defined -- or determined -- not by a number of theoretical reflections but by reference to a set of rules for valid consequences.

Yet it must be admitted that two requirements are frequently made for a valid and formal consequence, which can hardly be regarded simply as rules of consequence.   One states that the consequent must be understood formally (formaliter intelligitur) in the antecedent.[9]   This definition of the formal consequence seems only to occur in British works of the fourteenth century,[10] though the idea is found in Parisian works in the thirteenth century as well — even if not applied to the concept of formal consequence, something apparently only established in the fourteenth century.

The other idea occurs less frequently, perhaps, but is far from rare.   It is that a consequence is valid and formal if it is impossible that whatever the antecedent signifies is the case, without that which the consequent signifies also being the case.[11]   Now, this requirement for a consequent raises an interesting question, for it is exactly in this manner that Jean Buridan defines a valid consequence.[12]   Are we, then, confronted here with a British influence on Paris or a Parisian one on England?   I do not know: all the British treatises containing this requirement are seemingly later than Buridan. On the other hand, Buridan expressly ascribes the definition to 'some people' (alii), and he is slightly critrical of it.

However we answer this question, it should at least warn us against drawing too firm a line between British and Parisian developments regarding the theory of consequences. The same lesson can be learned from another description of the formal consequence which Rodolphus gives, viz., that it is a consequence in which the same mode of arguing holds for all terms and for any matter.[13] This statement is quite common in the Parisian works, and Rodolphus would probably have got it from one of them, since it hardly occurs at all in the other British texts.

Besides the two requirements just mentioned there are a number of rules that are nearly always listed at the beginning of the British treatises and that our authors evidently consider to be central for understanding what a consequence is. Among the most noteworthy of these rules is the one that asserts that if the antecedent is true, then the consequent must be, or necessarily is, true too. Nearly all our treatises add the verse: 'ex falsis verum, ex veris nil nisi verum.' Such a rule causes us no surprise: it displays an obvious similarity to the modern concept of implication. Still, we should notice the modal element in it, which brings it closer to the modern idea of strict implication than to that of material implication. In the same line is another medieval rule, which states that from the (contradictory) opposite of the consequent the opposite of the antecedent follows. Further rules that occur in all our texts are the two: that whatever follows from the consequent follows from the antecedent; and that whatever precedes the antecedent precedes the consequent.[14] These rules, too, are well-known from modern propositional calculi; they are often called respectively 'suffixing' and 'prefixing' or 'the laws of syllogism'.

We would nowadays say that the four or five rules already mentioned belong to the logic of propositions. Our medieval authors would probably rather say that they are rules for consequences with sentences in which the syncategoremes 'si' or 'nisi' occur. To these rules several of our treatises add a number for consequences from superior to inferior or vice versa, frequently combined with rules about consequences between universal, particular, and singular propositions.[15] Other works, however, do not grant these rules such a prominent place but only list them in later chapters.[16]

The rules to which I have briefly referred so far are those most frequently occurring in the opening chapters of our treatises and those by which our authors appear to want to describe what a consequence is. We notice that several among them are either identical with or similar to theses of modern propositional calculi. Still, some of them contain a modal element, and there are among the rules some belonging both to what we would call the logic of propositions and to the logic of terms. These two facts make it impossible simply to identify the modern concept of material implications with the medieval one of consequence.

Besides the rules already mentioned our texts enumerate a considerable number of other rules for consequences. The earliest works simply arrange these in various chapters, with no apparent order among the chapters. Such treatises contain chapters on exclusive, exceptive, copulative, disjunctive, and conditional sentences. In addition they contain chapters on the words that produce confusions (confusiones) in the suppositions of the terms of various sentences, and chapters containing rules that are said to be taken from Aristotle's Peri hermeneias and which cover various forms of opposition.[17] In contrast, other works, all of which seem to have been composed around or after the middle of the century, attempt to establish some organisation. Most frequently this is done by drawing a distinction between general and special rules (generales-speciales).[18] The precise meanings of these two terms are nowhere expressly stated. The most natural interpretation on the basis of their use is that a general rule is one that is valid for all sentences, whereas a special one concerns only sentences containing particular syncategoremes. Anyway, the special rules are frequently such as hold for, for example, exclusive sentences (those containing e.g., 'tantum'), and only for them, or for exceptive ones (those containing, e.g., 'praeter'), or disjunctive, conjunctive, conditional ones, etc. Further special rules are those valid for propositions containing such syncategoremes as 'omnis' and 'aliquis'. The general rules, on the other hand, will frequently be those mentioned before by which our texts describe what a consequence is, and in addition the rules for syllogistic consequences, and sometimes also the rules for sentences containing oppositions ('non', 'nullus', etc.). Yet, it must be admitted that it is far from clear what the background for this distinction between general and special rules is.

Anyway, the majority of the rules contained in our treatises on consequences are such as describe consequences valid for sentences in which various syncategoremes occur. In other words: our texts primarily discuss what effects the insertion of a syncategoreme into a proposition has upon its relations with other sentences. Or more directly: the greater part of the texts on consequences is taken up with discussions of various syncategoremes.

This observation can lead us on to a question about the origin of this genre of texts entitled De consequentiis, which seems to spring out of the earth in England rather suddenly around 1300. We may ask: In which other genres do we find discussions of the same type and contents? Evidently in the treatises on syncategoremes, but it is unclear how this genre might be the matrix for the creation of a new genre on consequences. It is much more likely that our genre is connected with the thirteenth-century collections of sophisms -- primarily of British origin — which are arranged as discussions of various syncategoremes. The discussions in these sophisms frequently concern the effect which the occurrence of a certain syncatego-reme in a proposition has with regard to the inferences that may be drawn from them. The works I have in mind are those that Alain de Libera has discussed in his paper,[19] and in this connection I think that the three genres which he carefully distinguished, viz., sophismata, distinctiones, and abstractiones, are of equal interest. Primarily, I am thinking here of the collection normally referred to as Magister Abstractionum or Abstractiones Richardi Sophistae. It is impossible to argue convincingly here for the affinity between such sophisms and the British treatises on consequences, since the text of the sophisms is so far known only to a few people. To me, however, the similarity between several passages in the Magister Abstractio-num and, for example, Walter Burley's work on consequences and other early treatises is so striking that a connection between the two genres seems to me indisputable. The day it will be possible to put all these texts down on a table beside each other and read them together, I suppose that no further arguments will be needed to prove the close relationship between the treatises on consequences and these sophisms. The similarity is still present in later works, e.g. in the discussions about the validity of various rules of consequences which occur in Martinus' Objectiones consequentiae or in Ralph Strode's work on consequences.

Now, seemingly the English literature of sophisms is connected with the disputations on sophisms which were part of the training that (undergraduate) students had to go through at Oxford.[20] Frequently the written form of these sophisms takes its point of departure from a proposition that raises a logical problem. During the discussion of it, one or more rules of consequence are adduced to settle or clarify the problem. In the discussions in the treatises on consequences things seem to be, so to speak, turned upside down: here a rule is first set out and then its contents are explained or illustrated by its application to a problematic sentence.[21]

Obviously, if the rules of consequence played such an important role in the solution of sophisms, there would sooner or later arise a demand for a manual or simply a checklist of such rules. This, I suggest, is the background for the creation of the genre of tracts on consequences. It is impossible to prove this assumption, but it may explain various facts connected with our genre. First, the elementary approach to the problems, mentioned above, has an explanation: for if our treatises are designed for the use of undergraduates, we should expect precisely such a level. Secondly, it would help us to understand why the genre enjoyed such a success in England, but not in Paris, since exercise in sophisms was not part of the training of undergraduates in Paris. Further, we should not overlook that this is precisely the reason Walter Burley gives for composing his text on consequences. In the opening lines of his work Burley says that we use consequences when we prove or disprove sophisms, and therefore we need to know a lot about their nature.[22] William of Sutton repeats Burley's phrase and goes on to say that his treatise has been composed for the _juniores_, i.e. the undergraduates.[23] Finally, the assumption of a connection between the British texts on consequences and the British practice of training students in debating sophisms that concentrate upon the nature of the various syncategoremes is indirectly reinforced by the fact that Jean Buridan's Parisian treatise on consequences contains far less material about syncategoremes -- and much more about the syllogism than the British ones.

There are admittedly some British works on consequences which are rather different from those hitherto discussed. They are Ockham's _Summa logicae_ and a sort of commentary on it, ascribed, probably falsely, to Thomas Bradwardine. Together with them belong the two Pseudo-Ockham manuals of logic, the _Elementarium logicae_ and the _Tractatus minor_, and the recently edited _Logica 'Ad rudium'_.[24] These texts, roughly speaking, begin with a chapter on general rules of consequences, which contains rules of the same kind as those by which the tracts I have spoken about so far determine what a consequence is. After that the texts now under discussion continue with chapters comprising special rules, generally speaking, identical with various

loci or rules known from the study of topics. It seems, however, that texts
with such contents were composed only in the period ca. 1325-1340, and only
under the influence from Ockham.[25] At least, I know only one text from the
second half of the fourteenth century,[26] which partly belongs to this
tradition and partly to the more common one which I spoke about earlier.
All other British texts on consequences, both those earlier than ca. 1325 and
those composed after ca. 1340, seem to belong to the type that is mainly
concerned with setting out rules for consequences connected with various
syncategoremes.

Hence, I think that the deviant works just mentioned do not constitute a
serious objection against the assumption that the primary background for the
creation of the genre De consequentiis in England was the practice of
training undergraduate students in sophisms concerned with the nature of
various syncategoremes. Yet, it must be admitted that we still need
something that will explain why this genre — together with several other new
genres -- arose precisely around 1300 and not earlier.

Notes

[1] See below, pp. 297-307.

[2] E.g., William of Sutton, Consequences (no. 5 in the appendix), MS Wien,
VPL 4698, fol. 134^r; 'Oxford-consequences' (no. 6), MSS Vat. Pal. lat. 1049,
fol. 105rb; Vat. lat. 3065, fol. 12rb; Martinus Anglicus, Cons. (no. 9), fol. 36^r;
Richard Billingham, Cons. (no. 7), MS Oxford, Bodl. Lib. lat. misc. e. 100, fol.
56^r; Richard Lavenham, Cons.(no. 13), § 1; Petrus de Candia, Cons. (no. 15),
fol. 34vb; Anon., Cons. 'Quoniam consequentiarum' (no. 12), fol. 141^r.

[3] E.g., Anon., Cons. 'Consequentia est habitudo' (no. 2), § 1; Rodolphus
Anglicus, Cons. (no. 14), fol. 87^v; cf. Ralph Strode, Cons. (no. 10), 1.1.01.

[4] Walter Burley, Cons. (no. 1), cap. 1; Anon., Cons. 'Consequentia est
habitudo' (no. 2); Anon., Cons. 'In omni consequentia' (no. 3); Martinus
Anglicus, Cons. (no. 9), fol. 36.

[5] 'Oxford-consequences' (no. 6), MS Vat. Pal. lat. 1049, fol. 105rb;
Robert Fland, Cons. (no. 8), § 1; Billingham, Cons. (no. 7), fol. 56^r;

Lavenham, Cons. (no. 13), § 5; Richard Ferrybridge, Cons. (no. 11), cap. 1,2; Strode, Cons. (no. 10), 1.1.03-04.

[6] Lavenham, Cons. (no. 13), § 5; Rodolphus Ang., Cons. (no. 14), fol. 87[v].

[7] Sutton, Cons. (no. 5), fol. 136[v]; 'Oxf.-cons.' (no. 6), MS Vat. Pal. lat. 1049, fol. 107[vb]; cf. Fland, Cons. (no. 8), § 6.

[8] E.g., Burley, Cons. (no. 1), §§ 37, 66, 67; Sutton, Cons. (no. 5), fol. 134[v].

[9] 'Oxf.-cons.' (no. 6), MS Vat. Pal. lat. 1049, fol. 105[rb]; Fland, Cons. (no. 8), §§ 1-3; Billingham, Cons. (no. 7), fol. 56[r]; Lavenham, Cons. (no. 13), § 2; cf. Sutton, Cons. (no. 5), fol. 136[v]; cf. Strode, Cons. (no. 10), 1.1.03.

[10] Cf. Paul V. Spade, 'Five Logical Tracts by Richard Lavenham' in J.R. O'Donnell ed., Essays in Honor of Anton Charles Pegis (Toronto, 1974), pp. 70-124; ibid., pp. 77 et seq.

[11] Lavenham, Cons. (no. 13), § 7; Rodolphus Ang., Cons. (no. 14), fol. 87[v]; Ferrybridge, Cons. (no. 11), cap. 1,4; Strode, Cons. (no. 10), 1.1.01; 'Oxf.-cons.' (no. 6), MS Vat. Pal. lat. 1049, fol. 107va; Anon., Cons. 'Tractaturus' (no. 17), fol. 36[r].

[12] H. Hubien ed., Iohannis Buridani Tractatus de consequentiis (Philosophes médiévaux 16; Louvain-Paris, 1976), pars. 1, cap. 3, p. 22 (47 et seq.).

[13] Rodolphus, Cons. (no. 14), fol. 87[v].

[14] E.g., Burley, Cons. (no. 1), §§ 1-16; Anon., Cons. 'Consequentia est habitudo' (no. 2), §§ 2, 12-19; Sutton, Cons. (no. 5), fol. 134[r]; 'Oxf.-cons.' (no. 6), MS Vat. Pal. lat. 1049, fols. 105[vb]-106[ra]; Martinus Ang., Cons. (no. 9), fol. 36[r-v]; Lavenham, Cons. (no. 13), §§ 7-15; Rodolphus, Cons. (no. 14), fol. 87[v].

[15] Burley, Cons. (no. 1), §§ 17-20, 26-31; Anon., Cons. 'Consequentia est habitudo' (no. 2), §§ 3-11; Sutton, Cons. (no. 5), fol. 134[r]; 'Oxf.-cons.' (no. 6),

MS Vat. Pal. lat. 1049, fol. 105[rb-va]; Rodolphus, Cons. (no. 14), fol. 88[r-v].

[16] Fland, Cons. (no. 8), §§ 38-42; Martinus Ang., Cons. (no. 9), fol. 37[r]; Billingham, Cons. (no. 7), fol. 56[v]; Lavenham, Cons. (no. 13), §§ 17-31; Ferrybridge, Cons. (no. 11), cap. 1,1.

[17] E.g., Burley, Cons. (no. 1); Sutton, Cons. (no. 5); 'Oxf.-cons.' (no. 6); Rodolphus, Cons. (no. 14).

[18] E.g., Fland, Cons. (no. 8); Martinus Ang., Cons. (no. 9); Billingham, Cons. (no. 7); Lavenham, Cons. (no. 13).

[19] 'La littérature des abstractiones et la tradition logique d'Oxford'; see above, pp. 63-114.

[20] Cf. Edith D. Sylla, 'The Oxford Calculators' in Norman Kretzmann, Anthony Kenny, Jan Pinborg eds., The Cambridge History of Later Medieval Philosophy (Cambridge, 1982), pp. 540-63; ibid., pp. 542 et seq.

[21] E.g., Burley, Cons. (no. 1), §§ 27-31; Anon., Cons. 'In omni consequentia' (no. 3), §§ 23-28.

[22] Burley, Cons. (no. 1), § 1.

[23] Sutton, Cons. (no. 5), fol. 134[r].

[24] Cf. E. Buytaert, 'The Elementarium logicae of Ockham', Franciscan Studies 25 (1965) 151-276; idem, 'The Tractatus logicae minor of Ockham', Franciscan Studies 24 (1964) 34-100; L.M. de Rijk ed., Anonymi auctoris Franciscani Logica 'Ad rudium' (Artistarium 1; Nijmegen, 1981); Bradwardine: no. 4.

[25] Cf. N.J. Green-Pedersen, 'Bradwardine (?) on Ockham's Doctrine of Consequences: An Edition', CIMAGL 42 (1982) 85-150; ibid., pp. 89-91.

[26] Anon., Cons. 'Quoniam consequentiarum' (no. 12).

Preliminary List of Fourteenth-Century Works
on Consequences connected with England

1. <u>Incipit</u>: Quia in sophismatibus probando et improbando consequentiis utimur, ideo circa naturam consequentiarum multa oportet scire. Et ideo sciendum quod haec regula est bona: quicquid sequitur ad consequens...

<u>Expl.</u>: ...bene valet ratione materiae, scilicet ratione talium propositionum, sed non formaliter, quia non tenet in omni materia praemissis isto modo dispositis. Quare non valet obiectio.

<u>Author</u>: Walter Burley.

<u>Date</u>: ca. 1300.

<u>Edition</u>: N.J. Green-Pedersen, 'Walter Burley's "De consequentiis". An Edition', <u>Franciscan Studies</u> 40 (1980) 102-66.

<u>MSS</u>: Brugge, Stadsbib. 500, fols. 95^r-101vb; Cambridge, Gonville & Caius Coll. 434/434, fols. 1ra-6ra; Firenze, Bib. Med. Laur., S. Crucis, Plut. XII, sin. 2, fols. 203vb-212rb; London, Brit. Lib., Royal 12.F.XIX, fols. 116ra-122rb; Oxford, Bodl. Lib., Digby 24, fols. 47ra-55rb; Paris, BN lat. 6441, fols. 18vb-22rb.

2. <u>Incipit</u>: Consequentia est habitudo inter antecedens et consequens. Antecedens est illud ad quod sequitur aliud. Consequens est illud quod sequitur ex alio. Ut hic 'si homo est, animal est'...

<u>Expl.</u>: ... ubi est praedicatio eiusdem de se non valet consequentia, sicut patet hic: ista consequentia non valet 'homo albus est homo albus, ergo homo est homo [est homo] albus.'

<u>Author</u>: Anonymous.

<u>Date</u>: ca. 1300.

<u>Edition</u>: N.J. Green-Pedersen, 'Two Early Anonymous Tracts on Consequences', <u>CIMAGL</u> 35 (1980) 1-28; ibid., pp. 4-11.

MS: London, Brit. Lib., Royal 12.F.XIX, fols. 111ra-112rb.   The text is possibly incomplete.

3. Incipit: In omni consequentia bona quicquid sequitur ad consequens sequitur ad antecedens; ut sequitur 'Socrates currit, ergo animal currit' et sequitur 'animal currit, ergo substantia currit'...

Expl.: ...Et quando accipitur: ad negationem copulativae etc.   Dico quod verum est nisi partes copulativae sunt ordinatae sicut antecedens et consequens.   Ergo etc.

Author: Anonymous.

Date: ca. 1300.

Edition: N.J. Green-Pedersen, 'Two Early Anonymous Tracts on Consequences', CIMAGL 35 (1980) 1-28; ibid., pp. 12-28.

MS: Paris, BN lat. 16130, fols. 118va-120vb.

4. Incipit: Circa scientiam consequentiarum aliqua praeambula sunt praemittenda.   Primo ponenda est definitio consequentiarum, secundo divisio earundem, et aliquae conclusiones sunt subiungendae.

Expl.: ...quia includunt diversum intellectum praedicandi 'entis'.   Et quod hoc sit mens Aristotelis patet diligenter intuenti textum ibidem.

Author: Very doubtful ascription to Thomas Bradwardine.

Date: 1325-1340.

Edition: N.J. Green-Pedersen, 'Bradwardine (?) on Ockham's Doctrine of Consequences: An Edition', CIMAGL 42 (1982) 85-150.

MSS: Liège, Bib. Univ. 1140, fols. 205ra-211ra; Vat. Pal. lat. 1049, fols. 117vb-127rb.

4A. Commentary-Incipit: Quaeritur circa librum consequentiarum utrum in bona consequentia antecedens possit esse verum et quod consequens non sit verum.

Argitur quod non: quorum unum includit alterum formaliter unum non potest esse...

Expl.: ...potest fuisse malus vel erit malus. Ideo bene tenet, et hoc etiam tenet respectu aliorum possibilium quae actu non sunt etc.

Anonymous questions, earlier than 1376.

MS.: Vat. Pal. lat. 1049, fols. 109vb-117vb.

5. Incipit: Quoniam in sophismatibus probandis et improbandis utimur consequentiis, quocirca ut iuniorum in dialectica collatione probitas amminetur aliqua in hoc opere de consequentiis videamus. Est autem consequentia antecedens et consequens cum consequentiae nota...

Expl.: ...'tu differs ab omni homine', id est 'tu es et omnis homo est, et tu non es omnis homo', et sic de singulis. Ne igitur prolixitas alicui taedium generaret haec de consequentiis sufficiant.

Author: Some commentaries ascribe it to William of Sutton, which is possibly correct; a few ascribe it to Thomas Manlevelt, which is unlikely. All the manuscripts of the treatise are apparently anonymous. In the German universities of the fifteenth century this work was often used together with Manlevelt's Suppositiones and Confusiones.

Date: ca. 1340.

MSS: Edinburgh, Univ. Lib. 138, fols. 82^{r}-87^{r}; Erfurt, WAB, Ampl. 4° 245, fols. 188^{r}-207^{v}; Ampl. 4° 271 (?); Klagenfurt, Bisch. Bib. XXIX.e.1, fols. 11^{v}-17^{v}; Kraków, Bib. Jag. 1894, fols. 158^{v}-208^{v}; 2178, fols. 60^{r}-82^{v}; 2591, fols. 93^{v}-111^{r}; Praha, Met. Kap. 1382 (M.XXIX), fols. 27^{r}-41^{v}; Stát. Knih. 2605 (XIV.F.20), fols. 60^{r}-69^{r}; Wien, ÖNB, VPL 4698, fols. 134^{r}-138^{r}; VPL 5196, fols. 85^{r}-100^{v}; VPL 5248, fols. 32^{v}-38^{r}; Wrocław, Bib. Univ. IV.Q.6, fols. 74^{r}-88^{r}; Zeitz, Domherrenbib. LXVIII (74), fols. 25^{r}-62^{v}.

5A. Commentaries - (a) Incipit: Circa initium consequentiarum primo quaeritur utrum nomine (?) consequentiarum sit assignandum aliquod subiectum ubi (!) non. Illa quaestio praesupponit unum et quaerit reliquum. Primo praesupponit...

Expl.: ...vel Sortes est homo, igitur Sortes non differt ab homine. Et sic est finis etc. Expliciunt disputata consequentiarum magistri Maulfelt etc.

Anonymous questions, fifteenth century.

MS: München, BSB, clm. 14896, fols. 187va-218ra.

(b) Incipit: Circa initium consequentiarum...

Fifteenth-century anonymous questions, which seem from the catalogue to be a commentary on our work.

MS: Praha, Met. Kap. 1391 (M.XXXVIII), fols. 42^{r}-46^{v}.

(c) Incipit: Circa initium libri consequentiarum quaeritur utrum consequentia sit subiectum libri consequentiarum...

Fifteenth-century anonymous questions, presumably on our work.

MS: Zeitz, Domherrenbib. LXIII (59), fols. 128^{v}-181^{r}.

(d) Incipit: Circa materiam consequentiarum nota quod argumentatio consideratur dupliciter, uno modo secundum se, alio modo secundum suas partes...

Expl.: ...in fine dat naturam exponendae propositionis ratione illius verbi 'desinit' de quo postea procedebit (?) circa materiam *** (?) et sic est finis materiae quantum sequitur.

Fifteenth-century anonymous questions, Erfurt.

MSS: Erfurt, WAB, Ampl. 4° 241, fols. 55^{v}-64^{v}; 4° 263.

(e) Incipit: Circa principium illius libri quaeruntur tria, primo quae causa, secundo quis titulus, et tertio cui parti philosophiae supponatur. Quantum ad primum sciendum quod huius operis...

Expl.: ...et simili modo de aliis, et dictio (?) vel non intellegibiles, quia earum exponentes non possunt intelligi esse verae.

Fifteenth-century, anonymous.

MS: Wien, Dom. Konv. 160/190, fols. 100vb-109va.

(f) Incipit: Circa tractatum de consequentiis primo proponitur hoc
sophisma 'verum est falsum'. Prima positio sic, et faciam
argumentum primo per modum obligationis: ponitur quod '**a**'
significat...

Expl.: ...earum exponentes non possunt intellegi, et vere ne igitur
prolixitas reportantium argumentum prohibebit (?).

Fifteenth-century, anonymous.

MS: Kraków, Bib. Jag. 687, fols. 1ra-18rb.

(g) Incipit: Iste est alter libellus parvae logicae, et est tertius in
ordine...

Expl.: ...cum partibus contradicentibus. Et sic est finis huius operis.
Deo gratias...

Fifteenth-century, anonymous, Erfurt.

MS: Erfurt, WAB, Ampl. 12° 13a, fols. 81^v-103^r.

(h) Incipit: Iste liber cuius subiectum est...

Expl.: ... illam propositionem etc. est finis huius operis.

Anonymous, dated 1413.

MS: Praha, Met. Kap. 1382 (M.XXIX), fols. 96^v-142^r.

(i) Incipit: Paucitas instructionis in logica est magnum impedimen-
tum in cognitione veritatis. Hanc propositionem scribit
Commentator in III. Metaphysicae...

Expl.: ...et alia implicite, quae implicatur in illo verbo 'differt', igitur tales exponuntur per tres affirmativas.

Fourteenth-century, anonymous.

MSS: Berlin, St. Bib. Preuss. Kult. lat. fol. 41 (974), fols. 14ra-33vb (dated 1344); Paris, BN lat. 14715, fols. 59vb-78rb (ascribed to Albert of Saxony, an ascription which I find very doubtful).

6. Incipit: Consequentia est quoddam aggregatum ex antecedente et consequente ad idem consequens cum nota consequentiae. Et sunt notae consequentiae 'ergo', 'ideo', 'quia', 'igitur', 'idcirco'. Consequentiarum alia formalis et bona et quaedam materialis...

Expl.: ...quia idem est 'omnis homo est animal' et 'omne animal est homo.' Respondetur quod termini idem significant, tamen non propositiones.

Author: Anonymous, 'Consequentiae secundum modum Oxoniae'.

Date: ca. 1350 (?).

MSS: Cambridge, Corpus Christi Coll. 244/245, fols. 6^r-13^r; 378, fols. 10^r-30^r; Oxford, Bodl. Lib. lat. misc. e. 79, fols. 4va-7vb; Padova, Bib. Antoniana 407 (?); Bib. Univ. 1123, fols. 1vb-3va (?); Pistoia, Archivio Cap. C. 61, fols. 83va-84vb; Vat. lat. 3065, fols. 12rb-14vb; 4269, fols. 187^v-192^r; Vat. Pal. lat. 1049, fols. 105rb-108rb; Vicenza, Bib. Bertol. 211 (306), fols. 98^v-102^r; Worcester, Cath. Lib. F. 118, fols. 4va-8ra. NB: The texts of these manuscripts differ greatly from each other. We should rather speak of a common stock of material than of a single work. The beginning and end of the work is here quoted from MS Vat. Pal. lat. 1049, which is apparently the earliest of the manuscripts.

6A. Commentary - Incipit: Utilem quandam mixtionem de consequentiarum obiectionibus restat titulare et regularum prius positarum intellectum quodammodo declarare. Et primo istius regulae: ab inferiori...

Expl.: ...tertio exceptive, ut 'omnis homo praeter Sortem currit'; quarto propositiones pluralis numeri, ut 'duo homines habent duo capita.' Ergo regula falsa est etc.

Fifteenth-century work, anonymous.

MSS: Oxford, New Coll. 289, fols. 25^r-33^v; Worcester, Cath. Lib. F. 118, fols. 15va-19vb.

7. Incipit: Consequentia est quoddam aggregatum ex antecedente et consequente et nota consequentiae. Et sunt notae consequentiae scilicet 'si', 'quia', 'igitur' et 'ergo' et consimiles. Est praeter consequentiam in condicionalibus et causalibus antecedens illud quod praecedit notam...

Expl.: ...igitur est impossibilis. De propositione contingenti sic 'homo currit' ista significat quod 'homo currit' est propositio sic contingit esse, ergo 'homo currit' est propositio contingens.

Author: Richard Billingham.

Date: ca. 1350.

MSS: Barcelona, Arch. Coron. Aragón, Ripoll 166, fols. 1^r-5^r; Gdansk, Munic. Lib. cod. 2181, fols. 68^r-71^v; Oxford, Bodl. Lib. lat. misc. e. 100, fols. 56^r-62^r; Roma, Bib. Casanatense 5445, fol. 108A^v-119^v; Salamanca, Bib. Univ. 1882, fols. 120^r-123^v; Toledo, Bib. Cabildo 94-27, fols. 70^r-86^v.

7A. Commentaries - (a) Incipit: Consequentia est quoddam etc. Contra regulam arguitur: et videtur quod regula sit falsa. Et arguitur sic: nullum complexum est definibile...

Expl.: ...et in contingenti, ubi accidens est inseparabile. Quare non. Et haec dicta sufficiant.

Anonymous, fifteenth-century work.

MS: Roma, Bib. Casanatense 5445, fols. 131^r-155^v.

(b) Incipit: Consequentia est etc. Hic ponitur talis conclusio quod nulla consequentia definitur. Et probatur sic: nullum complexum definitur, consequentia...

Anonymous, fifteenth-century work.

<u>MS</u>: Segovia, Bib. Cabildo, Vitrina 31, pars media, fols. 5^r-93^v.

(c) <u>Incipit</u>: Rogasti me, Fernande alumne ob ludicationem tui ingenii
⟨ut⟩ in <u>Consequentias</u> Berlingham aliquid de penuria mei
intellectus traderem... Consequentia est etc. Tractatus iste
potest dividi in praeambulam et tractatum, licet non consuevit
dividi...

Anonymous, fifteenth-century work.

<u>MS</u>: Salamanca, Bib. Univ. 1735, fols. 3^r-74^v.

8. <u>Incipit</u>: Nota quod consequentia dividitur duobus modis, nam quaedam est
formalis et quaedam materialis. Ad cognoscendum quando consequentia est
formalis dantur regulae generales. Prima est ista: ubi consequens intellegitur
in antecedente formaliter...

<u>Expl.</u>: ...nec procedit contra regulam, quia si differt ab aliquo impossibili
sufficit quod aliquid sit in-possibili vel aliquod sit impossibile.

<u>Author</u>: Robert Fland.

<u>Date</u>: 1335-1370.

<u>Edition</u>: Paul V. Spade, 'Robert Fland's <u>Consequentiae</u>: An Edition',
<u>Mediaeval Studies</u> 38 (1976) 54-84.

<u>MS</u>: Brugge, Stadsbib. 497, fols. 41ra-43rb.

9. <u>Incipit</u>: Consequentia est aggregatum ex antecedente et consequente et
nota consequentiae. Est autem antecedens illud quod praecedit notam
consequentiae, consequens vero est quod sequitur notam consequentiae...

<u>Expl.</u>: ...ex impossibili arguendo, quarum autem bonitas in practica
obiectionum totum (?) in tractatu immediate sequenti melius apparebit. Et sic
est finis Deo gratias.

<u>Author</u>: Martinus Anglicus (hardly = Martin of Alnwick).

Date: ca. 1350-1360 (?).

MS: Wien, ÖNB, VPL 4698, fols. 36^r-39^v.

9A. Commentary - Incipit: Consequentarium bonarum quaedam sunt obiectiones ponendae et quaedam solvendae. Prima regula est haec: arguendo ab inferiori ad suum superius cum negatione praeposita non valet consequentia...

Expl.: ...et tamen non sequitur quod sit disiunctiva, quia ista 'homo est' significat quod iste homo vel iste homo est. Et sic de obiectionibus ad praesens dicta sufficiant usque ad tractatum paralogismorum.

Probably written by Martin himself.

MSS: Cambridge, Gonville & Caius Coll. 182/215, pp. 48-69; Corpus Christi Coll. 244/245, fols. 33^v-38^v; 378, fols. 58^r-64^v; Oxford, Bodl. Lib. lat. misc. e. 79, fols. 24ra-32va; Padova, Bibl. Univ. 1123, fols. 14ra-16ra; Toledo, Bib. Cabildo 94-28, fols. 73^v-89^r; Venezia, Bib. Marc., Z.L. 277, fols. 6^r-12^r; Vat. lat. 2189, fols. 116^v-119^v; 3065, fols. 14vb-21rb; Wien, ÖNB, VPL 4698, fols. 48^v-56^r; Wrocław, Bib. Univ. IV.Q.3, fols. 197^r-203^v.

9B. Commentary on the 'Obiectiones' - Incipit: Postquam studiosi iuvenes intellexisse coeperunt tractatulos positivos in obiectionibus consequentiarum speculando consueverant delectari ut arguere tentantes et respondere...

Expl.:...obiectiones in aliis tractatibus quos prius pueris tradidi scripserim fortiores.

Probably a fifteenth-century work.

MS: Vat. lat. 3065, fols. 116vb-123va.

10. Incipit: Consequentia dicitur/est illatio consequentis ex antecedente. Et quia poterit aliquod consequens inferri debite ex antecedente vel indebite, secundum hoc dicitur aliqua consequentia bona...

Expl.:...cuius necessitas patet per impossibilitatem copulativae sibi oppositae. Et sic de aliis, nec amplius plura dicuntur. Et sic est finis consequentiarum.

Author: Ralph Strode.

Date: ca. 1360 (?).

Edition: W.K. Seaton, 'An Edition and Translation of the Tractatus de consequentiis by Ralph Strode...' (Ph. D. diss., Univ. California, Berkeley, 1973; University Microfilms 75-6797, 1974).

MSS: For the numerous manuscripts see the edition mentioned above.

10A. Commentaries - (a) Incipit: Consequentia dicitur etc. Pro cuius descriptionis notitia intellegendum primo quod de consequentia quae sit multiplex reperitur opinio...

Expl.: ...falsitas, possibilitas aut impossibilitas. Et haec pro huius tractatus declaratione dicta sufficiant ad mei exercitum et iuvenum introductionem faciliorem.

Caietanum de Thienis, Declarationes in Consequentia R. Strodi.

Several manuscripts.

(b) Incipit: Iesum deum et hominem totiusque sapientiae fontem uberrimum mente, corde et ore, dilectissimi fratres....Tripartitum tractatum vobis tradere institui ut sic toti libello trinitas suffragetur...

Expl.: ...ferendo actum supra multitudinem totam vel partes eius. Et sic est finis.

Paul of Pergula, Dubia super Consequentias R. Strodi.

Numerous manuscripts.

(c) Incipit: Satis mens mea dubia est in determinando, mi Bernardo, si hodie apud senam urbem nostram...

Alexander Sermoneta, In Consequentias R. Strodi.

Various manuscripts.

11. **Incipit:** Consequentiarum quaedam est bona et formalis, quaedam bona et non formalis. Duplex est autem consequentia bona et formalis: una ut est consequentia syllogistica seu discursoria, quod idem est...

Expl.: ...sicut manifeste apparere potest bene repicienti casum. Et ita patet solutio huius consequentiae et aliarum praemissarum Dei gratia cuius regnum manet per infinita saecula saeculorum.

Author: Richard Ferrybridge.

Date: ca. 1360 (?).

Edition: Lorenzo Pozzi, Le 'Consequentiae' nella logica medievale (Padova, 1978), pp. 262-80 (extracts).

MSS: Klagenfurt, Stud. Bib., Pap. 168, fols. 49^r-60^v; Kraków, Bib. Jag. 2660, fols. 2^r-16^v; Padova, Bib. Univ. 1123, fols. 31rb-36vb; Praha, Stát. Knih. 1008 (V.H.31), fols. 67^r-74^v; Roma, Bib. Casanatense 85 (D.IV.3), fols. 24ra-40rb; Vat. lat. 2189, fols. 105^v-116^v; 3065, fols. 43rb-54va; 9369, fols. 122^r-135^v.

11A. **Commentary** - **Incipit:** Consequentiarum quaedam etc. Circa primam divisionem notandum quod secundum hunc virum consequentiam est propositio categorica vel hypothetica...

Expl.: ...de aliis duabus consequentiis satis dicit magister in littera.

Caietanus de Thienis, Super Consequentias R. Ferrybridge.

MSS: Klagenfurt, Stud. Bib., Pap. 168, fols. 92^r-94^v; Mantova, Bib. Com. A.III.12, fols. 150va-156va (?); Vat. lat. 2139, fols. 88^r-93^r.

12. **Incipit:** Quoniam consequentiarum notitia facit iuvenes esse frequenter in disputationibus quamplurimum habiles, ad informandum ergo eorundem...

Expl.: ...quodammodo de istis et etiam de istis poterit in consequentiis aliquantulum abundare necnon quamplurima.

Author: Anonymous.

Date: Before 1388, possibly ca. 1360.

MS: Barcelona, Arch. Coron. Aragón, Ripoll 141, fols. 20^r-35^v.

13. Incipit: Consequentia est antecedens et consequens ad illud formaliter vel materialiter sequens cum aliqua nota consequentiae.   Notae consequentiae vocantur tales coniunctiones 'si', 'ergo', 'ideo', 'igitur'....

Expl.: ...contradictorium istius disiunctivae 'tu es Oxoniis vel tu es Londoniis' est hoc 'tu non est Oxoniis, et tu non es Londoniis.'

Author: Richard of Lavenham.

Date: ca. 1370 (?).

Edition: Paul V. Spade, 'Five Logical Tracts by Richard Lavenham' in J.R. O'Donnell ed., Essays in Honour of Anton Charles Pegis (Toronto, 1974), pp. 70-124.

MS: London, Brit. Lib., Sloane 3899, fols. 6^v-12^v.

14. Incipit: Consequentia est quaedam habitudo vel sequela in qua consequens se habet ad antecedens.   Pro quo sciendum est quod in argumento tria oportet considerare, scilicet illam propositionem vel...

Expl.: ...et ecce vero tantum isto termino rationali perficitur secundae (?) exponens, et qui terminus fuit sequens verbum in universali.

Author: Rodolphus Anglicus.

Date: ca. 1370 (?).

MSS: Erfurt, WAB, Ampl. 4° 271, fols. 141^r-151^r; Kraków, Bib. Jag. 2660, fols. 38^r-50^r (?); Wien, ÖNB, VPL 4698, fols. 87^v-97^v.

15. Incipit: Consequentia est aggregatum ex antecedente et consequente cum nota illationis.   Antecedens enim est propositio ex qua mediante nota illatum

est consequens. Consequens est...

Expl.: ...id est per sensum vel intellectum, ut 'ille est homo.' Sic ergo patet quo modo uniuscuiusque problematis fiat probatio.

Author: Petrus de Candia (Alexander V).

Date: 1370-1380 (?).

MS: Vat. lat. 3065, fols. 34vb-39va.

16. Incipit: Consequentiarum quaedam est formalis, quaedam est materialis. Consequentia formalis est cuius consequens est de intellectu antecedentis, cuiusmodi est haec 'homo currit, ergo homo movetur'...

Expl.: ...appellationem quam importet iste terminus 'Sortes' etc. Patet responsio ad plura talia sophismata. Et sic hactenus dicta sufficiant.

Author: John of Holland.

Date: 1370-1380 (?).

MSS: Kraków, Bib. Jag. 2660, fols. 24^r-36^r; Wien, ÖNB, VPL 4698, fols. 138^V-145^V (incompl.).

17. Incipit: Tractaturus de consequentiis, praemissis quibusdam — utpote quid est antecedens, quid consequens, quid consequentia, quid nota consequentiae -- cum aliquibus consequentiae divisionibus...

Expl.: ...quia de his videbitur ad partem nominatim in sophismatibus. Et haec pro nunc sufficiant. Expliciunt consequentiae.

Author: Anonymous.

Date: 1370-1380 (?).

MS: Barcelona, Arch. Coron. Aragón, Ripoll 141, fols. 36^r-41^V.

12

English Obligationes Texts after Roger Swyneshed:
The Tracts beginning 'Obligatio est quaedam ars'

E.J. Ashworth
University of Waterloo

Introduction

In this paper I hope to shed some light on the development of obligationes in
England by examining a number of texts which all have the same incipit,
'Obligatio est quaedam ars'.   A list of the manuscripts and early printed
books I have used, together with the sigla I have adopted, will be found in
Appendix A.[1]   In Appendix B I have given a list of other relevant
manuscripts which I was unable to consult for reasons of time.[2]   My paper
has three parts.   Part One contains a general survey of the texts, with an
account of their relationship to each other and to the Logica oxoniensis text.
Part Two contains a discussion of the doctrines and influence of Billingham's
Ars obligatoria and the almost identical treatise found in the Logica
oxoniensis.   Part Three contains a detailed analysis, with references, of the
texts discussed in Part Two.

It seems appropriate to begin with some further remarks about the incipit
itself.   The fullest version is found in Richard Billingham, who wrote:[3]

Obligatio est quaedam ars mediante qua aliquis opponens potest ligare
respondentem ut ad suum bene placitum respondeat ad obligationem sibi
positam; vel obligatio est oratio mediante qua aliquis obligatus tenetur
affirmative vel negative ad obligationem respondere.
(Obligation is an art whereby some opponent can bind a respondent to
reply at the opponent's pleasure to the obligatory sentence posited to

The Rise of British Logic, ed. P. Osmund Lewry, O.P., Papers in Mediaeval
Studies 7 (Toronto: Pontifical Institute of Mediaeval Studies, 1985), pp. 309-
333.   © P.I.M.S., 1985.

him. Alternatively, an obligation is a sentence by virtue of which someone who is obligated is committed to reply affirmatively or negatively to the obligatory sentence.)

As can be seen from the appendices, a number of variations in this _incipit_ were possible. A and D replaced 'opponens potest ligare' in Billingham's first definition with the phrase 'obligatus tenetur' from the second definition; and a number of authors added 'affirmative vel negative' to the first definition. Despite these minor variations, there is no doubt that the texts listed in Appendix A have basically the same _incipit_; but, as I shall show, it does not follow from this that the texts listed were otherwise identical, or even similar.

Part One: General Survey

1. Roger Swyneshed

Before I can approach the question of how to classify the texts we are concerned with, it is necessary to say something about the doctrines of Roger Swyneshed. His _Obligationes_, which 'was written after roughly 1330 and certainly before 1335',[4] presented new and controversial theories about the basic rules for obligational disputes, and these theories provide us with a convenient touchstone for the assessment of all subsequent authors. Swyneshed's innovations stemmed from his definition of a relevant proposition. Previous authors had defined a relevant proposition as one which stood in a logical relationship, whether that of following from or that of being inconsistent with, to the initial _positum_ together with any proposition which had already been granted, or which was the negation of a correctly denied proposition. They then specified that any proposed proposition which was relevant as following (_pertinens sequens_) should be granted, and that any proposed proposition which was relevant as inconsistent (_pertinens repugnans_) should be denied. All irrelevant propositions were to be treated as they would be treated outside the disputation. As the obligational disputation proceeded, an increasing number of propositions had to be taken in to account by the respondent who wanted to know whether a newly proposed proposition was relevant or not. Swyneshed, however, stipulated that a proposition was relevant or irrelevant solely by virtue of its logical relationship to the _positum_. At no point did subsequent propositions need to be considered. This stipulation led him to formulate two new rules. First, one can deny a conjunction even though one has already granted both its conjuncts. This happens when the initial *positum* is false, and is followed by a true proposition. The *positum* must be granted because it is possible, and the second proposition must be granted because it is irrelevant and true, but their conjunction is (on Swyneshed's view) irrelevant, and since it is false, it must be denied. The second rule, that one can grant a disjunction even though each disjunct has been denied, is a corollary of the first rule, based on the logical equivalence between a negated conjunction and the disjunction of the negated conjuncts.

2. Martinus Anglicus

Of all the texts beginning 'Obligatio est quaedam ars', only one contains a detailed and explicit discussion of Swyneshed's innovations.[5] This is the treatise by Martinus Anglicus, which is found in two copies (see Appendix A). Martinus drew a distinction between two types of *responsio* which could be given to propositions within an obligational disputation. One is the *antiqua responsio*, stemming from Burley, and the other, which he calls *magis nova*, is that developed by Swyneshed.[6] Martinus lays out Swyneshed's rules, and he give lengthy examples of how they apply in practice.[7] What is more, he clearly approves of them, for he says 'Iuxta istam responsionem poteris omnia inconvenientia in obligationibus effugere.'[8] Nor is it only with respect to his discussion of Swyneshed that his work differs from the other texts I shall examine. His presentation of definitions and rules is quite different, and his work contains none of the sophisms which characterize the *Logica oxoniensis*. The only hint of any relationship between Martinus Anglicus and the *Logica oxoniensis* is found in Δ, which briefly discussed three examples also discussed by Martinus (see Part Three, Section A, I.3). There is thus no evidence to support De Rijk's conjecture that the *obligationes* belonging to the *Logica oxoniensis* stems from the work of Martinus Anglicus.[9]

The close relationship between Martinus Anglicus and Roger Swyneshed raises certain problems for the identification of the author. De Rijk has argued that Martinus must be Martin of Alnwick, who was first heard of as a Franciscan friar resident in the Oxford convent in 1300 and who died in 1336.[10] The evidence cited by De Rijk mostly has to do with the authorship of a number of theological questions, some found in a manuscript said to date from the beginning of the fourteenth century. We are thus asked to suppose

that one and the same man was first active in theology and then, very near
the end of his life, turned back to topics belonging to the arts faculty. I do
not find this plausible. My doubts are supported by work done on other
logical treatises by Martinus Anglicus. N.J. Green-Pedersen has suggested
that the Consequentiae (which is cited in the Obligationes[11]) dates from ca.
1350[12]; and in a joint paper Wilson and Spade have suggested that Martinus
Anglicus, as the probable author of the Obiectiones consequentiarum, should
be identified with Martin Bilond.[13] It seems likely that there were at least
two Englishmen known as 'Martinus Anglicus', one a theologian, and one a
logician who wrote after Swyneshed.

3. The Logica cantabrigiensis

I now turn to the obligationes belonging to the Logica cantabrigiensis.[14]
This is found in one manuscript source and one early printed source (see
Appendix A). The work is very short, and it contains no sophisms at all. It
has three sections (For references, see Part Three, Section A.). Section one
gives definitions and rules. Both the presentation and the contents are the
same as in the Logica oxoniensis. Section three deals briefly with depositio,
a topic for which the Logica oxoniensis itself has no standard treatment.
The second and longest section discusses impositio in a way which I found
both interesting and original. One noteworthy feature is the attention paid
to conditionals and consequences; and another feature is the introduction of
the notion of sequestratio. The author emphasizes that when a new
significatio is imposed on a proposition, the impositor must be very careful to
make sure that the old significatio has been laid aside. This is done through
the use of such exclusive terms as 'solum' and 'tantum'. Thus, if the
impositor says 'Impono quod ista propositio "Deus est" solum significat
hominem esse asinum', it follows that 'suam primam significationem
sequestrari'.[15] The same material is found in the early printed text given
the title 'Logici' by the Short Title Catalogue,[16] though this text adds a
section on problems to do with mental propositions.[17]

4. Richard Billingham and the Logica oxoniensis

The largest group of texts and the one I am most closely concerned
with, includes the Ars obligatoria by Richard Billingham, who was a fellow of
Merton College in 1344, a position he still held in 1361, and regent master of
arts in 1349. De Rijk has listed several manuscripts,[18] and I used the one

from Salamanca which begins 'Incipit ars obligatoria a berlingano magistro edita'.[19]   De Rijk reports another manuscript in which the _obligationes_ immediately follow other works attributed to Billingham, but otherwise the texts are anonymous.   I shall assume that the ascription of the _Ars obligatoria_ to Richard Billingham is not problematic.   This assumption can be supported to some extent by a consideration of the relationship between the _Ars obligatoria_ and other texts which can be dated.   First, I think there is a relationship between the _Ars obligatoria_ and the section on _obligationes_ in Albert of Saxony's _Perutilis logica_.[20]   There are sixteen sophisms in the _Ars obligatoria_, nine of which appear in Albert of Saxony.   Of these nine, two were in Burley,[21] but I know of no earlier source for the others.   Whereas the _Ars obligatoria_ is a short, straightforward text, bearing no trace of doctrinal influence by Albert, Albert's text is lengthy and eclectic.   He takes sophisms from a variety of sources, including Burley and Swyneshed, and he frequently mentions alternative interpretations and solutions.   Hence, I think that the _Ars obligatoria_ influenced Albert, rather than the reverse.   If this is the case, we know that the _Ars obligatoria_ must have been written well before 1360, since William Buser's _Obligationes_, which is heavily dependent on Albert's work, was written in 1360.[22]   My second reason for dating the _Ars obligatoria_ before 1360, at a time when Billingham was active, stems from a consideration of John Wyclif, who was a fellow of Merton in 1356 and the Master of Balliol in 1360.   In the brief and obviously derivative treatment of _obligationes_ found in the _Tractatus de logica_ we find Billingham's package of definitions and rules, and three of the six sophisms are basically Billingham's.[23]   Wyclif's editor, Dziewicki, has postulated that Wyclif wrote his _Tractatus de logica_ at the beginning of his Oxford career, and before 1362.[24]

If one takes Billingham's _Ars obligatoria_ and compares it with the anonymous _obligationes_ texts which belong to the _Logica oxoniensis_, the results are startling.[25]   Provided that one ignores the minor additions, emendations and omissions that one would expect to find in copies of a working logical text, the initial package of rules and definitions is the same. The sequence of sophisms for both simple and composite _positio_ is also the same, except in the case of the two last sophisms for similars and dissimilars. Together the rules, definitions and sophisms for _positio_ comprise the bulk of the texts.   The genuine differences come in the last two sections of Billingham's text.   First, unlike the _Logica oxoniensis_, he has a section on _impositio_, but it is very brief, occupying about one typed page.   Second, his brief section on _depositio_ contains a non-standard set of rules, and no

sophisms at all. However, although five of the Oxford texts contain the
same package of five sophisms for depositio, they each give their own rules,
so there was no standard set. My general conclusion, then, is that apart
from the section on depositio, the Oxford obligationes just is Billingham's Ars
obligatoria.

Part Two: Doctrines and Influence of Billingham's 'Ars obligatoria'

I shall now consider the doctrinal importance of Billingham's logic, and
its influence on other logicians. There are two issues on which he took an
independent position, one having to do with inconsistency, and one having to
do with the rules for conjunctions. I shall begin with the most complicated
issue, that of inconsistency. In order to understand the problem, we have to
consider the basic rules for the type of obligational disputation known as
positio. The opponent began by putting forward an initial proposition, called
the positum; and two rules apparently governed the respondent's reply: (1)
Any positum which is possible must be admitted; (2) Any positum which has
been admitted must be granted. The first rule obviously debars any logically
inconsistent propositions of the form 'P and not P', and semantically
inconsistent posita were not an issue, except for Burley. However, there are
at least three kinds of pragmatically inconsistent propositions which were
recognised as problematic. (1) Some propositions, such as 'Nihil est tibi
positum' (Nothing is posited to you) are inconsistent with the making of the
positio or, as Wyclif put it, with the opponent's act.[27] (2) Some propositions,
such as 'Tu non es' (You do not exist) are inconsistent with the making of
the admissio, that is, with the respondent's act. (3) Some propositions such
as 'Tu curris et nulla copulativa est tibi posita' (You are running and no
conjunction is posited to you) are inconsistent with the positum itself, i.e.
with its syntactic properties.

One possible response to these types of pragmatic inconsistency was to
restrict the first rule, so that it read 'possibile licet falsum non repugnans
obligationi nec admissioni nec his simul est admittendum' (A possible, though
false, proposition should be admitted so long as it is not inconsistent with
the obligatio or the admissio or both of those together).[28] That is, no
pragmatically inconsistent positum could be admitted. This response was
preferred by Albert of Saxony. Another response, preferred by Buser and
Paul of Venice, was to accept both rules in an unrestricted manner. That is,
they admitted and granted the initial posita, and then they denied everything

which was logically inconsistent with these posita.[29]   A third response which, as we shall see, was somewhat similar to Billingham's, is found in Swyneshed, who stated that any positum which was inconsistent with the positio should be admitted but treated as irrelevant.   That is, it could be granted or denied as seemed appropriate.[30]

Billingham's own view seems to have been that inconsistent posita should be admitted and then denied.   Certainly this is the view criticized by Paul of Venice, who wrote that he saw no point in admitting a positum if it were then to be denied.[31]   However, there are only two places at which Billingham is relatively explicit about his intentions.   First, he added to his statement of the rules the rubric: 'Omnes istae regulae habent intelligi si non sit obligatio in contrarium' (All these rules must be understood to have the clause 'provided that there is no contrary obligato' added to them).[32]   Only two of the Oxford treatises followed him here (see Part Three, Section B 6). Second, in his section on conjunctions he stated that every conjunction from which the opposite of the positum followed should be denied; and he used as his example 'Tu curris et nulla copulativa est tibi posita' which, he said, implied 'Aliqua copulativa est tibi posita.'[33]   Here he was followed by all the Oxford treatises except one which omitted the rule and example altogether (see Part Three, Section C III.1).

Further clues to Billingham's intentions are afforded by an examination of his sophisms.   There are three which are relevant to the question of pragmatic inconsistency.   The first, 'Nulla propositio est tibi posita' (see Part Three, Section C I.2), is treated in a way which, at first sight, seems at odds with the treatment of 'Tu curris et nulla copulativa est tibi posita' in that the positum is granted and the inference to 'Aliqua propositio est tibi posita' is blocked.[34]   He granted the validity of the inference:

> Ista propositio est tibi posita, demonstrata ista 'Nulla propositio est tibi posita', et ista propositio est aliqua propositio; ergo aliqua propositio est tibi posita.
> (This proposition is posited to you, indicating 'No proposition is posited to you', and this proposition is some proposition; therefore some proposition is posited to you.);

but he denied the major premiss.   The Oxford texts other then A and B explained that the premiss should be denied because it was inconsistent with the <u>positum</u>, a solution which could also have been offered in the case of the conjunction example. Wyclif took the example a little further. If the opponent argues 'ego pono tibi istam proposicionem; ergo ista proposicio est tibi posita' (I posit this proposition to you; therefore this proposition is posited to you), the inference should be granted and the antecedent denied, again because it is inconsistent with the case.[35] Unlike Swynesned, who doubted the <u>positum</u>,[36] and Albert of Saxony, who refused to admit it,[37] Billingham and his followers clearly did not see this sophism as posing any problems of pragmatic inconsistency.

The second relevant sophism is 'Tu non es.' Here we find a difference between the treatment accorded it by Billingham and that found in the Oxford texts. Billingham himself said that the <u>positum</u> must be admitted because it is possible. Then he argued that it must be denied when it is proposed, and that this denial does not violate the second rule for <u>positio</u> since the rule is understood to apply only to a consistent <u>positio</u>.[38] Text F followed Billingham; <u>A</u> and <u>C</u> gave Billingham's reply as an alternative to the solution of granting the <u>positum</u>; and <u>B</u>, <u>D</u> and <u>E</u> granted the positum (for references, see Part Three, Section C I.1). It was then, of course, necessary to deny any proposition which implied the truth of the <u>positum</u>.[39]

Finally there is the sophism:

Pono tibi istas duas propositiones esse similes significando praecise, 'Tibi concluditur' et 'Tu nescis tibi concludi.'
(I posit to you that these propositions, given their normal signification, are similar with respect to their truth-value: 'The argument goes against you' and 'You do not know that the argument goes against you' -- see Part Three, Section C V.1).

The Oxford texts all give the standard solution, that these propositions should not be similar in falsity because of the force of 'know', and that they must therefore both be granted when they are proposed. Billingham, however, seems to have taken 'Tibi concluditur' (The argument goes against you) as being paradoxical, or something one cannot properly grant at the beginning of an obligational disputation. He described the two propositions as ones which 'cannot be similar in truth nor in falsity' and he said that one should deny both 'The argument goes against you' and 'You do not know that the argument goes against you.' At the same time, you should grant that each of these propositions is true, in order to evade the contradiction which arises when they are granted to be false.[40]

The other issue on which Billingham took an apparently original position was that of conjunction rules. He stated that although each categorical part of some conjunction was to be granted, it did not follow that the whole conjunction was to be granted: 'Notandum est quod licet utraque categorica alicuius copulativae sit concedenda, non tamen propter hoc tota copulativa est concedenda.'[41] He was followed in this by all texts belonging to the Logica oxoniensis.[42] One might think that Billingham was espousing Swyneshed's view, but this is not the case. Billingham's example makes it clear that he meant only that a conjunction might not be concessible at a point in a disputation where each conjunct would be concessible. His example was the conjunction 'You are in Segovia and you are sitting down' (other texts have 'Rome'). If 'You are in Segovia' is the false positum and 'You are sitting down' is true, each should be granted when proposed. But if their conjunction is proposed immediately after the positum, it must be denied, because at that point it is false and irrelevant. The principle was stated more clearly by the early printed text, E, which said (sig. C vii^r):

> Et nota quod licet utraque pars copulativae sit concedenda per se, non tamen sequitur quod copulativa sit concedenda antequam proponantur ambae partes.

Paul of Venice discussed the principle at some length, and argued that it had been formulated in a misleading manner. As it stood, it seemed to collapse into Swyneshed's view.[43]

I shall finish with a few remarks about the influence of Billingham and the Logica oxoniensis. Generally speaking, it seems to have been slight. Apart from Wyclif, no named author, including John of Holland and Paul of Venice in the Logica parva, adopted Billingham's organization of the material. There was a little discussion of Billingham's definition of obligatio, of his attitude to inconsistent posita, and of his conjunction rules, but one cannot claim that these topics loomed large in the literature. The most striking influence is that of the sophisms themselves, a number of which reappear in Albert of Saxony (see Part Three, Section B). I suspect that the apparent popularity (judging by the number of extant manuscripts) of the Logica oxoniensis in the fifteenth century, a period when people had on the whole ceased to write original obligationes treatises, stems solely from its character as a convenient brief compendium.

Part Three: Analysis of Texts

Section A: Table of Contents

I. Introduction to 'Positio'

After the incipit, we find the following topics discussed. I am using Billingham's organization as the standard for comparison.

1. The species of 'obligatio'

Billingham (fol. 89^V) lists three species, positio, depositio, and impositio. He also mentions suppositio. A (fol. 18ra) lists positio and depositio, but adds impositio after the first two rules have been stated. The remaining texts have just positio and depositio; B, fol. 14^r; C, fol. 48^r; D, fol. 62^V; E, fol. 95vb; F, sig. C v^r.

2. Definitions

Both B (fol. 14^r) and C (fol. 48^r) give definitions of positio and depositio. The other texts omit depositio. In D (fol. 62^V) and F (sig. C v^r) the definition of positio follows the listing of the species of obligatio, as it does in B and C. In A (fol. 18ra) the definition follows the reference to impositio. In Billingham himself (fol. 90^{r-v}) and in E (fol. 96rb) the definition of positio comes after the rules. A noted that the positum could be possible or impossible, but in the latter case it should not be admitted.

In C we find a definition of positum added at the bottom of fol. 48^r: 'Positum est illud quod manet dempto verbo significanti actum ponendi.' The same definition is found in F (sig. C v^V) after the rules. See also LSC sig. C i^V. A similar definition of the obligatum is found in MS Oxford, Magdalen College 92, fol. 163^r.

A (fol. 18va) also has a definition of 'tempus obligationis' which follows the last rule.

3. Rules

For details, see Section B.

In A the first two rules are separated from the others by the introduction of impositio and the definitions of positio and of simple versus composite positio (fol. 18^{ra-rb}). One sophism and three examples of the rules are discussed at some length (fols. 18va-19ra). The sophism, 'Reliquum istorum est verum', is found in Martinus, fols. 71^v-73^r (There is no fol. 72).[44] The first example, 'Aliquis istorum currit', is found in Martinus (fol. 74^r), as is the second, 'Antichristus est coloratus' (Martinus, fol. 74^v).[45]

4. Simple and composite 'positio'

See Billingham, fol. 90^v. Simple positio occurs when the positum is a categorical proposition; composite positio occurs when the positum is a hypothetical proposition. These notions are defined after the rules (as in Billingham) in B (fol. 14^v) and E (fol. 96rb). In A (fol. 18rb) the definition occurs after the definition of positio and before the third rule. In C (fol. 48^r), D (fol. 62^v) and F (sig. C v^r) the definitions occur before the rules. These three sources add the remark 'Unde in ista specie obligationis, solum possibile est admittendum et impossibile reiiciendum atque negandum' (d).

Billingham adds 'temporalis' to 'copulativa' and 'disiunctiva'.

5. The functions of the opponent and respondent

Billingham (fol. 90^v) wrote:

Opus opponentis est ponere et proponere quousque videat respondentem male respondere; et opus respondentis est recipere positum et servare ne videatur deduci ad aliquod inconveniens. Et si positum sit impossibile, negandum est; <si> positum est possibile, concedendum est.

The last clause was omitted by D (fol. 63^r) and by E (fol. 96rb). B (fol. 14^v) says: 'Si impossibile, debet negare casum.' A (fol. 19ra) adds 'Si dubium, dubitari.' C (fol. 49^r) and F (sig. C v^v) are like Billingham.

II. Sophisms for Simple 'Positio'

For a list, see Section C.

III. Sophisms and Rules for Composite 'Positio'

Both conjunctions and disjunctions were discussed. I have omitted the sophisms (or examples) in the section on disjunctions from my list in Section

C, since they are of little interest.

Billingham, fols. 92^V-93^V; A, fols. 20rb-21rb; B, fols. 16^V-17^r; C, fols. 53^V-54^V; D, fol. 64^V; E, fol. 97^{ra-va}; F, sig. C vii^{r-v}.

IV. Interchangeable Propositions

Billingham, fols. 93^V-94^r; A, fol. 21^{rb-va}; B, fol. 17^{r-v}; C, fols. 53^V-54^V; D, fol. 65^r; E, fol. 97^{va-vb}; F, sig. C vii^V-viii^r.

V. Similar and Dissimilar Propositions

Billingham, fol. 94r-v; A, fols. 21va-22va; B, fols. 17^V-18^V; C, fols. 54^V-56^r; D, fol. 65^{r-v}; E, fols. 97vb-98rb; F, sig. C viii^{r-v}.

VI. 'Impositio'

This section is found only in Billingham (fols. 94^V-95^r) and A (fol. 22vb). The presentation is different, but there are no significant doctrinal differences.

C gives the rule that replies should not be varied because of a new impositio, at the end of the section on interchangeable propositions (fol. 54^V), as does F (sig. C viii^r).

VII. 'Depositio'

Billingham, fol. 95^{r-v}. He finishes (fol. 95^V) with an analysis of the three types of necessary disjunction: cf. Martinus, fol. 78^V.

For other treatments of depositio, see A, fols. 23ra-24ra; C, fols. 56^r-57^r; D, fol. 66^{r-v}; E, fol. 98^{rb-vb}; F, sig, C viii^V-D i^V.

B has no section on depositio. Neither does Wyclif.

Section B. Rules for 'Positio'

1. 'Omne tibi positum sub forma positi propositum scitum a te esse positum non repugnans posito <positionis> et a te admissum durante tempore obligationis est a te concedendum.'

Billingham, fol. 89^V. He added that the rule must be followed 'si bene velis respondere.' This phrase also appears in A, fol. 18ra; Wyclif, p. 69; and MS Worcester Cathedral F. 118.[46]

The clause 'ubi positum non repugnat positioni' is found in B, fol. 14^r (with 'si' for 'ubi'); C, fol. 48^r; and E, sig. C v^r. Cf. LSC, sig. C i^v. The other sources lack the clause: A. fol. 18ra; D, fol. 62^v; E, fol. 96ra. However, A cites it in sophism one: fol. 19ra.

2. 'Omne repugnans formaliter tibi posito est a te negandum.'

Billingham, fol. 89^v; B, fol. 14^r; C, fol. 48^r; D, fol. 62^v; E, fol. 96ra. The rule appears in third place in E, sig. C v^r; as it does in Wyclif, p. 70, and LSC, sig. C i^v. It is in fourth place in A (fol. 18rb), which has 'Omne possibile non repugnans est admittibile' as its second rule (fol. 18ra).

3. 'Omne sequens formaliter ex tibi posito est a te concedendum.'

Billingham, fol. 89^v; A, fol. 18rb; B, fol. 14^r; C, fol. 48^r; D, fol. 62^v; E, fol. 96ra. The rule appears in second place in E, sig. C v^r, as it does in Wyclif, p. 69, and LSC, sig. C i^v.

4. 'Omne sequens formaliter ex a te concesso vel a te concessis non repugnantibus est a te concedendum durante tempore obligationis.'

Billingham, fols. 89^v-90^r; A, fol. 18rb; B, fol. 14^r; C, fol. 48^v; D, fol. 62^v; E, fol. 96ra; E, sig. C v^r.

The rule was rejected by Swyneshed.

5. 'Omnis propositio formaliter sequens ex tibi posito cum opposito bene negati vel oppositis bene negatorum est concedenda durante tempore obligationis.'

Billingham, fol. 90^r; A, fol. 18rb; B, fol. 14^r; D, fol. 63^r; E sig. C v^r. E (fol. 96ra) has just the singular case. C (fol. 48^v) gives two rules, one for the singular case and one for the plural.

The rule was rejected by Swyneshed.

At this point a sixth rule was added by D (fol. 63^r): 'Omne repugnans tibi posito et opposito (MS concesso) bene negati vel cum oppositis bene negatorum est negandum.' See also C, fol. 48^v.

6.   'Ad omne impertinens respondendum est secundum sui qualitatem.'

Billingham, fol. 90^r. He added the definition: 'Pertinens est illud quod est sequens vel repugnans, et impertinens est illud quod nec est sequens vel repugnans.' See also C, fol. 48^v-49^r; D, fol. 63^r; E, fol. 96ra, B, (fol. 14^{r-v}) and F (sig. C v^r) defined relevance in relation to the casus: cf. Wyclif, p. 70.   Only A (fol. 18va) gave an account of relevance which was full enough to rule out Swyneshed's narrow definition.

The rule is in fourth place in LSC, sig. C i^v.

After this rule Billingham added 'Omnes istae regulae habent intelligi si non sit obligatio in contrarium.' See also C (fol. 49^r); D (fol. 63^r).

7.   'Propter possibile positum non est concedendum impossibile nec negandum necessarium.'

Billingham, fol. 90^r; B, fol. 14^v; C, fol. 49^r; D, fol. 63^r; E, sig. C v^{r-v}. Some sources specify 'impossibile per se' and 'necessarium per se': A, fol. 18va; E, fol. 96rb; Wyclif, p. 71. E (fol. 96rb) added as a ninth rule that the impossible per accidens could be granted and the necessary per accidens denied.

8.   'Duo contradictoria inter se contradicentia non sunt concedenda simul nec neganda ab eodem infra tempus obligationis.'

Billingham, fol. 90^r; A, fol. 18va; B, fol. 14^v; D, fol. 63^r; Wyclif, p. 71. Billingham used a and b as examples of contradictories and specified that one a should be every a: see E, fol. 96rb; F, sig. C v^v; LSC, sig. C ii^r.

C (fol 49^r) reversed the order of the last two rules.

Section C. Sophisms

I.   Sophisms for Simple 'Positio'

1.   'Tu non es.'

Billingham, fol. 90^v; A, fol. 19^{ra-rb}; B, fol. 14^v (Vos non estis); C, fol. 49^{r-v}; D, fol. 63^{r-v}; E, fol. 96rb ('Tu non es homo', very brief treatment); F, sig. C v^v (Vos non estis).   Cf. Wyclif, pp. 71-72 (Tu es mortuus); Albert of Saxony, fol. 49rb; Strode, fol. 83^{va-vb}.

QUANTITY	DESCRIPTION	LIST PRICE	DISCOUNT	NET PRICE	TOTAL
1	LEWRY:Rise of British Logic PREPAID WITH CHEQUE #3620 OF 15 May 1985:THANK YOU	750			

BOOKS NOT RETURNABLE

750 gm

US$

PACKING SLIP

A 4537

2. 'Nulla propositio est tibi posita.'

Billingham, fols. 90^V-90^r; A, fol. 19rb (third sophism); C, fol. 49^V (vobis); D, fol. 63^V; E, fol. 96rb; F, sig. C v^V ('vobis', third sophism). The sophism is not in B. See also Wyclif, pp. 72-73; Burley, 3.17; Albert of Saxony, fol. 49rb; and many others.

3. 'Omnis homo currit' followed by 'Tu curris.'

Billingham, fol. 91^r; A, fol. 19rb ('Omnis homo est Romae, Tu es Romae', second sophism); C, fols. 49^V-50^r (Vos estis Romae); E, fol. 96rb-^{va}; F, sig. C v^V ('Vos estis Romae', second sophism). The sophism is not in B or D. See also Albert of Saxony, fol. 49va.

4. 'Omnis homo currit' followed by 'Hanc esse falsam, "Omnis homo currit".'

Billingham, fol. 91^r; A, fol. 19rb-^{va}; B, fol. 15^V (sixth sophism); C, fol. 50^{r-v}; D, fol. 63^V ('Non omnis homo currit' est vera); E, fol. 96va ('Illa est falsa, "Tu curris"', corollary of sophism three); F, sig. C v^V-vi^r. See also Logici, sig. P iiii^r (Omnis homo est Oxonii; haec est falsa, 'Omnis homo est Oxonii').

5. 'Homo est asinus', replaced by '"Homo est asinus" est tibi positum.'

Billingham, fol. 91^{r-v}; A, fol. 19va; B, fols. 14^V-15^r (second sophism); C, fol. 50^V; E, fol. 96va-^{vb}; F, sig. C. vi^r. The sophism is not in D. Cf. Wyclif, p. 73; Albert of Saxony, fol. 49vb.

6. 'Tu es Segoviae' followed by 'Tu es Segoniae in hoc instanti.'

Billingham, fol. 91^V; A, fol. 19va-^{vb} (Tu es Romae); B, fol. 15^r ('Vos estis Romae', third sophism); C, fols. 50^V-51^r (Vos estis Romae); D, fol. 63^V ('Tu es Romae', sixth sophism); E, fol. 96vb (Tu es Romae); F, sig. C vi^r (Vos estis Romae). See also Strode, fol. 88ra-^{rb} (Tu es Romae).

7. 'Aliqua res non est.'

Billingham, fol. 91^V; A, fol. 19vb; B, fol. 15^{r-v} (fourth sophism); C, fol. 51^V (ninth sophism); E, fol. 96vb; F, sig. C vi^{r-v} (ninth sophism). See also

Logici, sig. P v^r; Albert of Saxony, fol. 49va.

8. 'Tu differs a chimera.'

Billingham, fols. 91^v-92^r; A, fols. 19vb-20ra; B, fol. 15^v ('Vos differtis a chimera', fifth sophism); C, fols. 51^v-52^r ('Vos differtis a chimera', tenth sophism); D, fol. 64^r (ninth sophism); E, fol. 96vb; F, sig. C vi^v ('Vos differtis a chimera', tenth sophism). See also Logici, sig. P v^v; Albert of Saxony, fol. 49va.

There are other sophisms for positio which are not found in Billingham:

1. 'Pono vobis istam, "Omnis homo est Romae";...quaero ubi vos estis.'

C, fol. 51^r (seventh sophism); E, sig. C vi^r (seventh sophism). See also Logici, sig. P iiii^v.

2. 'Alter istorum currit': is it consistent with 'Uterque istorum currit'?

C, fol. 51^r (eighth sophism); D, fols. 63^v-64^r (seventh sophism); E, sig. C vi^r (eighth sophism). See also Logici, sig. P v^r.

3. 'Tu curris et "Tu non curris" est tibi positum.'

D, fol. 64^r (eighth sophism).

II. Sophisms for Exclusive 'Positio'
1. 'Tantum homo est asinus est tibi positum' (This sophism depends on the lack of punctuation).

Billingham, fol. 92^r; A, fol. 20ra; B, fols. 15^v-16^r (vobis); C, fol. 52^r (vobis); E, fol. 97ra; F sig. C vi^v (Tantum homo est leo est vobis positum). The sophism is not found in D. See also Logici, sig. P v^v; Paul of Venice, Logica magna, fols. 187ra-r^b. Cf. another version in Buser, fol. 76va-v^b.

2. 'Ponatur quod Sortes credat propositionem veram et Plato similiter, et nullus alius in mundo credat propositionem veram a Sorte et Platone. Tunc proponitur "Tantum alter istorum credit propositionem veram".' Is this consistent with 'Uterque istorum credit propositionem veram'?

Billingham, fol. 92^r; A, fol. 20^{ra-rb}; B, fol. 16^r; C, fol. 52^{r-v}; D, fol. 64^r; E, fol. 97ra; F, sig. C vi^v. See also Logici, sig. P vi^r.

III. Sophisms for Conjunctive 'Positio'

1. 'Tu curris et nulla copulativa est tibi posita.'

Billingham, fol. 92^v; A, fol. 20va; C, fols. 52^v-53^r (vobis); D, fol. 64^v; E, fol. 97rb; F, sig. C vii^r (vobis). See also Logici, sig. Q i^r; Albert of Saxony, fol. 50va.

2. 'Aliquis homo est Segoviae et nullus alius a te est Segoviae.'

Billingham, fol. 92^v; A, fol. 20va (Romae); B, fol. 16^v (nullus alius a vobis est Romae); C, fol. 53^r (nullus alius a vobis est Romae); D, fol. 64^v (Romae); E, fol. 97rb (Romae); F, sig. C vii^r (Nullus homo alius vel alia a vobis est Romae). See also Logici, sig. Q i^r; Albert of Saxony, fol. 50va.

IV. Sophisms for Similar and Dissimilar Propositions

1. 'Pono tibi istas duas propositiones esse similes significando praecise, "Tibi concluditur", "Tu nescis tibi concludi".'

Billingham, fol. 94^r; A, fols. 21vb-22ra; B, fol. 17^v-18^r (vobis); C, fol. 55^r (vobis); D, fol. 65^r; E, fol. 97vb; F, sig. C viii^r (vobis). See also Burley, 3.96-3.97; Albert of Saxony, fols. 49vb-50ra; Strode, fol. 93ra.

2. 'Pono quod duae propositiones sunt dissimiles significando praecise scilicet haec "Deus est" et "Homo est animal".'

Billingham, fol. 94^v; A, fol. 22rb; B, fol. 18^r; C, fol. 55^v; E, fol. 98ra; F, sig. C viii^v. The sophism is not found in D.

There are two other sophisms which are not found in Billingham:

3. 'Pono tibi istas propositiones esse dissimiles, scilicet "Homo est asinus" et "Quaelibet propositio est similis illi", solum primarie significando.'

A, fol. 22^{rb-va}; B, fol. 18^r; C, fol. 55^v; D, fol. 65^v; E, fol. 98ra; F, sig. C viii^v. The sophism is used as an example by Paul of Venice, Logica magna, fol. 190vb.

4. 'Pono tibi istas propositiones esse dissimiles, primarie significando, "Omnis homo currit" et "Quaelibet istarum est vera", scilicet demonstrando per illud pronomen "istarum" omnes singulares istius universalis.'

A, fol. 22va; B, fol. 18^{r-v}; C, fols. 55^{v}-56^{r}; D, fol. 65^{v}; E, fol. 98^{ra-rb}; F, sig. C viii^{v}.

V. Sophisms for 'Depositio'

These are not in Billingham's text. I quote them from A.

1. 'Aliquis homo non est Romae' followed by 'Tu es aliquis homo.'

A, fol. 23rb; C, fol. 56^{v} (Vos estis); D, fol. 66^{r}; E, fol. 98va; F, sig. D i^{r} (Vos estis). See Albert of Saxony, fol. 51va. The text has 'rationalis' for 'Romae', which must be an error.

2. 'Aliquae propositiones non sunt similes.'

A, fol. 23va; C, fol. 56^{v}; D, fol. 66^{r-v}; E, fol. 98va; F, sig. D i^{r}. See also Logici, sig. R v^{r-v}. The sophism is given a completely different treatment in Albert of Saxony, fol. 51va.

3. 'Antichristus est albus vel Antichristus est coloratus.'

A, fol. 23^{va-vb}; C, fols. 56^{v}-57^{r}; D, fol. 66^{v}; E, fol. 98^{va-vb}; F, sig. D i^{v}. See also Logici, sig. R iv^{v}-v^{r}.

4. '"Rex sedet et aliquis homo sedet, et quaelibet istarum est tibi deposita", demonstrando illas tres propositiones.'

A, fol. 23vb; C, fol. 57^{r} (vobis); D, fol. 66^{v}; E, fol. 98vb; F, sig. D i^{v} (vobis).

5. 'Aliquis homo currit vel nullus homo qui est Sortes currit.'

A, fol. 23vb; C, fol. 57^{r}; D, fol. 66^{v}; E, fol. 98vb; F, sig. D i^{v}. See also Logici, sig. R v^{v}.

APPENDIX A

Manuscripts and Early Printed Texts Used, with Sigla

I. Oxford Logic

Billingham: Richard Billingham, Ars obligatoria, MS Salamanca, Bib. Univ. 1735, fols. 89^r-95^v.

A: MS Oxford, Bodl. Lib. Lat. misc. e 79, fols. 18ra-24ra.
Incipit: 'Obligatio est quaedam ars mediante qua quis obligatus tenetur respondere affirmative vel negative, scilicet ad bene placitum opponentis, ad propositionem sibi propositam.'

B: MS Cambridge, Corpus Christi Coll. 244/245, fols. 13^v-18^v.
Incipit: Obligatio est quaedam ars mediante qua quis opponens potest ligare respondentem ut ad placitum suum respondeat affirmative vel negative.'

C: MS Cambridge, Corpus Christi Coll. 378, fols. 48^r-57^r. Fol. 57^v is blank.
Incipit: 'Obligatio est quaedam ars mediante qua (MS: in qua) quis opponens potest obligare respondentem ut ad placitum suum respondeat affirmative vel negative ad propositionem sibi positam vel depositam.'

D: MS Città del Vaticano, Bib. Apost. Vat., Urb. lat. 1419, fols. 62^v-66^v.
Incipit: 'Obligatio est quaedam ars mediante qua quis obligatus tenetur affirmative respondere vel negative ad propositionem sibi obligatam.'

E: MS Città del Vaticano, Bib. Apost. Vat., Vat. lat. 3065, fols. 95vb-98vb.
Incipit: 'Obligatio est ars quaedam mediante qua quis obligans potest respondentem ligare ut ad placitum suum respondeat ad propositionem sibi propositam et positam.'

F: Libellus sophistarum ad usum Oxoniensem (Londoniis, 1510), sig. C v^r-D i^v.
Incipit: 'Obligatio est quaedam ars mediante qua quis opponens potest ligare respondentem ut ad placitum suam respondeat affirmative vel negative ad propositionem sibi positam vel depositam.'

II. Other Sources

1. Martinus Anglicus: MS Wien, ÖNB, VPL 4698, fols. 71^r-78^v.

Incipit: 'Obligatio est quaedam ars qua mediante opponens potest ligare respondentem ut ad placitum suum respondeat.'

For an anonymous copy see MS Kraków, Bib. Jag. 2602, fols. 127^r-131^r.

2. LSC: Libellus sophistarum ad usum Cantabrigiensem (Londoniis, 1524), sig. C i^v-iii^r.

Incipit: 'Obligatio est quaedam ars mediante qua quis opponens potest ligare respondentem ut ad placitum suum respondeat affirmative vel negative ad propositionem sibi propositam.'

See also MS Cambridge, Gonville and Caius Coll. 182/215, pp. 42-47.

3. Logici: <Q>uoniam ex terminis <Theodoric Rood: Oxford, ca. 1483>, sig. O v^v-R vi^r.

Incipit: 'Obligatio est ars quaedam per quam opponens potest obligare respondentem ut ad placitum sibi respondeat affirmative vel negative ad propositionem sibi positam, impositam vel depositam. Vel obligatio est oratio composita ex signis obligationis et obligato....'

4. MS Oxford, Magdalen Coll. 92, fols. 163^r-165^r.

Incipit: 'Obligatio est ars oratio (MS: o^o) mediante qua quis tenetur affirmative vel negative respondere ad obligatum.'

This text is unlike any of the others examined.

APPENDIX B
Other Relevant Manuscripts (not seen)

1. Billingham:[47] MSS Barcelona, Arch. Coron. Aragón, Ripoll 166, fols. 49^r-54^r; Roma, Bib. Casanatense 5445, fols. 119^v-131^v; Toledo, Bib. Cabildo 94-27, fol. 63^r (opening lines only); 94-28, fols. 167^r-171^v (an adaptation).

2. Logica oxoniensis: MSS Padova, Bib. Univ. 1123, fols. 3vb-5va; Worcester Cathedral F. 118, fols. 8vb-10ra; Roma, Bib. Angelica 1053, fols. 36^v-39^v; Città del Vaticano, Bib. Apost. Vat., Vat. lat. 4269, fols. 192^v-196^r;[48] Padova, Bib. Antoniana 407.[49]

Notes

1 See above, pp. 327-328.

2 See above, p. 328.

3 Billingham, fol. 89^v. Both definitions are discussed by William Buser, MS Oxford, Bodl. Lib., Canon. class. lat. 278, fol. 72ra, and Paul of Venice, Logica magna (Venetiis, 1499), fol. 177va. The second definition is found in Roger Swyneshed: see P.V. Spade, 'Roger Swyneshed's Obligationes. Edition and Comments', Archives d'histoire doctrinale et littéraire du Moyen Âge 44 (1977) 252, § 6. For full bibliography, references and discussion of this and other topics to do with obligationes see E.J. Ashworth ed., Paul of Venice, Logica magna. Part II. Fascicule 8. Tractatus de obligationibus (British Academy: Classical and Medieval Logic Texts; forthcoming).

4 Spade, 'Roger Swyneshed's Obligationes...', p. 246.

5 There is one text associated with Wyclif, and hence with the Logica oxoniensis, which takes up the topic: see M.H. Dziewicki ed., Johannis Wyclif Miscellanea philosophica 2 (London, 1905; repr. New York-London-Frankfurt am Main, 1966), pp. 152-56. The two other modi respondendi discussed in this fragment seem to be garbled versions of standard moves made by Billingham and others.

6 Robert Fland also made this distinction between the antiqua responsio and the nova responsio: see P.V. Spade, 'Robert Fland's Obligationes: An Edition', Mediaeval Studies 42 (1980) 45, §§ 13, 14, p. 46, § 20. The parallels between the two treatises are extremely close, though Martinus lacks a section on impositio. However, given the current state of research, it is impossible to tell which of the two authors influenced the other.

7 For a full discussion see E.J. Ashworth, 'The Problems of Relevance and Order in Obligational Disputations: Some Late Fourteenth Century Views', Medioevo (forthcoming). When I wrote this paper I did not realize that the anonymous author of the treatise found in a Cracow manuscript was in fact Martinus Anglicus.

8 Martinus, fol. 76^r.

9 See L.M. de Rijk, 'Logica Oxoniensis: An Attempt to Reconstruct a Fifteenth Century Oxford Manual of Logic', Medioevo 3 (1977) 164.   In another work he mistakenly identifies text C as being by Martinus: see idem, ed., Some 14th Century Tracts on the Probationes terminorum: Martin of Alnwick O.F.M., Richard Billingham, Edward Upton and Others (Artistarium 3; Nijmegen, 1982), p. *40*.   Contrary to what De Rijk says, the text does not seem to be incomplete, for it ends in the same way as texts D and E.   De Rijk made the same identification and remarks in an earlier paper: see idem, 'The Place of Billingham's "Speculum puerorum" in 14th and 15th Century Logical Tradition with the Edition of Some Alternative Tracts', Studia Mediewistyczne 16 (1975) 118.   Equally mistaken is the tentative attribution of text D to Martinus Anglicus in the Vatican Library catalogue.

10 See De Rijk, Some 14th Century Tracts, pp. *6*-*7*.

11 Martinus, fol. 77^r.

12 See N.J. Green-Pedersen, 'Early British Treatises on Consequences', above, p. 303.

13 G.A Wilson and P.V. Spade, 'Richard Lavenham's Treatise Scire: An Edition with Remarks on the Identification of Martin (?) Bilond's Obiectiones consequentiarum', Mediaeval Studies 46 (1984) 1-30.

14 For discussion of the Logica cantabrigiensis, see L.M. de Rijk, 'Logica Cantabrigiensis -- A Fifteenth Century Cambridge Manual of Logic', Revue internationale de philosophie.   Grabmann 29e année, 113 (1975) 297-315; and E.J. Ashworth, 'The "Libelli sophistarum" and the Use of Medieval Logic Texts at Oxford and Cambridge in the Early Sixteenth Century', Vivarium 17 (1979) 134-58.

15 LSC, sig. C ii^v.

16 Logici, sig. Q ii^r.   For a discussion of this text, see E.J. Ashworth, 'A Note on Paul of Venice and the Oxford Logica of 1483', Medioevo 4 (1978) 93-99.   In my analysis of the obligationes I failed to distinguish the section on impositio from the sections on interchangeable propositions and on similar and dissimilar propositions (sig. Q iiii^r-R iii^r).   The latter sections are a mixture of material from the Logica oxoniensis and Paul of Venice.

[17] Logici, sig. Q iii^r-iiii^r.

[18] L.M. de Rijk, 'Richard Billingham's Works on Logic', Vivarium 15 (1976) 132.   De Rijk nowhere relates Billingham's text to the Logica oxoniensis.

[19] Billingham, fol. 89^r.

[20] Albertus de Saxonia, Perutilis logica, tract. 6, pars 2, cap. 1-6 (Venetiis, 1522; repr. Documenta Semiotica, serie 6, Philosophica; Hildesheim-New York, 1974), fols. 46va-51vb.   For details of the sophisms, see Part Three, Section C (above, pp. 322-326). Two sophisms on disjunction have been omitted from this section.

[21] For Burley's text see Romuald Green, The Logical Treatise 'De obligationibus'.   An Introduction with Critical texts of William of Sherwood and Walter Burley (Franciscan Institute Publications: St. Bonaventure, N.Y., forthcoming).

[22] See C.H. Kneepkens, 'The Mysterious Buser Again: William Buser of Heusden and the "Obligatones" tract "Ob rogatum"' in A. Maierù ed., English Logic in Italy in the 14th and 15th Centuries: Acts of the 5th European Symposium on Medieval Logic and Semantics, Rome 10-14 November 1980 (History of Logic 1; Naples, 1982), p. 149.

[23] See M.H. Dziewicki ed., Johannis Wyclif, Tractatus de logica 1, cap. 22 (London, 1893; repr. New York-London-Frankfurt am Main, 1966), pp. 69-74.

[24] Ibid., p. vii.

[25] For discussion of the Logica oxoniensis, see De Rijk, 'Logica Oxoniensis...' and Ashworth, 'The "Libelli sophistarum"..'. In the latter paper (p. 156) I mistakenly suggested that the printed tract was not that found in the Logica oxoniensis. I made this judgment because the printed tract was obviously closely related to texts B and C, the two Corpus Christi College manuscripts, which De Rijk did not discuss in his account of the Logica oxoniensis.

26 Billingham, fols. 94^v-95^r.

27 Wyclif, Tractatus 1, cap. 22, pp. 72-73.

28 See Albert of Saxony, Perutilis logica, tract. 6, pars 2, cap. 4 (Venetiis, 1522), fol. 49rb.

29 Buser, MS Oxford, Bodl. Lib., Canon. class. lat. 278, fol. 76rb. Paul of Venice, Logica magna (Venetiis, 1499), fol. 180va. See also Ralph Strode, Obligationes in Consequentie Strodi etc. (Venetiis, 1517), fols. 78vb-79ra.

30 Spade, 'Roger Swyneshed's Obligationes...', p. 265, §§ 62, 64.

31 Paul of Venice, Logica magna (Venetiis, 1499), fol. 180va.

32 Billingham, fol. 90^r.

33 Ibid., fol. 92^v.

34 F said that the positum should be denied, but this seems to be a mistake since the rest of the argument is the same as in the other Oxford texts.

35 Wyclif, Tractatus 1, cap. 22, pp. 72-73.

36 Spade, 'Roger Swyneshed's Obligationes...', p. 256, § 28, p. 271, § 92.

37 Albert of Saxony, Perutilis logica, tract. 6, pars 2, cap. 4 (Venetiis, 1522), fol 49rb.

38 Billingham, fol. 90^v. He gave as an alternative the solution that the positum should be denied (by which he meant, I think, 'not admitted') because it included the logical contradiction 'Tu es et tu non es.'

39 For further remarks see Wyclif, Tractatus 1, cap. 22, p. 71. Line 26 should probably read: 'Deinde, ipsa proposita, concedatur. Si proponitur: tu es vivus, negatur.'

40 Billingham wrote (fol. 94^r): 'Huic dicitur admittendo positum, et negatur ista "Tibi concluditur", et ista "Tu nescis tibi concludi", quia sequitur, et conceditur quod utraque istarum est vera. Et sic est respondendum quando ponuntur aliquae propositiones esse similes solum significando praecise, quae non possunt esse similes in falsitate nec in veritate, cuiusmodi sunt istae duae.' It was a standard move to allow P to be granted (or denied) when 'P is true' was denied (or granted): see Paul, Logica magna, fol. 180ra. I owe the translation of 'Tibi concluditur' to Paul Spade.

41 Ibid., fol. 92^v.

42 A, fol. 20rb; B, fol. 16^v; C, fol. 52^v; D, fol. 64^v; E, fol. 97ra; F, sig. C vii^r. See also Albert of Saxony, Perutilis logica, tract. 3, cap. 5 'De propositionibus hypotheticis' (Venetiis, 1522), fol. 19rb; and John of Holland, Obligationes, in MS Kraków, Bib. Jag. 2132, fol. 102^r.

43 Paul of Venice, Logica magna (Venetiis, 1499), fol. 189^{va-vb}.

44 See also Burley, De obligationibus, 3.07, ed. Green (forthcoming), and others.

45 See also ibid., 3.28; Albert of Saxony, Perutilis logica, tract. 6, pars 2, cap. 2 (Venetiis, 1522), fol. 47va.

46 As cited by De Rijk, 'Logica Oxoniensis...', p. 127.

47 See De Rijk, 'Richard Billingham's Works...', p. 132.

48 This list comes from De Rijk, 'Logica Oxoniensis...', p. 162.

49 See A, Maierù, 'Le ms. Oxford, Canonici misc. 219 et la Logica de Strode' in idem, English Logic in Italy, p. 92.

I would like to thank the Social Sciences and Humanities Research Council of Canada for the generous grants which enabled me to visit libraries in Oxford and Cracow; the Master and Fellows of Corpus Christi College, Cambridge, for providing me with microfilms of manuscripts from their library; and Mr. Julian Deahl for allowing me to consult his transcripts from the Oxford logic.

13

'I promise a penny that I do not promise':
The Realist/Nominalist Debate over Intensional Propositions
in Fourteenth-Century British Logic
and its Contemporary Relevance

Stephen Read
University of St. Andrews

1. Wyclif

Suppose I promise you one or other of these pennies I have in my hand. Did I promise you this one (pointing to one of them)? No. Did I promise you the other? No. So I did not promise you either of them. But it certainly was not any other penny that I promised. So I promised you one or other of these pennies, neither of which I promised you. So I promised you a penny which I did not promise.

John Wyclif treats this sophism at length in the third chapter of the third treatise in his Logicae continuatio.[1] He takes a resolutely realist stand, defending the claim that what is promised in such a promise is the universal, not a singular. This is not always so, he notes. One can promise a particular, if one says, for example, 'I promise the other of these two pennies' (pointing to one of them). Even so, although it is an individual which has been primarily and distinctly promised, the universal has still been promised secondarily and confusedly, since 'I promise a penny' is entailed by 'I promise this penny.' But in the case of 'I promise you a penny', or 'I promise you one or other of these pennies', no individual penny has been explicitly and distinctly promised. Wyclif describes the two kinds of promise as, respectively, distinct and confused (Burleigh called them determinate and indeterminate).[2]

The Rise of British Logic, ed. P. Osmund Lewry, O.P., Papers in Mediaeval Studies 7 (Toronto: Pontifical Institute of Mediaeval Studies, 1985), pp. 335-359. © P.I.M.S., 1985.

If, however, it is the universal and not any singular which has been promised, in what way am I bound by the promise? What am I obliged thereby to give? Since I have promised the universal, I have, in a sense, promised every singular. But I am not obliged to pay every singular, for they were not promised explicitly. All I need pay is what I explicitly promised, namely, the universal, and I can pay the universal by giving any singular penny. Indeed, it can only be given by giving a singular:

> The execution of ⟨such⟩ acts requires singulars....For a lord can promise me a horse even if he has none, and the gift is worth much to me. But his servant does not deliver me a horse unless he has a singular....[3]
> Because a universal cannot be given or possessed except by a singular, it is necessary that the promiser give a singular; and then it follows that he, by giving the universal, fulfils the promise.... I may have a penny already (if I have some penny), but not because of that promise, and so I claim the universal be given to me by him who promised.[4]

How then does Wyclif use such an account to solve the sophism? It is for such a purpose that logicians, both medieval and contemporary, develop a semantic theory. The main planks of the medieval theory were the twin notions of signification and supposition. Taking 'signification' in some loose and unanalysed sense of 'what an expression means', Wyclif describes supposition as the signification of one extreme in a categorical (atomic) proposition in relation to the other extreme.[5] Supposition therefore both depends on the analysis of atomic propositions into two components, subject and predicate, and belongs to a term only in the context of its occurrence in a particular proposition, in contrast to its signification.

The theory of supposition is straightforwardly a semantic theory, that is, a description of propositions whereby one can explain why those propositions have the conditions of truth that they do. Thus, for example, Wyclif distinguishes material from simple and from personal supposition, so that, in relation to its predicate, the term 'I' in 'I is a pronoun' means itself and has material supposition. Wyclif commonly indicates such supposition by prefixing the particle 'li' to the expression, and so explains the truth of 'Li ego est pronomen.'[6]

Wyclif describes simple supposition as that possessed by a term in relation to a universal outside the mind, in contrast with personal, when it relates to one or more individuals. Thus supposition serves to tell us which objects are involved in the truth-conditions of a particular proposition -- whether it be expressions, real universals, or individuals. Hence, to take the distinction mentioned earlier between promising a penny in general, and promising this particular penny, in the first case the term 'penny' supposits simply, and the proposition is true if what is said is true of the universal penny; whereas in the second, the term 'penny' or 'this penny', supposits personally, and indeed has singular personal supposition, since it supposits for one singular, and the proposition is true if what is said is true of this particular penny:

> By promising a singular firstly and distinctly, a universal is promised secondarily and confusedly, and conversely. So just as it follows: 'A signifies a man, so it signifies an animal'; so too it follows: 'I promise you this penny, so I promise you a penny.'[7]

Wyclif can now present his solution to the sophism. When I ask, 'Did I promise this penny?', 'this penny' has singular supposition, and the answer is correctly, 'No'; so too when I ask, 'Did I promise the other?' Thus 'I promised this penny' and 'I promised the other penny' can both be false, even though 'I promised one or other of these pennies' is true. For in this last proposition, the phrase 'one or other of these pennies' has simple supposition and supposits for a universal; not, it is true, for the universal penny, or at least not primarily — it supposits for it secondarily, since 'I promised a penny' is entailed -- but for a restricted universal, namely, one or other of these two pennies.

Is the universal penny a third penny over and above the two pennies in my hand? Of course not. Wyclif has already dismissed this misunderstanding in the previous chapter. In order to count individuals, one must refer to them using terms with personal supposition; but one cannot refer to a universal that way, but only with a term with simple supposition. So to add a third man to Socrates and Plato, namely, the universal, exhibits a fallacy of equivocation.

So it is possible to understand 'Either of these pennies is promised' and 'Neither of these is promised' in this way: just as there is no contradiction between 'Man is a species' and 'No man is a species', because of the change from simple supposition to personal,[8] so neither is

there in the given case, since the same point applies.   And indeed, even
if I wish it not to be the universal, it will be despite me.[9]

2.   Ockham

Wyclif was a realist: he believed there are universals outside the mind.
But those, as they are often called, nominalists denied this.   For them the
only universals were linguistic, both spoken and written and also, drawing
inspiration from Aristotle's De interpretatione, mental.   Thus Ockham, the
most famous exponent of the doctrine, claimed that the only universals,
except derivatively, were in the mind, and were specifically, acts of
understanding.

Sophisms such as the one above were therefore a challenge to the
nominalist, and Ockham faced that challenge both in his Commentary on the
Sentences and in his Summa logicae.   In the former, he considers thirteen
arguments in favour of Scotus' claim that there is something universal really
existing outside the mind in every singular.   The seventh argument points out
that when an agent intends something, he cannot intend just a singular act,
for no more one act than another, and so, in intending indefinitely many
singulars, he would always fail to carry out his intention; hence the object of
his intention must be a universal.   The case is similar, says Ockham, to the
thought that when someone promises another person a horse, he must promise
him either a singular, or a universal, or a concept.   But it cannot be a
singular, for no more one horse than another, and so he could never fulfil
the promise -- he would needs give any horse whatever.   Nor can it be a
concept, for then he could fulfil the promise by simply imparting the concept,
and without giving anything real at all, which is absurd.   Hence, it seems, a
proper account of what we may call intensional propositions, is impossible
without admitting real universals outside the mind.

Ockham had already met with a similar problem concerning the predicates
of universal affirmative propositions.   One might be inclined to argue that
every man is either any man or none, since he is no more one than another.
In the technical terms of the theory of semantics, for what does 'animal'
supposit in the proposition, 'Every man is an animal'?   It cannot supposit for
any singular animal, nor for a concept, for whichever was chosen would
result in the wrong truth-conditions.   Hence, it seems, a proper account of
universal affirmative propossitions is impossible without admitting real

universals outside the mind.[10]

The nominalists' inspiration (on which I have commented elsewhere[11]) was to use a certain form of internal disjunction. For Ockham, a written or spoken general term gained its sense by being attached conventionally to the appropriate mental general term. But in what did the sense of that mental term consist? Ockham's nominalism required that he insist that its sense was no more than a relation to the individuals which fall under it. Such a one-many relation was called by the medievals a 'confused' one.[12] The sense of the term could be captured by a disjunction: 'penny' simply means 'this penny or that penny, and so on'.

There are two crucial aspects of this account of meaning to bear in mind later. The first is that the semantic contribution of a general term is an array of singulars, not an unexplained universal. The universal is, for Ockham, the act of understanding the general term, and that act has for its (only) object the array of singulars themselves: it is a 'confused cognition of singulars'.[13] Secondly, although a proposition about a disjunction of individuals is sometimes equivalent to a disjunction of propositions, since, for example, 'I give you this horse or that horse and so on' is equivalent to 'I give you this horse or I give you that horse, and so on', and 'Plato was this man or that man, and so on' is equivalent to 'Plato was this man or Plato was that man, and so on', this equivalence fails in other cases, such as 'Every man is an animal' and 'I promise you a horse.' Each disjunct of the form 'Every man is this animal' and 'I promise you this horse' is, or may be seen in suitable circumstances to be, false, even though the corresponding propositions with an internal, or nominal, disjunction are true.

Ockham's answer to the puzzle provoked by the seventh argument can now be stated. To give the truth-conditions of, for example, 'I promise a horse', we must say for what 'horse' here supposits. Since what I promise, and what I am held to pay you, is a horse, an individual, 'horse' must supposit for individuals; but not for any particular individual, but confusedly for any individual horse. Thus the object which enters the truth-condition is not a concept, or any other sort of universal (which Ockham rejects), but an individual. However, the theory is able to explain how it is not any specific or, in the terminology of the time, any determinate horse which makes the proposition true, since there is merely confused supposition for horses.

Surprisingly, Ockham fails to extend this solution to the seventh argument itself.   One would expect him to say that in the same way what the agent intends is some act or other of the appropriate sort, so that in 'An agent intends a deed', 'deed' supposits merely confusedly.   However, what he does say is that the agent intends precisely that determinate deed which he actually performs.   Wyclif makes a similar move — though one perhaps more in keeping with his realism.   Right at the end of his chapter, having neatly parried all objections, he quite unnecessarily suggests an alternative response: that God knows which particular penny my confused promise obliges me to give, 'for it cannot be a matter of indifference for God.   But I do not know which; and so there is a singular which I ought to give....'[14]   But these implausible claims are rendered unnecessary by the analysis each in his own way applies to the sophism.

3. Burleigh

In the course of his discussion of the 'promising' objection, Ockham suggests that it is really an ironical suggestion which hardly bears scrutiny:

> This lighthearted point would not be offered here were it not for the fact that some people, reputed to know about logic, reflect on such childish matters and in consequence say many absurd things about the supposition of terms....[15]

From similar remarks in Walter Burleigh's writings about the same topic, it seems clear that each intended his insults for the other.   In his commentary on Aristotle's Physics Burleigh wrote:

> But these points would not be adduced here were it not for the fact that certain people, claiming to know logic better than all mortals say that when I say, 'I promise you an ox', I promise you one singular thing outside the mind, but I do not promise this ox, or this, because in the proposition 'I promise you an ox', 'ox' stands merely confusedly, and hence does not supposit disjunctively for singular oxen, but supposits disjointly.[16]

The task Burleigh has set himself at this point in his commentary, is to show that there is something outside the mind which is not singular; and the third argument he adduces, is that contracts, promises and so on are not always about individuals. No individual ox can have been promised, since no particular ox can justifiably be demanded; and if you owe me a florin, there is no particular florin you must give me.

However, this shows only that 'ox' and so on do not supposit determinately. He needs an argument to show that they cannot have merely confused supposition either. He produces three. Let me take the second one first. 'All logicians up to the present day', he says, have laid down that a general term is ony able to supposit confusedly if there is a syncategorematic term signifying many preceding it. For example, it is the syncategorematic term 'every' which makes 'man' supposit confusedly and distributively, and 'animal' supposit merely confusedly, in 'Every man is an animal.' But there is no such term in the present case.

Ockham's reply is, of course, that the rule is too narrow. Merely confused supposition is produced not only by such a syncategorematic term, but also by certain verbs, that is, categorematic expressions.

> So it should be known that whenever in such a proposition in the present, past or future tense there occurs a verb in virtue of which it is meant that some proposition will be true or must be true, and where there occurs a general term in the predicate such that it does not follow that a proposition resulting from substituting for that general term a singular contained under it is true, then that general term...does not supposit determinately, for it is not permissible to descend to singulars by a disjuction of propositions, but only by a proposition with a disjoint extreme or part thereof.[17]

(Indeed, Burleigh is quite wrong to claim that all logicians up to his time had taken such a narrow view. We read in the Tractatus de univocatione Monacensis, dating from the end of the twelfth century:

> When it is said, 'Health is wished for', it is wrong to ask, 'Which health?', because with such a verb that word occurs confusedly.... For the same reason, no anaphoric relation can be made to such a phrase, because an anaphoric relation needs to be fixed and referred to some determinate suppositum. But the word occurs confusedly.[18])

The first argument tries to make nonsense of the idea that a term can supposit for singulars without suppositing for any singulars in particular. If there is nothing outside the mind except singulars, and I promise you something outside the mind, but no singular is promised, it would seem to follow that I promise both something and nothing. We can best understand what has gone wrong here by considering it along with the third argument. 'I promise you an ox' is equivalent, says Burleigh, to 'Some ox I promise you', in which 'ox' clearly supposits personally and indeed determinately, and so must be false in the situation we are considering. Ockham's reply is to deny the equivalence of 'I promise you an ox' and 'An ox to you I promise'; the second entails the first, he says, but not vice versa. And consequently, although there is nothing I promise you, it does not follow that I promise you nothing. Thus it is a travesty of Ockham's doctrine to suggest that he is committed to the joint truth of 'Something outside the mind is promised to you' and 'Nothing outside the mind is promised to you.' We certainly need an explanation of why one proposition in the active mood is not equivalent to its apparent passive form. But the claim that in the passive sentence 'ox' supposits determinately and in the active merely confusedly provides that explanation, for Ockham's theory of personal supposition is founded on the notion of descent, and a term only has merely confused supposition when one form of descent which is permissible under a term with determinate supposition is not permissible for it.

Nonetheless, the failure of the inference should give one pause, for it seems to run counter to the widely accepted rule, that from an active proposition the corresponding passive proposition can be inferred. William Heytesbury, writing a few years later, raised the problem explicitly.[19] The explanation he gives is that not just any passive proposition can be inferred, but only one appropriately expressed, in this case, 'To you is promised a penny.' Here 'penny' is preceded by the verb 'promise', which confers on it the correct mode of supposition, merely confused, and so the inference is good. We must return later to this important question of word order, on which Heytesbury's explanation depends.

We can see then that Burleigh's arguments in favour of real universals can be countered by Ockham. And indeed, it is clear that the easy confidence with which Burleigh expounds the realist analysis of 'I promise you an ox' in the commentary on the Physics, and in the early treatise on supposition,[20] is no longer present in his later work, De puritate artis logicae. Once again, Burleigh does not distinguish the apparent active and passive forms. But he considers as an objection to the claim that simple supposition occurs when a term supposits for its significate, that if 'horse' in 'A horse is promised to you' has simple supposition, then the proposition would be false, for in general neither a universal nor a concept in the mind is promised, but a horse. His reply seems to allow two possibilities: on the one hand, we may maintain the view that 'horse' has simple supposition, but realise that one cannot infer from the fact that a horse is what is given in fulfilling the promise that it is a singular that is promised, for a universal is also given whenever a singular is given, and can only be given in that way; so it is not contrary to intuition to take 'horse' to supposit for a universal. Alternatively, it seems, we can follow those who maintain that nothing but singulars exist outside the mind, in which case, says Burleigh, if no determinate (singular) thing was promised, then every future and possible horse is promised, only under a disjunction and indeterminately;[21] and the promise will be fulfilled by the gift of any horse whatever.

4. Frege

What we have seen then is a conflict over the articulation of a semantic theory capable of dealing with intensional propositions such as 'I promise you a penny', a conflict between those who wish to make reference in the expression of truth-conditions only to individual objects, and those who are willing to countenance reference there to another kind of entity, based on (as Burleigh puts it) 'some sort of identity other than numerical identity'.[22] Interestingly, the very same conflict has run through semantic theory in the present century, though I am inclined to think the similarity has too often gone unremarked.[23]   One reason is that the leading proponent of the individuals-only doctrine, namely, Russell, was happy to admit universals as the reference of predicates; another is the misguided thought that Frege's invocation of senses can be emasculated and its ontological commitments revoked.

The contrast between Russell and Frege over semantics is that whereas Frege thought it necessary to distinguish two components, sense and reference, in meaning, Russell maintained that only one was needed, and indeed that Frege's notion of sense actually resulted in incoherence. Frege based his belief on two arguments, or at least Dummett finds two in his writings.[24]   It is questionable whether one of these is really to be found in Frege. But something very close to it does occur in Bradley,[25] who points out that the use of a name presupposes the reidentification of its referent. The name must have associated with it, therefore, certain criteria, not only for identifying a particular kind of thing, but also for reidentifying one particular instance of that kind. These criteria constitute the sense of the name.

I wish here, however, to concentrate on the other argument, which is more famous, and directly, though inexplicitly, involves intensional propositions. A remark first on the epithet 'intensional' to mark off a certain class of problematic expressions. I adopt this one as the best of a bad bunch. For 'intensional' would naturally be taken to mean either that there is reference here to intensions, rather than extensions, or that the principle of extensionality, otherwise known as Leibniz' Law fails. But Russell denies that there are intensions to which to make reference, and both Frege and Russell maintain, in the face of the challenge to it from these problematic expressions, that Leibniz' Law is universally valid, that is, that two coreferential expressions can be substituted one for the other wherever they occur, _salva veritate_. Quine is totally at odds with them in believing that Leibniz' Law fails in certain contexts; and it is Quine who gave us the other term most popularly used (and abused), that of an 'opaque' context. An opaque context is an expression containing an argument-place for propositions, such that extensional positions in substituted propositions lose their extensionality on substitution in the context. [26] Thus 'opaque' is a theory-laden term — laden with Quine's antipathy to Leibniz' Law. (It also fails to cover the intensionality of the non-propositional context 'I promise....', of which more later.) So I use the term 'intensional' advisedly, to refer to those cases which at least appear to be possible counterexamples to Leibniz' Law.

Frege's argument concerns the proposition
   (1) S knows that Hesperus is Hesperus,
where S is a Babylonian ignorant of the fact that Hesperus is Phosphorus. (1) is true, let us suppose, because S understands the proposition, 'Hesperus is Hesperus' (or some Babylonian equivalent), and can immediately see that it is true. Since Hesperus is Phosphorus, 'Hesperus' and 'Phosphorus' refer to the same object, namely, Venus, and so, if Leibniz' Law is universally valid, the above true proposition (1) should entail
   (2) S knows that Hesperus is Phosphorus,
which results from (1) by the substitution of one coreferential expression for

another. However, by hypothesis, S̲ lacks this knowledge.

Frege's solution is not to reject Leibniz' Law, but to infer that 'Hesperus', as it occurs in (1) and (2), must have some semantic function other than that of simply referring to Hesperus. There must be another semantic component besides customary object of reference, namely, indirect reference or sense. 'Hesperus' here refers to its sense, a sense it does not share with 'Phosphorus'. So, in this position, 'Hesperus' and 'Phosphorus' are not coreferential, and Leibniz' Law emerges unscathed. There is some sort of identity other than numerical identity: Hesperus and Phosphorus are numerically identical, but not identical in the world of sense. Leibniz' Law of the Indiscernibility of Identicals discerns whether it is Hesperus or Phosphorus which S̲ knows Hesperus to be, and so they are not, in the relevant sense, identical.

(This presentation of Frege's argument is consciously at odds with Dummett's, for Dummett claims that the need for a notion of sense must be prior to its application to 'opaque contexts'.[27] But first, Dummett does not make it at all clear what can be wrong with taking the problems generated by these contexts, themselves to demonstrate the existence of the notion of sense; secondly, Frege's discussion clearly concerns knowledge of the truth of certain propositions, and so cannot be divorced from intensionality; and lastly, Dummett's own account of Frege's argument, as showing the need for the notion of sense independently of consideration of the application of Leibniz' Law to intensional contexts, itself requires attribution to Frege, without any textual warrant, of a principle of transparency of sense whose justification, if any, would appear to be Leibniz' Law, namely, 'that, if someone knows the senses of two words, and the two words have the same sense, he must know that they have the same sense....'[28] By Leibniz' Law and Frege's doctrine of indirect reference, we can move from 'S̲ knows that A̲ and A̲ have the same sense' and 'The sense of A̲ is the sense of B̲' to 'S̲ knows that A̲ and B̲ have the same sense.' So Frege's doctrine of sense as indirect reference justifies the principle of transparency of sense. But Dummett gives no independent warrant for the principle on the basis of which it could be adduced in support of that doctrine itself.)

However, the concept of identity here needs a little more attention. Surely Burleigh's conception of an identity other than numerical identity is, one might say, a wider sense, whereby, for example, Red Rum is identical

with L'Escargot, in their both being horses, or in their both winning the
Grand National; whereas the sense in which Hesperus and Phosphorus are not
identical must be a narrower sense of identity, and indeed a puzzling sense,
for if Hesperus is not Phosphorus, then it would seem that Phosphorus is not
Phosphorus, by a straightforward application of Leibniz' Law. But the fault
here is in not taking 'identity' seriously enough. When we say that Red Rum
is identical with L'Escargot, it is tempting to take this relation as simply an
equivalence relation, but not a congruence: a congruence being any relation
which satisfies Leibniz' Law — of the Indiscernibility of Congruents; for Red
Rum and L'Escargot differ in many of their properties. In order to take
identity seriously here we have to change our ontology: if Red Rum and
L'Escargot are the same horse, in that they are both the winner of the
Grand National, then that winner has only the properties which are shared by
the horses that win, and our ontology now contains a new object -- the
winner of the Grand National. This is the concept of identity which Burleigh
had: for 'horse' in his example supposited for that thing which has all the
properties shared by individual horses. But in just the same way, if we are
led by Frege's argument to introduce a concept of identity other than
numerical identity, in which Hesperus is not Phosphorus, then our ontology is
not that of planets, but one of senses. For if not, either Leibniz' Law will
fail, or this is not identity at all, but only an equivalence relation.

Frege also wishes to infer from his argument concerning the semantic
import of 'Hesperus' in (1), what it is that one knows when one understands
the proposition

(3) Hesperus is Phosphorus.

For the falsity of (2) shows that one can understand (3) without knowing that
it is true. For Frege, as for the medievals, the semantic import of an
expression served two functions: it was needed in the theoretical description
of the truth-conditions of propositions containing the expression; but further,
since understanding was construed as (implicit) knowledge of the conditions
under which such propositions were true, it appeared in the theoretical
description of that knowledge. The medieval equivalent was the conception
of the priority of mental language. Hence if understanding 'Hesperus is
Phosphorus' devolves on, inter alia, understanding 'Hesperus', and understanding 'Hesperus' is construed as knowing its semantic import, and moreover, its
semantic import is what it refers to, then the argument that, in the
preservation of Leibniz' Law, 'Hesperus' in (1) must refer to a sense, shows
that understanding must consist in a knowledge of senses, not of customary

referents.

Frege's solution of Wyclif's sophism can now be seen.   In 'I promise you one or other of these pennies', the phrase 'one or other of these pennies' refers not to any sort of penny, but to its customary sense.   On the level of reference, $F(\underline{a}$ or $\underline{b})$ is equivalent to $\underline{Fa}$ or $\underline{Fb}$; so solution of the sophism requires that on the level of sense, this not be so, that is, that 'the sense of' not distribute over 'or'.   But this is entirely true: the referent of '$\underline{a}$ or $\underline{b}$' is the referent of '$\underline{a}$' or the referent of '$\underline{b}$', whereas the sense of '$\underline{a}$ or $\underline{b}$' is neither the sense of '$\underline{a}$' nor the sense of '$\underline{b}$'.   Hence there is no inconsistency between the two conjuncts of 'I promised you one of these pennies, neither of which I promised you', and one cannot infer that I promised a penny which I did not promise.

5.   Russell

Russell, however, eschewed senses.   For him, there was only one semantic component, reference to those and only those objects recognised by zoology.   This is perhaps obscured, as I said, by his treatment of ordinary proper names as disguised descriptions, where that description appears to encapsulate a sense for the name.   But Russell is quite adamant that the truth-conditions of a proposition result from the meaning of its constituents, and descriptions do not have meaning in themselves: they contribute only indirectly to the meaning of the proposition as a whole.   The meaning of the proposition is composed from the meanings of its constituents, and the description itself is not one of those constituents.   The real constituents are, on the other hand, logically proper names, whose meaning is the object to which they refer, and on the other, predicates or (propositional) functions, whose meanings are universals.

Where Frege resorts to sense in the solution of sophisms, Russell relies on a distinction between logical and grammatical form.   Grammatically, a description, for example, may appear to be a constituent of a proposition; indeed, grammatically, it is a constituent.   But logically it is not.   Hence the logical form of Frege's problematic proposition,

(2) $\underline{S}$ knows that Hesperus is Phosphorus,

is not its grammatical form.   Otherwise the truth-conditions of (2) would be the same as (1), for they would have the same constituents, and so would be equivalent.   Hence Russell is committed to the necessary truth of all identities between logically proper names,[29] and in cases such as (2) can account for its inequivalence to (1) only by insisting that one or both of 'Hesperus' and 'Phosphorus' are disguised descriptions, abbreviating, for example, 'the morning star' or 'the planet visible near the Sun in the morning'. (2) is then found to be ambiguous, for Russell's analysis of descriptions can be performed either on the contained proposition, or on the whole of (2). Thus, though (2) is grammatically unambiguous, it is logically ambiguous, one of the resulting propositions, namely, that which gives the description substituted for 'Phosphorus' wide scope (or, as Russell called it, a primary occurrence), being entailed by (1) in conjunction with (3), and so being true, and the other, giving the description narrow scope (or a secondary occurrence), being not so entailed, being in fact false, and expressing what was originally intended by the ambiguous expression (2).

Indeed, it has become common, following Quine's practice, to express the sense of (2) in which 'Phosphorus' has wide scope by

Phosphorus is such that $\underline{S}$ knows Hesperus to be it,

leaving the ambiguous form (2) to express canonically that sense in which the description has narrow scope. These intuitions about the logical function of a preposed noun phrase are just those we saw expressed by Ockham and Heytesbury. For Ockham pointed out that when the noun is placed first, no sign precedes it which can provide and explanation of why it should not supposit determinately.[30] Hence in 'A horse is promised you', 'horse' supposits determinately for a particular horse, which is why, in the sort of casus we are considering, it is literally false, since all its instances, 'Red Rum is promised you' and so on, are false.

I have compared Burleigh's and Wyclif's account of intensional propositions to Frege's, both on the ground that their semantic theories embrace both individuals and other sorts of thing, and in terms of the particular detail of their semantic description of the problematic propositions. Russell and Ockham are similar in their mutual resistance to reference by names to anything but individuals. But are their detailed semantic theories any closer than this general methodological stance? Can we delineate a useful similarity between their precise description of intensional propositions? Let us take, for reasons that will become clear in the next section, the example proposition,

(4) I promise to give you a penny,

where no singular is promised. Then Russell sees here an embedded proposition, so that the generality present in 'a penny' can be confined to a narrow scope:

$Pr(\exists x(Px \ \& \ Gx))$

or, using the restricted quantifier, defined by $(\exists x : \Phi) \Psi = df(\exists x)(\Phi x \Psi)$,

$Pr((\exists x : Px) Gx)$,

or again, using Price's many sorted logic,[31]

$Pr((\exists p)Gp)$.

Now, without its being truth-functional, it is nonetheless true that the truth-conditions of this formula depend on the truth-conditions of its parts (just as 'necessarily $\underline{p}$' is for Frege and Russell, extensional without its being truth-function[32]); and the truth-conditions of $(\exists x : Px)Gx$ are, expressed aong the simplified lines of truth-value semantics, that there be some object of which 'P' and 'G' are true.

Ockham's description may at first glance appear rather different. His claim is that 'penny' in (4) has merely confused supposition, and thus that its semantic contribution to truth-conditions is a nominal disjunction ranging over pennies:

(5) I promise to give you this penny or that penny and so on. However, two observations will reveal that this articulation of the truth-conditions is the same as Russell's. First, remember that we noted earlier that

I give you this penny or that penny and so on

is (logically) equivalent to

I give you this penny or I give you that penny and so on;

so that (5) is equivalent to

I promise to give you this penny or to give you that penny and so on. No particular penny is promised, nor may it be demanded. But nonetheless the promise requires the giving of some penny or other. Secondly, let us tidy up the rather inelegant medieval expression, 'I give you this penny or I give you that penny and so on, for all pennies', by

$$\bigvee_{\underline{p} \text{ is a penny}} \text{I give you } \underline{p}.$$

Then the possibly infinite disjunction '$\bigvee_{\Phi} \Psi$' behaves exactly like the restricted quantifier '$(\exists x : \Phi) \Psi$'. Ockham's and Russell's articulation of the truth-conditions of intensional propositions differ only notationally.

6. Realism vs. Nominalism

I have argued that not only is the overall view of semantics adopted by on the one hand Frege and on the other Russell, mirrored in the contrast between the realists and the nominalists in the fourteenth century; but also that the analysis which each of these parties makes of the problematic intensional propositions is the same. My aim here is not primarily to use some prevailing contemporary view to make sense of the medieval debate -- I think it is clear as it stands. On the contrary, my aim is to attempt to breathe new life into a twentieth-century debate which I think has reached an impasse.

One thought which one might hope to use to this end is that semantics must respect not only truth-conditions, but also intuition. Recall first how Ockham threw out the suggestion that 'animal' in 'Every man is an animal' supposits for a concept in the mind, on the grounds that clearly no man is a concept in the mind;[33] and the similar suggestion that in 'Someone promises to give another some horse', 'horse' supposits for a concept in the mind, which appears to lead to truth-conditions whereby the proposition would be false, for he promised a real thing -- and moreover would result in the absurdity that 'he could keep the promise by not giving a real horse but only a concept.'[34] Now the accusation that this move results in the wrong truth-conditions is simply wrong; it is precisely the misapplication of Leibniz' Law which the realist is using his appeal to universals to block. That 'animal' supposits for a concept in the mind when used as predicate of a universal affirmative proposition, and 'concept in the mind' supposits for the same thing in some other context, is no warrant whatever for substituting the latter for the former in that universal proposition. In the same way, Frege's claim that 'Hesperus' in (1) refers not to Hesperus, but to the sense of 'Hesperus', does not permit us to substitute 'the sense of "Hesperus"' for 'Hesperus' in (1). For there is no reason to suppose -- and, indeed, every reason to suppose otherwise -- that 'the sense of "Hesperus"', in that context, refers to the sense of 'Hesperus'.

The same considerations show that there is no problem regarding truth-conditions for the realist over apparent coreference within and outwith an intensional context. The phenomenon is used by, for example, Currie,[35] to show that Frege's claim that expressions in intensional contexts refer to their customary senses, must be mistaken. Consider

Copernicus thought that Venus is a planet, and it is a planet.

Currie claims that this makes sense only if 'Venus' and 'it' are coreferential, while on Frege's theory they are not. The Fregean response must, however, be the same as Burleigh's and Wyclif's: that on the contrary, the theory explains how the proposition makes sense only by attributing a different reference to the two expressions in their context. If indeed they were given the same reference, absurdity would result (by some invalid substitution); the intuition that they are coreferential is mistaken, but that mistake is explained by the relationship, in the theory, between expressions within and outwith intensional contexts, namely, that oblique reference is customary sense. Currie's objection is as insensitive to Frege's theory as were Ockham's arguments to the realist's.

So neither Frege's, nor Burleigh's, nor Wyclif's, semantics is actually inconsistent. What one can say is that it has a decidedly unintuitive feel, similar to that oddity on which Frege remarks when he points out that the concept horse is not a concept. But I think this oddity is also the basis of a problem which Heytesbury, no friend to the realists, faces when he considers the objection that if no penny was owed, then no penny need be paid -- and indeed that if one is, it fails to discharge the debt. Heytesbury writes:

It may be supposed, for example, that someone, no [particular] penny promising to you, promises you a penny. Later he may pay you a penny, and it is argued: he pays you a penny, therefore either he pays you a penny which he promised or a penny which he did not promise. If he pays you a penny which he promised, and only pays you penny Δ, then he promised you penny Δ, and so penny Δ was promised to you. If he pays you a penny which he did not promise, then he promised a penny which he did not pay, and has not paid. So he is still obliged to pay you a penny.[36]

So if there was no particular penny, such as penny Δ, which he promised, then paying any other penny, which he did not promise, must fail to pay off the debt.

Heytesbury's response is: 'for in paying Δ he fulfils that promise, even though he does not pay the penny which he promised, since none was promised.'[37] The promise is fulfilled, but not, it seems, by paying what was owed, for nothing in particular was owed.

But this shows that the discordance with intuition cuts both ways. For

Heytesbury is concerned to resist the conclusion that if one promises a penny then a penny was promised, for he shares that intuition (on which I remarked earlier), that a preposed noun phrase refers to something determinately. Hence what was promised is not what was given. So the nominalistae also find they cannot resolve conflicting intuitions. The realists are forced to say that no real penny was (explicitly) promised, but that what was promised, the universal, can only be given by giving a real, individual penny; and the nominalists seem equally forced to deny that a real penny was promised, since in 'A penny was promised', 'penny' has escaped from the 'confusing' power of 'promise', and the proposition is false. Either way, intuition suffers.

In fact, it is Pseudo-Campsall who respects our intuitions best.[38] The problem, he says, is with the rule that a term not affected by a negation, a universal sign, or any other expression, such as 'promise', has determinate supposition. But that rule is incorrect even for future-tense propositions, for descent on 'man' in 'Socrates will be a man' can only be made disiunctim. Hence, since 'A horse is promised you' is equivalent to a future-tense proposition (an Ockhamist suggestion which Wyclif rejected[39]), we should concede that 'horse' there has merely confused supposition too.

So I do not see any decisive argument of this sort coming from the medievals to settle the dispute. The nominalist and the realist can each articulate a semantic theory which is equally at odds with intuition. However, there is one obvious point on which the Russellian account looks likely to fail, where it may help to appeal to its nominalist forebears (but where the account is ultimately doomed to failure, I fear). This concerns the proposition at the heart of the sophistical dispute in this paper, namely,

(6) I promise you a penny.

When I showed the similarity between the Russellian and Ockhamist accounts, I quite consciously took an example which contained an embedded proposition; for this embedding was crucial to the scope distinction on which Russell's appeal to a hidden logical form depended. But in (6) there is no embedded proposition. Quine, when discussing a similar example, suggests that logical analysis will reveal such an embedding: so that 'I want a sloop' is elliptical for 'I wish to have a sloop', and (6) is elliptical for 'I promise to give you a penny.'[40] This procedure, however, even if faintly plausible here, fails in general. For the same intensionality is found in 'I am looking for a horse'[41] (for which Quine might desperately suggest 'I am striving to find a horse', in line with his analysis of 'Ernest is hunting lions' as 'Ernest is striving to find lions'); in 'Judas hated Christ', [42] and in many other cases.[43]   Lakoff once desperately invented new lexemes WURF and GLIP, yielding 'Oedipus WURFs to GLIP his mother' as a lexical decomposition of 'Oedipus admires his mother', in order to provide such an analysis.[44]   I think we might christen the search for such hidden embeddings, the WURFs-to GLIP syndrome.   It must clearly fail.

Here Ockham's theory of personal supposition has a power which Russell's semantics lacks.   As I showed, when there is an embedded proposition, a nominal disjunction behaves logically in the same way as a restricted existential quantifier with narrow scope.   But Ockham allowed a nominal disjunction to replace any general term — recall   that the nominal disjunction in fact gives, for Ockham, the signification of the general term.   Hence Ockham can explain the truth-conditions of (6) as following from a recognition that 'penny' there has merely confused supposition, and that the semantic contribution of such a term is a nominal disjunction.

But this move will fail, for two reasons.   First, consider 'Judas hated Christ.'   Paul of Pergula pointed out that this was true, yet the result of substituting 'God' for 'Christ' was false, for Judas loved God.[45]   However, 'Christ' cannot here be replaced by any such disjunction: it is a discrete term and must have discrete supposition, if it has personal supposition at all. The case is similar to that which Russell reaches with (2) if 'Hesperus' and 'Phosphorus' are in fact logically proper names.   For Russell and Ockham, any term in such problematic positions can only be handled if it admits some sort of analysis and is not atomic.

Secondly, the talk of merely confused supposition for 'penny' in (6) is (excuse the pun) a promissory note, which needs to be redeemed.   For it requires some account of how the truth of (6) depends on the semantics of a nominal disjunction.   Recall the formula

$$\text{Pr}(\ (\exists x)(Px\ \&\ Gx))$$

which appeared at one point in my Russellian account of (4).   I observed that $\text{Pr}(\phi)$ is not a truth-functional context; neither is $\square(\phi)$.   However, modal logicians who presented $\square(\phi)$ as the form of, say, '9 is necessarily odd', had not then completed the task of analysing modality.   What was further required was an account of how in general the truth of $\square(\phi)$ depends, non-truth-functionally, on the truth of ϕ.   That account was given by Kripke.

Similarly the full story about Pr(Φ) has not been given until we receive an account of how the truth of Pr(Φ) depends on that of Φ. And so too with (6). We saw that

(7) I give you this penny or that penny and so on

is equivalent to

I give you this penny or I give you that penny and so on,

and so the semantics of (7) is unproblematic. But when Ockham tells us that 'penny' in (6) has merely confused supposition he has not yet told us how the truth of (6) depends on the semantic values of its constituents. All the hard work remains to be done, and nothing in Ockham's account of the truth-conditions of propositions in Part II of his Summa logicae deals with such cases.

One might here turn to Lesniewski's Ontology for help. For D.P. Henry has repeatedly claimed superiority for Ontology in the explication of supposition theory on the grounds that it contains a nominal disjunction which modern classical logic lacks.[46] There is, however, no help forthcoming from this quarter. For the nominal disjunction ' a u b' is introduced by a contextual definition; and that definition only gives it sense in the context c ε a u b, in such a way that it is equivalent to a propositional disjunction: c ε a u b. ≡ . c ε a .v. c ε b.

In contrast, Wyclif's and Frege's analysis of (6) as containing a phrase referring to a universal, or a sense, immediately subsumes that proposition under their general account of truth-conditions. One cannot conclude from this , of course, that the Fregean analysis is right, for that approach may also meet insuperable problems.[47] I conclude, however, that it is to the realist distinction between two realms of semantic entities, a realm of reference and a realm of sense, that we should turn, in order to find an account of the semantics of intensional propositions with any hope of success.[48]

Notes

[1] M.H. Dziewicki ed., Iohannis Wyclif Tractatus de logica, 3 vols. (Wyclif Society; London, 1893-1899; repr. New York-London, Frankfurt am Main, 1966), 2.55-72.

2 Ibid., p. 59; P. Boehner ed., Walter Burleigh, De puritate artis logicae tractatus longior (Franciscan Institute Publications, Text Series 9; St. Bonaventure, N.Y., 1955), tract. 1, pars 1, cap. 3, ad 2, p. 15.

3 Wyclif, Tractatus, tract. 3, cap. 3, ed. cit., 2.63.

4 Ibid., 2.62.

5 Wyclif here uses the characterisation of supposition which S.F. Brown, 'Walter Burleigh's Treatise De suppositionibus and its influence on William of Ockham', Franciscan Studies 32 (1972) 15-64, argues was Burleigh's notable invention (ibid., p. 21).

6 Wyclif, Tractatus, cap. 12, ed. cit. 1.39.

7 Ibid., tract. 3, cap. 3, 2.64.

8 The sense requires that we read 'propter supposicionis simplicis mutacionem in personalem' in place of Dziewicki's '...singularis...pluralem'.

9 Ibid., 2.67.

10 P. Boehner, G. Gál and S. Brown, eds., Guillelmi de Ockham Summa logicae (Guillelmi de Ockham Opera philosophica 1; St. Bonaventure, N.Y., 1974), pars 1, cap. 66 p. 201. But see above, section 6, pp. 349-354.

11 G. Priest and S. Read, 'Merely Confused Supposition: A Theoretical Advance or a Mere Confusion?', Franciscan Studies 40 (1980) 265-97, section 3 (ibid., pp. 274-77).

12 See, e.g., L.M. de Rijk, Logica modernorum, 2 vols. in 3 (Wijsgerige Teksten en Studies 6, 16; Assen, 1962-1967), 2.1, pp. 582, 592.

13 See, e.g., A. Gambatese and S. Brown, eds., Guillelmi de Ockham Expositio in librum Perihermeneias (Guillelmi de Ockham Opera philosophica 2; St. Bonaventure, N.Y., 1978), lib. 1, proem. § 6, p. 352.

14 Wyclif, Tractatus, tract. 3, cap. 3, ed. cit., 2.72.

[15] S. Brown ed., Guillelmi de Ockham Scriptum in librum primum Sententiarum Ordinatio (Guillelmi de Ockham Opera theologica 1-4; St. Bonaventure, N.Y., 1967-1979), dist. 2, q. 4, 2.146.

[16] Walter Burley (Gualterii Burlei), In Physicam Aristotelis expositio et quaestiones (Venice, 1501; repr. Hildesheim-New York, 1972), fol. 8vb.

[17] Ockham, Summa logicae, pars 1, cap. 72, ed. cit., p. 220.

[18] Ed. De Rijk, Logica modernorum 2.2, p. 340 (2-9). The same point is made in the Tractatus Anagnini, 3 (ed., ibid., p. 280), and in the Fallacie Parvipontane, 1 (ed. De Rijk, Logica modernorum 1, p. 569).

[19] Tractatus Gulielmi Hentisberi de sensu composito et diviso, Regulae eiusdem cum sophismatibus, etc. (Bonetus Locatellus: Venice, 1494), Sophisma IV, 'Omnis homo est unus solus homo', fol. 90^{rb-va}.

[20] For editions see notes 16 and 5, above. The following chronology is plausible: Ockham, Scriptum in librum Sententiarum Ordinatio (second redaction), 1319-21; Burleigh, a revision of book 1 of In Physicam Aristotelis expositio, before 1324; Ockham, Summa logicae, 1323; Burleigh, De puritate artis logicae tractatus longior, 1325-28. (See Brown ed., Ockham in 1 Sent., 1.34*-36*; J.A. Weisheipl, 'Ockham and some Mertonians', Mediaeval Studies 30 (1968), 163-213, ibid., pp. 180-82; Boehner et al., eds., Ockham, Summa logicae, pp. 47*-56*; Boehner ed., Burleigh, De puritate artis logicae, p. VIII.)

[21] On the medieval sense of 'determinate', see, e.g., N. Kretzmann transl. and ed., William of Sherwood's Introduction to Logic (Minneapolis, Minn., 1966), pp. 115-116; De Rijk, Logica modernorum 2.1, p. 582.

[22] Burleigh, De puritate artis logicae, pars 1, cap. 3, ed. cit., p. 14.

[23] Exceptions are P.T. Geach, 'A Medieval Discussion of Intentionality' in idem, Logic Matters (Oxford, 1972), § 4.2, pp. 129-38; J. Trentman, ed., Vincent Ferrer, Tractatus de suppositionibus (Grammatica speculativa 2; Stuttgart-Bad Canstatt, 1977), Introduction I and IV, pp. 15, 41-49; E.P. Bos, 'Mental Verbs in Terminist Logic (John Buridan, Albert of Saxony, Marsilius of Inghen)', Vivarium 16 (1978) 56-69, ibid., p. 69.

24 See M.A.E. Dummett, 'Frege's distinction between sense and reference' in idem, Truth and other Enigmas (London, 1978), pp. 124-30; idem, 'What is a theory of meaning? (I) 'in S. Guttenplan ed., Mind and Language (Oxford, 1975), pp. 124-25; idem, 'What is a theory of meaning? (II)' in G. Evans and J. McDowell eds., Truth and Meaning: Essays in Semantics (Oxford, 1976), p. 128.   Dummett gives no textual reference to Frege's works; one argument is clearly to be found in 'On Sense and Reference' in, e.g., P.T. Geach and M. Black, Translations from the Philosophical Writings of Gottlob Frege (Oxford, 1952), pp. 55-78; the other may perhaps be found hinted at in the footnote on p. 58 of the same article of Frege's, but is really a reconstruction according to Fregean themes. (My thanks to Greg Currie for help here.)   More recently, Dummett has attributed two further arguments, with textual references, to Frege: see M.A.E. Dummett, The Interpretation of Frege's Philosophy (London, 1981), p. 533, n. 1.

25 F.H. Bradley, The Principles of Logic (Oxford, 1887), § 17.

26 W.V.O. Quine, Word and Object (Studies in Communication; Cambridge, Mass., 1960), p. 144. Quine contrasts opacity with transparency, and claims to take the latter term from A.N. Whitehead and B. Russell. However, their informal use -- Principia mathematica 1, 2nd ed. (Cambridge, 1925), p. 655. -- concerned truth-functionality, not extensionality in the present sense, that is, the substitution of coreferential singular terms salva veritate. (See further, note 32 below.)

27 See M.A.E. Dummett, Frege: Philosophy of Language (London, 1973), p. 90.

28 Ibid., p. 95.

29 B. Russell, 'The Philosophy of Logical Atomism' in Logic and Knowledge: Essays 1901-1950, ed. R.C. Marsh (London, 1956), p. 245.

30 Ockham, Summa logicae, pars 1, cap. 72, ed. cit., pp. 214 (19)-215 (23), 219 (139)-221 (205); see also Geach, 'A Medieval Discussion...'.

31 R. Price, 'William of Ockham and Suppositio personalis', Franciscan Studies 30 (1970) 131-40.

32 There is a modern sophism which appears to show that any extensional propositional context permitting the substitution of logical equivalents is truth-fuctional: see, e.g., W.G. Lycan, 'The Extensionality of Cause, Space and Time', Mind 83 (1974) 498-511. This is clearly not the case; and so the argument must indeed be — somehow -- sophistical.

33 Ockham, Summa logicae, pars 1, cap. 66, ed. cit., pp. 199-205.

34 Ockham, In 1 Sent., dist. 2, q. 4, ed. cit., 2.145-46.

35 G. Currie, Frege: An introduction to his philosophy (Brighton-Totowa, N.J., 1982), pp. 91-92.

36 Heytesbury, Sophisma IV (Venice, 1494), fol. 90va.

37 Ibid.

38 E.A. Synan, 'The Universal and Supposition in a Logica attributed to Richard of Campsall' in J.R. O'Donnell ed., Nine Medieval Thinkers (Studies and Texts 1; Toronto, 1955), pp. 183-232, ibid., p. 219; critical edition idem, Pseudo-Richard of Campsall, Logica Campsale Anglici ualde utilis et realis contra Ocham, cap. 56 (.34-.37) in idem ed., The Works of Richard of Campsall 2 (Studies and Texts 58; Toronto, 1982), pp. 385-386.

39 Wyclif, Tractatus, tract. 3, cap. 3, ed. cit., 2.60.

40 W.V.O. Quine, 'Quantifiers and Propositional Attitudes' in L. Linsky ed., Reference and Modality (Oxford, 1971), pp. 101-11, ibid., p. 102.

41 See De Rijk, ed., Summa Sophistarum elencorum, Logica modernorum 1.89.

42 See M.A. Brown ed., Paul of Pergula, Logica, tract. 3, § 17d, in idem ed., Paul of Pergula, Logica and Tractatus de sensu composito et diviso (Franciscan Institute Publications, Text Series 13; St. Bonaventure, N.Y.-Louvain-Paderborn, 1961), pp. 78-79.

43 Incidentally, I might point out here, since the matter arose in discussion at the Symposium, that in this paper I have concentrated on one

aspect of intensional propositions. But they exhibit another problematic aspect, namely, intentional existence: an example relevant here would be, 'The Philistines worshipped Baal', which must be given truth-conditions whereby it is true even though Baal did not exist.

[44] G. Lakoff, 'Linguistics and Natural Logic', Synthese 22 (1970) 151–271, ibid., p. 221.

[45] Paul of Pergula, Logica, tract. 3, § 17d, ed. cit., pp. 78–79.

[46] D.P. Henry, Medieval Logic and Metaphysics: A Modern Introduction (London, 1972), p. 52.

[47] Crispin Wright and others have reminded me that Frege claims that terms such as 'a penny' in (6) not only refer to their customary sense, but also act as quantifiers, and so are second-level. It is, therefore, unclear quite what a Fregean should say is the syntax of (6), and until that question is settled, one cannot be sure how his semantics will apply to it. I cannot deal with this question in the present paper.

[48] This is a revised version of a paper presented to the Sixth European Symposium on Medieval Logic and Semantics held at Balliol College, Oxford in June 1983. I am grateful to all who have commented on it there and since, and in particular to Dr. Hermann Weidemann for valuable advice.

14

L'influence des Regulae solvendi sophismata
de Guillaume Heytesbury:
l'Expositio de tribus praedicamentis de Magister Mesinus

Graziella Federici Vescovini
University of Sassari

On ne connaît l'influence, en Italie, de la logique anglaise du XIVe siècle
(dont témoignent les polémiques acharnées des jeunes humanistes florentins)
que par les écrits de ses adversaires.[1] Par ailleurs la connaissance que nous
en avons du côté britannique, est très imparfaite. Il s'agit pourtant, dans
une certaine mesure, de la secta Nominalium dont parlait Leibniz, qui
l'appréciait et l'estimait au point d'écrire que l'école des nominalistes était
non seulement la plus profonde, mais aussi la mieux adaptée aux exigences de
ceux qui voulaient, à son époque, reformer la philosophie. En effet ils
avaient eu le mérite, selon Leibniz, de séparer la dialectique de l'ontologie,
s'affranchissant aussi de la tutelle d'Aristote.[2]

Il faut souligner surtout que l'on n'a pas identifié, à l'exception de
Guillame d'Ockham, les chefs de file de cette école, que leurs noms sont
incertains et que leurs ouvrages n'ont pas été clairement identifiés. C'est
dire que nous sommes encore aux préalables de notre recherche.

Ainsi que notre ami, le regretté Jan Pinborg, l'avait remarqué,[3] l'une des
consequences de l'extraordinaire succès de la logique anglaise en Italie au
XIVe siècle, a été que la plupart des plus importants parmi les traites anglais
de logique, ont été diffusés dans leurs exemplaires italiens plutôt qu'en
anglais. De plus ces textes ont été élaborés et commentés par des disciples
italiens, dont cependant on ne sait pas grand-chose. L'initiative de nos
collègues, dont Jan Pinborg, Lambert de Rijk et le père Lewry, qui a abouti

The Rise of British Logic, ed. P. Osmund Lewry, O.P., Papers in Mediaeval
Studies 7 (Toronto: Pontifical Institute of Mediaeval Studies, 1985), pp. 361-
379. © P.I.M.S., 1985.

aussi bien au volume du Ve Simposium de logique médiévale de Rome, par les soins d'Alfonso Maierù,[4] qu'à notre rencontre à Oxford, est d'autant plus louable.

On sait que Leonardo Bruni dans son Dialogus ad Petrum Histrum,[5] définissait ces dialecticiens 'l'équipe d'outre-Océan qui a foncé sur la dialectique' et, ajoute-t-il, 'leurs noms me font trembler: Farabrich, Buser, Occam et d'autres encore du même genre, si bien qu'il me semble qu'ils ont tiré leurs noms de l'armée de Radamante.'

Maintenant que nous connaissons un peu mieux ces textes, ces attaques nous paraissent superficielles, voire même de mauvaise foi, relevant d'une intolérance envers des écoles et des enseignements que l'on voulait nier.[6] En termes généraux il s'agit d'après nous, plutôt que d'une simple polémique verbale entre deux adversaires, de l'ébauche de certaines formes nouvelles d'une philosophie du langage, lesquelles se développent[7] sur des plans, dans des directions, avec des buts différents: les formes des partisans des logiciens anglais étaient très elaborées et très complexes, tandis que celles des premiers humanistes étaient beaucoup plus simples. Il suffit que l'on pense à la logique de Lorenzo Valla,[8] par example, pour avoir un document témoignant de la façon dont les differentes théories du langage, commun ou scientifique, avec leurs formes logiques et rhétoriques ont pu se rencontrer et se mêler en aboutissant à des résultats surprenants.

Pour revenir à la citation de Leonardo Bruni, nous savons encore très peu de choses à propos de Farabrich, éxcepté les recherches plus récentes, dont celles de Francesco del Punta.[9]

Nous avons déjà consacrée une étude à l'identification de Buser, après avoir tout d'abord recherché les manuscrits du traité De obligationibus, et notre enquête[10] a été le point de départ des travaux rémarquables de C.H. Kneepkens lequel, ayant trouvé deux autres manuscrits, a réussi à identifier le mystérieux Buser. Celui-ci ne serait pas un britannique, mais un hollandais, Guillaume Buser de Heusden, qui a enseigné à Paris[11] et dont les ouvrages circulaient aussi à Florence.

En revanche, on a beaucoup écrit sur l'influence de Guillaume d'Occam à telle enseigne qu'on a fini par ramener tout l'école de la logique anglaise du XIVe siècle en Italie à l'école occamiste. Et même si on reconnaît l'importance, notamment dans cette direction, des études de Cesare Vasoli, présentées dans le livre[12] qu'il a consacré aux polémiques occamistes dans les milieux florentins, et étayées par la publication et l'étude du petit poème en vers latin d'inspiration virgilienne de Francesco Landini (L'Aveugle des Orgues), où l'auteur fait l'éloge d'Occam, cette tendance n'est plus acceptée par tout le monde et on est en train de déceler d'autres ecoles et d'autres traditions.

Dans le poème de Landini on trouve une défense assez surprenante des logiciens 'modernes' britanniques contre leurs détracteurs humanistes, et le poète imagine que c'est Occam lui-même l'auteur de son texte, lequel nous ramène au coeur même de la querelle entre les logiciens modernes du XIVe siècle et les humanistes.

L'école anglaise, cependant, apparaît très différenciée et articulée.[13] Par example les études de De Rijk et de Maierù ont démontré l'importance de l'influence qu'a exercée en Italie Richard Billingham, par la diffusion de plusieurs rédactions manuscrites de son Speculum puerorum. Ce texte -- a déclaré De Rijk[14] -- est à la base des différentes rédactions de l'oeuvre De veritate ac falsitate propositionis. Dans le troisième volume de la série Artistarium [15] Lambert Marie de Rijk vient de publier les éditions critiques des différentes rédactions de l'oeuvre de Richard Billingham (Recensio de probationibus terminorum) et surtout, outre la Recensio altera, la Recensio italica du traité Terminus est in quem sive Speculum puerorum, une rédaction autre que celle éditée par le même De Rijk dans la revue Medioevo. Elle témoigne de l'extraordinaire influence que ce texte de Billingham a exercée en Europe centrale et en Italie dans le XIVe et le XVe siècle par l'intermédiaire aussi de l'oeuvre de Jean Venator (1373-1414 environ), jusqu'à l'activité de Pierre de Mantoue. En outre, on a souligné l'importance au XVe siècle, de la Logica oxoniensis, qui parait composée d'une série d'élaborations, pour la plupart anonymes, de textes de maîtres renommmés.[16]

Nous en sommes encore aux préalables de la recherches à propos de l'emprise de britannica sophismata, des textes, des commentaires, de canaux par lesquels ils aboutirent à la culture italienne et y pénétrèrent avec tant de vigeur, bien que récemment Norman Kretzmann en analysant les sophismata de Ricardus Kilvington[17] en ait montré les différences par rapport à ceux de Guillaume Heytesbury et bien que Henri Braakhuis vienne d'étudier le commentaire de Paul de la Pergula des sophismata de Guillaume Heytesbury.[18]

Qui sont, en effet, ceux que — pour prendre un example — Sassolo da Prato, dans un texte assez connu, appellé 'nos maitres' et dont il dit qu'ils ont délaissé Aristote en lui préférant des monstres et des êtres étranges aux noms bizarres tels que 'Esborum', 'Entisberum', 'Occam'?[19] Comment pourrait-on identifier ces disciples?

II

C'est justement le but de notre communication que d'étudier quelques-uns de ces logiciens-philosophes ou savants italiens, disciples d'un certain 'Esborum', 'Entisberum' (il s'agit de Guillaume Heytesbury dont le latin italianisé de l'époque déformait le nom, le transformant en 'Entisberus', 'Esberus', 'Tisberus').

Non seulement les Sophismata mais aussi les Regulae solvendi sophismata de Heytsbury, ont joui en Italie d'une renommé extraordinaire, que démontrent, d'un côté la diffusion des exemplaires manuscrits de ses ouvrages (qu'il serait bon d'étudier de près), et de l'autre le succès indéniable de ces mêmes ouvrages de Heytesbury dans l'enseignement universitaire, dont témoignent les commentaires ou les expositiones de son texte par ces professeurs italiens auxquels sans doute faisait allusion Sassolo da Prato.

C'est justement de ces commentaires (dont par ailleurs on ne sait pas grand-chose) que nous allons parler maintenant.

Nous avons déjà consacré une recherche préalable à la diffusion des manuscrits de l'Expositio par Angelus de Fossombrone du De tribus praedicamentis de Guillaume Heytesbury.[20] L'Expositio fait ressortir l'intérêt que les philosophes et les maîtres ès arts italiens témoignaient pour la façon dont les règles de la logique terministe permettaient d'approcher les problèmes physiques du mouvement et de la vitesse qu'ils ne réussissaient pas à résoudre à l'aide de l'interprétation réaliste de la logique d'Aristote.

C'est en effet justement sur le VIe traité des Regulae solvendi sophismata, où il est question explicitement des trois formes du mouvement (de motu locali, de motu augmentationis, de motu alterationis), que ces maîtres concentrent leur attention. Et aussi le texte d'Angelus a eu deux titres: _Expositio de tribus praedicamentis_, mais aussi _De velocitate motuum_, ce qui ne manqua pas d'engendrer une certaine confusion, car on put croire qu'il s'agissait de deux ouvrages différents dont l'un aurait été le commentaire de _Regulae_ et l'autre un traité indépendant.

La renommée de l'_Expositio_ d'Angelus de Fossombrone fut telle qu'on voulut aussi l'imprimer mais aussi bien dans les manuscrits que dans le texte imprimé, ce commentaire de l'oeuvre de Guillaume Heytesbury est publié avec l'_Expositio_ d'un autre maître.

Il s'agit là de ce 'Magister Mesinus' ou 'Messinus', qui pourrait bien être, d'après nous, un autre de ces _hii nostri_ dont parle Sassolo da Prato lesquels ont délaissé Aristote pour suivre _Entisberus_ (c'est-à-dire Heytesbury).

Le titre _De tribus praedicamentis_ correspond à l'_incipit_ du VIe traité de Guillaume Heytesbury: 'Tria sunt predicamenta vel genera in quibus contingit motum fieri proprium, mutatur enim localiter, quantitative aut qualitative.'[21]

Le sujet du traité _De tribus praedicamentis_ est donc en réalité _De velocitate motuum_. Si le titre a changé, c'est qu'il correspond davantage à l'_incipit_ du VIe traite des _Regulae_ et au fait que le livre de Heytesbury est divisé en trois parties concernant respectivement la _mutatio localiter, quantitative et qualitative._

Il s'agit là d'un découpage lourd de conséquences pour les exposés des maîtres italiens de la fin du XIVe siècle et du début du XVe, parce que dans les copies manuscrites de l'exposé du _De tribus praedicamentis_ de Guillaume, on remarque la collaboration de plusieurs maîtres. Par exemple, dans certaines collections, les trois premières parties comprennent l'exposé d'Ange suivi de celui de Mesinus, sur la deuxième et troisième partie du traité de Guillaume, et de celui de Gaetanus de Thiene sur la troisième partie de Mesinus.

C'est dire que l'_Expositio_ se brise en des fragments d'auteurs différents, ce qui aboutit à des ensembles complexes de textes, que les maîtres ont rédigés à différentes époques, dans des contextes divers d'après les exigences de multiples écoles philosophiques et scientifiques. Par conséquent tout discours concernant la reconstruction des exemplaires des _expositiones_ par l'un ou par l'autre des maîtres, est très complexe du point de vue philologique: c'est le cas, notamment, de l'exposé de Mesinus.

Il reste donc que les manuscrits aussi bien que les textes imprimés des expositiones de VIe traité des Regulae de Guillaume prêtent à certaines confusions en ce qui concerne leur attribution. Autrement dit, des recherches préalables sur les manuscrits de l'Expositio rédigée par les maîtres dont nous avons parlé (Angelus par exemple ou Magister Messinus) nous ont paru indispensables malgré le succès des éditions de la fin du XVe siècle.

En effet, c'est justement dans ces éditions que nous avons remarqué l'inversion des textes que nous a poussée à remonter aux sources manuscrites pour établir la paternité de chaque exposé, l'un par rapport à l'autre. Autrement dit, on a confondu l'Expositio de Mesinus et celui d'Ange, dans le texte duquel le commentaire de Mesinus avait été inséré.

C'est un cas exemplaire, à ce propos, que celui de l'édition de l'exposé d'Ange publié sans date avec l'exposé de Gaetanus de Thiene des Regulae, lesquelles par contre ont été datées '1483' par Paulus Aurelius Floch de Firmo. Dans ce texte d'Angelus on a inséré le texte de l'Expositio de Mesinus, dont la deuxième partie est consacrée à la vitesse du motus augmentationis.

Comme nous avons déjà parlé de tout ceci dans un autre essai,[22] nous croyons pouvoir passer tout de suite à l'examen ponctuel de la tradition manuscrite de l'exposé de Magister Mesinus, telle que nous la connaissons aujourd'hui, sans tenir compte du fait que ce texte a été inséré dans un texte d'Angelus. Nous reconnaîtrons en Mesinus un autre disciple des Regulae de Guillaume. Il va de soi que la recherche reste ouverte et que d'autres données pourront s'y ajouter pour parachever ou modifier notre conclusion.

III

Qui était Magister Mesinus? Comment l'identifier? Peut-on identifier notre Magister Mesinus, l'auteur de l'Expositio avec ce 'Magister Mesinus', 'Messinus', 'Masinus', qui est probablement aussi le 'Massius', 'Maxius', 'Misinus', 'Mexinus', 'Maxinus de Choderoncho'[23] dont parlent Dallari et

Maiocchi?

Dallari dit qu'en 1382-1385 un maitre ès arts 'Masius de Choderoncho' (Coderonco) avait été nommé ad lecturam loycae, ce qui serait en accord aussi bien avec son exposé du texte de Guillaume, qu'avec ses autres ouvrages de logicien.   De même, Maxinus de Coderoncho est celui qui est ellectus ad lecturam loycae pour l'année 1385-1386 en Bologne.   En 1386-1387 Dallari cite un certain Magister Misinus de Choderoncho 'qui legit in studio Bononiae lecturam loycae et philosophiae.'[24]

Étant donné les déformations dialectales des noms italiens latinisés dans cette periode, nous sommes de l'avis que c'est au même maître que Dallari fait allusion.   Par ailleurs, dans le ms. Oxford, Bodleian Library, Canonici classici latini 278 (s. xiv)[25] on lit, avant l'incipit des oeuvres de Mesinus: 'Questiones super duos libros Peryermeneias recollecte ab reverendo artium doctore Magistro Masino de Coderoncho legenti in studio Bononiensi sub anno Domini 1387 ut iam patet.'   Et aussi on lit la même chose à la fin du commentaire du premier livre.[26]

En outre, d'après les documents rassemblés par Maiocchi pour L'Université de Pavie,[27] il ressort qu'un Magister Mesinus enseignait la philosophie naturelle et l'astrologie à Pavie en 1390-1391, tandis qu'en 1392-1392 ce même magister Misinus de Coderoncho s'adonnait à Bologne 'ad lecturam astrologiae', 'ad lecturam medicinae in nonis'.

En ce qui concerne les matières enseignées, le curriculum parait plausible et conforme par example à l'organisation des matières enseignées par les maîtres ès arts, de la philosophie et de la médecine dans les universités de l'Italie du Nord.[28]

C'est pourquoi nous serions d'avis d'identifier l'auteur de l'Expositio de tribus praedicamentis avec ce maître, même si un supplément d'enquête pourrait toujours être utile.

IV

Magister Mesinus a-t-il écrit autre chose, outre l'Expositio?   Nos recherches[29] nous ont amenée à lui attribuer un remarquable commentaire

sous forme de Doutes (Dubia) ou de Questions 'Super quaestionem Johannis de
Casale de intensione et remissione formarum', c'est-à-dire un texte assez
important de philosophie naturelle qui méritérait qu'on l'étudie davantage
(Anneliese Maier et Marshall Clagett lui ont consacré quelques mots).

Mesinus a donc rédigé les Dubia super quaestionem Johannis de Casali.
Voci l'incipit:

Postulato Dei suffragio necnon genitricis gloriose Virginis Marie et
beatorum Apostolorum Petri et Pauli totius aure celestis quibus semper
flecto genua multis lecturus questionem Ioannis de Casali quedam dubia
que eam legendo occurrent in quorum quibusdam aliter videtur michi fore
dicendum discutiam, pro primo ergo dubio queritur utrum bene describitur
hic terminus latitudo uniformiter difformis sic....

Je signale cinq manuscrits: Bologna, Bib. Univ. 1227 (2410), fols. 101ra-163va;
Madrid, Escorial, Real Bib. f.II.8, fols. 1^r-49^r; Padova, Bib. Anton. 431 (scaff.
XX) (miscel.; s. xiv-xv), fols. 69ra-83rb; Civico Museo 169, fols. 1ra-46^v
(incomplet et anonyme); Venezia, Bib. Marc. lat. class. XI, cod. 21
(Valentinelli 4.234) (=lat. VI. 25), fols. 1^r-76^r. L'exemplaire de ms. Padova,
Bib. Anton. 431 est joint au commentaire anonyme, peut-etre d'Antonio de
Scarperia, sur les sophismata fols. 85ra-114vb). Il a le même incipit:

Tractatus sophismatum. Obrogatum quorundam scholarium deo favente
conscribam sophismata ex parte diversorum sincategorematum difficultatem
habentia, talem ordinem servando....

Mais les commentaires les plus nombreux qui nous sont parvenus
concernent son enseignement de la logique: il a écrit un commentaire au Peri
hermeneyas et l'Expositio de tribus praedicamentis.

Je ne connais que deux exemplaires des Quaestiones in librum de
interpretatione dont voici l'incipit du texte: 'Utrum enunciatio sit subiectum
libri Periermeneias et arguitur primo quod sic auctoritate communi
expositorum huius libri.' Les exemplaires sont: mss. Oxford, Bodl. Lib.,
Canon. class. lat. 278 (s. xiv), fols. 38ra-63vb, et Viterbo, Bib. Capitolare 56
(D.52) (miscel.; s. xv), fols. 14ra-36rb.[30] L'exemplaire d'Oxford nous semble
très intéressant aussi parce qu'il comprend à la fin une Tabula[31] qui résume
tous les sophismes discutés dans le texte Periermeneias: en outre, il est

contemporain de l'activité de professeur de Mesinus à Bologne en 1387.

Nous donnerons à la fin de cet essai une liste des manuscrits de l'Expositio de tribus praedicamentis de Guillaume par Mesinus en soulignant que tous les exemplaires ne sont pas complets, que quelques-uns sont anonymes, que quelques-uns ont été attribués à Angelus de Fossombrone[32] ou à Gaetanus de Thienis. Voici l'incipit des trois parties de l'Expositio de Mesinus:

Mesini de tribus predicamentis, incipit (I): 'Dubium est utrum omnis motus verus et proprie dictus....'

explicit: '...in eodem tempore ceteris aliis paribus.'

incipit (II): 'De velocitate ergo motus augmentationis augmentatio communiter dicta vocatur rarefactio....'

explicit: '...est dificultas quare transeo ad alia.'

incipit (III): 'De velocitate ergo alterationis, etc. Quantum ad velocitatem alterationis penes quid ipsa habeat attendi tres recitantur positiones (opiniones)....'

explicit (différant): '...per totam horam', suivi du Complementum de Gaietanus de Thienis, 'Contra hanc positionem arguitur multipliciter....'

ou: '...ad punctum sibi immediatum.', suivi du Complementum: 'Sequitur complementum expositionis predicte secundum Gaetanum de Thienis. (inc.:) Contra hanc positionem arguitur multipliciter... (expl.:) ...ille alterationes etiam sunt equales quibus mediantibus latitudines equales inducuntur subiectis inequalibus licet non ita proprie quare etc. Et sic terminatur capitulum de motu alterationis ad laudem gloriosi dei et eius beatissime Matris Amen.'

Manuscrits de l'Expositio de tribus praedicamentis
de Guillaume Heytesbury par Mesinus de Coderonco

1. Belluno, Seminario Gregoriano 33 (s. xv), fols. 21r-33v: entremêlé à l'exposé d'Angelus et suivi du Complementum Gaetanis de Thienis:-

fol. 21r: 'Et hoc de motu locali secundum magistrum Angelum de

Fossambruno. Incipit de motu augmentationis secundum Masinum.
II. De velocitate motus augmentationis dicitur quod augmentatio communiter dicta vocatur rarefactio....';

fols. 27^V-31^r: 'III. De velocitate autem alterationis quantum ad velocitatem alterationis penes quid ipsa habeat attendi tres recitantur positiones...per totam horam.';

fols. 31^r-33^V, Complementum Gaetani de Thienis: 'Contra hanc positionem arguitur multipliciter...; ille alterationes etiam sunt equales quibus mediantibus latitudines equales inducuntur subiectis inequalibus licet non ita proprie quare etc. (suivi par l'explicit erroné:) et hic finit totus tractatus de tribus predicamentis secundum clarissimum doctorem magistrum Angelum de Fosambruno scriptus per me Georgium Rugarlum de Brugo Valistari 1460 die septima septembris.'

A la fin, au fol. 77^V commence anonyme le premier traité de l'exposé de Mesinus, probablement suivi du texte complet de la deuxième et troisième partie (fols. 77^V-102^V): 'Dubium est utrum omnis motus verus et proprie dictus.' Mais nous n'avons pu contrôler les derniers folios du manuscrit.

2. Milano, Bib. Ambros. O.51 super, comprend seulement la deuxième partie sur la vitesse de motu augmentationis, fols. 39ra-52ra, et il a été confondu avec l'exposé d'Angelus, anonyme.

3. Oxford, Bodl. Lib., Canonici class. lat. 278 (s. xiv ex.-xv), fols. 95^r-115^r: texte complet suivi des trois parties, suivies du Complementum de Gaetanus de Thienis:-

fol. 95ra, Tractatus Mesini super tractata de tribus predicamentis, incipit (I): 'Dubium est utrum omnis motus verus et proprie dictus....';

fol. 104ra (II): '<De> velocitate ergo motus augmentationis, augmentatio communiter dicta....';

fol. 111^V (III): '<De> velocitate ergo alteracionis etc. Quantum ad velocitatem alterationis penes quid ipsa habeat attendi....';

fol. 115^r: '...punctum sibi immediatum.';

fol. 115^V blanc;

fol. 116^r-118^V: 'Hic incipit complementum tractatus Misini super tribus predicamentis Tisberi secundum Gayetanum de Thienis. Contra hanc positionem arguitur multipliciter. Primo quia in ea sequitur quod....; inducuntur subiectis inequalibus licet non ita proprie quare etc. Et sic terminatur capitulum de motu alterationis ad laudem gloriosi dei.'

Au fol. 119$^\text{v}$ on lit: 'Liber est mei Bernardini Cepolle physici veronensis quem emi a Johanne Andrea Bolderio pro libris duabus denariorum parvorum die 17 Ianuarii 1475.'

4. Oxford, Bodl. Lib., Canonici misc. 456 (s. xv), suivi du Complementum Gaetanis de Thienis, fols. 93$^\text{rb}$-123$^\text{vb}$:-

fol. 93$^\text{rb}$: 'Expositiones Messini viri doctissimi in capitulum de tribus predicamentis Hentisberi acutissimi incipiunt foeliciter.
(I) Dubium est utrum omnis motus verus et proprie dictus....';
fol. 106$^\text{rb}$: '...ceteris aliis paribus. (II) De velocitate motus augmentationis augmentatio communiter dicta vocatur rarefactio....';
fol. 115$^\text{va}$: '...quare transeo ad alia. (III) De velocitate ergo alterationis quantum ad velocitatem alterationis penes quid ipsa habeat attendi tres recitantur positiones....';
fol. 120$^\text{ra}$: '...ex quo ad utrumque alteratio per totam horam. (incipit Complementum:) Contra hanc positionem arguitur multipliciter primo quia ex ea sequitur....';
fol. 123$^\text{vb}$: '...licet non ita proprie quare etc. Finis expositionum Messini viri doctissimi in capitulum de tribus predicamentis acutissimi Hentisberi per me Ludovicum ser Angeli de Auximo Ferrarie studentem. Ad laudem dei sueque genitricis Marie et omnium sanctorum atque sanctarum et vita eterna fruentium hoc opus completum fuit 1467 6$^\text{o}$ kalendas....'

5. Padova, Civico Museo 169 (s. xiv ex.-xv in.), fols. 48$^\text{va}$-65$^\text{ra}$, Expositio complet des trois parties suivi du Complementum Gaetanis de Thienis, fols. 65$^\text{ra}$-67$^\text{rb}$:-

fol. 48$^\text{va}$: 'Incipit Expositio Mesini super tractatu Entisberi de tribus predicamentis. (I) Dubium est utrum omnis motus verus et proprie dictus....';
fol. 56$^\text{va}$: '...aliis paribus. (II) <D>e velocitate ergo motus augmentationis augmentatio communiter dicta vocatur rarefactio....';
fol. 62$^\text{ra}$: '...quare transeo ad alia. (III) <D>e velocitate ergo alterationis etc. Quantum ad velocitatem alterationis penes quid ipsa habeat attendi tres recitantur positiones....';
fol. 65$^\text{ra}$: '...ad punctum sibi immediatum. Sequitur complementum expositionis predicte secundum Gaytanum de Thienis. Contra hanc positionem arguitur multipliciter....';

fol. 67rb: '...subiectis inequalibus licet non ita proprie quare etc. Et sic terminatur capitulum de motu alterationis ad laudem gloriosi dei amen.'

6. Città del Vaticano, Bib. Apost. Vat., Chig. E.VI.197 (s. xv), fols. 161vb-173rb, Expositio de Mesinus (anonyme), seulement de la deuxième et troisième partie, suivi du Complementum Gaetanis de Thienis:-

fol. 161va, la fin de l'exposé d'Angelus de Fossombrone: '...nullo modo confertur b ergo etc. Explicit de motu locali incipit de motu augmentationis.';

fol. 161vb: '(II) De velocitate motus augmentationis dicitur quod augmentatio coommuniter dicta vocatur rarefactio....';

fol. 167vb: '...transeo ad alia. (Suit explicit erroné:) Explicit de velocitate motus augmentationis Angeli de Fossinfronio 1468 die 17 hora 12 mensis iunii. (III) <D>e velocitate motus alterationis quantum ad velocitatem alterationis penes quid ipsa habeat attendi tres recitantur opiniones....';

fol. 170vb: '...ad punctum sibi immediatum. Sequitur complementum expositionis secundum autenticum doctorem Gaetanus de Thienis. Contra hanc positionem arguitur multipliciter....';

fol. 173rb: '...quibus mediantibus equales latitudines inducuntur in subiectis inequalibus licet non ita proprie quare etc. Et sic terminatur capitulum de motu alterationis. Iste liber est mei Magistri Bernardini Antonii de Spanochiis artium doctoris quem propria manu transcripsi anno Domini 1468.'

7. Venezia, Bib. Marc. lat.VI.105 (2656) (s. xv), fols. 47rb-65ra, l'Expositio complet des trois parties par Mesinus, suivi du Complementum Gaetani de Thienis:-

fol. 47rb: 'Incipit sententia super de tribus predicamentis Magistri Messini. (I) Dubium est utrum omnis motus verus et proprie dictus....';

fol. 54vb: '...ceteris paribus. (II) De velocitate augmentationis. Augmentiatio communiter dicta appellatur rarefactio....';

fol. 60ra: '...ideo ad alia pertranseam.';

fol. 60rb: '(III) De velocitate ergo alterationis quantum ad velocitatem alterationis penes quid habeat ipsa attendi....';

fol. 63ra: '...per totam horam. (Ici on trouve tout de suite l'incipit du Complementum de Gaetanus de Thienis:) Sed contra positionem arguitur multipliciter....';

fol. 65ra: '...inequalibus licet non sint ita proprie sed relinquitur potentia. Et hec sufficiant Deo gratias Deo gratias. Et sic est finis scripti super de tribus predicamentis Hentisberi editi, initiatur a Messino et completur a Gayetano de Thienis amen.'

8. Venezia, Bib. Marc. lat.VI.160 (2816) (s. xv environ), fols. 241ra-248ra, 255ra-275rb: ce manuscrit contient deux exemplaires de l'Expositio de Mesinus (anonymes); le premier est l'exposé de la deuxième et de la troisième partie et est precédé de l'Expositio d'Angelus de Fossombrone (fols. 224rb-239rb), 'Angelus de Frosempronio autor. Incipit. In omni predicamento potest esse mutatio....'33:-

fol. 241ra: '(II) De velocitate motus augmentationis. Augmentatio communiter dicta vocatur rarefactio quoniam....';

fol. 246ra: '...(III) De velocitate motus alterationis tres sunt opiniones.... (explicit fol. 248ra).

Suit le De reactione d'Angelus de Fossombrone. Après, on a un deuxième exemplaire complet des trois parties de l'Expositio de Mesinus:-

fol. 255ra: '(I) Dubium est utrum motus verus et proprie dictus....';

fol. 263vb: '...(II) De velocitate ergo motus augmentationis. Augmentatio communiter dicta vocatur rarefactio....';

fol. 269vb '...(III) De velocitate ergo alterationis etc. Quantum ad velocitatem alterationis penes quid ipsa habeat attendi tres recitantur positiones quarum prima....';

fol. 275rb: '...Et sic terminatur capitulum de motu alterationis ad laudem gloriosi dei et eius beatissime Matris Amen.'

Notes

[1] Cf. E. Garin, 'La cultura fiorentina nella seconda metà del Trecento e i barbari britanni' dans L'età nuova (Napoli, 1969), pp. 139-66; C. Vasoli, '"Antichi" contro "moderni"' dans La dialettica e la retorica dell'Umanesimo: "Invenzione" e "Metodo" nella cultura del XV e XVI secolo (Milano. 1960), pp. 9-27. Cf. aussi W.J. Courtenay, 'The Early Stages in the Introduction of Oxford Logic into Italy' dans A. Maierù éd., English Logic in Italy in the

14th and 15th Centuries: Acts of the 5th European Symposium on Medieval Logic and Semantics, Rome, 10-14 November 1980 (History of Logic 1; Napoli, 1982), pp. 13-32, ibid., p. 14.

2 Dissertatio praeliminaris in Marii Nizolii De veris principiis et vera ratione philosophandi contra pseudo-philosophos libri IV dans Gottfried Wilhelm Leibniz, Philosophische Schriften 2 (Gottfried Wilhelm Leibniz, Samtliche Schriften und Briefe 6 Reihe; Berlin, 1966), p. 427 (20-22): '...secta Nominalium, omnium inter Scholasticas profundissima et hodiernae reformatae philosophandi rationi congruentissima....' Cf. aussi B. Hauréau, De la philosophie scolastique 2.2 (Paris, 1880), p. 487.

3 J. Pinborg, 'A Logical Treatise ascribed to Bradwardine' dans A. Maierù et A. Paravicini Bagliani, éd., Studi sul XIV secolo in memoria di Anneliese Maier (Storia e Letteratura 151; Roma, 1981), p. 27.

4 Maierù éd., English Logic in Italy (cf. n. 1).

5 Leonardo Bruni Aretino, Ad Petrum Paulum Histrum dialogus dans E. Garin éd., Prosatori latini del Quattrocento (La letteratura italiana, storia e testi 13; Milano-Napoli, 1952), pp. 58, 60: 'Nam etiam illa barbaria, quae trans oceanum habitat, in illam [dialecticam] impetum fecit. At quae gentes, dii boni? Quorum etiam nomina perhorresco: Farabrich, Buser, Occam....'

6 Cf. en cette direction F. Corvino, 'l'evoluzione dell' aristotelismo nel passaggio dal Medioevo al Rinascimento' dans Aristotelismo veneto e scienza moderna (Atti del 25º Anno Accademico del Centro per la Storia della tradizione aristotelica nel Veneto) 2 (Padova, 1983), pp. 567-68. Sur l'ignorance de nos jours, encore en matière des fondements de la pensée médiévale, pas seulement linguistiques, conséquence de cette polémique des humanistes, cf. R. Jakobson, Lo sviluppo della semiotica (Milano, 1978), p. 77.

7 Pour une évaluation de la logique du Moyen Age en général, cf. E.A. Moody, 'The Medieval Contribution to Logic', Studium generale 19 (1966) 443-52; J. Pinborg, 'Some Problems of Semantic Representations in Medieval Logic' dans H. Parret éd., History of Linguistic Thought and Contemporary Linguistics (Foundations of Communications; Berlin-New York, 1976), pp. 254-78.

[8] A propos du rapport entre la dialectique de Lorenzo Valla et la tradition nominaliste, cf. G. Zippel éd., Lorenzo Valla, Repastinatio dialectice et philosophie 1 (Padova, 1982), p. LXXXVII; F. Bottin, La scienza degli occamisti. La scienza tardo-medievale dalle origini del paradigma nominalista alla rivoluzione scientifica (Studi di Filosofia e Storia della filosofia 4; Rimini, 1982), cap. VIII, pp. 277-313. Evidemment à ce sujet, comme a remarqué aussi R. Fubini, la question est encore sub judice; cf. idem, 'Umanesimo ed enciclopedismo. A proposito di contributi recenti su Giorgio Valla', Il pensiero politico 16 (1983) 251-69. Cf. aussi R. Waswo, 'The reaction of Juan Luis Vives to Valla's Philosophy of Language', Bibliothèque d'Humanisme et Renaissance 42 (1980) 595-609, qui parle d'un langage bâti sur une ontologie de Lorenzo Valla, interprétation qui ne semble pas exacte parce que la doctrine du langage commun de Lorenzo Valla paraît renvoyer plutôt à un empirisme. Cf. aussi E. Garin, 'Retorica e "Studia humanitatis" nella cultura del Quattrocento' dans B. Vickers éd., Rhetoric Revalued: Papers from the International Society for the History of Rhetoric (Medieval & Renaissance texts and studies 19; International Society for History of Rhetoric Monograph 1; Binghamton, N.Y., 1982), pp. 225-39.

[9] F. del Punta, 'La Logica di R. Feribrigge nella tradizione manoscritta italiana' dans Maierù éd., English Logic in Italy, pp. 53-85.

[10] G. Federici Vescovini, 'A la recherche du mystérieux Buser. A propos de trois copies manuscrites de la même oeuvre: le De obligationibus de "Buser" ou "Busel"' dans H.A.G. Braakhuis, C.H. Kneepkens, L.M. de Rijk éd., English Logic and Semantics from the End of the Twelfth Century to the Time of Ockham and Burleigh: Acts of the 4th European Symposium on Mediaeval Logic and Semantics. Leiden-Nijmegen. 23-27 April 1979 (Artistarium Supplementa 1; Nijmegen, 1981), pp. 443-57.

[11] C.H. Kneepkens, 'The Mysterious Buser Again: William Buser of Heusden and the Obligationes Tract Ob rogatum' dans Maierù, English Logic in Italy, pp. 147-66. En 1364 Buser avait été nommé aussi Recteur de l'Université de Paris; cf. ibid., pp. 148-52.

[12] C. Vasoli, 'Polemiche occamiste', Rinascimento 3 (1952) 119-41; idem, Guglielmo d'Occam (Firenze, 1953), pp. 57-68.

[13] Cf. J. Pinborg, 'The English Contribution to Logic before Ockham',

Synthese 40 (1979) 19-42.

[14] L.M. de Rijk, 'Another "Speculum puerorum" attributed to Richard Billingham: Introduction and Text', Medioevo 1 (1975) 203.

[15] L.M. de Rijk éd., Some 14th Century Tracts on the Probationes Terminorum: Martin of Alnwich O.F.M., Richard Billingham, Edward Upton and Others (Artistarium 3; Nijmegen, 1982).

[16] De Rijk, 'Another "Speculum puerorum"...' édition, pp. 213-35; idem, 'Semantics in Richard Billingham and Johannes Venator' dans Maierù éd., English Logic in Italy, pp. 167-83; idem, 'Logica Oxoniensis: An Attempt to Reconstruct a Fifteenth Century Oxford Manual of Logic', Medioevo 3 (1977) 121-64.

[17] N. Kretzmann, 'Richard Kilvington and the Logic of Instantaneous Speed' dans Maierù et Paravicini Bagliani éd., Studi sul secolo XIV in memoria di Anneliese Maier, pp. 144-78. Cf. aussi F. Bottin, 'Un testo fondamentale nell'ambito della "nuova fisica" di Oxford: i Sophismata di Richard Kilmington' dans A. Zimmermann éd., 'Antiqui' und Moderni' (Miscellanea mediaevalia 9; Berlin-New York, 1974), pp. 201-205; S. Knuuttila et A.I. Lehtinen, 'Plato in infinitum remisse incipit esse albus: New Texts on the Late Medieval Discussion on the Concept of Infinity in Sophismata Literature' dans E. Saarinen, R. Hilpinen, I Niinilnoto, M.P. Hintikka éd., Essays in Honour of Jaako Hintikka (Synthese Library 124; Dordrecht-Boston-London, 1979), pp. 309-29.

[18] H.A.G. Braakhuis, 'Paul of Pergula's Commentary on the Sophismata of William of Heytesbury' dans Maierù éd., English Logic in Italy, pp. 343-57. A propos de la thèse que les sophismata représentent un genre spécifique, une typologie différente par rapport aux quaestiones pour l'analyse des problèmes philosophiques et scientifiques au XIVe siècle, cf. J.E. Murdoch, 'Mathematics and Sophisms in Late Medieval Natural Philosophy' dans Les genres littéraires dans les sources théologiques et philosophiges médiévales, definition, critique et exploitation: Actes du Colloque international de Louvain-la-Neuve, 25-27 mai 1981 (Publications de l'Institut d'Études Médiévales 2e série: Textes, Études, Congrès, vol. 5; Louvain-la-Neuve, 1982), pp. 85-100, ibid., p. 100.

[19] Saxolus Pratensis ad amicum suum. De Victorini Feltrensis vita et disciplina dans E. Garin éd., Il pensiero pedagogico dello Umanesimo (Firenze, 1958), p. 520: 'At hi nostri graviores haec ut levia inepta, nugatoria reiiciunt. Quid? Aristotelem ipsum ducem, nonne etiam desertum habent? cum huic anteponant monstra illa et portenta Esborum, Entisberum, Occham, Bridan: hiisque auctoribus, contendunt nonnulli acutiores hodie in disserendo atque in reliqua philosophia perspicienda homines reddi, quam temporibus Aristotelis.' Cf. aussi C. Guasti, Intorno alla vita e all'insegnamento di Vittorino da Feltre. Lettere di Sassolo pratese volgarizzate (Firenze, 1869), p. 57. A propos de Sassolo, cf. aussi P.L. Rose, The Italian Renaissance of Mathematics: studies on humanists and mathematicians from Petrarch to Galileo (Travaux d'humanisme et Renaissance 145; Genève, 1975), pp. 16-17.

[20] G. Federici Vescovini, 'Il commento di Angelo di Fossombrone al De tribus praedicamentis di Guglielmo Heytesbury' dans Maierù éd., English Logic in Italy, pp. 359-74.

[21] Heytesbury, Regulae solvendi sophismata, ms. Firenze, Bib. Riccardiana 821 (s. xv; daté en Perugia 1472), fols. 1ra-30va. Il s'agit d'un remarquable exemplaire suivi de l'exposé d'Ange de Fossambruno.

[22] A ce propos nous renvoyons à notre étude; cf. n. 20.

[23] Cf. aussi M. Clagett, The Science of Mechanics in the Middle Ages (Publications in medieval science 4; Madison, Ws., 1959), pp. 646-48, qui affirme que notre maître ne doit pas être identifié avec 'Misino di m. Bonfantino dalle Pecore', maître bolonais en 1372 selon G.N.P. Alidosi, I dottori bolognesi di teologia. filosophia. medicina e d'arti liberali dall'anno 1000 per tutto Marzo del 1623 (Bologna, 1623), p. 140.

[24] U. Dallari, I rotuli dei dottori legista e artisti dello Studio bolognese 1 (Bologna, 1888), p. 5; 4 (Bologna, 1924), pp. 11, 12, 17.

[25] Ms. Oxford, Bodl. Lib., Canon. class. lat. 278, fol. 37ra.

[26] Ibid., fol. 57rb.

[27] R. Maiocchi, Codice diplomatico dell'Università di Pavia 1 (Pavia, 1905), p. 186.

28 Cf. aussi pour le curriculum du Studium medicinae de Bologne, les
remarques de N.G. Siraisi, Taddeo Alderotti and his Pupils: Two Generations
of Italian Medical Learning (Princeton, N.J., 1981), pp. 6, 23, 139-46: les arts
libéraux, la logique et l'astrologie étaient considérés comme matières très
importantes pour devenir maîtres en médecine.

29 Pour des détails à propos de cette question de Mesinus, cf. ma
recherche, G. Federici Vescovini, 'Duns Scoto e Biagio Pelacani a Padova'
dans Regnum hominis et regnum Dei. (Acta quarti Congressus Scotistici
internationalis. Patavii 24-29 septembris 1976), 2 Sectio specialis: La
tradizione scotista veneto-padovana (Roma, 1978), pp. 187-198; idem, 'Il
commento di Angelo da Fossombrone...', pp. 367-70; idem, "Arti" e filosofia
nel secolo XIV. Studi sulla tradizione aristotelica e i "moderni" (Firenze,
1983), p. 59.

30 Le codex Viterbo, Bib. Capitolare 56 (D. 52) est un cartaceo,
miscellaneus, XVe siècle, dont les oeuvres ont été copiées en 1456-1457 par
le frère Franciscus Maria Settara, qui deviendra éveque de Viterbo. On peut
lire cette référence à la fin des Regulae supra consequentiis Rodulphi Strodi,
aussi à l'explicit des Termini naturales domini Burlei ('Expliciunt termini
naturales domini Burlei per me fratrem Franciscum Mariam Septaram aliquando
eram magister studii in Conventu Papie anno domini millesimo quadrigentesimo
LVII [?] die XXa mensis februarii'; et à la fin: 'Expliciunt utilia ac preclara
dubia super consequentiis Strode compilate per acutissimum logicantem
dominum magistrum Paulum Pergulensem artium et sacre theologie professorem
meritissimum et completa et scripta per me fratrem Franciscum Mariam de
Septara ordinis minorum...1456.') Les Quaestiones De interpretatione de
Mesinus au contraire ne portent pas de date (fol. 14ra): 'Queritur primo pro
cognitione traditorum in hoc libro peryermeneias utrum enunciatio sit
subiectum libri peryermeneias et arguitur primo quod sic auctoritate communi
expositorum huius libri; (fol. 36rb): '...similiter verificate. Et hec dicta sint
ad presens sufficientia etc. Expliciunt questiones Mesini super libro
periermeneias Aristotelis Deo gratias.' L'oeuvre de Mesinus est precédée
(fols. 1ra-13ra) de: 'Obligationes M. Rodulfi Strode Anglici compilate per me
Paulum de...famosissimi artium et medicine doctoris'; incipit: 'Redargutum
dicimus respondentem qui solius argumentationis virtute....' A la fin on peut
lire une date, '1435'. A propos de Strode, cf. W.K. Seaton, 'An Edition and
Translation of the Tractatus de Consequentiis by Ralph Strode, Fourteenth
Century Logician and Friend of Geoffrey Chaucer' (Univ. of California,

Berkeley, Ph.D. diss., 1973); et A. Maierù, 'Le ms. Oxford, Canonici misc. 219 et la Logica de Strode' dans idem éd., English Logic in Italy, pp. 87-110.

31 A la fin du deuxième livre on peut lire (fol. 63ra): 'Et multe similes consequenter sunt verificabiles de quibus aliis tactis in isto libro quia iam cum correctione cuiuscumque melius dicentis tanta dicta sufficiant. De quibus expliciunt questiones super libro peryermeneias recollecte sub reverendo doctore magistro Misino de Coderonco Deo gratias.' Suit au fol. 63va la Tabula des questions: 'Incipit tabula questionum magistri Masini de Coderonco super libro peryermeneias valde utilium.' Après les titres des seize questions du premier livre on lit: 'Expliciunt questiones primi libri, incipit secundi....Expliciunt questiones secundi libri peryermeneias.' Puis on a une tabula des sophismata qui ont été discutés dans ces questions: 'Incipit tabula sophismatum in his ipsis questionibus positorum.' Dans la columna du même folio (fol. 63vb), on peut lire: 'Explicit tabula questionum peryermeneias et sophismatum datarum per reverendum artium doctorem magistrum Masinum de Coderonco tunc legentem sub anno Domini Millesimo trecentesimo octogesimo septimo in Kristo patris et Domini Domini Urbani divina providentia pape VI Deo gratias Amen.'

32 A ce sujet nous renvoyons à notre étude sur l'exposé d'Angelus, maintenant dans Federici Vescovini, "Arti" e filosofia nel secolo XIV (cf. n. 29), p. 69.

33 Cet exemplaire n'avait pas été signalé par moi dans mon étude consacrée à l'exposé d'Ange parce qu'il m'avait échappé; je le signale maintenant.

15

Peter of Mantua and his Rejection of _Ampliatio_ and _Restrictio_

E.P. Bos

University of Leiden*

Medieval handbooks of logic discussing properties of terms like _suppositio,_ _ampliatio, appellatio, restrictio,_ and _alienatio,_[1] do not always interpret them in the same way. Sometimes, one or other is omitted from the discussion, or a specific property is rejected as such; sometimes, a property is given different names by different logicians or is to be found within different theoretical frameworks.

As I have already indicated, notions which receive different interpretations from different logicians include _ampliatio_ and its counterpart, _restrictio._ (These two notions, by the way, have not received much attention from modern scholars).[2] Now, the Italian logician and physicist Peter of Mantua (d. 1399)[3] does not admit either of these properties of terms into his theory. In this paper I shall try to show: (1) that Peter criticizes and rejects _ampliatio_ and _restrictio_ and how he does so; futhermore, that Peter has foremost in mind the interpretations of these notions advanced by the Parisian masters Albert of Saxony[4] and Marsilius of Inghen;[5]

(2) that Peter's rejection is _based_ on his theory of knowledge (and on its metaphysical aspects), in which he differs from, for example, Albert and Marsilius, but in which he is probably in general agreement with some English logicians. I shall try to show that Peter's theory of knowledge determines his rejection of _ampliatio_ in the same ways as it does his interpretation of _appellatio._[6]

Peter's tract on ampliations, in the incunable edition, has the following composition:[7]

The _Rise of British Logic,_ ed. P. Osmund Lewry, O.P., Papers in Mediaeval Studies 7 (Toronto: Pontifical Institute of Mediaeval Studies, 1985), pp. 381-399. © P.I.M.S., 1985.

1. Four axioms (presuppositiones): fol. 14^{ra}(13)–14^{rb}(20);
2. An objection, followed by Peter's reply: fol. 14^{rb}(20)–14^{va}(14);
3. Three notes: fols. 14^{va}(14)–15^{ra}(21);
4. An objection followed by Peter's reply: fol. 15^{ra}(21)–15^{rb}(30);
5. Peter's general conclusion on ampliatio and restrictio: fol. 15^{rb}(30)–15^{va}(17);
6. A set of objections, with Peter's replies: fols. 15^{ra}(17)–16^{ra}(35);
7. A problem (dubium) is raised and solved by Peter. The dubium is interspersed with objections and replies: fols. 16ra–17^{ra}(35).[8]

The opening sentence of Peter's tract is: 'Numquid sit ampliatio?' (Is ampliation possible?) — I provisionally define 'ampliatio' here as the enlargement of the reference of a term. This question is immediately followed by the four axioms. The first and the third, on the one hand, and the second and the fourth, on the other, are related. The first axiom runs as follows:[9]

Suppositio est statio termini in oratione connexi pro supposito, vel suppositis, in quod, vel in que, trasit vis termini, a quo habet ut supponat.
(Supposition is a term's standing in a proposition for a thing, or for things, to which thing, or to which things, the power excercised by another term extends, in virtue of which latter term the former term has supposition.)

It is clear from his tract on suppositions[10] that by 'another term' Peter means the verb of the proposition, be it a substantival or an adjectival verb — A substantival verb is, for example, 'est' (is); an adjectival verb, 'est albus' (is white). The verb causes the term's supposition for things according to the tense of the verb. A term's supposition is in no respect determined by the term itself.

Closely connected with the first axiom is Peter's third:[11]

...nullus terminus ampliat se ipsum.
(Ampliation of a term by the term itself is impossible.)

Here Peter means to say, as will become clear below,[12] that a term's ampliation, if the term is indeed capable of ampliation, depends on the verb with which it is construed in a proposition.

Now, Peter's second axiom is:[13]

...ista propositio et consimiles cathegorice de disiuncta copula sunt
affirmative: 'Quodlibet est vel non est', 'Chimera est vel non est.'
(the following and similar categorical propositions with a disjunct copula
are affirmative: 'Each thing is or is not', 'A chimera is or is not.')

Here Peter means that the quality (affirmative or negative) of the whole
proposition is determined by the first copula. Otherwise, Peter subsequently
adds, the proposition would be affirmative and negative at the same time.

The English logician 'Johannes Venator' (or John Hunt[e]man)[14] comments
on this subject in his Logica,[15] composed in the early 1380's: 'Likewise,' he
says, 'all logicians call this [i.e., the first copula - E.P.B.] the principal verb
of a categorical proposition. In virtue of this verb the understanding is true
or false.[16] Peter's fourth axiom reflects this interpretation:[17]

...quilibet terminus supponens respectu huius verbi 'est' per se sumpti
supponit solum pro eo quod est.
(each term having supposition with regard to the verb 'is' taken for
itself, only supposits for a thing that exists.)

Here Peter refers to his primary interpretation of 'esse' as existere. The
formula 'quod est', as referring in this respect to existence, seems to be
accepted by all medieval logicians. 'Esse' here is taken in its function of
denoting existence.[18]

For Peter of Mantua, 'Each thing is' means: 'Each thing exists.' 'Esse'
(to be) is explained here as 'to exist'; the copula is, what I call here,
'extensionally' interpreted, in contradistiction to, what I call, an 'intensional'
interpretation of the copula, according to which the copula joins the
predicate term to the subject term and does not denote existence.[19] If this
'is' means what is actually the fact, it cannot at the same time, for the
same intellect that utters a single proposition, not actually be the fact.

These four propositions are sufficient basis for Peter to reject the truth
of these five propositions:[20]

1. Adam est mortuus (Adam is dead);
2. Aliquid est corruptum (Something is corrupted);
3. Chimera est intelligibilis (A chimera is intelligible);
4. Antechristus (sic) est generandus (The Antichrist is to be generated);
5. Aliquid est futurum (Something is future).

First, I single out proposition (3), 'Chimera est intelligibilis.' The correct analysis is on Peter's view: 'Chimera est intelligibile quod est' (A chimera is some existing intelligible thing). This proposition is false, because a chimera does not exist: the subject term does not have supposition. Our main interest here is Peter's alternative analysis of the predicate in view of the copula, to be contradistinguished from other logicians' interpretations of such a proposition.

According to the same line of thought, propositions (1) and (4) are considered to be false by Peter. Propositions (2) and (5) are false as well, Peter thinks, because one cannot simultaneously say that if something exists, it is corrupted or to be generated. Clearly, the copula 'est' here is ultimately decisive for the truth of the proposition; the predicate (Peter means the terms that come after the copula) is separated from it. The copula consignifies time; the predicate contains no indication of tense.

An opponent proposes, however, that 'est mortuus' and 'est generandus' should be interpreted as one single verb. This objection is rejected by Peter. His main points are: first, that if this argument is accepted, participles of past and future tense, as well as nouns ending in '-bilis',[21] would occur separately in Latin to no purpose (frustra);[22] secondly, Peter says that a verb does not possess gender — it consignifies time.

Then follow three notes in hypothetical form. The first runs:[23]

...terminus non ampliatur nisi supponat, si ampliari possit.
(a term can only be ampliated if it supposits -- on the proviso that it can indeed be ampliated.)

This note eliminates the possibility of ampliation of, for example, 'chimera' in 'Chimera potest esse' (A chimera can exist), or in 'Chimera erit' (A chimera will exist), because a chimera is not realisable in the future, nor can it be actualised by any power or cause whatever.

In his second note Peter describes how ampliation (when it is possible) takes place:[24]

...si ampliatur li 'homo' in ista propositione (sc. 'Homo fuit'[25]), aut ampliatur copulative aut disiunctive aut disiunctim aut copulatim.
(If the term 'man' is ampliated in the proposition [viz. 'A man was'], it is ampliated either copulatively or disjunctively or disjunctly or in copulation.)

Peter comments:[26] If copulative, two contradictory propositions would be true at the same time, viz., 'Omne creans de necessitate est Deus' (Every creating thing necessarily is God) and 'Aliquod creans non de necessitate est Deus' (Some creating thing is not necessarily God).   The second proposition is clearly false.

If disiunctive, these same contradictory propositions would be false at the same time (the connective in this case is 'vel' [or]).

If copulatim, then there follows from the initial proposition 'Homo fuit' a proposition whose subject term stands in conjunction, viz., 'Homo qui est, fuit' (A man who is and was, was).   This is a contradiction, Peter says, for the assumption is that at the present a man is not.

If disiunctim, the analysis of the initial proposition is: 'Homo qui est vel fuit, fuit' (A man who is or was, was).   This analysis is one that closely resembles the interpretations of Albert and Marsilius, as is confirmed by the fact that Peter gives somewhat later in his tract the definitions of ampliation offered by both Parisian logicians.   The analysis is false, Peter argues, for the case assumed is that at present a man is not.

Peter's third note is:[27]

Item, si aliquo modo terminus ampliaretur, ampliaretur (1) ex eo quod supponeret pro eo quod est vel erit, aut pro eo quod est vel fuit; (2) aut ex eo quod supponeret pro supposito, vel suppositis, diversarum differentiarum temporum;[28] (3) vel quia supponeret pro aliquo, vel pro aliquibus, ultra ea que actualiter sunt.
(Further, if in some way or other a term was to be ampliated, it would be so on one of three grounds: (1) the term would supposit for what is

or will be, or for what is or has been; or (2) the term would supposit
for a thing or things -- for which it stands -- having different time-
distinctions; or (3) the term would supposit for a thing, or things -- for
which it stands -- over and above that which actually exists.)

The second ground mentioned by Peter closely resembles the one used by
Marsilius of Inghen;[29] the third is almost literally the same as Albert of
Saxony's definition.[30]   All these proposed grounds are rejected by Peter
because the same proposition would be affirmative and negative, assertoric
and modal, etc., at the same time,[31] and, as I have pointed out above,[32] the
proposition is determined by the first verb, which makes the intellect true or
false.

Peter concludes[33] that a term having supposition in respect to a verb of
a specific tense only supposits according to the tense of the verb.   This
applies not only, Peter says, to the copula in past, present and future tense,
but also to, what I call here, 'modal verbs' such as 'potest' (can), 'contingit'
(happens to be), 'intelligitur' (is understood), 'significat' (signifies).[34]

His general conclusion is:[35]

Ideo dicitur generaliter quod nullus terminus ampliat aut constringit alium
terminum.
(Therefore it should be said generally that no term can ampliate or
restrict another term.)

Peter apparently means that his opponents interpret a term's supposition
without paying serious attention to the proposition in which it occurs, even
though the term is acknowledged by the opponents to have supposition in a
proposition.   A proposition is, according to Peter, denominated from the tense
of the verb.[36]   The opponents, it is implied, primarily interpret terms as
having signification in respect to present things.   Even after having taken
into consideration the function of the copula or modality, this signification in
respect to present things is in the opponents' view still active.   The
opponents define time-distinction and modalities in terms of each other,
especially in regard to the present.

In Peter's view, his opponents hypostatize a term.   Albert of Saxony (one
of the philosophers under attack by Peter) calls[37] 'acceptio' (acceptance) the

generic term of 'ampliatio' -- acceptio is a use of a term before its supposition in a proposition is determined. Peter's criticism of Albert is justified, I think. But the same criticism applies to Marsilius of Inghen, though Marsilius explicitly rejects 'acceptio' as a generic term of 'ampliatio'[38] in his criticism of Albert. In Marsilius' theory as well, ampliatio is the use of a term primarily irrespective of the tense of the verb.

The argument involves, to my mind, different conceptions of the proposition, held by Peter on the one hand and the Parisian masters on the other. Peter says[39] that a proposition is denominated from the copula (and in the case of a categorical proposition with a disjunct copula, it is denominated from the first copula). The verification of a term takes place by way of the copula. In contradistinction, the two Parisian masters interpret a proposition primarily in function of the terms themselves. They do not fully appreciate the implications of the tense of the verb, it is Peter's contention, and so do not acknowledge the mutable nature of things, which is the prime concern of our language. (It must be commented here that in Peter's view language is primarily the language of physics.[40]) Peter, moreover, is one of the many medieval philosophers to interpret the copula as having tense. He conceives of esse per se as referring to existence.[41]

So far I have concentrated on Peter's interpretation of propositions with any form of 'esse'. What, then, is Peter's interpretation of modal verbs? Peter mentions here four: 'potest' (can), 'contingit' (happens to be), 'intelligitur' (is understood) and 'significat' (signifies). In these cases, as in the case of the copulas 'erat', 'est', 'erit', Peter says a term has supposition in virtue of the verb. As I understand Peter's theory, modal verbs and copulas are unequal in nature: 'intelligitur', 'potest' and (probably) 'contingit' are not linked with actual things in time in the way that copulas are. 'Intelligitur', 'significat' and 'potest' signify a knowing subject's signification of things outside the mind; the copulas refer to things themselves as past, present, or future.

It should be kept in mind, as Maierù has correctly pointed out,[43] that Peter of Mantua maintains a strict distinction between mental terms, on the one hand, and spoken and written terms, on the other. On the conventional level, the verb plays a dominant part.

After Peter's conclusion about a term's supposition, an opponent is

presented as raising three problems.[44] From the first and second of these
we may conclude that in the opponent's view a term like 'homo' in 'Omnis
homo fuit' possesses an atemporal character because of ampliation. In his
third objection he brings into discussion 'potest' and 'scitur' (is known), and
so, by implication, 'significatur'. He says:

Item, si terminus supponens respectu alicuius termini sequitur vim istius
termini, sequitur quod album significatur per istum terminum 'nigrum'.
Quia: sit Sortes niger, qui potest esse albus, tunc Sortes niger
significatur per li 'nigrum'; et Sortes potest esse albus, igitur album[45]
significatur per li 'nigrum'. Et consequenter sequitur quod ista 'Sortes
albus currit' Sortem nigrum currere significat, quia Sortem album currere
ista significat; et Sortem album currere intelligitur esse Sortim nigrum
currere: igitur, etc. Patet consequentia et minor sequitur ex positione.

Item sequitur quod regem sedere scitur a te, et tamen nullus rex
sedet, quia regem currere scitur a te. Ponatur quod nullus rex sedeat,
sed quod omnis rex currat: tunc patet secunda pars. Et prima arguitur,
quia omnem regem currere scitur a te; et omnem regem currere
intelligitur aut potest esse regem sedere: igitur sequitur quod regem
sedere scitur a te. Consequens tamen falsum, quia nichil scitur nisi
verum.

Etiam sequitur quod Antechristum (sic) esse scitur a te, quia quod
Antechristus erit, scitur a te; et quod Antechristus erit est Antechristum
esse vel potest esse Antechristum esse: igitur Antechristum esse est
scitum a te.

Item sequitur quod chimeram esse scitur a te,[46] quia chimeram
imtelligi scitur a te: igitur, etc.

(Further, if a term having supposition with regard to another term
follows the power exercised by the latter term, it follows that the white
is signified by the term 'black'. For: suppose that Sortes is black, while
he can be white, then the black Sortes is signified by the term 'black';
and Sortes can be white, therefore the white is signified by the term
'black'. Consequently it is argued that 'The white Sortes is running'
signifies that the black Sortes is running, because this proposition 'The
white Sortes is running' signifies that the white Sortes is running; and
that the white Sortes is running is understood as that the black Sortes is
running: therefore, etc. The inference is valid; the minor premiss follows
from the assumption -- viz. that the white is signified by the term
'black'.

Further, this follows: that a king is sitting is known by you, and yet no king is sitting, for that a king is running is known by you. Let it be assumed that no king is sitting, but that every king is running: then the second part of the latter consequence is evident. This is the proof of the first part: that every king is running, is known by you; and that every king is running is understood by you, or it is possible that a king is sitting: therefore, that a king is sitting is known by you. The consequent, however, is false, for only the true is known.

Further, this follows, that the Antichrist exists is known by you, for that the Antichrist will exist is known by you; and that proposition 'The Antichrist will exist' means that the Antichrist exists, or this proposition can mean that the Antichrist exists: therefore that the Antichrist exists is known by you.

Further, this follows, that a chimera exists is known by you, for that a chimera is understood is known by you: therefore, etc.)

An opponent tries to reduce Peter's view to absurdity. First, he reformulates Peter's principal claim that a term's supposition is determined by the verb. Then, the opponent introduces a well-known sophism, 'Nigrum potest esse album' ('The black can be white' -- on the assumption that Sortes now is black, while he can be white). This sophism, by the way, is one of the starting-points in the development of the theory of _ampliatio_. [47]

According to the opponent, Peter's conception of possibility has nothing to do with actuality. In the opponent's view, Peter cannot explain that what now actually is black, can be white: for, as is said by the opponent, on Peter's theory the white is signified by the term 'black'. So, what is understood by the term A is understood by the term B, and while what is known is the true (_verum_), on Peter's theory, it is implied, the opponent says, that the intellect knows what is false according to the case assumed. To the opponent's mind, Peter is forced to admit that A _is_ identical with B, while A _can_ be B.

From his answer to the objection, it becomes clear that Peter's interpretation of 'potest' lacks reference to any (non-modal) time-distinction. He conceives of it as a pure and irreducible notion, functioning as a modal verb atemporally. It cannot be defined in terms of actuality: rather, actuality is to be defined in terms of potentiality. Under the concept of possibility, categorical expressions such as 'white' or 'black' are no longer distinctive of things.

    Peter's criticism is primarily directed against Albert of Saxony and Marsilius of Inghen, as has already been indicated.[48]   Marsilius' tract on ampliation is instructive for a Parisian interpretation of 'potest'.   Marsilius says:[49]

> ...That can be accepted in two senses. First, in a strict way: then it ampliates a term only to things which are or can be. Secondly, in a broader sense: then it ampliates a term to all its significates which are or can be in the future or could have been in the past. So in this case it ampliates a term to stand for its significates which were and are not.

In their analysis of terms causing ampliation, both Albert and Marsilius interpret 'potest' according to the strict sense. Both senses, however, are different from Peter of Mantua's interpretation, whereby 'potest' is conceived of as irreducible.

    To the opponent's objections quoted above, Peter replies:[50]

> Ad aliud, cum arguitur quod album significatur per istum terminum 'nigrum', dicitur concedendo. Et consimiliter conceditur quod ista 'Sortes currit' Sortem sedere significat. Et ultra conceditur ista conclusio quod regem sedere scitur a te, et tamen nullus rex sedet de virtute sermonis. Et cum concluditur quod nichil scitur nisi verum, conceditur quod tantum verum scitur, quia tantum illud quod intelligitur esse verum scitur. Verumtamen, iste non est communis modus loquendi, quamvis sit verus habita significatione terminorum.
>
>   Sed de hoc est magis videndum in <u>Tractatu de veritate et falsitate,</u> quia hoc dato multi modi arguendi propositiones esse veras vel falsas non sunt boni.
>
>   Et ita dicitur ad alias conclusiones ibi illatas.
>
>   (To the third argument, viz., that the white is signified by the term 'black', I concede this conclusion. Likewise, I concede that 'Sortes is running' signifies that Sortes is sitting. Further, I concede as false by virtue of the expression the conclusion that a king is known by you and yet no king is sitting. When it is claimed that only the true is known, I concede this, for only what is understood to be true is known. However, this is not the common use of language, although this mode is true

according to the primary signification of the term.

For more about this subject, see my _Tract on truth and falsity_, since, on the assumption made here, many ways of proving propositions to be true or false are not valid.

The other conclusions by my opponent should be criticized in a similar fashion.)

Peter's comments that the opponent's conclusion is correct de virtute sermonis (by virtue of the expression; Kretzmann: 'with respect to discourse'), that is, the supposition is apparently determined by grammar,[51] but the logician's intention in framing the statement is different.

Here, Peter primarily discusses the semantics of 'intelligitur'. At the beginning of his tract, the proposition 'Chimera est intelligibilis' is under scrutiny.[52] This proposition is false, because the term 'chimera' does not have supposition. Our main interest in the proposition is to see how Peter analyses 'est intelligibilis', namely, into 'est intelligibile quod est'. If, for example, the proposition 'Sortes est intelligibilis' is true, knowledge is of an existing thing, for the analysis is: 'Sortes est intelligibile quod est.' In his reply to the objection, Peter presents what I call a 'complementary' interpretation of knowledge. This interpretation understands knowledge of what is understood to be true, irrespective of existence. It is the intellectum, that is, the thing as far as it is understood, which is understood, not the thing as existing.

In Peter's conception, knowledge and signification on the mental level are linked. We may conclude that, as far as signification is supposition, that is to say, in those cases where a term is used in a proposition, be it written or spoken, signification is linked with existence. Peter's conception of signification is broader, however, than could be discussed in this paper which is primarily about the denotative use of names.

In Albert's theory, which Peter criticizes, verbs denoting an inner act of the mind, such as 'intelligo', 'scio', 'cognosco', 'significo', etc., ampliate a term that is construed with the verb and follows it, to supposit for all time-distinctions indifferently, namely, past, present, future and possibility.[53] Marsilius of Inghen adds to this list of time-distinctions, imaginability.[54] In consequence of this view, Albert defines 'ampliatio' as 'acceptio', which is a sort of hypostatization of a term. Marsilius rejects the use of 'acceptio' as the generic term of 'ampliatio', but introduces the notion of supposition of a term for different time-distinctions simultaneously — including at least the present time (This is the core of his definition of 'ampliatio'). This use of a term is, in the final analysis, the same as Albert's.

Peter of Mantua opposed this view: on his account, a term's supposition is determined by the tense of the copula. Knowledge of a true proposition is primarily knowledge of mutable things existing in time; any other denotative knowledge is secondary. Peter draws the full implications of the mutability of things. This emphasis on the function of the verb in consignifying time, causes Peter to reject the notion of ampliation. I thus conclude that, according to Peter's tract, a name can be used in a way in which existence is not implied. De Rijk calls this 'indefinitely'.[55] On the other hand, a name can be used definitely, or indexically, where existence is implied.

Both these uses bear upon the _denotation_ of the term. The _descriptive_ use of names, that is, when the content or intentional aspect of the term is considered, is discussed in Peter's tract on appellations.[56] In my paper on that tract, I concluded that Peter takes full account of the immanent and mutable character of forms, realized in concrete individual things. The knowing-subject forms in his mind a concept of a form which is constantly changing in the thing outside the mind. Forms are successively acquired and lost, Peter says. In his tract on truth and falsity, Peter refers to the 'intensio et remissio qualitatum' (intension and remission of qualities). It becomes clear, I think, that on Peter's theory a quality in the mind — being abstracted from matter — never truly corresponds to changing forms in nature, possessing degrees, with intension and remission. Any naive metaphysical realism is alien to our philosopher. If this interpretation is correct, attaching truth-value to propositions will be difficult, of course. Things -- that is, forms existing in matter -- are ultimately contingent: 'quodlibet ens est possibile' (each being is contingent), says Peter in his tract on truth and falsity.[57] This _posse_ (contingency) of things is irreducible to other things; rather, other things are reducible to it.

Now, the following scheme of the use of names may be given:

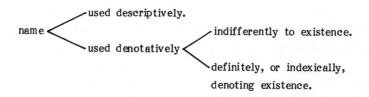

name
— used descriptively.
— used denotatively
— indifferently to existence.
— definitely, or indexically, denoting existence.

In conclusion, some remarks about Peter of Mantua's position in the history of logic: Peter's criticism and rejection of ampliation and restriction is for a large part directed against the Parisian masters Albert of Saxony and Marsilius of Inghen. In his tract on appellations, Peter again makes Albert the object of his attack. As is well-known, English logicians were highly influential in fourteenth- and fifteenth-century Italian logic.[58] Is Peter of Mantua dependent on English logicians too, and, if so, on whom? My present insight into English and Italian logic does not allow me to be precise in regard to this question. However, I do wish to mention here some points of agreement with the _Logica_ of 'Johannes Venator Anglicus', John Hunt(e)man.[59] (Items 1, 2 and 6, below, are attested in notes added in the margin of the manuscript used for this comparison):

1. Both deny the distribution of 'homo' in 'Omnis homo est animal' for all present, past and future men: the supposition here, because of the tense of the verb, is only for present men.[60]

2. Both logicians interpret a categorical proposition with a disjunct copula according to the _first_ copula.[61] (This is, perhaps, a _common_ interpretation of logicians).

3. Both interpret 'potest' as an irreducible verb.[62]

4. Both interpret 'Album erit hoc' and 'Hoc erit album' as identical.[63]

5. Both make a clear distinction between _significatio-suppositio_ and _verificatio_.[64] I shall clarify this distinction by an example, 'Omnis homo est albus' (Every man is white). The term 'man' is _verified_ of a man who is white; it _supposits_ for all present men; it _signifies_ all men of the present, past and future.

6. Both distinguish between a _terminus distributus_ (i.e., the distributive signification of a term outside a proposition) and a _terminus_ having _suppositio distributiva_ (the distribution of a term within a proposition).[65]

I was unable to find an _explicit_ rejection of ampliation and restriction in John's _Logic_, but the items cited show that John's views come close to this

rejection. John, too, emphasized the part played by the tense of the verb —
and of the first copula in propositions with a disjunct copula — so the basis
for John's possible rejection of ampliation and restriction is there.

How exactly Peter's originality and/or dependency is to be evaluated,
can only be said after further study of Peter of Mantua's tracts, which have
not until now received the attention they deserve.

Notes

*I am grateful to my colleagues K. v. Dooren, R.E. de Gruiter and H.A.
Krop (all of Leiden) for their comments on an earlier draft of the text, and
to Mr. J. Deahl (Leiden) for the correction of my English.

1 For medieval lists of these properties of terms, see, e.g., Ph. Boehner,
Medieval Logic (Manchester-Chicago, 1952), p. 117; E.P. Bos ed., Marsilius of
Inghen. Treatises on the Properties of Terms: A First Critical Edition of the
Suppositiones, Ampliationes, Appellationes, Restrictiones and Alienationes with
Introduction, Translation, Notes, and Appendices (Dordrecht-Boston, 1983), p.
46.

2 Some short remarks on ampliatio are to be found in: I.M. Bocheński,
Formale Logik (Orbis academicus; Freiburg-Munich, 1956), pp. 199-202, §§
28.01-28.12; transl. I. Thomas, A History of Formal Logic (Notre Dame, Ind.,
1961), pp. 173-75; W. & M. Kneale, The Development of Logic (Oxford, 1962),
pp. 261-62; E.J. Ashworth, Language and Logic in the Post-Medieval Period
(Synthese Historical Library 12; Dordrecht-Boston, 1974), pp. 89-92; N.
Kretzmann, A. Kenny and J. Pinborg eds., The Cambridge History of Later
Medieval Philosophy (Cambridge, 1982), esp. A. de Libera, 'The Oxford and
Paris traditions in logic', ibid., pp. 174-87; Bos, Marsilius of Inghen. Treatises,
pp. 211-20.

3 On Peter's life, see A. Maierù, 'Il problema del significato nella logica
di Pietro da Mantova' in A. Zimmermann ed., Antiqui und Moderni:
Traditionsbewusstsein und Fortschrittsbewusstsein im späten Mittelalter
(Miscellanea medievalia 9; Berlin-New York), pp. 155-170, ibid., pp. 155-57;
and esp. Th. E. James, 'Peter Alboini of Mantua: Philosopher-Humanist',
Journal of the History of Philosophy 12 (1974) 161-70, to which the reader is

referred for all relevant sources.

4 Albert of Saxony taught philosophy at Paris from (at least) 24 May 1351 to 1362, before leaving for the University of Vienna. See G. Heidingsfelder, Albert von Sachsen, sein Lebensgang und sein Kommentar zur Nikomachischen Ethik des Aristoteles (BGPTM 22, Heft 3-4, 2 Aufl.; Münster i. W., 1927), p. 7ff.

5 Marsilius of Inghen (ca. 1340-1396) was a master of the University of Paris (until 1377); after leaving Paris he may have stayed some time in Italy. From 1386 till his death he was active as a master and the first rector of the University of Heidelberg. See Bos, Marsilius of Inghen. Treatises, pp. 8-9.

6 For Peter's interpretation of appellatio, see E.P. Bos, 'Peter of Mantua's Tract on "Apellatio" and His Interpretation of Immanent Forms' in A. Maierù ed., English Logic in Italy in the 14th and 15th Centuries: Acts of the 5th European Symposium on Medieval Logic and Semantics, Rome, 10-14 November 1980 (History of Logic 1; Naples, 1982), pp. 231-52.

7 The text I have used for this paper is that of the incunable edition of Peter's Logica with Burley on the Analytica: Scriptum excellentissimi doctoris magistri Galteri Burlei super libro Posteriorum. Viri preclarissimi ac subtilissimi logici magistri Petri Mantuani Logica (Padua, 1477). The copy used was that preserved in the British Library. I have compared this text with the manuscripts of Peter's Logica known to me, and I have noted deviations from the incunable where necessary. For a list of the manuscripts, see Bos, 'Peter of Mantua's Tract...', p. 232, n. 8.

I thought it desirable to number the leaves of this unfoliated text with Arabic figures. This seemed to afford an easier system of reference -- and moreover, one that is more often used in early printed books themselves -- than the combinations of letters and Roman numerals at the foot of the folios, indicating the signatures of the gatherings in the 1477 edition. So, I have foliated Peter's tract on ampliations (sig. b vi^{ra}-c i^{ra}), fols. 14ra-17ra. Each column of the edition contains the same number of lines, viz. 39; lines of text are indicated here by bracketed numbers following those of the folios.

8 In this survey I have omitted to mention those objections and replies that do not substantially affect Peter's line of thought.

9 Peter of Mantua, Logica (Padua, 1477), fol. 14^{ra}(14-18).

10 Ibid., fol. 1ra, esp. (31-38).

11 Ibid., fol. 14^{ra}(38)-14^{rb}(1).

12 See above, pp. 385-387.

13 Peter of Mantua, Logica (Padua, 1477), fol. 14ra (18-38), citation (19-23).

14 For the identification of this 'Johannes Venator', see L.M. de Rijk, 'Semantics in Richard Billingham and Johannes Venator' in Maierù ed., English Logic in Italy, pp. 167-183, ibid., p. 168.

15 For the text of Venator's Logica, I have used MS Città del Vaticano, Bib. Apost. Vat., Vat. lat. 2130. fols. 49^{r}-141^{r}.

16 Ibid., fol. 92vb: 'Similiter apud omnes logicos illud dicitur verbum principale alicuius propositionis categorice. Quo habito habetur intellectus verus vel falsus.' A note in the margin adds: 'Nota quod hinc potuit forte accipere Petrus de Mantua opinionem quam tenet in Logica sua, tractatu de ampliationibus' (From this text Peter of Mantua might have taken the view he holds in his Logic, viz., in his tract on ampliations).

17 Peter of Mantua, Logica (Padua, 1477), fol. 14rb (2-5).

18 Cf. A. Maierù, Terminologia logica della tarda scolastica (Lessico Intelletuale Europeo 8; Rome, 1972), p. 199.

19 Cf. Ashworth, Language and Logic, pp. 68-69.

20 Peter of Mantua, Logica (Padua, 1477), fol. 14rb (5-11).

21 One could think of, e.g., 'intelligibilis' (intelligible); see the third proposition of the list, rejected by Peter.

22 Another reply is inspired by grammatical considerations; I shall not discuss it here.

23 Peter of Mantua, _Logica_ (Padua, 1477), fol. 14va (15-16).

24 Ibid., fol. 14va (37)-14vb (1).

25 Addition from fol. 14va (26). [E.P.B.]

26 Ibid., fol. 14vb (25).

27 Ibid., fols. 14vb (39)-15ra (21), citation (39-8).

28 'temporum', MS Venezia, Bib. Padr. Red. 457, fol. 8vb] 'terminis' incun.

29 Bos ed., _Marsilius of Inghen. Treatises_, p. 98 (5-6): 'Ampliatio est suppositio termini pro suis significatis respectu diversorum temporum indifferenter' (Ampliation is a term's supposition for its significates with regard to different times without distinction).

30 _Albertus de Saxonia. Perutilis logica_ (Venice, 1522; repr. Documenta semiotica, series 6, philosophica, Hildesheim-New York, 1974), tract. 2, cap. 10, fol. 15rb (46-49): '...ampliatio est acceptio alicuius termini pro aliquo, vel pro aliquibus, ultra hoc quod actualiter est' (ampliation is the acceptance of a term for some thing, or some things, beyond what actually exists).

31 See also above, p. 384.

32 See above, p. 383.

33 Peter of Mantua, _Logica_ (Padua, 1477), fol. 15rb (31)-15va (17).

34 Peter unfortunately discusses at one single level modal and non-modal copulas. See also above, p. 387.

35 Peter of Mantua, _Logica_ (Padua, 1477), fol. 15va (15-16).

36 See also above, p. 387.

[37] Albert of Saxony, Perutilis logica (Venice, 1522), tract. 2, cap. 10, fol. 15rb (46–47).

[38] Bos ed., Marsilius of Inghen. Treatises, p. 100.

[39] See also above, p. 386.

[40] One is reminded of W.V.O. Quine, Word and Object (Studies in Communication; Cambridge, Mass., 1960), p. 4.

[41] For post-medieval logicians' interpretation of esse, see Ashworth, Language and Logic, pp. 68–69.

[42] Peter does not discuss 'contingit' in his tract. The verb is discussed in Albertus de Saxonia. Sophismata, obligationes ac insolubilia (Paris, 1502; repr. Hildesheim-New York, 1975), pars 4, Sophismata xxviii-xxx, sig. c v^{r-v}.

[43] Maierù, Terminologia logica, p. 159.

[44] Peter of Mantua, Logica (Padua, 1477), fol. 15va (17)-15vb (29), citation (36–29).

[45] 'album', MS Vat. lat. 2135, fol. 10va] 'albus' incun.

[46] 'a te', ibid., om. incun.

[47] Cf., e.g., Ashworth, Logic and Language, p. 90,

[48] See above, pp. 381, 386–387.

[49] Bos ed., Marsilius of Inghen. Treatises, p. 120 (5–13).

[50] Peter of Mantua, Logica (Padua, 1477), fol. 16ra (18–35).

[51] Cf. N. Kretzmann, 'Semantics, History of' in P. Edwards ed., The Encyclopedia of Philosophy 7 (New York-London, 1967), pp. 358–406, ibid., p. 372.

[52] See above, p. 384.

53 Albert of Saxony, Perutilis logica (Venice, 1522), tract. 2, cap. 10, fol. 15vb (19-53), rule VII of his chapter on ampliation.

54 Bos ed., Marsilius of Inghen, Treatises, p. 102. See too Joel Biard, 'La signification d'objets imaginaires dans quelques textes anglais du XIVe siècle', above, pp. 272-273.

55 See De Rijk, 'Semantics in Richard Billingham...', pp. 178-83.

56 See Bos, 'Peter of Mantua's Tract...'.

57 Peter of Mantua, Logica (Padua, 1477), fol. 53rb (11).

58 See, e.g., Maierù ed., English Logic in Italy.

59 Cf. above, nn. 14 and 15.

60 Venator, Logica, MS Vat. lat. 2130, fol. 91ra; Peter of Mantua, Logica (Padua, 1477), tract. de suppositionibus, fol. 1va.

61 See above, p. 383.

62 See above, pp. 389-390, and Venator, Logica, MS Vat. lat. 2130, fol. 49ra.

63 Paul of Mantua, Logica (Padua, 1477), fol. 16ra (5-6); Venator, Logica, MS Vat. lat. 2130, fol. 92vb, the same conclusion.

64 Venator, ibid., fol. 90vb; Paul of Mantua, Logica (Padua, 1477), tract. de supp., fol. 1va.

65 Venator, Logica, MS Vat. lat. 2130, fol. 90vb.

Participants in the Sixth European Symposium on
Medieval Logic and Semantics

Jennifer Ashworth, Department of Philosophy, University of Waterloo, Waterloo, Ontario, Canada N2L 3G1.

Joël Biard, 13 rue Charles Friedel, F-75020 Paris, France.

Egbert Peter Bos, Filosofisch Instituut, Rijksuniversiteit, Matthias de Vrieshof 4, Postbus 9515, NL-2300 RA Leiden, The Netherlands.

Francesco Bottin, Università di Padova Istituto di Storia della Filosofia, Piazza Capitaniato 3, I-35100 Padova, Italy.

H.A.G. Braakhuis, Katholieke Universiteit Filosofisch Instituut, Thomas Aquinostraat 3, Postbus 9108, NL-6500 HK Nijmegen, The Netherlands.

Alessandro Conti, via Zampiano 6, I-07024 La Maddalena (SS), Italy.

Julian G. Deahl, c/o E.J. Brill, Oude Rijn 33a, Postbus 9000, NL-2300 PA Leiden, The Netherlands.

Sten Ebbesen, Københavns Universitet Institut for graesk og latinsk Middelalderfilologi, Njalsgade 90, tr. 1,2, DK-2300 København S, Denmark.

Graziella Federici Vescovini, Lungopo Antonelli 11, I-10100 Torino, Italy.

P.T. Geach, Department of Philosophy, University of Leeds, Leeds, England LS2 9JT.

Niels Jørgen Green-Pedersen, Københavns Universitet Institut for graesk og latinsk Middelalderfilologi, Njalsgade 90, tr. 1,2, DK-2300 København S, Denmark.

Desmond Paul Henry, Department of Philosophy, University of Manchester, Manchester, England M13 9PL.

Yukio Iwakuma, Kyoto University Research Institute for Humanistic Studies, Yushida-Ushinomiya-cho, Sakyo-ku, Kyoto, 606 Japan.

Klaus Jacobi, Krieler Strasse 60, D-5000 Köln 41, Germany.

Ludger Kaczmarek, Westfälische Wilhelms-Universität Institut für Allgemeine Sprachwissenschaft, Bispinghof 17, D-4400 Münster, Germany.

Elisabeth Karger, 9 rue Custine, F-75018 Paris, France.

Anthony Kenny, Balliol College, Oxford, England OX1 3BJ.

C.H. Kneepkens, Katholieke Universiteit Instituut voor Oude Letteren, Erasmuslaan 40, NL-6526 GG Nijmegen, The Netherlands.

Ria van der Lecq, Leliestraat 57, NL-2313 BE Leiden, The Netherlands.

P. Osmund Lewry, O.P., Blackfriars, Oxford, England OX1 3LY, and Pontifical Institute of Mediaeval Studies, 59 Queen's Park Crescent East, Toronto, Ontario, Canada M5S 2C4.

Alain de Libera, 34 rue de Provence, F-74009 Paris, France.

Christopher Martin, Department of Philosophy, State University of New York at Stony Brook, Stony Brook, NY 11794, U.S.A.

Francesco del Punta, Università degli studi di Pisa, Dipartimento di Filosofia, Piazza Torricelli 2, I-56100 Pisa, Italy.

Stephen Read, Department of Logic and Metaphysics, University of St Andrews, St Andrews, Fife, Scotland KY16 9AL.

Jeroen van Rijen, Centrale Interfaculteit, Erasmus Universiteit Rotterdam, Postbus 1738, NL-3000 DR Rotterdam, The Netherlands.

Georgette Sinkler, Sage School of Philosophy, Cornell University, Ithaca, NY 14853-0205, U.S.A.

Frank Vleeskens, Centrale Interfaculteit, Erasmus Universiteit Rotterdam,

Postbus 1738, NL-3000 DR Rotterdam, The Netherlands.

Hermann Weidemann, Schulte-Bernd-Strasse 55, D-4400 Münster-Roxel, Germany.